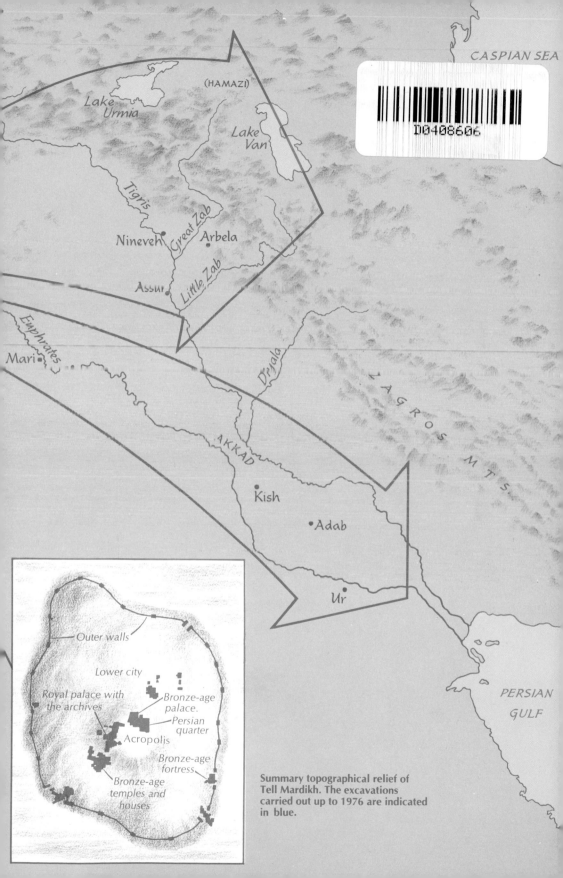

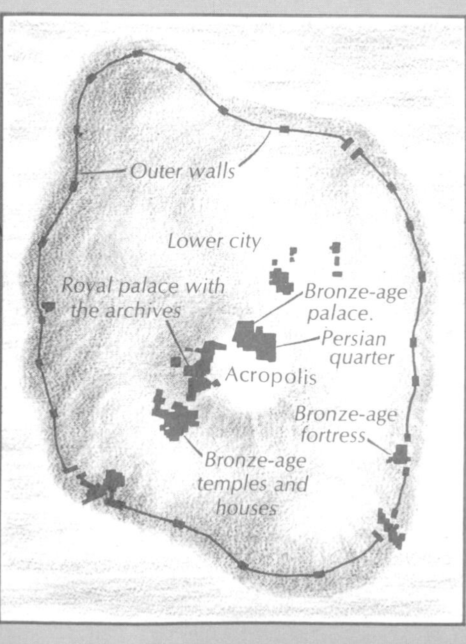

Summary topographical relief of Tell Mardikh. The excavations carried out up to 1976 are indicated in blue.

THE ARCHIVES OF EBLA

The courtyard room at Ebla where the archives of early Bronze Age tablets were found

THE ARCHIVES OF EBLA

An Empire Inscribed in Clay

GIOVANNI PETTINATO

with an Afterword by
MITCHELL DAHOOD, S.J.

Doubleday & Company, Inc.
Garden City, New York

To my wife Agatha

and my children, Marcello, Daniela, and Stefania,

the real sacrificial victims of the Ebla discoveries

Library of Congress Cataloging in Publication Data

Pettinato, Giovanni.
The archives of Ebla.

Translation of Ebla. Un impero inciso nell'argilla.
Bibliography: p. 323
Includes indexes.
1. Ebla, Syria. 2. Ebla tablets. I. Title.
DS99.E25P47313 939'.4
ISBN: 0-385-13152-6
Library of Congress Catalog Card Number 77–16939

Photographs by Giovanni Pettinato
Frontispiece photographs by David Noel Freedman, University of Michigan
This book, except "Ebla, Ugarit, and the Bible" by Mitchell Dahood, S.J., was originally published in Italian under the title *Ebla. Un impero inciso nell'argilla*
© 1979 Arnoldo Mondadori, with some parts omitted, Editore S.p.A., Milano

9 8 7 6 5 4 3

Contents

List of Illustrations ix

List of Abbreviations x

Preface xiii

CHAPTER I EBLA: THE MEANING OF A DISCOVERY 1
1. The novelties from the texts 3
2. Description of the texts 7

CHAPTER II THE FINDING OF EBLA 13
1. Ebla in Mesopotamian and non-Mesopotamian documents 15
2. Theories about the location of Ebla 20
3. The archaeological discovery of Ebla 22
4. The philological rediscovery of Ebla and the identification of Tell Mardikh with Ebla 23
   4.1. The finding of the Ibbiṭ-Lim statue 23
   4.2. First consequences and reactions 28

CHAPTER III THE ROYAL ARCHIVES 31
1. The discovery: 1974, 1975, 1976 32
2. The importance of an archive for the reconstruction of a civilization 36
3. The tablets of Ebla: manufacture, quantity, study 39
4. Typology of the texts 42
5. Archive science 48

CHAPTER IV THE WRITING AND LANGUAGE OF EBLA 53
1. Mesopotamian cuneiform system 54
2. Toward the identification of a new language 55
3. Structure of the language of Ebla 57
   3.1. Writing and phonetics 59
   3.2. The noun and the nominal formation 61
   3.3. The pronominal system 62
      3.3.1. Independent personal pronouns 62

3.3.2. Suffixes of personal pronouns 63
3.3.3. Other pronouns 63
3.4. Prepositions 63
3.5. Conjunctions and adverbs 63
3.6. Verbal system 63
3.7. Syntax and style 65
4. The position of Eblaite among the Semitic languages 65

CHAPTER V THE DYNASTY OF EBLA AND ITS HISTORICAL DOCUMENTS 67
1. Reconstruction of the dynasty and historical synchronisms 69
2. The king, the queen, the queen mother, and the princes 74
3. The "Elders" and the king 92
4. International politics 95
4.1. Alliances 96
4.2. Wars 99
4.3. Treaties 103
4.4. The political expansion of Ebla 105

CHAPTER VI SOCIETY 113
1. The division of power 114
1.1. The social classes 114
1.2. The administration 122
2. The division of space 134
2.1. Settlements and population 134
2.2. Division of the city 136
2.2.1. Political divisions 143
2.2.2. Topography of Ebla 145
3. The division of time 145
3.1. Systems of dating 145
3.2. Calendars 147
3.2.1. The old calendar 147
3.2.2. The new calendar 150

CHAPTER VII THE ECONOMY 155
1. Economic resources 156
1.1. Agriculture 157
1.2. Cattle breeding 162
1.3. Industry 165
1.4. Alloys of metals: an example of advanced technology 172
2. Models of production 179

3. Units of measure 180
3.1. Dry and liquid measures 181
3.2. Weights 181
3.3. Surfaces 182
3.4 Numbering systems 182
4. Commerce 184
4.1. Models of exchange 185
4.1.1. Barter 185
4.1.2. Purchase and sale 186
4.1.3. "Tributes" 188
4.2. Value of exchange: prices and currency 195
4.2.1. The value of goods and the dynamics of prices 196
4.3. Commercial goods: import-export 202
4.4. Commercial empire 225

CHAPTER VIII CULTURE 229
1. The school 230
1.1. Structure and curriculum 231
1.2. Documents of the school 232
2. Higher culture 233
2.1. Lists of cuneiform signs 234
2.2. Syllabaries 234
2.3. Dictionaries and vocabularies 235
2.4. Encyclopedias 237
2.5. Literary texts 238
3. Scientific congresses and cultural exchanges 239

CHAPTER IX RELIGION 243
1. The pantheon 245
1.1. The gods 245
1.2. Forms of syncretism 249
1.3. Borrowings 251
2. Worship 252
2.1. Priests and places of worship 252
2.2. The offerings 253
2.3. The feasts 256
2.4. Incantations, hymns, and myths 258
3. Popular Religion 260

CHAPTER X CONCLUSION: PROBLEMS AND PROSPECTS RAISED BY THE DISCOVERY OF EBLA 263

AFTERWORD EBLA, UGARIT, AND THE BIBLE
Mitchell Dahood, S.J. 271

BIBLIOGRAPHY 323

INDEXES
1. Names of Persons 327
2. Names of Places and Rivers 329
3. Names of Gods
4. Ebla Texts Cited 332
5. Biblical Texts Cited 337
6. Index of Subjects 342
7. Hebrew Words in Afterword
8. Eblaite Words in Afterword
9. Ugaritic Words in Afterword

LIST OF ILLUSTRATIONS

The courtyard room at Ebla where the archives of early Bronze Age tablets were found ii
Principal commercial routes of Syria about 1910 5
Criteria for composing a tablet (obverse) 10
Criteria for composing a tablet (reverse) 11
Example of cuneiform text transliterated 12
Synoptic view of the attestations of Ebla in Near Eastern literature 19
Hypotheses regarding the location of Ebla 20
Copy of the inscription on the statue of Ibbiṭ-Lim, king of Ebla 26
Plan of palace G. of Ebla and the location of the archives 33
Principal archives of the third millennium B.C. found in the Near East 38
Copy of text TM.74.G.120 (obverse) 43
Reconstruction of the wooden shelves of the Ebla library 49
Copy of a cuneiform text 59
The greatest holders of power during the reign of Ibbi-Sipiš 80
Diverse positions of the greatest extension of power 81
The fortunes of Ebrium's children 82–83
Allocations of sheep for diverse purposes in various months 91
Military route of Enna-Dagan against Iblul-Il, king of Mari and Assur 100
The great powers in the middle of the third millennium and their zones of influence 108
The makeup of Eblaite society 119
Gold tribute paid by the royal governors 124
The governors of state under the first four kings of the dynasty 126
The governors and the overseers at the time of Arennum 131
The administrative cadres of Ebla 132
The city of Ebla at the time of King Ibbi-Sipiš 137
Allotments of sheep for various purposes in the 12 months of the year 149
Geography of the agricultural crops of present-day Syria 158
Ecological zones of the origin of wild barley in the Near East 159
Percentages of tin in the bronze alloys 173
Percentages of tin in relation to the physical characteristics of the bronze alloys 175
Summary outline of unitary weights of the bronze objects 177
Mean weight measures of the bronze objects 178
Units of measure of the weights 182
Tribute paid by the governors and the king to the state treasury 189
Tribute paid by the governors 193
Value of textiles in silver shekels 197
Relationship of prices among the various products 198–199
Lines of expansion of cuneiform writing in the third millennium 268

LIST OF ABBREVIATIONS

AfO	= *Archiv für Orientforschung*
AIUON	= *Annali dell'Istituto Universitario Orientale di Napoli*
AS	= *Assyriological Studies*
AT	= D. J. Wiseman, *The Alalakh Tablets,* London 1953
ATHE	= B. Kienast, *Die altassyrischen Texte des Orientalischen Seminars der Universität Heidelberg und der Sammlung Erlenmeyer,* Berlin 1960
ATU	= A. Falkenstein, *Archaische Texte aus Uruk,* Berlin 1936
BA	= *Biblical Archeologist*
BIN	= *Babylonian Inscriptions in the Collection of J. B. Nies*
CAD	= *The Assyrian Dictionary of the Oriental Institute of the University of Chicago*
*CAH*³	= *The Cambridge Ancient History,* Third Edition
CHM	= *Cahiers d'Histoire Mondiale*
GS	= H. Klengel, *Geschichte Syriens,* Berlin 1965
IAS	= R. Biggs, *Inscriptions from Tell Abu Ṣalabikh,* Chicago 1974
IRSA	= E. Sollberger—J. R. Kupper, *Inscriptions Royales sumériennes et akkadiennes,* Paris 1971
ITT	= *Inventaire des tablettes de Tello*
JCS	= *Journal of Cuneiform Studies*
KAV	= *Keilschrifttexte aus Assur verschiedenen Inhalts*
LSS	= *Leipziger semitistische Studien*
MAIS	= *Missione Archeologica Italiana in Siria*
MSL	= *Materialien zum sumerischen Lexikon*
NEB	= *New English Bible*
OECT	= *Oxford Editions of Cuneiform Texts*
OIP	= *The University of Chicago Oriental Institute Publications*
OrAn	= *Oriens Antiquus*
OrNS	= *Orientalia Nova Series*
R	= H. C. Rawlinson, *The Cuneiform Inscriptions of Western Asia*
RA	= *Revue d'Assyriologie et d'Archéologie orientale*
RBI	= *Rivista Biblica Italiana*
Rép.Géogr.	= *Répertoire Géographique des Textes Cunéiformes*
RlA	= *Reallexikon der Assyriologie*
RPARA	= *Rendiconti della Pontificia Accademia Romana di Archeologia*
RSO	= *Rivista degli Studi Orientali*
RSV	= *Revised Standard Version*

SAK = F. Thureau-Dangin, *Die sumerischen und akkadischen Königsinschriften,* Leipzig 1907
SMS = *Syro-Mesopotamian Studies*
UET = *Ur Excavations Texts*
UF = *Ugarit-Forschungen*
UT = C. H. Gordon, *Ugaritic Textbook,* Rome 1965
UNL = G. Pettinato, *Untersuchungen zur neusumerischen Landwirtschaft,* Napoli 1967
TM. = Tell Mardikh
WdM = *Wörterbuch der Mythologie*
ZA = *Zeitschrift für Assyriologie*

Preface

Undertaking to write a book about the archives of a vanished empire, I fully agree with my colleague Karlheinz Deller of Heidelberg who, in the library of the Oriental Seminary at the end of a profitable colloquium in July 1976 on the revolutionary documents from Ebla, told me, "Indeed, you must be eternally grateful to divine providence for having guided your steps and prepared you for the very difficult task as the epigrapher of Ebla." As a matter of fact, one must be a trained Semitist and also have a good grasp of cuneiform in general and of Sumerian in particular before approaching the Ebla texts.

It so happened that I received my first formation in Semitics at the Pontifical Biblical Institute in Rome under the direction of Alfred Pohl, Mitchell Dahood, and William L. Moran. Later I studied under Adam Falkenstein at the University of Heidelberg where I acquired the basic cuneiform and linguistic tools that, together with my training in Semitic languages, enabled me one day to become the decipherer of the language of Ebla.

My first encounter with Ebla, however, was by pure chance. For ten years I had been in Germany, at the University of Heidelberg, where after my doctorate I pursued a postgraduate career, serving first as annual instructor and later, after qualifying for university teaching in Germany, as university lecturer. My career as an academic now appeared pretty well settled; I had become a specialist in Neo-Sumerian economic texts.

Nonetheless, partly from nostalgia and partly from the desire not to lose contact with the Roman academic scene, I returned from time to time to the Eternal City, quite unaware that one of these visits would prove fateful.

One day in November 1969, in a Rome mantled by autumnal gray, I met the young archaeologist Paolo Matthiae at the Termini railroad station. It was then that I had occasion to speak with him for the first time about his excavations at Tell Mardikh in northern Syria. Given my interest in epigraphic finds, I still recall the question I put to him almost point-blank: "Paolo, have you found any cuneiform texts these years?" Paolo replied with his typical sly smile, "Come to my house this evening."

That evening of November 3 at nine-thirty sharp, I appeared at 25 Via Brescia in the Salaria quarter. Matthiae received me and had me take a seat in the dim light of the drawing room. A moment later I had under my eyes some photographs reproducing the inscription of the statue of Ibbiṭ-Lim, king of Ebla.

The excitement I experienced in running over the 26 lines incised in the basalt of a headless statue cannot be described. Ebla was a city without a face or a history but now for the first time she revealed herself through the words of one of her kings. Matthiae, who had dug at Tell Mardikh for six years and had long gazed at the mysterious signs of this inscription, had already guessed the presence of the word *EBLA* but wanted confirmation by a philologist. I confirmed that *EBLA* occurred at least twice, the first time as an adjective and the second as the name of the city. It was the first proof favoring the identification of Tell Mardikh with Ebla; Paolo Matthiae could begin to feel proud of that which some years later would develop into one of the great archaeological discoveries of the century.

To permit me to complete the decipherment of the inscription, he handed me those photographs, which I took with me that same evening on the train to Heidelberg. Five days later the translation of that important epigraphic document was ready for delivery to Rome. In his reply to me Matthiae expressed his enthusiasm and named me official epigrapher of Ebla. But another five years passed before I could again test my mettle against the ancient documents of Tell Mardikh-Ebla.

In August 1974 a telegram from Matthiae in Damascus reached me at Nus in Val d'Aosta: "Archive of 40 cuneiform tablets found. Stop. I await you in Syria. P. Matthiae."

In the first days of September I arrived by air in Damascus. Matthiae was there waiting for me in the hot night. From the airport we headed directly for Tell Mardikh where at two in the morning I was straightway set in front of the 40 tablets recovered. On the other side of the table stood all the archaeologists eager to know. Under the gaze of all I took the tablets, one by one, in my hand, from the smallest to the biggest. After some minutes of absolute silence, I looked up and candidly confessed: "The writing seems to correspond to the Mesopotamian script of the Fara period, but I don't understand a word."

Actually I did not think that I was looking at a new language, as was found to be the case six months later. During the following days I was able to single out some Sumerian verbal forms, but nonetheless failed to understand any one text completely. On my return to Rome I began the systematic study of the 40 tablets.

Will this have been chance or providence? Surely the Eblaites had looked on me with consideration; if, in fact, 40 texts could appear somewhat meager, it was precisely their scantiness that permitted an intense examination of the material. I still recall the two months from November 1974 till January 1975 passed in my small room in the Poggio Ameno quarter of Rome where, together with my colleague Giovanni Garbini, I sought to find the key to the decipherment of the new texts. By April 23 I was able to announce in a public lecture at Rome's Pontifical Biblical Institute that the Ebla texts were written in a language of the Northwest Semitic group, more precisely in Old Canaanite.

The reactions both in Italy and abroad were marked by critical skepticism. One scholar was heard to say, "Pettinato is inventing a new language."

In the summer of 1975 another telegram from Matthiae invited me to come to Syria as the result of the recovery of the administrative archive, consisting of nearly 1,000 texts and fragments.

The study on the site already permitted the drawing of two very important conclusions: the first concerned the identification of Tell Mardikh with Ebla, the second confirmed the accuracy of the decipherment of the new language.

While I was bent over transcribing these texts in a small room of the mission's compound—it was the evening of September 30, 1975—Dr. Alessandro De Maigret arrived on the run and out of breath with the news that in the square he was digging he lit upon a huge quantity of tablets. Furnished with kerosene lamps, we set out at eight in the evening for the sector in question and through a hole one could catch a glimpse of a heap of large, dust-covered tablets incised with cuneiform signs. I descended to a depth of eight meters and, cautiously drawing near, I began to look through the first text that cropped out, half-covered by the sand of centuries.

This time the emotion is inexpressible because in the ten columns that appeared I could several times distinctly read the words en-*eb-la*^{ki}, "king of Ebla":

"The city of Arga
(is) in the hands
of the king
of Ebla;
the city of Ladainu
(is) in the hands
of the king
of Ebla;
the city of Irrulaba
(is) in the hands
of the king
of Ebla" . . .

We stood before some historical texts that left no further room for doubt. Throughout the night the archaeologists continued to excavate and the following morning the first layer of what was the nucleus of the royal library of Ebla could be sighted. The analysis of the contents of thousands of tablets and fragments revealed untold aspects of a buried civilization, of a vanished empire.

This book aims to present the treasure of the royal archives of Ebla—some 20,000 tablets, chips, and fragments—just as it appears at the beginning of the studies. Therefore no conclusions will be offered but rather the uncertainties; the texts will be allowed to speak for themselves. The interest in Ebla is great, to be sure, but no less considerable is the accompanying skepticism.

The information extracted from the texts is arousing great enthusiasm, but equally remarkable has been the speed with which this information has been forthcoming. This has been made possible by constant study and collaboration.

I am grateful to Professor Matthiae for having entrusted me with the challenging position of epigrapher of the mission and to his entire archaeological team for the zeal and sacrifice manifested in the recovery of the tablets of the archives. I also thank colleagues and Assyriologists, Semitists, and archaeologists who have constantly encouraged me to carry on with the work of decipherment and interpretation of the texts and have on occasion contributed decisively to resolve problems discussed in this book. I mention specifically K. Butz of Vienna and Munich, M. Civil of Chicago, K. Deller of Heidelberg, I. J. Gelb of Chicago, Th. Jacobsen and W. L. Moran of Cambridge, Massachusetts, H. Waetzoldt of Heidelberg, and E. Sollberger of London among foreign scholars. Among the Italians, L. Cagni of Naples, S. Picchioni of Bologna, G. Garbini of Pisa, F. Pennacchietti of Venice, A. Roccati of Torino, M. Dahood of Rome, E. Acquaro of Bologna, M. Tosi of Naples, and A. De Maigret of Rome.

A most cordial word of thanks also goes to the authorities of the Arab Republic of Syria, in particular to Dr. Afif Bahnassi, director general of antiquities, Dr. Adnan Bounni, Dr. Kassem Tueir, and to Messrs. Mahmoud Heretani and Wahid Khayata for their kindness and the assistance granted me.

I would finally mention and thank my collaborators and students for the time dedicated to discussions and the filing of the Ebla tablets: F. Pomponio, G. Biga, L. Fozzati, M. Fransos, P. Mander, E. Arcari, A. Puglia, and G. Visicato.

I dedicate this book to my children who, together with my wife, have paid the price for the sacrifice demanded by Ebla. My desire is that for them and Ebla better days lie ahead!

GIOVANNI PETTINATO

Rome, 31 May 1978

AUTHOR'S NOTE: In the transliterations of the cuneiform texts that follow, the Eblaite words are written in italics; Sumerian words are written in Roman type with a space between the letters. Words for which we have no exact reading are written in capital letters. The Sumerian word k i, "place," which occurs frequently, marks a word as a place name.

G.P.

Rome, Italy, July 1980

THE ARCHIVES OF EBLA

CHAPTER I

Ebla: the Meaning of a Discovery

1. The novelties from the texts. 2. Description of the texts.

Flying over that small corner of the world situated between the Nile and the chain of the Zagros mountains, one notices the landscape grow harsher and the color scorch as it extends eastward. The great sweep of desert, broken at the beginning by the fertile banks of the Nile, then only by the play of shadows created by the barren reliefs burnt by the sun, yields to the green plain lapped by the Tigris and the Euphrates. Immediately after, the landscape loses its softness and appears to grow angry with itself in the stretch of valleys and dales of the Zagros. This is the region, customarily called the ancient Near East, extending along the Fertile Crescent, yesterday the theater of glorious civilizations and today of international archaeological expeditions. This vast territory may, under the historico-geographical profile, be compared to an unfinished painting; despite the enormous labor of archaeologists and philologists, the strokes appear now firm and then shaded, the contours precise or hardly traced, and often the bare canvas shows through. In brief, a composition not brought to a finish, but already framed and hung; for its lacunae, it was accepted as an abstract painting.

This comparison may give an idea of the situation in which both the scholar and the tourist find themselves; zones perfectly illuminated alternate with zones in shadows where nothing stands out. Hence the continuing effort to wrest from the darkness of mystery and void new inhabited centers, new historical periods, new events that will allow ancient civilizations to arise from the sleep of death.

The exciting adventure of archaeologists and, in some happy instances, of philologists encounters, however, the hard and arid reality of the excavation terrain hidden by a landscape so reluctant to yield its secrets as to appear to the human eye terribly boring with its flat and barren stretches.

Northern Syria beautifully illustrates the truth of the observation that in this epic struggle men do not always come out on top. While Mesopotamia and Egypt have revealed enough of their secrets to permit tracing their history across five millennia, beginning at 3000 B.C., northern Syria has remained till now an enigma, especially during the third millennium, which elsewhere is relatively well documented. If the frontier zone is excluded—consider fabled Mari on the Euphrates, Chagar Bazar, and Tell Brak in the Ḫabur valley, all touched by the expansion of Mesopotamian civilization—the center of northern Syria appeared as terrain unaccountably unexplored.

Who could ever have imagined that a hillock of 56 hectares (140 acres) 70 kilometers (42 miles) from Aleppo along the road leading to Ḥama and finally to Damascus concealed the capital of an empire as immense as it was unknown? The recovery of the royal library alone with its thousands of tablets and fragments could open our eyes to a world heretofore completely unknown.

1. THE NOVELTIES FROM THE TEXTS

Ebla is the subject of our story. Ebla: a name till very recently known only to a handful of scholars dedicated to the study of the ancient Near East. Not even the exact location of this city was known; all that was known—apart from the numerous hypotheses on its identification—were the bare notices transmitted by the Mesopotamian texts of the Sumerians and Akkadians. Now, however, the name of Ebla is destined to become part of that common cultural patrimony and already has claims on titles used of the Babylonian, Assyrian, and Hittite empires. One will discourse on Eblaite civilization just as one has discoursed on Sumerian civilization. A new world is opening up to scholarship and to the modern public because the combined efforts of archaeologists and philologists have succeeded in bringing to light tablets of clay which let the kings and functionaries and scribes of Ebla speak to us.

The excavations at Tell Mardikh have definitively laid to rest the oft-repeated statement that made third-millennium Syria a land of nomads, the exact opposite of the great urban development of the Nile valley and of Mesopotamia. Now the texts are setting matters straight, furnishing the dossier of numerous commercial and political relationships with lands and kingdoms, some of which were till now considered legendary. The Mesopotamian-centered vision of a large part of the history of the ancient Near East must be refocused; it was not only Mesopotamia which took and gave, as archaeological researches in Iran are also proving.

The picture now emerging exceeds the expectations of even the most optimistic scholars; it is not only Ebla and its empire that are being recovered, but in a surprising fashion the world of the third-millennium Near East with all its interrelationships and differentiations. In brief, a much more detailed and complex picture is being gradually revealed.

The archives exhumed at Ebla beginning in 1974 describe a state structure admirably adequate for the complex administration of a power of imperial dimensions, a sign of a still older process of maturation and development whose final results are becoming visible.

In this region and at such a remote epoch one would have expected an empire governed by an absolute monarch directly invested with authority by the gods. Again Ebla disproves and surprises: the political system expresses power under the form of an oligarchy which is exercised through organs with specific functions and duties to control and balance the political and administrative management. A political model which, in the moment it is projected on a vast area subject to Ebla's influence through a far-reaching commercial network, calls to mind the city-state of the Italian Renaissance or of the Hanseatic League.

The king of Ebla (can one still call him "king"?) was elected every seven years and with him was also chosen the head of the administration. Alongside these offices we find a "senate" composed of elders organized in "axes" (which recall the *"fasces"* of the Etruscan and Roman magistrates), each with two representatives. In the official records the former kings are also present, perhaps as members of another body respected for its experience and its knowledge.

From a first analysis—and this is all that can be claimed at this stage of research—it appears evident that great care was taken to balance the powers of the great families owning the large estates and making their voices heard in the chambers of government. The whole system entered into crisis when King Ebrium, reelected four times in a row to the highest office, in an excess of nepotism entrusted all the villages surrounding the capital to his numerous sons. Ibbi-Sipiš, son of Ebrium, succeeded his father on the throne and did not disappoint: his son got elected head of the administration.

In the seventy years covered by the documents of the Royal Archives (the texts actually refer to only five sovereigns, the last two being precisely Ebrium and Ibbi-Sipiš), this reign is the most troubled and teeming with reforms; the new calendar is introduced and among personal names those composed with the divine element *ya,* an abbreviated form of *yau,* supplant those with *il.*

We do not know the outcome of these political-cultural transformations. All that can be said is that Dubuḫu-hada, Ibbi-Sipiš' son, who held important posts while his father was king and was led to believe that he would succeed him on the throne, was not named king.

Another element of Eblaite society which stands out and makes it look like a city-state of Western European tradition is its division of the population into two large categories, the d u m u - n i t a d u m u - n i t a *Ebla*^{ki}, "the sons of Ebla" and the b a r - a n, "the foreigners." The category of foreigners appears very motley: slaves, prisoners of war, objects of purchase and sale, as well as mercenaries who made up Ebla's army.

Nevertheless, in this peculiar society women enjoyed a prominent role. In one of the top positions stands the *maliktum,* "the queen," whose solemn function is to consecrate the king. Not much more can be asserted at the present time other than that she enjoyed ample privileges and disposed of enormous wealth. Woman's decisive role is registered also at the productive level. In the great commercial state of Ebla, exporter of textiles to all areas of the Near East, the numerous spinning mills, concentrated in large part together with the mills in the suburbs, gave work to women, who received a salary in measures of barley. The women are indicated in the texts by the Sumerian ideogram d a m, "woman, lady," never by g e m é, "slave, servant." This distinction is important in revealing the surprising modernity of Ebla which, clearly a forerunner in the classic horizon of the Near East, has lent itself to facile and foreseeable representations of the role of women.

The direct participation of women in the process of production is certainly a striking aspect, but it gets lost in that great commercial phenomenon of Ebla so shrewdly organized; though still few, the data are nonetheless significant.

Figure I, 1 Principal commercial routes of Syria about 1910 (from E. Wirth, *Syrien*)

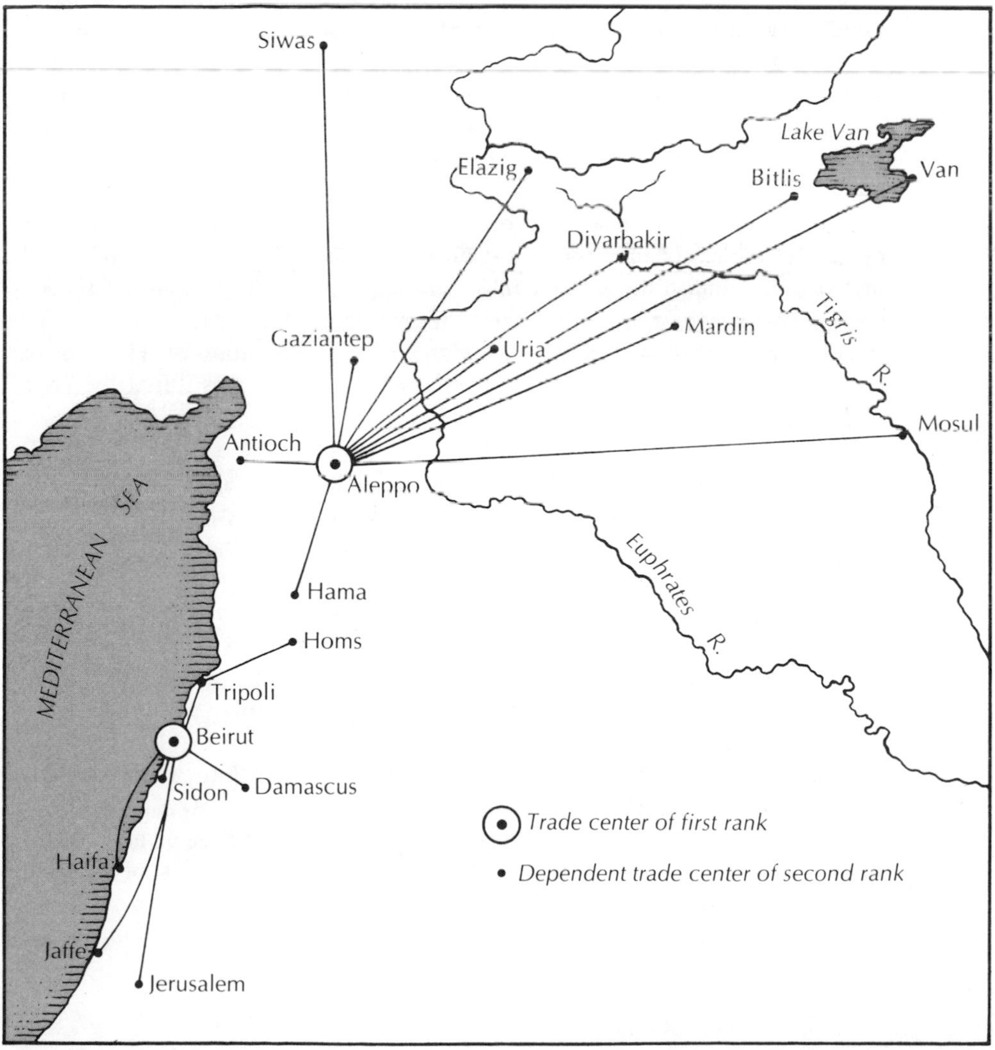

The commercial tradition of Syria is well known for recent epochs; Syrian merchants traversed the Roman empire even during the turbulent and unsafe periods of the massive invasions by the barbarians. Not even the fall of the Roman empire dampened their spirit of initiative; sources attest the influence of Syrian merchants and their commercial colony in Paris during the Merovingian epoch (sixth century A.D.). Data being fished up by underwater archaeology will doubtless supply further proof regarding the maritime routes of these merchants from Syria. Moreover, there is no need to appeal to a period so distant from that in question to find proof of this ancient vocation; the Phoenician expansion offers the most shining illustration of this fact when, at the beginning of the Iron Age, the Syrian hinterland was overrun by the great upheavals resulting from the so-called "invasions of the Sea Peoples."

In what way do the Ebla tablets add to this already exuberant picture of economic data? The rare combination of the antiquity of the texts (mid third millennium), of their quantity and precision, with the vastness of the area of commerical influence leaves little to be desired from the scholar's point of view. These tablets record the volume of debit and credit specifying the socio-functional origin and destination of the goods put into the commercial circuit, and not infrequently the modalities which regulated these local and international exchanges.

A panorama of such a remote epoch unexpectedly unfolds before our eyes. The tablets of clay speak not only of an enormous number of cities in Syria and Palestine of 3000 B.C., among which one recognizes places that subsequently will have great importance, but also of cities in Anatolia, Mesopotamia, Cyprus, of the distant kingdom of Ḫamazi in northern Iran that supplied the mercenary troops that constituted the core of Ebla's army.

Was this vast area amenable to the formation of a true "empire," granted the ambiguity of the term? It would seem that talk of a real "empire" would be premature, but one may speak of a definable political unity as an "area of commerce" and hence subject to the play of supply and demand made by the strongest party.

The international treaties, such as that with Ashur (the ancestors of the Assyrian empire), exhibit an aspect of carefully studied political equilibrium. They guarantee the respect of local autonomy even when they secure in fact an effective position of privilege for Ebla, especially from the commercial standpoint.

However, when need be, Ebla knows how to move into action, as the war conducted against Mari demonstrates. This famous city on the Middle Euphrates, the gateway to Mesopotamia, is by force of arms brought back into the sphere of Eblaite influence, provoking a series of internal and foreign reactions.

What did Ebla, the "imperial" city of 260,000 inhabitants, import and export? In addition to various kinds of foodstuffs, which circulated in traffic over short and medium distance, there are the goods that traveled over medium and long distance and which may be said to have characterized the great commercial power of Ebla: metals, handmade objects of wood and, above all, textiles. This last particular cannot but call to mind the economic expansion of the Italian cities of the Renaissance which imported semifinished and unbleached fabrics only to export them as costly finished products which were able to gain popularity on the international market both for the quality achieved and for the quantity which could meet any demand.

Production organized on these terms had need for precise systems of quantitative and qualitative measurements. In Ebla one sees the conditions designed to promote the process of monetization. There exist, in fact, standard measures for weights and exact models of classification to indicate the quality of certain goods, such as clothes or even the purity of gold. Silver serves as the basic metal of exchange and other goods are evaluated in reference to it. In brief, a new chapter on the history of money and economic practice can now be written.

2. DESCRIPTION OF THE TEXTS

But it is not only the society with its economy that draws the scholar's admiration as this forgotten city is restored to history. The culture of Ebla opens up new areas of information and interrogation.

The language itself spoken by the Eblaites caused the first great surprise; it was assumed that in this region Akkadian was the spoken or at least the written language. Even this assumption has proven false, just like that which denied an intense urbanization. Eblaite in reality belongs to an archaic phase of the Northwest Semitic languages, which include Ugaritic of 1400–1200 B.C., Phoenician, and Biblical Hebrew. Besides those of a historical-administrative and commercial nature, many documents were composed in this language, which shows that culture was a primary concern at Ebla. Various dictionaries and specialized encyclopedias listing birds, fishes, professions, etc. have been found. But the most pleasant surprise is provided by the vocabularies, the oldest on record, which make a vital contribution for understanding the new language. The professors at Ebla placed after the Sumerian word the corresponding

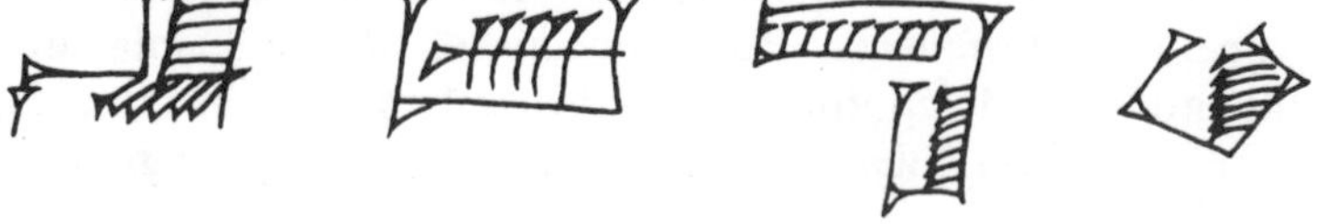

Eblaite term, sometimes even adding the pronunciation of the foreign (Sumerian) word.

At this point the legitimate question arises: Why do the Eblaites translate the Sumerian words? A reply to this query necessarily entails a discussion of the kind of writing used by the scribes to compose the documents of their own culture.

The four cuneiform signs reproduced here in the writing of the Eblaites are transliterated EN.EB.LA.KI and are translated "king of Ebla." Their importance for the identification of Tell Mardikh with Ebla and for the recognition of this new and unexpected civilization may hence be termed historic.

But the purpose of beginning this chapter with some of the signs in which the tablets of the royal archives were composed is to show the reader the kind of writing employed by the ancient scribes which today is called "cuneiform writing."

Used for the first time in 1700 by E. Kämpfer, the term "cuneiform" serves to indicate all those systems of writing in which the graphic signs are composed of *cunei* "wedges," arranged in very varied groupings. One could speak up to now of Babylonian (or, better, Sumero-Akkadian), Hittite, Hurrian, Urartian, Elamite, Persian, or even Ugaritic cuneiform, to which Eblaite cuneiform must now be added.

All these systems resemble one another, but only in external appearances, insofar as they originated or at least arose under the impulse of cuneiform *par excellence,* namely Babylonian. This writing presumably originated in southern Babylonia, the southern Iraq of today, spread first throughout Mesopotamia and then the whole Near East, and lasted for about three thousand years; the latest surely datable cuneiform tablet goes back to about A.D. 50.

With the exception of a reference in one of Herodotus's works, cuneiform was completely lost to sight and sixteen hundred years had to pass before the European world became aware of its existence. It was the great Italian traveler Pietro della Valle who, in a letter of 1621 describing his visit to the ruins of Persepolis, mentions this form of writing and furnishes a copy of five of the signs.

After this phase of rediscovery of cuneiform writing follows a new period of silence, not to say oblivion. Only in 1778, when C. Niebuhr published faithful copies of inscriptions from Persepolis, did the period of decipherment begin, a task that occupied European scholars for nearly seventy years.

Now we are in the third period, at least so far as Sumero-Akkadian cuneiform is concerned; this consists of working out and evaluating some of the cuneiform documents. Peoples vanished for millennia are rising out of the ground and reporting in vivid detail their great cultures, their historical experiences, their economic structure, their religious beliefs.

The discovery of Ebla and her documents in cuneiform now bids us to retrace the various phases of the decipherment which will probably engage savants throughout the world for the next 50 years.

The Ebla texts are written on clay tablets of varying dimensions and shapes. From a purely external point of view, all the tablets from the smallest to the biggest are normally written on both sides divided by the scribes into vertical columns. In every column is found a varying number of lines called registers. The following example serves to illustrate a characteristic feature of cuneiform tablets, that is, the criteria by which the scribe composed every one of his documents:

Having divided the front side of the tablet into columns, the scribe began to write the first column, going from left to right. The lines of each column were written from the top down and when he reached the last line of the last column, the scribe did not turn the page, so to speak, as we do today, but lifted up the tablet like a sheet of a writing-pad. Then he reversed the writing process, so that the columns now read from right to left. He began at the top of the first column on the right of the reverse side which corresponds to the last column of the obverse, so that the first line of the reverse is the continuation of the last line of the obverse.

This example gives the general lines of procedure in composing a cuneiform tablet, but occasional exceptions to this practice are not excluded.

Though quite different from modern Western methods of writing, this manner of drawing up a document is coherent; no less coherent is the writing of cuneiform signs in the several registers of the columns. In writing from left to right, the scribe conforms to the nature of the wedges which go from left to right.

Occasionally the amount of text does not fill the whole tablet, so that some of the columns remain vacant. But above all in the large tablets with commercial transactions we notice that the scribe, while leaving some columns empty, prefers to carry over the concluding sums to the last column and this for archivistic necessity. I will stress below that the library tablets were arranged on shelves with the reverse of the tablet facing the center of the room. Now the reason becomes evident: on top one found the last column of the text so that the consultation of the final sums was easier.

In some tablets the sum is put directly on the spine corresponding to the last column, just as today the title of a book is also written on the spine. This way consultation was rendered simple insofar as there was no need to move the tablet in order to read the final column.

To this treatise on how a tablet was composed we attach a practical illustration showing how to read a tablet. The text is TM.75.G.2342, whose historical content will be examined later.

When dealing with the specific problem of the forms of writing used in

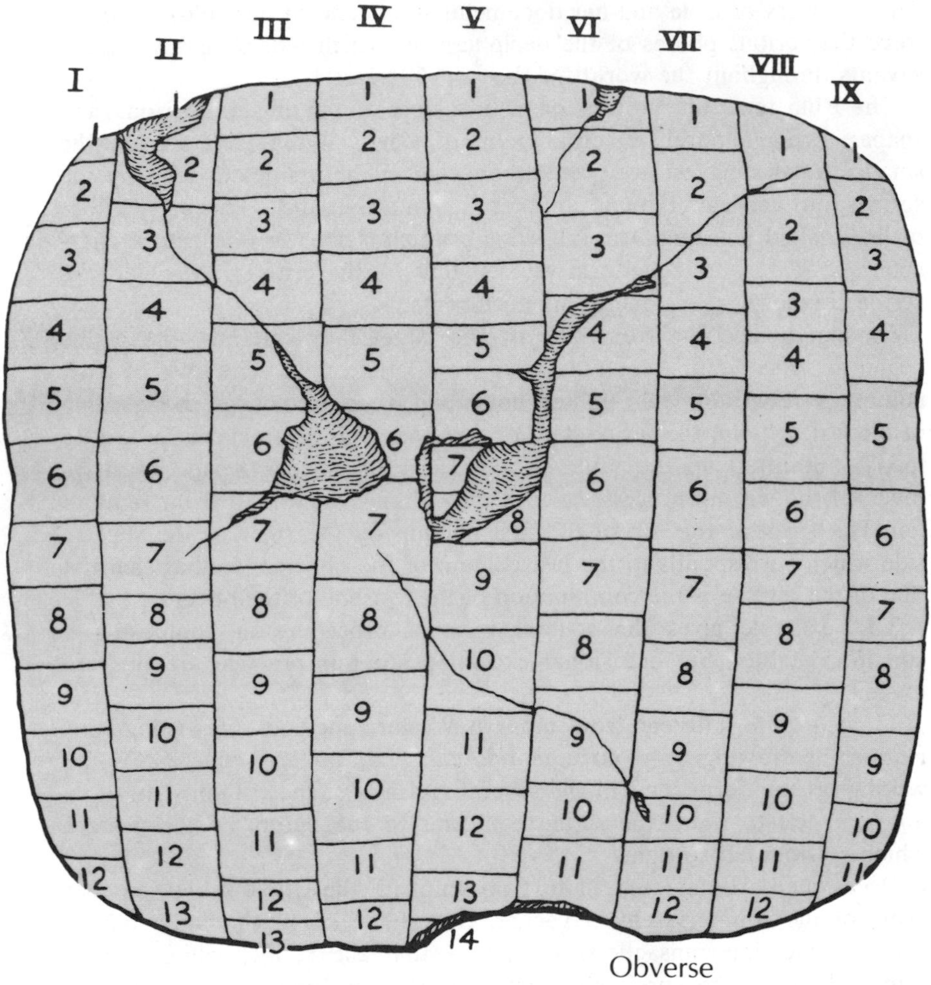

Figure I, 2 Criteria for composing a tablet (obverse)

Ebla and with the indications for a plausible dating of the tablets on purely paleographic grounds, it should be observed that the scribal tradition of Ebla presents similarities with the system of writing of Fara and Abu Salabikh. The similarities are such as to justify the position that the archives of Ebla are contemporary with the documents found in these two Mesopotamian cities and dating between 2600–2500 B.C.

Such a dating must, however, be further substantiated. First, it must be noted that the external shape of the tablets themselves is identical with that known from Fara and Abu Salabikh. The form of the signs is undeniably the same; a comparison of any tablet from Abu Salabikh with

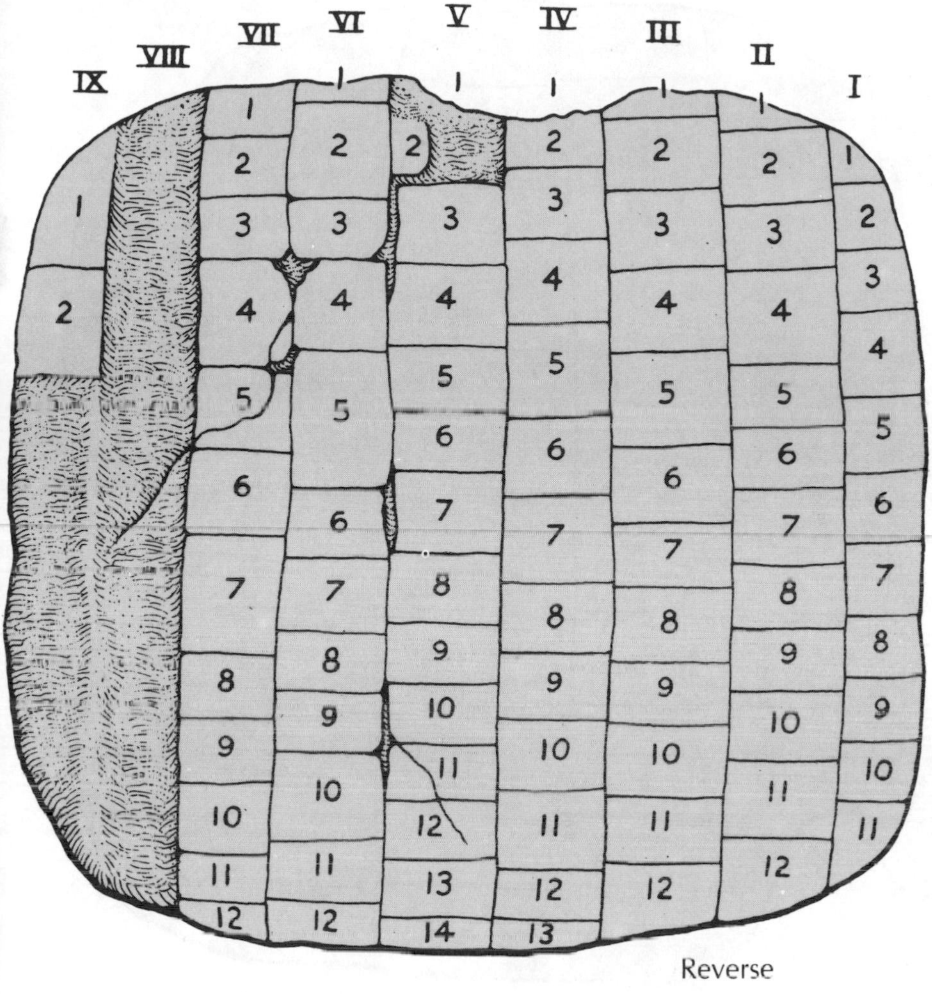

Figure I, 3 Criteria for composing a tablet (reverse)

one from Ebla will suffice to establish the identity of the signs in the two centers. Recognized with the first discoveries at Ebla in 1974, this identity was further confirmed when the great library came to light in 1975.

But the similarities do not end here; there are some lexical tablets at Ebla in which the number of columns and lines is identical to those in tablets of the same contents found in Abu Salabikh! To these merely formal aspects another consideration which is decisive must be added. In the Fara and Abu Salabikh documents the position occupied by the different signs in the individual registers is not constant in the sense that the signs are necessarily written in the order in which they are to be read. The

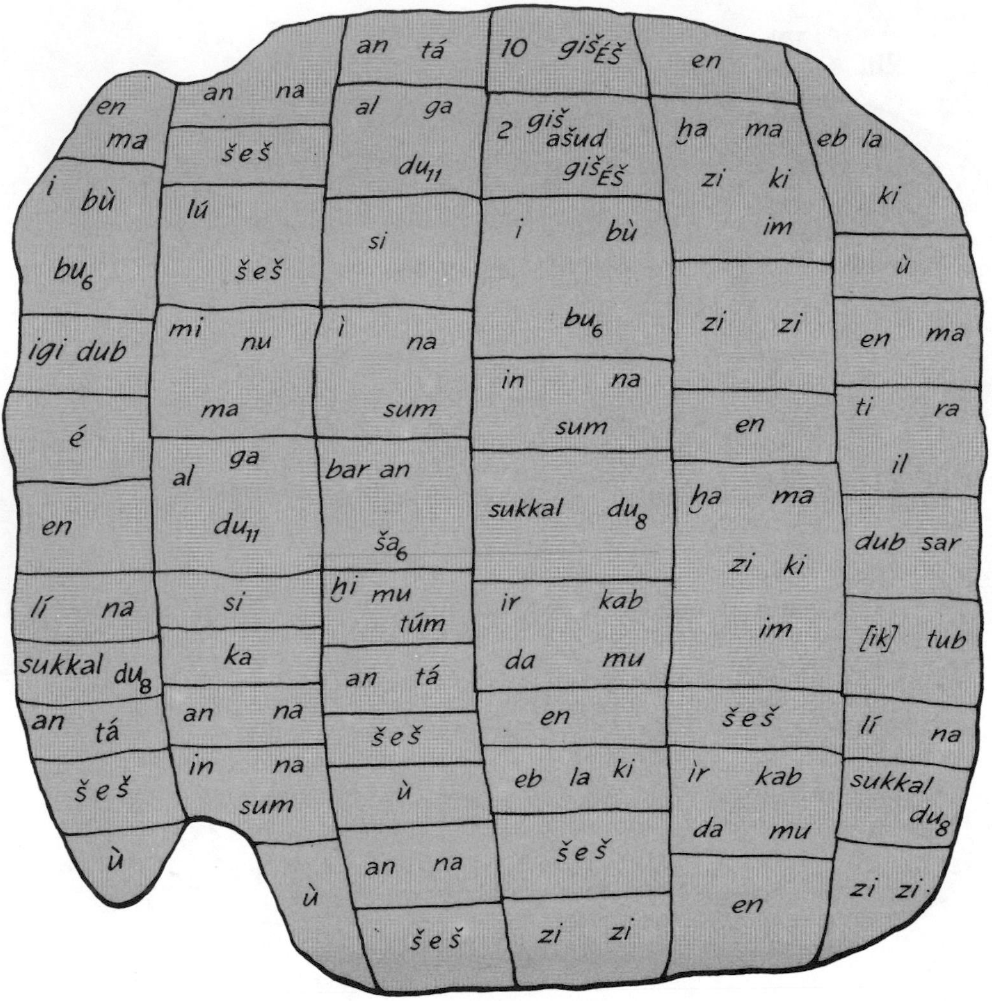

Figure I, 4 Example of cuneiform text transliterated (TM.75.G.2342, cf. p. 97f.)

same practice obtains at Ebla when Sumerian logograms are employed, but the situation is different when the Eblaites write syllabically.

From these diverse paleographic factors one conclusion appears plausible: the Ebla archives are contemporary with those of Fara and Abu Salabikh and should be dated on purely paleographic grounds to circa 2500 B.C. This requires giving up the 2350–2250 dates which I defended earlier because of mainly archaeological considerations.

CHAPTER II

The Finding of Ebla

1. Ebla in Mesopotamian and non-Mesopotamian documents. 2. Theories about the location of Ebla. 3. The archaeological discovery of Ebla. 4. The philological rediscovery of Ebla and the identification of Tell Mardikh with Ebla. 4.1. The finding of the Ibbiṭ-Lim statue. 4.2. First consequences and reactions.

"Never since the time of the creation of mankind did any king whatever set Arman and Ebla to sword and flame; *now* did Nergal open up the path for Naram-Sin the strong, and he gave him Arman and Ebla; he also presented him with Amanus, the Mountain of Cedars, and the Upper Sea. And with the weapon of Dagan who aggrandizes his kingdom, Naram-Sin the strong defeated Arman and Ebla, and from the banks of the Euphrates as far as Ulisum he subdued the peoples whom Dagan had given him, so that they carried the corvée-basket for his god Aba, and he could control the Amanus, the Mountain of Cedars."

It is Naram-Sin (2250 B.C.),[1] the king of Akkad, who is here recounting to his subjects and to posterity his roaring successes in distant lands, his conquests and his greatness. The strong and mighty Naram-Sin, the darling of the gods, has destroyed Arman and Ebla and has reached Amanus, the Cedar Mountain, and the Upper Sea.

The tone of the inscription is typically triumphalistic and Oriental, bringing us back enchanted to a distant past when valiant men were allied with gods in sensational exploits. And here appears Ebla, set to sword and torch, but still grand since no king "since the creation of mankind" had ever managed to conquer her. Only the destiny decreed by the gods permitted her destruction.

From this and other reports both within and outside of Mesopotamia, which will be reviewed in this chapter, one could collect, before the discovery of the royal archives, information about this city. Nonetheless, she continued to be without a face and without a history, so much so that no one knew where to locate her. That she was also the center of an immense empire was simply unthinkable.

1. EBLA IN MESOPOTAMIAN AND NON-MESOPOTAMIAN DOCUMENTS

The oldest references to Ebla in cuneiform literature from Mesopotamia date to the period of the Akkad Dynasty (2350–2150 B.C.). Sargon the Great, the founder of the dynasty, and his grandson Naram-Sin both tell us that they conquered Ebla, the former in a rather detached style, the latter euphorically. From an inscription of Sargon preserved not in the original but in copies of later periods we know that he conquered all of northern Syria as far as Lebanon and Turkey:

> "Sargon the king prostrated himself in prayer before Dagan in Tuttul. (He) gave him Upper Region: Mari, Iarmuti (and) Ebla as far as the forest of cedars and the mountain of silver."[2]

This report is directly confirmed by the geographical list of the Neo-Assyrian period[3] and indirectly by the "Legend of Sargon" according to which the king decided to undertake the military campaign toward northern Syria to secure the commercial route from Turkey to Mesopotamia against the ambushes of local kings.[4]

A hundred years later King Naram-Sin adorns himself with the prestigious title "Conqueror of Arman and Ebla,"[5] as well as affirming in the inscription cited above that he was the first king ever to destroy these two cities. In due course he also mentions the name of Arman's king, Rid(a)-Hadad, whom he took prisoner and bound to the pillars of the gate to his palace. The text thus continues:

> "At the time when Dagan decreed a (favorable) destiny for the mighty Naram-Sin and handed over to him Rida-Hadad, the king of Arman, whom he personally bound to the hinges of his palace, Naram-Sin had his statue sculpted in diorite and he dedicated it to Sin. Thus (speaks) the mighty Naram-Sin, the king of the four quarters: 'Dagan has given me Arman and Ebla and I have taken prisoner Rida-Hadad the king of Arman. Then I had my statue carved and I dedicated it to Sin. Let no one obliterate my name.' "[6]

It is interesting that the royal palace of third-millennium Ebla, unearthed since 1974 by the Italian expedition, shows undoubted traces of a huge conflagration and that Naram-Sin of Akkad was considered responsible for its fiery destruction. Artifacts found in the ruins of the palace would, on historical and artistic grounds, seem to support that conclusion. Historically, however, Naram-Sin's inscription raises some doubts; he does not, in fact, mention the king of Ebla but only the king of Arman. After the discovery of the royal archives of Ebla, which mention a number of the city's kings, this omission is surprising, to say the least. Secondly, Naram-Sin claims to be the first conqueror of Ebla. Leaving aside for the moment the colorful manner of Oriental rhetoric, it is certain that Sargon had conquered Ebla before him. Hence one must exercise caution when evaluating the affirmations of Naram-Sin. Finally, there is no avoiding the fact that the empire of Ebla flourished before 2350, so that the destruction of the palace might also have been the work of some other king.

The following attestations of Ebla belong to the period of the Second Dynasty of Lagash (2150–2110 B.C.). The governor Gudea maintained some commercial relations with Ursu in northern Syria whence he imported wood:

> "From the city of Ursu (situated on) the plateau of Ebla he imported pine logs, large fir-tees, trunks of plane-trees and mountain trees."[7]

In an economic text of the same period are mentioned three pieces of Ebla linen cloth each measuring 22.5 meters in length.[8]

Naturally the most frequent references to Ebla occur in the archives of the Third Dynasty of Ur (2112–2004 B.C.). First of all, Ebla appears together with Mari and Tuttul in a historical inscription of King Shusin, which leads one to think that Ebla was incorporated into the great Sumerian empire.[9] This hypothesis is enhanced by an unpublished text of the Third Dynasty of Ur coming from Nippur and dated to the seventh year of Amar-Suena's reign:

> "287,150 gur of barley as food for the men of Mari, the men of Ursu, and the men of Ebla; on the part of Luningirsu, Khuziru the messenger has received in his capacity as representative of the men of Tuttul and of the men of Iamatium. Seventh year of AS."

If I understand rightly the contents of this text, northern Syria, already at the time of Amar-Suena, the predecessor of Shusin, was divided into two administrative provinces with seats at Tuttul and Iamatium upon which depended the three centers of Mari, Ursu, and Ebla. The barley assigned as rations must surely have served for the functionaries of the empire.

In the economic texts of various provinces of the empire the mention of Eblaites visiting Sumer is frequent. These were either messengers or merchants or persons with no particular designation, almost always cited together with people of Mari, Ursu, Tuttul, and Iamatium.[10] In some cases the texts also give the names of certain Eblaites, such as Ili-Dagan, Shuri-Hadad, Nur-Ili, which prove exceptionally important for the question of the ethnic group at Ebla during this period.

At this period too one encounters the mention of the "canal of Ebla"[11] in the vicinity of the city of Adab, which suggests that a colony of Eblaites had settled in Sumer before the colony after which the canal was named. The oldest reference to this canal is found in an economic text of the First Dynasty of Lagash, hence about 2400 B.C. and predating the Akkad Dynasty. The data supplied by the royal archives of Ebla seem to confirm the hypothesis that a colony of Eblaites existed in the neighborhood of Adab, since Ebla had some commercial dealings with Adab as well as with Kish.

After the collapse of the Ur empire during the Isin Dynasty (2017–1994 B.C.) in southern Mesopotamia, Ebla continues to be mentioned. Thus one text from the time of Ishbi-Irra lists some leather pouches containing tablets of people coming from Mari and Ebla.[12] To this same period belongs the inclusion of the city of Ebla in the great Babylonian geographical list[13] and the mention of the "forest of Ebla" as the source of construction wood in the literary composition called "Nanna's Trip to Nippur."[14]

In the period of the First Dynasty of Babylon, Ebla seems not to have interested southern Mesopotamia. The sole mention is that of a personal name, *eb-la-a-num,* "the One of Ebla," in an economic text.[15]

In Assyria, however, Ebla is mentioned, even if rarely. A letter of the Old Assyrian period related that citizens of Ebla traveled to Kaniš in Cappadocia on business matters,[16] and another from the Middle Assyrian period mentions a royal messenger of Ebla who goes to Ashur.[17] In the theological schools of Assur at this same period the "goddess of Ebla" was known and accepted in the "list of divinities" as belonging to the official Assyrian pantheon.[18]

Outside of Mesopotamia proper, and more precisely in Syrian, Hittite, and Egyptian documentation, Ebla rarely figures and then only in relatively late texts. In the Syrian area the documents from Alalakh deserve special mention. Tablets of phase VII at Alalakh (eighteenth century B.C.) record trips of the king of Alalakh or of his messengers to Ebla.[19] One tablet contains the name of a year which commemorates a dynastic marriage:

> "Year (in which) Ammitaku, the king (of Alalakh), chose (as wife) for his son the daughter of the lord of Ebla."[20]

The closeness of bonds joining these two cities during this period is confirmed by another text which tells of the purchase of a house at Ebla by a merchant from Alalakh.[21] In phase IV of Alalakh (fifteenth century B.C.) a certain Ekhli-Teshup is mentioned as coming from Ebla.[22]

In the rich documentation of Ugarit (fourteenth to thirteenth centuries B.C.) Ebla remains absent, but its existence is indirectly attested by the personal name *ibln,* "the one of Ebla."[23]

In a still unpublished tablet from Emar during the years around

1310–1187 B.C. there is the surprising mention of an Eblaite, sure proof that the city continued to exist even after 1600 B.C.[24]

Beyond Syria, Hittite and Hurrian literature each record Ebla but once, and the same obtains for the great geographic list of Thutmosis III in the temple of Amon at Karnak.[25]

From this summary of references to Ebla in Mesopotamian and extra-Mesopotamian literature one sees its documentation for over a thousand years. But what is the face of Ebla revealed by these sources? The one sure datum is that Ebla was an important trade center for southern Mesopotamia (Gudea, Ur III) and for Turkey (Cappadocia). That it was also a significant political hub can be gathered only indirectly from the inscriptions of Sargon and Naram-Sin, at least for the third millennium. If the year name from Alalakh and the mention of "king of Ebla" in a Middle Assyrian letter are left aside, we know precious little about Ebla as a political entity in the second millennium.

Hence it is difficult to understand the silence of the very rich epigraphic sources of Mari and Ugarit, which has elsewhere been explained as due to the secondary role played by Ebla after 1800 because of the rise of the neighboring kingdom of Aleppo.[26] In addition to this purely historical explanation, there might be another of a political nature. By a kind of vendetta one prefers not to mention the age-old enemy or to transmit to posterity the memory of defeat or even the name of the conqueror. Hence Mari, repeatedly defeated by the mighty Ebla of the third millennium, categorically refuses to mention the name of the rival city.

To return to third-millennium Ebla, the Ebla of the royal archives, one need not be surprised at its not being mentioned in contemporary Mesopotamian sources. Perhaps later on, when Kish has been excavated, it will be possible to establish if Ebla is really missing or not in texts from Mesopotamia. At present the chanciness of epigraphic evidence does not permit writing Ebla's history on the basis of Mesopotamian documents. Fortune, however, has favored the Italians, granting them the chance to reconstruct the history of Ebla from its own witness, as well as to rewrite much of the history of the ancient Near East during the third millennium.[27]

If Mesopotamian and non-Mesopotamian records do not assist in the reconstruction of Ebla's history, they do help with their personal names of Eblaites to draw conclusions regarding the ethnic composition of Ebla in different historical periods. From these we know that during the Old Akkadian and Ur III periods the greater part of the population must have been Semitic, more precisely West Semitic, as appears from such names as Rida-Hadad, Guraya, Shuri-Hadad, Iṣṣi(n)-Dagan, etc. The contents of the royal archives also make it clear that the natives are Canaanites and not Amorites. After the year 2000 a Hurrian element joins the Semitic population, as can be seen from personal names witnessed at Alalakh

(Napa, Ekhli-Teshub, Milabite). In the present state of knowledge a hundred-percent certainty cannot be attained, but it is very probable that Hurrians were present at Ebla already in the third millennium.

Table II, 1

Synoptic View of the Attestations of Ebla in Near Eastern Literature

	Mesopotamia	*Egypt*	*Turkey—Syria*
2400	Lagaš I —economic texts	——	——
2350	Accad —Sargon, Naram-Sin —historical texts	——	——
2150	Lagaš II —Gudea —anniversary texts	——	——
2112	Ur III —historical and economic texts	——	——
2017	Isin —Ishbi-Irra —economic and literary texts	——	——
1900	——	——	Kaniš —economic texts
1700	——	——	Alalaḫ VI —economic texts
1400	Ashur —economic texts	——	Alalaḫ IV Ugarit
1300	——	Karnak —Thutmosis III —anniversary texts	Emar —economic texts

2. THEORIES ABOUT THE LOCATION OF EBLA

Before the recent finds rendered certain the identification of Tell Mardikh with Ebla, numerous proposals had been advanced to identify and situate the city. Basing themselves on information supplied mainly by Sumerian-Akkadian texts, scholars had to work with many unknowns. In fact, they had not yet identified the cities located in the environs of Ebla, Ursum for example, with the result that they have been going from unknown to unknown.

From the following list of proposed identifications set forth between 1914 and 1970, oné can see not only the inaccuracy, but also the rash-

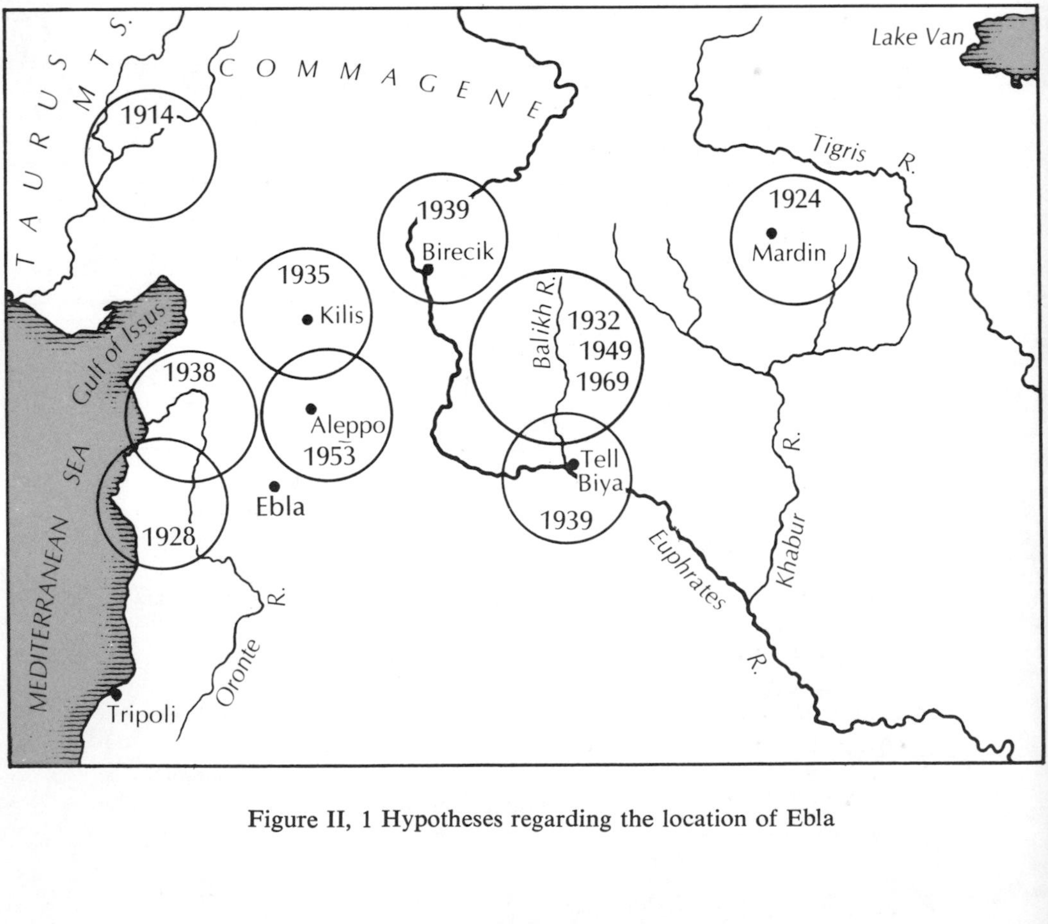

Figure II, 1 Hypotheses regarding the location of Ebla

ness of so many historical-geographical conclusions in the area of ancient Near Eastern studies.[28]

1914 A. Poebel proposes to situate Ebla in the zone between the Taurus range and Commagene.
1924 B. Landsberger localizes Ebla in the region of Mardin.
1928 Legrain-Gadd propose to place Ebla in the mountain between the gulf of Issos and Tripoli (Tarabulus).
1932 E. Unger identifies Ebla with Balikh.
1935 On the strength of a Middle-Assyrian letter, I. J. Gelb situates Ebla in the neighborhood of the modern city of Kilis in southern Turkey.
1936 Though citing a Hurrian text in which Ebla and Aleppo occur together, A. Ungnad does not commit himself.
1938 Returning to the problem, Gelb localizes Ebla in northern Syria and near the Mediterranean.
1939 W. F. Albright suggests the identification of Ebla with Tell el-Biya at the outlet of the Balikh river.
1939 Again tackling the problem, Landsberger proposes to set Ebla not far from Birecik in southern Turkey.
1949 J. Kupper proposes to place it in the Balikh valley.
1952 J. Lewy assigns Ebla to "the area today known as Bailan."
1952–53 E. Weidner thinks that Ebla was situated in northern Syria.
1953 A. Goetze proposes a site close to Aleppo.
1965 H. Klengel claims that Ebla lies to the northwest of Karkamis between the Euphrates and the mountain of Amanus.
1965 M. Liverani maintains that the epigraphic evidence allows a vacillation between a site east of the Euphrates and one in Syria proper.
1966 On the basis of information furnished by Gudea, A. Falkenstein does not see clear to localize Ebla much to the south of Taurus mountain.
1968 J. Bottéro looks for Ebla in the region of the Balikh river.
1970 M. Astour would identify Ebla with Tunanapa.

Though what is said here might be interpreted as heartless behavior toward living and deceased scholars, it should be stressed that prior to the discovery of the Ibbiṭ-Lim statue (see 4.1), no one thought to identify Ebla with Tell Mardikh. The prevailing opinion, in fact, sought the city in Turkey. Hence it was not a prophetic dream that led to the discovery of Ebla but pure and simple chance, an almost daily occurrence in Near Eastern archaeology. One need but recall that the great city of Akkad built by Sargon and his successors continues to elude the archaeologist's spade, despite frantic searches and rather explicit indications in cuneiform writings, to realize that the finding of Ebla and its ample archives is due in large measure to Dame Fortune.

3. THE ARCHAEOLOGICAL DISCOVERY OF EBLA

In the preface to the first volume of preliminary reports on the excavation of the Italian Archaeological Mission in Syria, Professor Matthiae sets out the motives and aims which led him to choose Tell Mardikh as the site for the dig: "A reconnaissance trip undertaken by the writer to preclassical sites south of Aleppo and north of Ḥama in September–October 1963 is at the origin of the creation of the Italian Archaeological Mission in Syria . . . In this reconnaissance trip I was able to visit and examine certain sites which I knew were particularly suited for an evaluation of the oldest urban culture in Syria. Two tells, situated relatively close to each other—Tell Mardikh and Tell Afis—and about seventy kilometers south of Aleppo, seemed after some surface exploration to offer sufficient guarantees that would justify efforts to clarify that important phase of Syria's history. It was the hope and wish of the writer and of his future collaborators that these sites would shed some light precisely on the origins of urban culture in that region of Syria and on the degree of relationships with the rest of northern Syria and with Mesopotamia and Syria."[29]

Tell Mardikh is a large tell, in form almost a trapezoid, covering some 140 acres. It consists of a central hillock—the Acropolis, somewhat roundish in shape and slightly tilted toward the south—of the quite extensive lower city in the shape of a ring, and of the enclosing wall of earth with four major depressions to the southwest, northwest, southeast, and northeast which seem to correspond to the four gates of the city.

In the excavations conducted regularly since 1964 one can fix the sequence of the settlements of the city and of its fortunes. To judge from the pottery found in sector B, Mardikh had its beginnings between 3500 and 3000 B.C. (Mardikh I). In proto-Syrian I (3000–2400 B.C.) the settlement still covered the Acropolis; in proto-Syrian II (2400–2000) Mardikh also extends down to the lower city. According to Matthiae this would be the period of the royal palace and its archives. In this period there are traces of two large-scale destructions, the first about 2250 and the second around 2000 B.C. In Old Syrian I (2000–1800) Mardikh's culture manifests enough characteristics different from those attested earlier to suggest a change of population. Old Syrian II (1800–1600) shows no break with the preceding period and ends with the definitive destruction of the city. After this phase the large city disappeared, but there are remains of smaller settlements both in the Middle Syrian (1600–1200) and in the New Syrian period (1200–530). In the Persian-Hellenistic epoch (530–60 B.C.), the city still preserves vestiges on the northern slope of the Acropolis with three quite distinct phases.[30]

4. THE PHILOLOGICAL REDISCOVERY OF EBLA AND THE IDENTIFICATION OF TELL MARDIKH WITH EBLA

Several times over the archaeologists of the Italian Archaeological Mission have underlined the perfect correspondence of the archaeological data regarding the phases of Mardikh's settlement with the philological information from Mesopotamian and non-Mesopotamian sources. Back in 1964 M. Liverani, in his work on preclassical tells, wrote that the archaeological situation answered to the textual data supplied us concerning ancient Ebla, without, however, hazarding the hypothesis of a possible identification of Tell Mardikh with Ebla.[31]

On the strength of the available archaeological evidence, such correspondences do not appear convincing. With regard to second-millennium Ebla the Mesopotamian sources are almost completely silent, even though the city enjoyed a marvelous reflowering, as the excavations have revealed. When one looks at third-millennium Ebla, the situation is even more desperate: in this period Ebla reached its greatest splendor, and yet contemporary Egyptian and Mesopotamian texts never mention it. From this observation it grows clear that only the recovery of local texts can guarantee certainty.

For five years the Italian mission had been digging at Mardikh, but it did not know nor could it suppose that it was digging the ancient city of Ebla. But in 1968 the first of three events which were to shake the world of culture came to light. With the finding of the statue of Ibbiṭ-Lim the first proof that Tell Mardikh could be Ebla was at hand.

4.1. THE FINDING OF THE IBBIṬ-LIM STATUE

P. Matthiae describes the discovery thus: "The opening up of the sector called G, in the southwest area of the Acropolis was undertaken to obtain some indications concerning the topography of the presumed approach to the Acropolis itself. Though this digging adduced only negative elements for an urban interpretation of the organization of the southwest slope of the citadel which hypothetically gave shape to the Acropolis, it led, however, to an unusually important discovery for the history of the city. The exploration of the limited area of the upper slope of the Acropolis called sector G did in fact bring to light the torso of a statue in basalt, TM.68.G.61. Its chief interest lies in the relatively well-preserved Akkadian cuneiform inscription on the upper part of the bust. In its present condition the torso measures 0.54 meters in height on the left side of the body which is more extensively preserved. At the height of the shoulders, which preserve their original dimensions, the statue is 0.47 meters wide. It is 0.21 meters thick at shoulder height corresponding to the beard while in the lower part of the fragment at the level of the break its thickness measures 0.23 meters."[32]

Since the statue, whose head had been removed, was not found in situ, its dating can only be approximate. While not categorically excluding an earlier date Matthiae, for historical-artistic reasons, tends to favor a date between 2000 and 1900 B.C.[33]

The 26-line cuneiform inscription[34] was added crosswise to the normal erect position of the statue. It begins on the figure back at the height of the spine, continues on the left shoulder and goes on to the chest as far as chin level to finish, after an empty space, on the right shoulder.

The text was written on one column in a rectangular space well demarcated on its four sides. The scribe took constant care always to fill the space at his disposal between the outer edges of the rectangular column, sometimes elongating the signs in an exaggerated manner, and was careful not to transgress the right edge of the column.

The script is cuneiform of the monumental type and the language is Akkadian, which belongs to the East Semitic group of languages. The number of peculiarities was such that in 1969 I began to think that we had indications of a new language, a new branch of the Akkadian language.

After the discovery of the royal archives of the third millennium, also written in cuneiform but in a West Semitic language—hence quite different from Akkadian—the inscription constitutes a very important element showing that the population and the culture itself of Ebla must have radically changed around 2000 B.C. The uncertainty and the crudeness of the script contrasting with the perfect execution of the writings from the royal archives also make one think that the new population succeeding that of 2500 B.C. must have had to learn anew the art of writing which had been completely forgotten.

1 *a-na* ^{d}[*eš*$_4$*-tár*] *ap-sà-am*
2 *i-bi-iṭ-li-im*
3 *mār ig-ri-iš-ḫe-epa*$_x$ *šàr*
4 *me-ki-im eb-la-i-im*
5 *ú-šé-ri-ib*
6 mu.sà.sà *ša* ^{d}*eš*$_4$*-tár*
7 *ša*$^?$ *ú-pí-a i-na eb-la*
8 *ma-za-zu-um*
9 *i-bi-iṭ-li-im*
10 *šu-um-šu a-na ba-la-ṭì-šu*
11 *ù ba-la-aṭ*
12 *me-er-e-šu* <*i-pu-uš-ma*>
13 ^{d}*eš*$_4$*-tár* {*u*}

14 *ta-ar-ta-šu-ma*
15 *ma-za-zu-ú*
16 IGI *^{d}eš$_{4}$-tár*
17 *bé-el-ti-šu*
18 *ú-ša-zi-iz iš-k[u$^{?}$]*
19 *šu-um-šu*
20 *ša ma-za-zi-[i]*
21 *šu*-ME MAŠ$^{?}$ ŠU$^{?}$[ ]
22 *me-er-e-[šu]*
23 *^{d}eš$_{4}$-[tár]*
24 *ú-lu-[ ]*
25 *šu-um-[šu$^{?}$]*
26 *ša i-[bi-iṭ-li-im]*

"For the [goddess Eštar], Ibbiṭ-Lim, brought in a basin (in the temple), the son of Igriš-Ḫepa, the king of Eblaite 'stock.' He, to whom the goddess Eštar has given the name, who has taken possession in Ebla, the above-mentioned Ibbiṭ-Lim, had a statue <sculpted> for his life and the life of his sons; Eštar was intensely pleased with him; he erected the statue before Eštar his lady . . . [ ]. The name of the statue is: . . . [ ] [his] sons [ ] Ešt[ar]; the name [?] of I[bbiṭ-Lim]."

The inscription, given here in an updated version,[35] is in a good state of preservation, except for line 1 and lines 20–26; hence the sense is quite clear. It divides into two unequal parts:

A. The offering of a votive gift to Eštar.
B. The dedication to Eštar of a statue of the king.

The first part, comprising only lines 1–5, records the offering to Eštar on Ibbiṭ-Lim's part of a basin for ritual ablutions.

The second part, however, embracing lines 6–26, deals with the dedication to the goddess Eštar of one or more statues of the king by King Ibbiṭ-Lim himself "for his own life and the life of his sons." It begins with an epithet of the king which reveals the close bond uniting him to the goddess Eštar and continues with a historical notice. A detailed account of the statue's carving then follows, and mention is made of Eštar's pleasure in the statue set before her. The inscription closes by mentioning the name, unfortunately unintelligible, given to the statue by Ibbiṭ-Lim.

The paleographic and linguistic arguments for dating the inscription fully accord with Matthiae's historical-artistic considerations for a 2000–1900 B.C. date.

The inscribed statue is important for a number of reasons, but here we

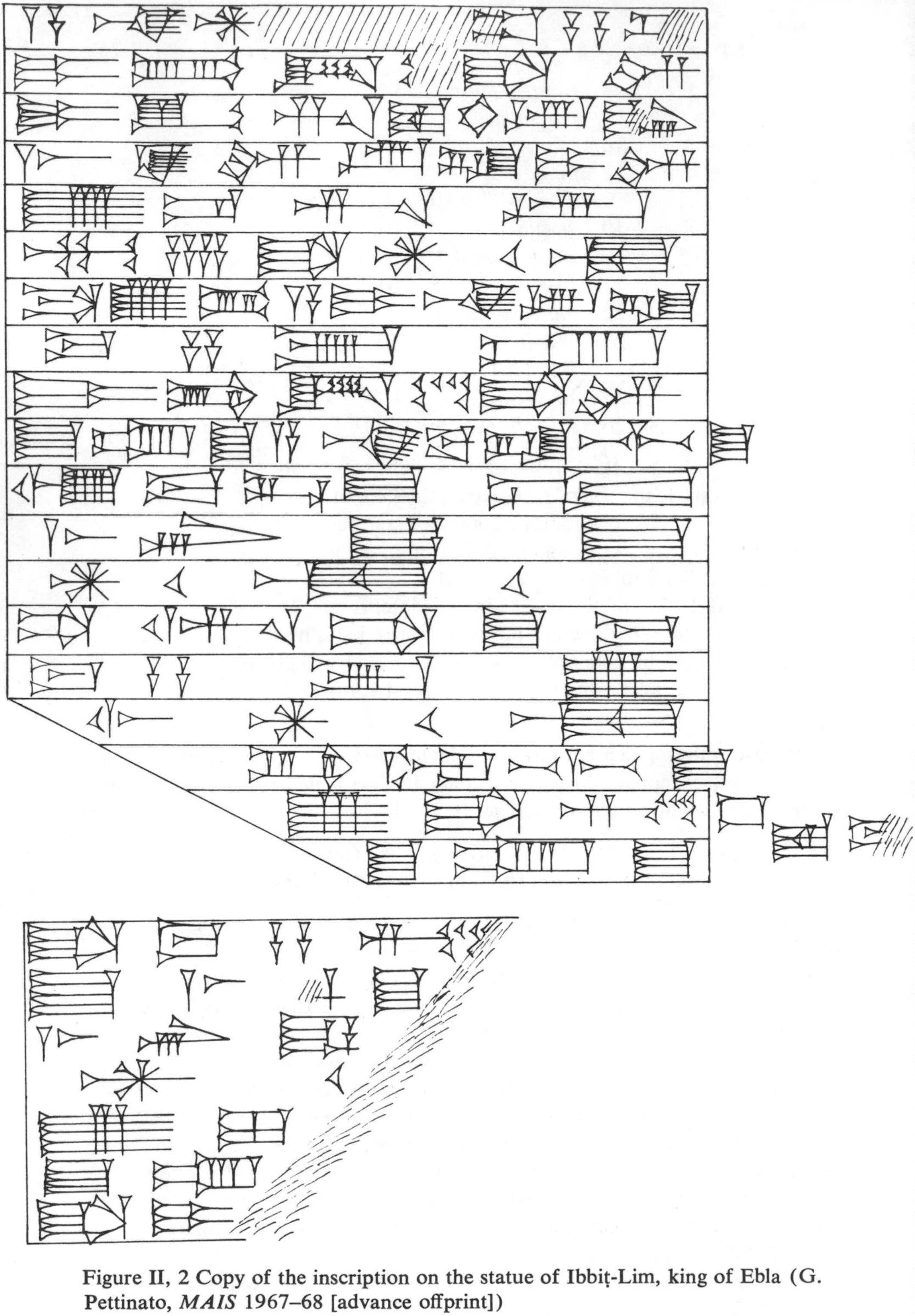

Figure II, 2 Copy of the inscription on the statue of Ibbiṭ-Lim, king of Ebla (G. Pettinato, *MAIS* 1967–68 [advance offprint])

shall dwell only on the contribution it makes to the history and geography of the ancient Near East.

Above all, it sheds new light on the history of northern Syria in general and of Ebla in particular around the period 2000–1900 B.C. From the inscription we learn the name of one of Ebla's kings, Ibbiṭ-Lim, and the name of his father Igriš-Ḫepa. The king's epithets are particularly interesting in that they permit some conclusions of considerable importance:

1. son of Igriš-Ḫepa;
2. king of Eblaite "stock";
3. he to whom Eštar gave his name;
4. he who took possession in Ebla.

Epithet number 2 in particular permits one to hold that in this period the kingdom of Ebla was based upon tribal unity following a tradition already verified at the time of the royal archives five hundred years earlier. From epithet four it emerges that Ibbiṭ-Lim was installed at Ebla, but the real meaning of this escapes us. Is it hinting at the fact that Ebla perhaps regained its independence under Ibbiṭ-Lim when he refounded the kingdom after a period of decline?

Another item that merits notice is the ethnic composition of Ebla. The king's father Igriš-Ḫepa has a hybrid Amorite-Hurrian name, while his son Ibbiṭ-Lim bears a pure Amorite name. This would indicate that Ebla stood at the crossroads of two ethnic components—Amorite and Hurrian—living peaceably in Ebla. Far from creating difficulties, this piece of information helps fill in our previous knowledge. The name of the first king known at Urshum, which always had close contacts with Ebla, is Shennam, a strictly Hurrian name. The date of the inscription thus synchronizes perfectly with what was known of this area before the discovery of the statue.

But the most stunning item is the mention of the elusive Ebla, appearing first as the ethnic adjective in "Eblaite stock" and later as the city name. For the first time it became possible to advance the hypothesis that Tell Mardikh was ancient Ebla. When working out the inscription in 1970 I cautiously wrote: "The discovery at Tell Mardikh of an inscription mentioning Ebla is certainly not enough to conclude that Tell Mardikh is the ancient city of Ebla; one must in fact await other and more numerous texts which might confirm such an identification. From now on, though, we must face such a problem to which a large bibliography has been dedicated before the finding of our inscription." And after having examined all the documentation on Ebla in Mespotamian and non-Mesopotamian literature, I concluded: "I hold it opportune to stress that the epigraphic evidence does not oppose the identification Ebla = Tell Mardikh; rather, some texts render it very probable."[36]

Basing himself on archaeological data, but relying more on philological information which I supplied, P. Matthiae also wrote in a similar vein: "The problem of the identification of the site can be considered as resolved during this last season by the discovery . . . of the torso of a male figure, carved in basalt and bearing a 26-line cuneiform inscription . . . Identification (of Ebla) with Tell Mardikh would suit the facts far better, and the floruit of Tell Mardikh corresponds to that of Ebla."[37]

4.2. FIRST CONSEQUENCES AND REACTIONS

What were the reactions of scholars to the proposed identification of Tell Mardikh with Ebla? As often happens, opinions were immediately divided; while some reacted with a somewhat exaggerated skepticism, others at least took the matter into consideration.

Having reviewed all the literary evidence, M. C. Astour in 1971 rejected the identification in unmistakable terms: "Knowing how uncritically geographical statements are often accepted and perpetuated, it may be worthwhile to warn fellow researchers against hastily adopting the widely announced but unfounded identification of Tell Mardikh with Ebla."[38] Since Astour's competence is widely appreciated, his words came as a harsh setback and gave rise to the Ebla "thriller."

In 1974 the German scholars D. O. Edzard and G. Farber, though with greater caution, also rejected the proposed identification: "There are no other proofs for an identification [of Ebla] with Tell Mardikh; from geographical and prosopographical grounds there are more convincing proofs for a connection between Ebla and Ursu."[39] Again in 1974 Anneliese Kammenhuber cannot bring herself to accept the equation: "The identification of Ebla with Tell Mardikh some sixty kilometers south of Aleppo is, in my opinion, not possible."[40]

The reason for this reluctance is not hard to find. Accepting the equation Tell Mardikh=Ebla would entail admitting that earlier historical reconstructions were mistaken, that so many geographical maps of the ancient Near East meticulously detailed would no longer serve. Scholars are known not to rush when admitting their error.

Other savants, however, were less categorical. Thus in 1970 H. Klengel[41] already connected Tell Mardikh with Ebla, albeit with a question mark, and in 1975 M. Heltzer[42] vigorously defended the identification suggested by the inscription.

The discovery of Ebla began amid skepticism and criticism, hardly good auspices for the finds to follow, especially in 1974 and 1975.

Notes

1. *AfO* 20, pp. 73–75=*UET* I, 275, obverse I 1 – II 33.
2. *AfO* 20, p. 38,=Sargon b2, 14–28/17–35=*MAIS* 67/68, p. 30.
3. *KAV*, 92=*AfO* 16, p. 4, with n. 63=*MAIS* 67/68, p. 30.
4. See H. Hirsch, *AfO* 20, p. 6 and n. 48.
5. *RA* 10, p. 101, n. 1=*SAK* 166d=*MAIS* 67/68, p. 30.
6. *AfO* 20, pp. 75ff.=*UET* I, 275 obverse III 1 – IV 6.
7. *Statue B* V 54–59=*MAIS* 67/68, p. 31.
8. *ITT* V 6748, 1.
9. *JCS* 21, p. 37.
10. For the attestations of Ebla in UR III, see most recently G. Pettinato, *RlA* V, p. 10, with reference to *MAIS* 67/68, pp. 29ff.; M. Heltzer, *AIUON* 35, pp. 298ff.; D. O. Edzard–G. Farber, *Rép. Geogr.* II, p. 39.
11. *MAIS* 67/68, p. 33.
12. *BIN* IX, 417, 2–3.
13. *MSL* XII, pp. 104, 272.
14. A. J. Ferrara, *Studia Pohl* II, pp. 48 and 50.
15. *MAIS* 67/68, p. 34.
16. B. Kienast, *ATHE* 32, pp. 17–18.
17. *KAV*, 107, 7–8.
18. III *R* 66, obverse 20d.
19. *MAIS* 67/68, p. 35.
20. *AT* 35.10.
21. *AT* 60.3.
22. *AT* 182.5.
23. *MAIS* 67/68, p. 36.
24. *RlA* V, p. 11.
25. *MAIS* 67/68, pp. 35–36.
26. *RlA* V, p. 11.
27. On the relationships between Ebla and Mari in the third millennium, see G. Pettinato, *Akkadica* 2 (1977), 20–28.
28. *MAIS* 67/68, pp. 36–37.
29. *MAIS* 64, p. 17.
30. *RlA* V, pp. 13–15.
31. *MAIS* 64, p. 122; see also P. Matthiae, *Archaeology* 1971, 60–61.
32. *MAIS* 67/68, pp. 1–2.
33. *MAIS* 67/68, p. 16.
34. *MAIS* 67/68, pp. 16ff.
35. M. Heltzer, *AIUON* 35, 289ff., has subsequently studied this inscription; cf. already *RlA* V, p. 11. The new reading in line 6 comes from a suggestion of E. Sollberger whom I warmly thank.
36. *MAIS* 67/68, pp. 29 and 37.
37. *Archaeology*, 1971, 60–61.
38. *UF* 3, 18.
39. *Rép. Geogr.* II, p. 40.
40. In J. Harmatta–G. Komoroczy, *Wirtschaft und Gesellschaft im Alten Vorderasien*, Budapest 1976, p. 221 and n. 138.
41. *G. S.* III, p. 32.
42. *AIUON* 35, p. 317.

CHAPTER III

The Royal Archives

1. The discovery: 1974, 1975, 1976. 2. The importance of an archive for the reconstruction of a civilization. 3. The tablets of Ebla: manufacture, quantity, study. 4. Typology of the texts. 5. Archive science.

During the first decade of digging at Tell Mardikh the inscribed finds brought to light by the Italian Archaeological Mission were few indeed; apart from the statue of Ibbiṭ-Lim discussed in the preceding chapter, only a score of fragments of tablets were recovered in the northern part of the Acropolis, and these out of level. Of these still unpublished documents some belong to the period after 2000 B.C., whereas others date from the era of the great archives.

This lack of textual finds seemed to strengthen the hypothesis that northern Syria to the west of the Euphrates had not been reached by the great, ever-expanding culture of Mesopotamia until after 2000 B.C., and that Tell Mardikh, despite the wealth of archaeological material found, was essentially poor in written evidence.

With this contingent and preconceived view of the situation, H. S. Drower could write in the 1971 edition of the *Cambridge Ancient History*[1] that nothing was known of the ethnic makeup of the inhabitants of third-millennium Syria or of the language they spoke; moreover, one could question their familiarity with writing at this epoch. Another scholar, Anneliese Kammenhuber, wrote in 1974: "Thus far in northern Syria at a certain distance from the Euphrates no cuneiform documents antedating the Ur III period have been found, for example, at Tell Mardikh. This is not necessarily due to chance but is rather indicative; at least it can now be explained why later on the Hittites and others adopted the cuneiform script of the Ur III type."[2]

If the scientific premises listed here are added to the scholarly skepticism regarding the proposed identification of Tell Mardikh with the ancient city of Ebla, then the diffidence which accompanied the great discovery of the royal archives becomes understandable.

1. THE DISCOVERY: 1974, 1975, 1976

Ancient Near Eastern studies took an unexpected and portentous turn in 1974–76 when Ebla began to reveal herself through her own written documents. The first lot of tablets came to light in August 1974 in the

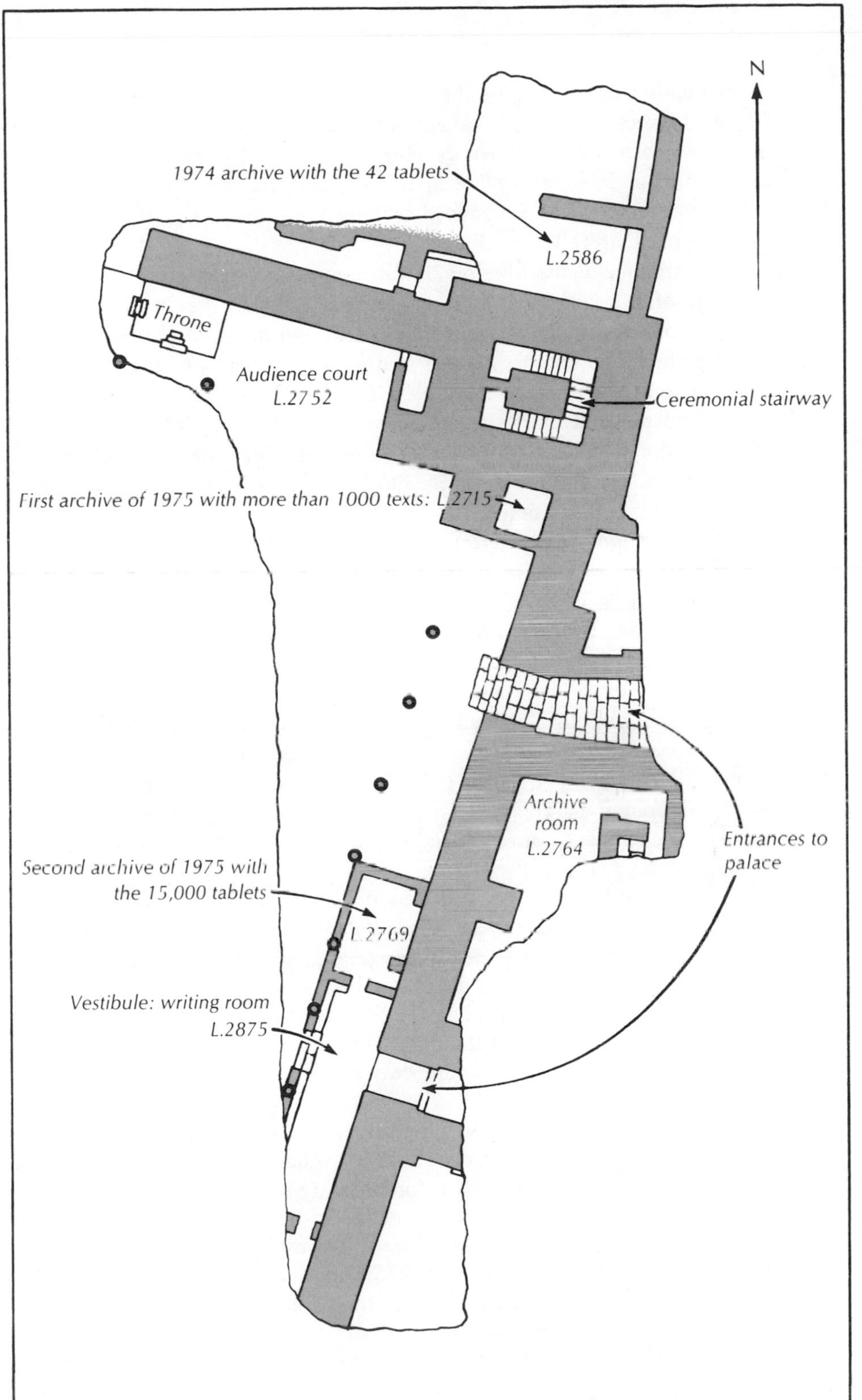

Figure III, 1 Plan of palace G. of Ebla and the location of the archives

room numbered L.2586. In the northwest wing of the royal palace the Italian Mission made an exceptional find; in one of the rooms it recovered carbonized wooden carvings—proof of Ebla's artistic maturity in the third millennium—while in the adjacent room it found some forty cuneiform tablets and fragments scattered on the floor, the first texts found in place at Tell Mardikh.[3]

As epigrapher of the Mission, I was summoned to interpret these writings, and after six months of study could report that they were composed in a very old Semitic language different from all heretofore attested. After the decipherment of the 26-line statue inscription found in 1967–68, which permitted the identification of Tell Mardikh with Ebla and which constituted the first of the three historic moments of Ebla's philological recovery, the decipherment of the language of Ebla with its revolutionary consequences for the study of Semitic languages in general followed as the second historical moment.[4]

Both these moments interested only the students of the ancient Near East, that is, the specialists. The mass media had not yet taken hold of Ebla and were in a sense unprepared for the upsetting reports coming at the close of the 1975 and 1976 seasons.

The year 1975, when the royal library was unearthed, marks the third historical moment. The Italian Mission intensified the excavation of the area on the Acropolis occupied by the royal palace, bringing to light "the audience court," and already in August discovered at the northern extremity of the court a room, L.2712, which turned out to be a small storeroom containing about a thousand tablets and fragments found amid the fill of unbaked bricks coming from the collapse following the conflagration.

In another room, L.2769, situated on the east side of the court and measuring 5.10 × 3.55 meters, the palace library properly speaking was found. Lined up against the north, east, and west walls and inclining toward the center of the room 14,000 tablets and fragments were discovered, still arranged on approximately two or three levels despite the sliding caused by destruction of the palace.

Both L.2712 and L.2769 were two areas outside the palace proper, which leads one to surmise that the courtyard was the open space where departing caravans were organized and returning caravans were received. From the palace interior, from L.2764 situated in the administrative quarter, some fragments were also forthcoming in 1975.[5]

The fateful date of October 1, 1975, is bound to the discovery of the library, but the approaching date of the dig's closing did not permit the recovery of all the tablets in L.2769 nor the clarification of how this area was connected with the interior of the palace.

The number of tablets recovered in the course of the 1975 work exceeded 15,000 units, and it was at this point that the mass media moved in. When press dispatches began to transmit the news about the sensational discovery of the royal archives of Ebla written in a heretofore unknown Northwest Semitic language from the second half of the third millennium B.C., the skepticism that had greeted the other phases of the finds continued to spread in the minds of scholars of the ancient world.

A very curious thing happened. At first the size of the discovery was put in doubt, so that the Parisian newspaper *Le Monde* wrote in December 1975 that the discovery of so many tablets in Syria was unthinkable. My subsequent lectures in European and American universities served to reduce the skepticism, which was partially replaced by a somewhat morbid interest in the epigraphic discovery of Ebla that almost got out of scientific control and began to be treated as an attractive curiosity.

In 1976 the excavation of L.2769 was resumed and another 600 fragments of tablets were recovered. In the immediately adjacent room, L.2875, which communicated with both the library and the interior of the palace, the Mission uncovered some 450 tablets and fragments. Precisely here was also found a jar full of clay and some instruments for writing and for canceling mistakes with lines or cross-hatching. The same season saw the completion of the clearing of L.2764, with the recovery of 500 tablets and fragments. Finally, on the pavement of the court was found a score of tablets arranged on one or two wooden planks which were completely burned; these must have served for transporting tablets from one place to another.

The discoveries made in 1975 and 1976 completely dispelled the doubts which had arisen earlier regarding both the identification of Tell Mardikh with Ebla and the correctness of the decipherment of the new Northwest Semitic language in which the documents were written.

So far as the identification of the site with ancient Ebla was concerned, the definitive reply was furnished by numerous historical documents, more precisely, by edicts and letters of state making mention of en-*eb-la*^{ki} "king of Ebla." Tal Mardikh—so the Arabs call it—a tiny village scarcely numbering 500 souls not far from the highway leading from Ḥama to Aleppo and near the turnoff to Saraqeb, is the ancient Ebla whose destruction was the boast of Naram-Sin, the sovereign of Akkad, and whose greatness we can now begin to appreciate, thanks to the discovery of the royal archives.

Dotted with so many important archaeological sites, such as Ugarit and Mari, Northern Syria can now show off a bigger and brighter jewel in Ebla.

Once the visitor to northern Syria interested in the historical problems of the ancient Near East reached the undulating plateau between Homs and Aleppo, he caught site of the tell of Kadesh with all its historic memories; it was here that the age-long power struggle between Egypt and the Hittite empire was decided in an epic encounter. But that concerns the second millennium. The recent recovery of the royal archives now confirms Syria's central role in the history of the entire Near East during the third millennium. Thanks to Ebla, Syria's central role brings to mind the political-commerical empire of Alexander the Great.

2. THE IMPORTANCE OF AN ARCHIVE FOR THE RECONSTRUCTION OF A CIVILIZATION

In a recent article[6] I wrote that Ebla has supplied the largest third-millennium archive uncovered to date; all the texts yielded by Mesopotamian soil from the Uruk period (2900 B.C.) to the Old Akkadian epoch (2150 B.C.) amount to about one fourth of the documents from Ebla.

Leaving aside considerations of quantity which, as will be seen, must be brought back into proper focus, we must stress that the recovery of an archive constitutes a priceless element for understanding and reconstructing a civilization. It is not a question of the primacy of philology over archaeology or vice versa, since both must be fully exploited if a clear picture of a civilization is to emerge, but it must not be overlooked that archaeology yields data much more difficult to interpret than those furnished by texts.

Unfortunately, the earliest civilizations must be reconstructed from archaeological finds alone; this obtains for prehistoric and protohistoric cultures as well. The finding of written evidence can, however, radically alter the picture. Taking third-millennium Syria as an illustration, the truth of the preceding statement becomes apparent. Despite numerous and important archaeological digs revealing a density of exceptional settlements in all this territory, the ethnic and linguistic composition of the inhabitants remained unknown.[7] Much less could one speculate on the structure of the state and its relationships with other states.

The royal archives of Ebla not only enable scholars to answer unsolved queries, but oblige them to see a period till now lost in prehistoric dusk in a historical dimension. Their discovery marks a turning point whose historical consequences at present can only be glimpsed. These archives compare not only in intrinsic worth but also in extent with the great cuneiform libraries of the first and second millennia B.C. found in Mesopotamia, such as those of Nineveh and Ashur of Boghazköy in Turkey, of Ugarit and Mari in Syria.[8]

The third millennium, on the other hand, has been very stingy with written evidence but, as Ebla shows, this has been essentially due to the chanciness of archaeological discoveries. Nor do indications lack for such a conclusion: archives of the Ur III empire (2000 B.C.) have been discovered in widely scattered provinces of the empire. Among these, the

Lagash archives have yielded more than 100,000 cuneiform tablets while the state archives of the capital Ur have never been located.[9]

To obtain a synoptic view of the archives in the Fertile Crescent dating to 3000–2100 B.C., attention must be fixed on Sumer in southern Mesopotamia; it is at Uruk, the legendary city of Gilgamesh, the Sumerian hero par excellence, that the oldest cuneiform writings have been found.[10] At this period—around 3000 B.C.—the writing is mainly pictographic, and yet the archives of Uruk, so far as they can be understood, describe a high civilization. In addition to economic texts, the archives yield lexical or school texts, signs of advanced intellectual endeavor.[11]

Nearest in time are the archives of Gemdet Nasr and Ur, the first in northern Babylonia not far from Baghdad,[12] the second in the heart of Sumer near modern Nasariya;[13] one is still dealing with texts difficult of comprehension and few in number, dating to the century 2800–2700 B.C. To 2600 B.C. date the archives of Fara,[14] ancient Shuruppak, the home of the Flood hero Utnapishtim, and those of Tell Abu Salabikh,[15] ancient Eresh. Besides economic and lexical documents, Fara and Abu Salabikh have yielded literary texts such as poems, myths, proverbs, and hymns; in other words, a complete picture of what writing can express. That writing was known during this period outside southern Mesopotamia is evident from the discovery of historical inscriptions and administrative documents at Mari in northern Mesopotamia.[16] It is precisely at this time that cuneiform script was employed to write a language other than Sumerian, namely, the Semitic language documented at Abu Salabikh and Mari.

Toward 2600 B.C. a cultural revolution of considerable proportions was taking place and one of its manifestations was the employment of the same script by diverse peoples of different tongues. The royal archives of Ebla not only confirm this event but attest it in a manner surpassing all expectations.

The archives of the first dynasty of Lagash[17] date to circa 2450 B.C. A five-city confederation with its capital at Girsu, this dynasty was ruled by kings considered unworthy to be included in the famous "Sumerian King List." And yet from Lagash come the great historical inscriptions, of which the inscription of Eannatum on the vulture stela is doubtless the most important, as well as a substantial number of economic texts. Writing had by this time become widespread throughout Mesopotamia, even though Nippur, Ur, and Adab have yielded few tablets.

With the rise of the dynasty of Akkad around 2350 B.C. the use of Akkadian, a Semitic language, became quite normal.[18] Different centers of Sumer, of the Diyala and of northern Mesopotamia such as Gasur (the Nuzi of later periods) all have their archives.

The third millennium closes with the second dynasty of Lagash (2150 B.C.), which marks the rebirth of Sumer after first being oppressed by the Akkadians and then by the Gutians. Famous above the others for their

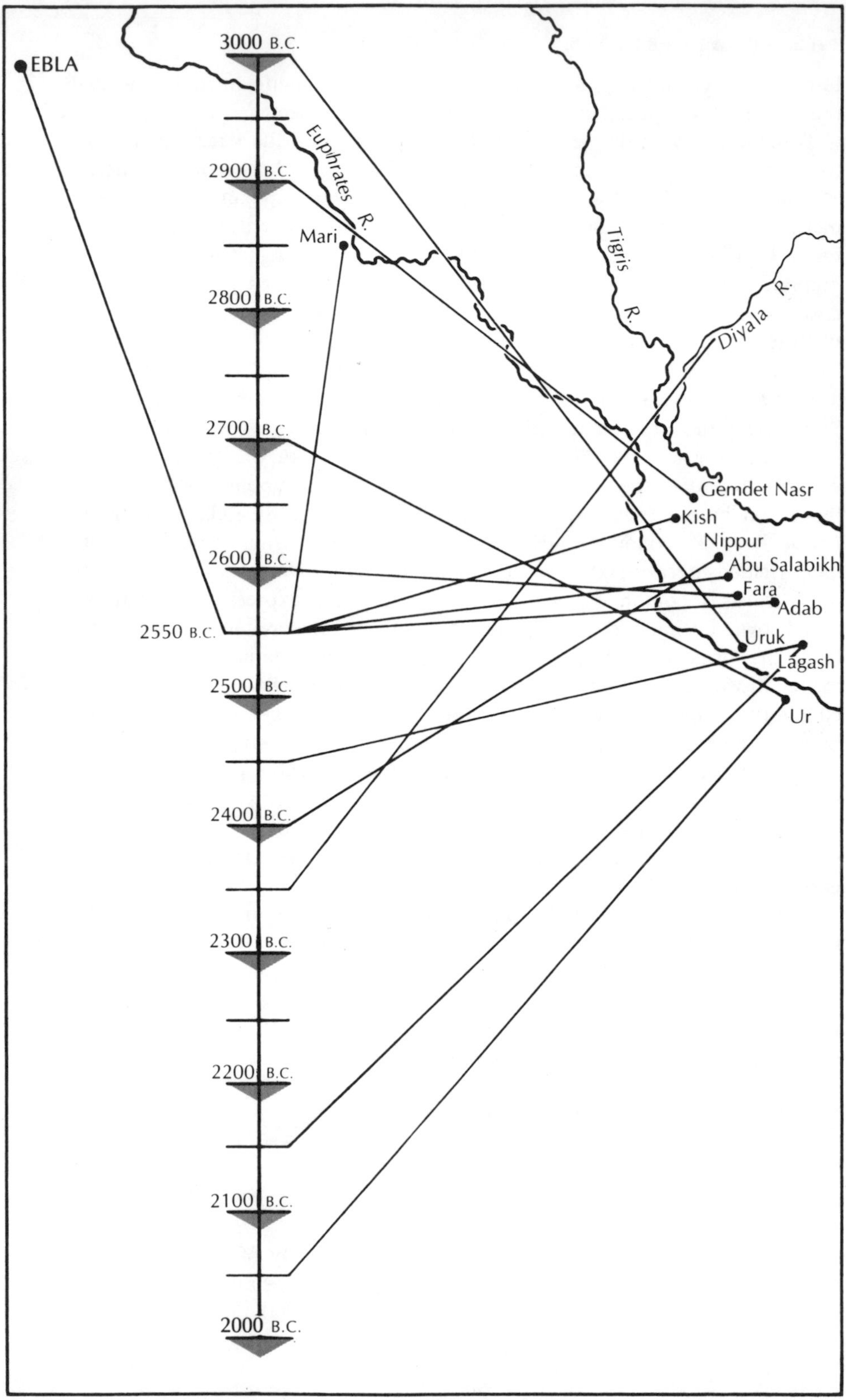

3000 B.C.
EBLA
Euphrates R.
2900 B.C.
Mari
Tigris R.
2800 B.C.
Diyala R.
2700 B.C.
Gemdet Nasr
Kish
Nippur
2600 B.C.
Abu Salabikh
Fara
Adab
2550 B.C.
Uruk
Lagash
2500 B.C.
Ur
2400 B.C.
2300 B.C.
2200 B.C.
2100 B.C.
2000 B.C.

literary maturity are the inscriptions of the governor Gudea, but these remain isolated monuments.

A comparison of all these archives with those of Ebla gives some idea of what has been called above the "chanciness" of the finds and to what extent good fortune has smiled upon the Italian Mission and with it the world of scholarship. All earlier archives, given their provincial character, cannot hold a candle to those of Ebla, the first real state archives of the third millennium in the Fertile Crescent. If this is true, then one conclusion stares us in the face: it is imperative to intensify archaeological excavations throughout the Near East, since the Ebla treasure cannot be unique, and surely many others lie hidden under the often arid soil of the ever-surprising Near East, rightly hymned as the cradle of civilization.

To return to our argument, the archives with their written documents found in various places and dating to several periods permit a much deeper penetration into a culture than essentially mute artistic artifacts can ever allow. Precisely to the lack of rich archives must be attributed the extremely limited knowledge of the ancient Near East.

3. THE TABLETS OF EBLA: MANUFACTURE, QUANTITY, STUDY

Like the vast majority of cuneiform tablets, the Ebla tablets are of terra-cotta. The clay is characteristic of Ebla and the kneading was done in the scribal quarters. It was mentioned above that in vestibule L.2875 was found a jar full of unbaked clay whose purpose is evident.[19]

Neither the form nor the dimensions of the various types are constant; there are round tablets, square tablets with roundish edges, squared rectangular tablets with thick borders. The dimensions vary for the round tablets from 2 to 10 centimeters in diameter while the square ones run about 15 centimeters per side, and those rectangular average 26 by 24 centimeters but at times reach 36 by 33 centimeters.

The most frequent type is represented by the square tablets with roundish edges, very similar to contemporary tablets from Fara and Abu Salabikh.

The discovery of the rectangular tablets now necessitates the coining of a new term to fit these documents, which are anything but "tablets." Neither English "tablet" nor French "tablette" nor Italian "tavoletta" reflect their size, whereas German "Tontafel," literally "table of clay," does give a better idea of their bulk. If the term "tablet" continues to appear in these pages, it will do so for want of a better term.

The tablets were written with a special stylus, perhaps of bone; several of these were found in vestibule L.2875.[20] After the tablet was inscribed,

Figure III, 2 Principal archives of the third millennium B.C. found in the Near East

it was baked in the sun. They were apparently not baked in special ovens, so that the varying hues are due to the greater or lesser intensity of the heat of the fire that destroyed the palace. The hues vary from white-beige to copper red to coal black. One should perhaps be eternally grateful to the king who destroyed Ebla by fire, which baked the tablets into a marvelous state of preservation. When the tablets of Ebla are compared with those of Abu Salabikh, it will be seen that the Italian Mission had a relatively easy task. To be sure, some few tablets were exposed to moisture, especially those on the floor of room L.2769, and were irreparably damaged, but the vast majority got well baked in the fire and hence were saved.

As regards the quantity of tablets found in 1974–76, the exact figure is not known, since not all the pieces had been catalogued at the end of 1976. The figure of 16,500 pieces given out by the Italian Archaeological Mission does not take into account the 23 cases awaiting inventory.[21]

Every artifact found in a dig receives a catalogue number regardless of its being whole or fragmentary. The same holds true for tablets, be they intact or broken. Thus the figure 16,500 should not be thought to apply only to complete tablets but to both tablets and fragments. The Italian Mission has in fact subdivided the epigraphic finds into tablets, fragments, and chips so that, taking into account the material still to be catalogued, one may speak of about 20,000 written documents.

It is obvious, however, that this does not answer the initial question about the quantity of the Ebla tablets, a question which concerns the number originally stored in the various places. The exact figure may never be determined, even after the restoration of the tablets, because numerous other factors must be considered, not the least of which is the capacity of the individual storerooms and the extent to which they were filled.

If one had to supply an approximate figure for the entire archive unearthed between 1974 and 1976, it would run no higher than 5,000 tablets. Thus so many exaggerations and consequent expectations must be deflated; at the same time, the irresolution with regard to a careful edition of the texts becomes difficult to understand. If the Ebla tablets are not put at the disposition of scholars within a reasonable period, the cause must be sought not in their mass but in other factors.

This discussion will surely dampen much misplaced enthusiasm, as if the value of the royal archives depended only or mainly on their bulk! But it solicits a calm and realistic evaluation of the situation, and the following data may facilitate the operation.

Of the 16,500 inventory numbers, about 2,000 are whole tablets, some 4,000 are fragments—often quite large—while about 10,000 are chips or very small fragments, usually with one or two cuneiform signs.

What did the philologist of the Mission do immediately after the finding of the tablets? It is important that this be made public so that the reader might know the grounds for certain reports concerning the contents of the texts which will be treated presently.

Were it necessary to spell out the various phases of a philologist's work once tablets have been found, the following steps would be indicated: 1. a logical catalogue, 2. transliteration of the cuneiform into Latin characters, 3. hand copy of the tablet, 4. elaboration and publication. These are the steps of a single work, indispensable when the material is not always at hand.

With the tablets found in 1974 the various phases were gone through in regular fashion, including that of deciphering the new Semitic language. Since only 40 tablets were involved, the process was carried out with unsurprising dispatch.

The discovery of the big archives in 1975 created a problem, but given the limited time at my disposition, I feel satisfied with the progress achieved. I was able to study archive L.2712 with calm and to complete on the spot of discovery the transliteration of some 200 tablets, but the mere 20 days at my disposition permitted only a quick reading of the mass of material issuing from room L.2769.

In 20 days of intense labor—rising at six and retiring at midnight—I was able to prepare a catalogue raisonné of all the pieces inventoried, some 5,000 tablets and fragments. Besides indicating the general content of the tablet, and for the economic texts the various types, I took care to note on every filing card the date (month and year), the verbal forms and other interesting items regarding personal and place names. On the basis of this card file it will be possible to program the critical edition of the texts that will for the first time permit the bringing together of texts of the same subject and of the same period in a systematic arrangement, something that the progress of Assyriological studies not only expects but categorically demands.

Because the head of the Mission put at my disposition around 350 photographs of texts from room L.2769, I was able to continue throughout 1976 the study of the material. This resulted in a number of articles and a complete card file of all the data furnished by the texts at my disposal. In the summer of 1976 I spent a month at the Aleppo Museum preparing the transliteration of all the known bilingual vocabularies and of a large part of the monolingual Sumerian texts. Thanks to the collaboration and enthusiasm of my student Dr. Giovanna Biga, the economic texts also received some attention and a few got transliterated. During a subsequent visit to Tell Mardikh from September 8 to 21, I got a view of the material brought to light by the current campaign as well as cataloguing in odd moments tablets of the 1975 season. The catalogue of all these texts was prepared and the transliteration of some 250 tablets completed.

Synthesizing the work accomplished during these eighteen months, the period after the great discovery of October 1975, I can look back with a certain satisfaction. On the credit side are a catalogue of about 6,000 tablets and fragments and the transliteration of some 800 texts of all types. Prolonged sojourns at the Aleppo Museum would have yielded even more, but they were not possible.

This book does not intend to indicate the priorities in the philological work on the royal archives of Ebla, but three objectives do seem urgent: 1. completion of the catalogue of the 23 cases to be inventoried; 2. photographing of all the texts; 3. careful restoration of the tablets.

4. TYPOLOGY OF THE TEXTS

A detailed description and an accurate evaluation of this epigraphic treasure will only be possible upon the completion of the work undertaken with such enthusiasm. But on the basis mainly of the catalogue readied in October 1975, we can already gain some idea of the wealth of information supplied by the texts discovered by the Italian Archaeological Mission in Syria.

When speaking about the typology of texts, an Assyriologist refers to the underlying structure of any text whatever and especially takes into account the key words used by scribes when annotating, for example, the economic proceedings or, more generally, he refers to the contents of the texts as outlined by the scholar on the basis, however, of subjective criteria.

Both procedures must obviously be adopted simultaneously, but the difficulties of matching criteria of judgment sometimes diametrically opposed—those adopted by a scribe 5,000 years ago and those of a modern reader might be such—counsel us to follow at least for the time being the objective principle of the contents of the texts.

Despite the title of this section, I shall briefly describe the contents of the royal archives of Ebla, postponing to the future a technical study of the typology of the texts. Though the lion's share belongs to the 1975 discovery, the 1974 and 1976 archives will not be ignored.

I. The 1974 archive consists of 42 tablets and fragments mainly of an administrative nature regarding the various branches of industry such as metals, wood, and textiles. One is dealing here with relatively small tablets, for the most part "receipts" which, besides their intrinsic value for the information furnished, are important for the historical notices, such as the date of the text ARE I 24 affixed to the end of the tablet:

I	1	6 gada-túg	6 materials of linen
	2	*puzur*$_4$*-ra-ìa*	Puzur-Ya

II	1	šu ba$_4$-ti	has received.
	2	DIŠ mu	Year
	3	DU	of the campaign (against)
rev.	1	*gàr-mu*^{ki}	Garmu.

The text consists of the entry that Puzur-Ya received six materials of linen in a specific year, namely, the year of the military campaign against the city of Garmu. From this tiny tablet emerges the information concerning linen weaving at Ebla and the report of a historical nature, even though added parenthetically.

The presence among the 1974 archive texts of lists of rations and goods to be delivered by messengers heading for various cities already gave a preview of how extensive were Ebla's relationships under King Ibbi-Sipiš. The cities recurring in the small archive include Kish in Mesopotamia, Tuttul, Mari, Nagar, and Zabalum.

One text fails to conform to the common pattern of the others; it is a school tablet containing a list of personal names attested at Ebla, and may well be the lesson of a student who had not only to write names but also to compose them.

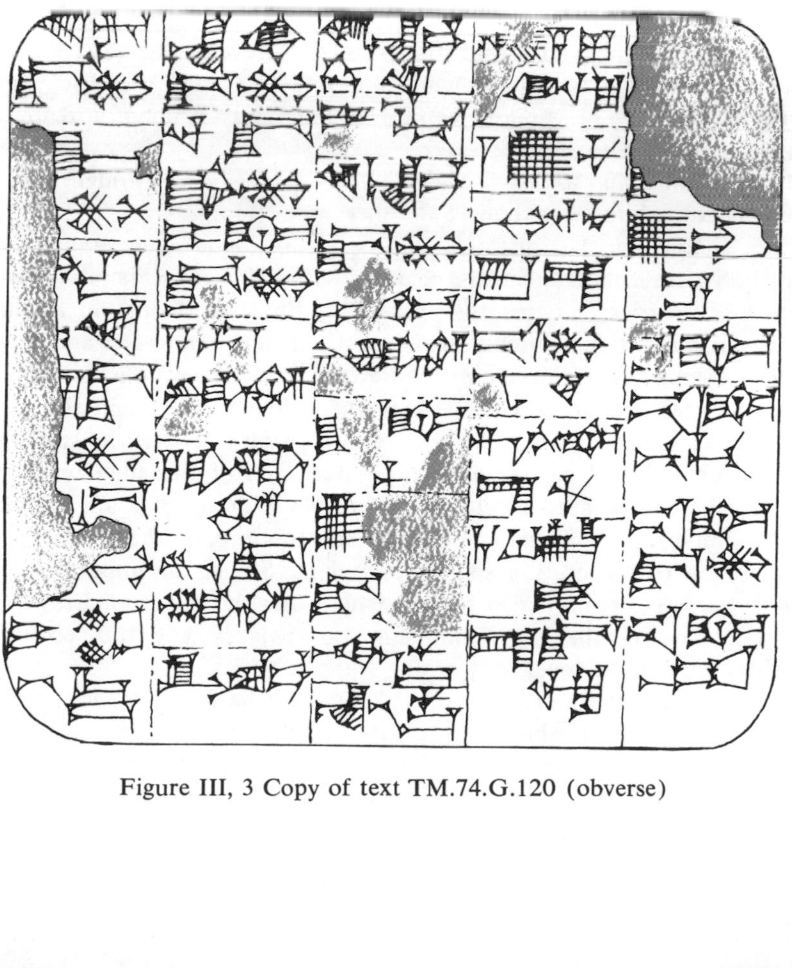

Figure III, 3 Copy of text TM.74.G.120 (obverse)

The tablet is divided into two parts; the first contains a series of names common in the Ebla onomasticon. Despite the interruptions, these names seem to be arranged on the basis of the second element, which is a divine name. A few examples:

iš$_x$-ar-Damu
en-àr-Damu
ḫa-qá-Damu
i-bí-Damu
iš$_x$-ru$_x$-ut-Damu

The second part follows the canons for the composition of personal name lists known from Mesopotamia. The student writes first the formative element of the name and then lists a group of names with that element. Thus, for example, he writes *ṭūbī,* "my good," and then follow:

ṭūbī-Ti
ṭūbī-Damu
ṭūbī-Ab
ṭūbī-Dalu

Precisely this tablet, I wrote in April 1975, reveals the existence of a scholastic tradition at Ebla which leads one to expect the discovery of further writings. This timidly expressed hope was brilliantly realized a scant five months later.[22]

II. We now come to 1975 when in three places were brought to light documents totaling more than 15,000 inventory numbers.

1. The greater part of this archive's documents are economic and administrative in character. Lists of rations for the royal family, for the state functionaries, and for the citizens of Ebla stand out. Such rations consist of quantities of bread, beer, wine, oil, meat of sheep and pigs as daily and monthly requirements. Moreover there are rations for messengers traveling to friendly cities, offerings for the temples and the divinities, lists of tributes paid to Ebla by various states, as well as catalogues of functionaries and personnel of the palace and of the state of Ebla in general. As will be seen in chapters V and VI, these texts are of fundamental importance for understanding the structure of the Eblaite state, the division of power, the society and daily life of an imperial capital 5,000 years ago. It may also be noted here that the city was divided into two large sectors, the first comprising four palaces, and the second the four quarters of the lower city which were named after the four gates of the city. These gates were in turn dedicated to the four principal gods of Ebla: Dagan, Baal, Resheph, and Sipiš. The four palaces employed 4,700 functionaries out of a total of 11,700 for the whole state of Ebla, which, according to one text, had 260,000 inhabitants.

Then there are numerous texts concerned with agriculture, mainly with the various kinds of wheat and barley, and viticulture and olive-growing, the raising of cattle, both large and small, with all their products, and with industry, metallurgical, textile, wood, and precious stones. Anticipating the results of Chapter VII, we can already deduce from the initial study of the material that Ebla was a highly industrialized state whose economy was not based on agriculture and sheep-rearing but rather on industrial products and international trade.

The accuracy of the scribes in recording all the phenomena regarding the administration of the city and their use of a precise terminology permit the sorting out of the different types of administrative texts and also dating them to a certain month or to a given period of the reign. From the clauses at the ends of administrative texts we learn that until the reign of Ibbi-Sipiš a monthly calendar, with month names all known, was current, which then was replaced by a totally different calendar.

Among the economic tablets, those dealing with international commerce (textiles and metals) occupy an important place. They turn out to be what archaeologists and philologists dream of finding and rarely succeed in finding. They describe not only the products traded but also indicate the persons and places for which the various goods were destined. It appears precisely from these texts that Ebla engaged in two kinds of commerce: the first designated as šu-bala-aka, "barter," and the second as nì-šám, "purchase and sale." We also learn that the coin of exchange, or of purchase and sale, could be silver but was more commonly gold, in the constant relationship of five pieces of silver to one of gold.

These tablets, which are impressive in external form—some reach 60 columns with about 3,000 lines—reveal the economic and geopolitical situation throughout the Near East in exemplary fashion; one document alone lists 260 geographical names, and these commercial documents may well permit the reconstruction of numerous dynasties and kingdoms linked by a tight commercial network.[23]

2. For their importance the historical and historical-juridical texts of the dynasty of Ebla occupy the second position. Typologically these separate into royal ordinances, edicts, letters of state or of state officials, lists of cities subject to Ebla, assignments of prebends to princes and functionaries. The most delightful surprise, because quite unexpected, is furnished by the international treaties concluded by Ebla with other powerful states. Pride of place belongs to the commercial treaty between Ebla and Ashur that will be more fully discussed later. Among the other treaties, that between Ebla and Emar looking to the marriage of the Eblaite royal princess Tište-Damu with the king of Emar, and the treaties between Ebla and Hama and between Ebla and Edu may be singled out. These will receive further notice in Chapter V, dealing with political alliances in the third millennium.

The juridical texts concern contracts of purchase and sale, division of goods and official loans.

Mention was made of some letters of state; the introduction in these letters differs from those thus far known in the Mesopotamian ambit:

en-ma	"Thus
NP	So and so
lí-na	to
NP	So and so
ší-ma	listen"

For the final verb "speak" of the Mesopotamian letters the Eblaites substitute the one more consonant with their culture: "listen." Nor do the novelties in the historical texts end here; among them, one in the form of a letter to the king describes the various phases and the favorable outcome of the military campaign conducted by the Eblaite general Enna-Dagan against the age-old and irrepressible rival city of Mari and her king Iblul-Il. The text is so stylized that I at once labeled it "Military Bulletin"; it remains unique in cuneiform literature.

This review cannot pass over a noticeable lacuna in the texts discovered: royal historical inscriptions, whether commemorative, narrative, or dedicatory, are conspicuous by their absence. This may be due to the fact that no inscribed royal statues belonging to this period have been found, whereas to the epoch around 2000 B.C. the Ibbiṭ-Lim statue contributes handsomely. New excavations will perhaps fill this void.[24]

3. Belonging in the third position, the lexical texts reveal Ebla as a most important cultural center. In addition to school exercises we possess scientific lists, some real encyclopedias containing lists of animals in general, fishes and birds in particular, lists of professions and personal names, of objects in stone, metal, and wood. All these lists are closely bound to the Mesopotamian tradition documented at Uruk, Fara, and Abu Salabikh. But the Eblaites were not content merely to transmit Sumerian lists already known; they began to compile catalogues in Old Canaanite itself, some of which, such as the geographical list of Ebla with its 289 names of cities, were also transmitted and recopied in Mesopotamia.

A characteristic of the Ebla scientific lists, to which Chapter VIII will be dedicated, is the redaction according to the principle of acrography, which orders the entries on the basis of the initial formative elements, a principle adopted many centuries later in Mesopotamia.

Among the various lexical texts, a prominent position is occupied by the syllabaries for learning Sumerian, grammatical texts with verbal paradigms, and finally bilingual vocabularies properly speaking in Sumerian and Eblaite, the first such bilinguals in history. This is perhaps the finest expression of the cultural maturity of Ebla, which has presented us with some works that are the equal of modern culture. Who would ever have dreamed that back in 2500 B.C. Syrian teachers and students passed their time in classrooms compiling vocabularies that the Italians would find 4,500 years later? I still remember the fateful moment on that sunny afternoon of 4 October 1975 when with vivid emotion I could announce to my archaeological colleagues that tablet TM.75G.2000 was a bilingual vocabulary. Thus Ebla was not only an economic power but a center of culture as well!

What impresses in these bilingual vocabularies is the modernity of their layout. Today vocabularies follow the alphabetical principle; at Ebla a similar procedure was adopted. Above mention was made of lists whose words are arranged according to acrographic criteria; the vocabularies show the same structure inasmuch as they contain, as will be seen subsequently, different sections clearly set off from one another by their initial elements. Another very interesting novelty furnished by some of the vocabularies is the occasional insertion between the Sumerian word and its Eblaite equivalent of the pronunciation of the foreign (Sumerian) word. Exactly as happens today in, say, English-Italian or German-Italian vocabularies.[25]

4. To the fourth position belong the literary texts, including at least 20 myths, some of them in several copies, which cast new light on religious beliefs in the Near East during the third millennium. Though the chief actors are the great Mesopotamian divinities Enlil and Enki, Utu, Suen and Inanna, very strong indications have surfaced that other great gods such as Marduk and Tiamat have their origins in the Northwest Semitic ambience.

Epic tales, hymns to divinities, incantations, rituals, and collections of proverbs round out the literary texts.

As will subsequently be explained, these form the most difficult texts of the royal archives of Ebla and their decipherment will take some years; I must confess that right now I understand only some disparate phrases, albeit highly important. Thus in the mythological introduction to the hymn of praise to the "lord of heaven and of earth" (lugal-an-ki) we find a fragment of the creation of the universe which immediately calls to mind Chapter 1 of Genesis. Another tablet speaks of Tiamat, the primordial element of the sea, whose battle with Marduk gave rise in Mesopotamia to the myth Enuma Elish.

What has been said thus far concerns the 1975 archives but with the footnote that 23 cases must still be catalogued; these may well add up to about 4,000 texts and fragments. So the surprises are not yet ended and the desire to know what treasures are still in store remains undiminished.[26]

III. In 1976 fortune again abetted the Italian Archaeological Mission, which brought to light more than 1,600 tablets and fragments. In September 1976 I was able to examine the first 500 numbers of inventory. In their classification the texts found align with those of 1975, with a certain prevalence of three types:

1. historical documents totaling 87; 2. documents concerning the raising of animals; 3. documents of a commercial nature.[27]

Among the historical texts are numerous official letters containing the new feature that different letters are written on the same tablet, in some instances two or even three, suggesting that these are not the original but the rough drafts preserved in the state archives. Also, the text of the above-mentioned treaties is not the original but the archive copy. These facts all shed light on the problem of archive science at Ebla.[28]

5. ARCHIVE SCIENCE

The recovery of a library immediately raises the question about archival criteria or the scribal preservation of the material with all the attendant problems.

This question interests not only the students of library science but all of us; the sole and the most ancient traditions that come to mind are those referring to the great library of Alexandria. The scanty information furnished with regard to the libraries of the Near East by the archaeologists who discovered them does not permit us to reconstruct the principles of cataloguing and conserving the written material.

Is it possible now to say something about archive science at Ebla? In this connection Professor Matthiae writes in his book: "The real archival criterion according to which the records were classified and set on the shelves can only be determined when the study of the texts is well advanced, when after the publication of a large part of the economic texts concerning the distribution of textiles and the payment of tributes it will be possible to compare the textual data with the archaeological data regarding the removal of the tablets in the archive room. In fact, of every tablet, whose position was not disturbed by the fire, the place of discovery was duly recorded with reference to the wall of the room and to the individual rows, as well as, obviously, to the level."[29]

This affirmation confirms once again how virulent in academe is the blight of individualism! There is no need to await the publication of a great proportion of texts to establish the archival criteria on the basis of the comparison of the archaeological with the epigraphic data. Using the catalogue raisonné of the contents of the tablets described above, one could and should undertake the work straightway. Notwithstanding, this could never be done accurately, since there will always be lacking one item of information: the precise position occupied by each tablet in the individual rows. To be sure, approximate criteria can be guessed at, but it will never be possible to identify the real criteria of Eblaite archive science.

That the tablets were not preserved helter-skelter is already obvious from the descriptions regarding their recovery in the separate rooms.

As regards the 1974 archive of 42 tablets found in L.2586, it appears very plausible that they were kept in the jar found in that room. Such a system of storage would coincide with Mesopotamian practice in all historical periods.

One encounters a different arrangement, however, in the rooms unearthed in 1975 and 1976.

In L.2712, the so-called small storeroom where administrative texts were kept, it is supposed that "the tablets were arranged on overhead shelves fixed to the north and east walls and perhaps formed by a wooden holder plastered with clay."[30]

In L.2764, however, it seems that the tablets were originally kept on brick benches along the north wall and the west wall,[31] the same situation as in L.2875.

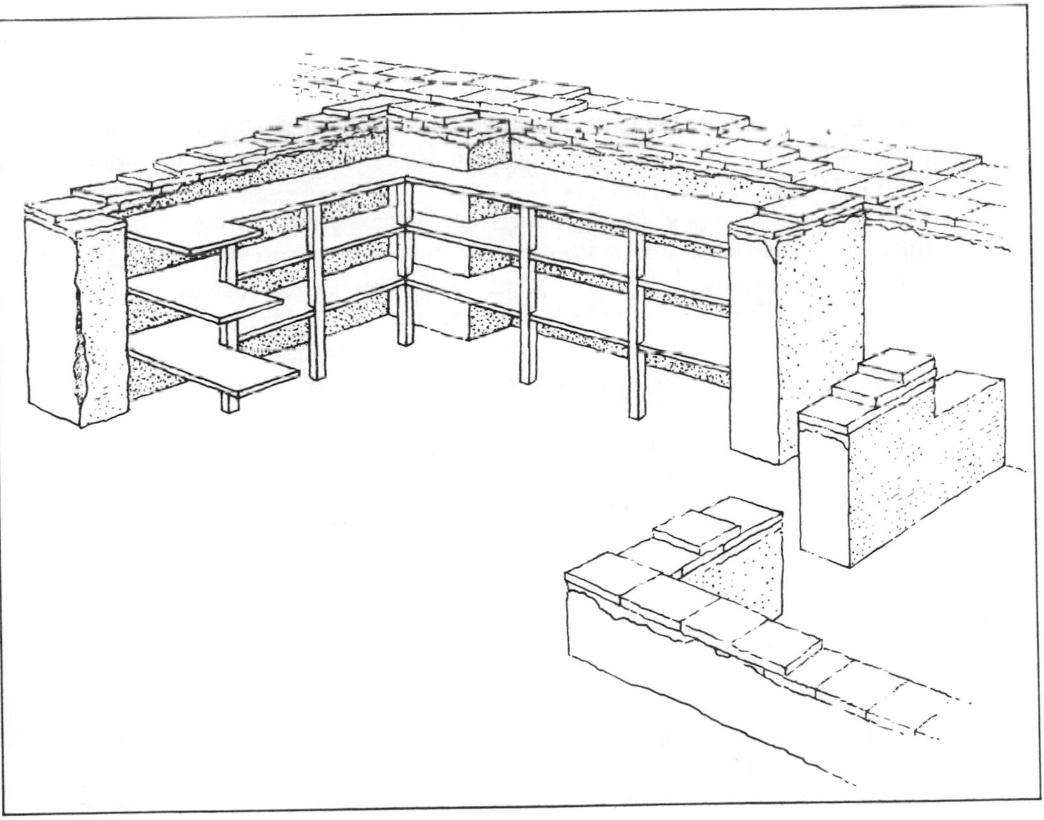

Figure III, 4 Reconstruction of the wooden shelves of the Ebla library [L.2459]

Different and under certain aspects more interesting is the storing of the tablets in L.2769, the library proper. Here, as it has correctly been reconstructed, the texts must have been arranged on sets of three shelves running along the east, north, and west walls. "The presence on the flooring of the room of holes of regular dimensions equally distant from the east, north, and west walls and in particular in the northeast corner leaves no doubt about the fixed fittings used for keeping the clay tablets. The east, north, and west walls of L.2769 must have been faced with sets of wooden shelves sustained by upright supports, also of wood, fixed in the floor. The shelves of the racks probably consisted of two planks 0.40 meters long laid side by side and, at least along the north wall, were supported by horizontal beams set along the surface of the master wall and fixed in the two corners at the end."[32]

Considering the arrangement of the tablets on the individual shelves, one can scarcely agree with the archaeologist Matthiae when he writes: "Till now in any case, some elements of archival interest can be supplied, based solely on archaeological observations. Thus it can be said that the square tablets were certainly housed on the intermediate shelves, while the roundish ones were placed on the top shelf of the north wall or deposited right on the floor under the shelves, especially near the north wall . . . The front face of the tablet—the obverse—was definitely turned toward the center of the room, and the records were always set in such a way that the first column of the obverse, given the height of the shelf and the size of the tablets, could conveniently be done without pulling out the tablets."[33]

A look at one of the many photographs which show the tablets at the moment of discovery suffices to convince one that the preceding observations are erroneous. The tablets were, in fact, arranged not with the obverse toward the center of the room but rather with the obverse toward the wall and the reverse toward the center of the room.

Apart from this observation, resulting from a simple glance at the photographs, it suffices to be knowledgeable of the structure of economic texts to understand that the most important column is precisely the last one, because it contains the final sums which form a kind of analytical index. On the reverse, conjoined to the final column, one often finds an indication of the month in which the transaction took place, and this is just what interested the scribes wanting to check the documents.

Without intending to evaluate the internal archival criteria, that is, according to what system the texts of different contents were preserved in the same room, we can already see from purely external criteria how far archive science had advanced at the time of Ebla.

But our curiosity is now so whetted that we must say something about the so-called internal criteria for preserving written material. As regards L.2769, I recall having gone down the opening made by the excavation the morning before the removal of the individual tablets began and having ascertained that the area of the north wall contained texts of a lexical character, while the east sector was reserved for the tablets of commercial nature. It seems, therefore, that the scribes had ordered the material also, and perhaps chiefly, on a basis of content. To us this would seem quite normal and no cause for surprise, but in the ambience of preclassical Oriental traditions it constitutes a fact of considerable importance for the history of library science, which in the future shall have to take due note of this.

Notes

1. *CAH*² I/2, pp. 319–321.
2. In J. Harmatta and G. Komoroczy, eds., *Wirtschaft und Gesellschaft im Alten Vorderasien* (Budapest, 1976), p. 246.
3. P. Matthiae, *OrNS* 44 (1975) 337–360.
4. G. Pettinato, *OrNS* 44 (1975) 361–374.
5. P. Matthiae, *ibid.*, 360; G. Pettinato, *ibid.*, 374, n. 107.
6. G. Pettinato, *RBI* 25 (1977) 225–226.
7. See note 1.
8. *RlA*, I, pp. 142–143; II, pp. 24–25.
9. G. Pettinato, *UNL* I/1, pp. 3ff.
10. A. Falkenstein, *Archaische Texte aus Uruk* (Berlin, 1936).
11. Falkenstein, *ibid.*, pp. 43ff.
12. S. Langdon, *Pictographic Inscriptions from Gemdet Nasr* (= *OECT* VII), (Oxford, 1928); A. Falkenstein, *Archaische Texte aus Uruk*, p. 13, n. 2.
13. E. Burrows, *Archaic Texts* (= *UET* II) (London, 1935).
14. A. Deimel, *Die Inschriften von Fara, I–II* (Leipzig, 1922–1924); R. Jestin, *Tablettes sumériennes de Šuruppak* (Paris, 1937); idem, *Nouvelles tablettes sumériennes de Šuruppak* (Paris, 1957). In general, see D. O. Edzard, *Zeitschrift für Assyriologie* 66 (1976), 156ff.
15. R. D. Biggs, *IAS* (= *OIP* 99) (Chicago, 1974).
16. G. Dossin, *Les inscriptions des temples de Ninni-Zaza et de (G)istarat,* in A. Parrot, *Mission Archéologique de Mari,* III (Paris, 1967), pp. 307–331.
17. J. Bauer, *Studia Pohl* 9 (Rome, 1972), pp. 27–28.
18. I. J. Gelb, *Materials for Assyrian Dictionary* 2 (Chicago, 1962), pp. 1ff.
19. See above on p. 6.
20. *Ibidem.*
21. *RBI* 25 (1977) 232ff.
22. *OrNS* 44 (1975) 371.
23. *RBI* 25 (1977) 228ff.
24. *Ibid.*, 230ff.
25. *Ibid.*, 231ff.
26. *Ibid.*, 231–232.
27. *Ibid.*, 233.
28. See paragraph 5.
29. *Ebla: Un impero ritrovato* (Turin, 1977), p. 170.
30. *Ibidem,* pp. 99–100.
31. *Ibidem,* p. 102.
32. *Ibidem,* pp. 100ff.
33. *Ibidem,* p. 106.

CHAPTER IV

The Writing and Language of Ebla

1. Mesopotamian cuneiform system. 2 Toward the identification of a new language. 3. Structure of the language of Ebla. 3.1. Writing and phonetics. 3.2 The noun and the nominal formation. 3.3. The pronominal system. 3.3.1. Independent personal pronouns. 3.3.2. Suffixes of personal pronouns. 3.3.3. Other pronouns. 3.4. Prepositions. 3.5. Conjunctions and adverbs. 3.6. Verbal system. 3.7. Syntax and style. 4. The position of Eblaite among the Semitic languages.

1. MESOPOTAMIAN CUNEIFORM SYSTEM

The Ebla texts are written in archaic cuneiform characters previously known from Fara and Abu Salabikh.[1] The Eblaites thus imported from the land of Sumer the cuneiform system of writing with which they composed all their documents.

In Ebla appears a kind of writing whose earliest attestations in Mesopotamia go back to Uruk IVa (3000 B.C.); these are clay tablets of small dimensions with imprints of graphic signs having the value of words or numbers. Since the reed stylus used for this purpose has the form of a pointed knife blade, it leaves an impression very similar to a wedge, whence the denomination "cuneiform." The graphic characters of this period and also of that following are, however, very figurative, so that the first phase of cuneiform is rightly called pictographic. The character indicating the "hand" is represented by the hand itself, the character indicating the "head" is represented by the head itself, etc. That it is not merely a question of figurative writing or of the antecedent of real writing is demonstrated by the fact that many graphic characters either bear no similarity to the object it stands for, such as the character indicating "sheep," or are so stylized that a possible or probable likeness with the object indicated is no longer verifiable. The Uruk IVa tablets contain, therefore, an autonomous system of writing and represent the oldest documents of writing, humanity's greatest invention and the beginning of civilization itself. In its first phase cuneiform writing was employed to record economic transactions; for this reason the graphic signs represent concrete objects. Later on it was also used for other purposes, such as narrating historical events, for religious or literary compositions. The preferred material always remained clay, inscriptions on stone or metal being very rare. The use of a different stylus and the need to simplify the characters led to a reduction of their number (some 2,000 characters at the start, 800 in the Fara period, around 500 in 2000 B.C.) and to such a stylizing that the figurative quality of the original signs disappeared. With the passage of time the cuneiform characters were shifted 90 degrees counterclockwise from the vertical position in which they stood at the beginning. Only in the monumental inscriptions did they preserve their original vertical position even in later periods.

As regards the internal structure of cuneiform, it should be observed that in the first phase only logograms were employed: to one character one word corresponds. Those who operated a merely logographic system of writing soon came to understand how limited were the possibilities of expression. At first one began to use the same logogram for words having some nexus between them, then to introduce some key words or clarifiers. Only in the Gemdet Nasr period do some syllabograms make their first appearance. The principle that permits the development of syllables is inherent in the structure of the language expressed with a particular writing: to accentuate the phonetic element to the detriment of the figurative factor, as, for example, in Sumerian the sign for "arrow" is used for the same-sounding ti "life" (homophony and poliphony are two of the outstanding characteristics of Sumerian). Babylonian cuneiform always remained a writing system that expressed words and syllables (logograms prevail in Sumerian, syllabograms in Akkadian).[2]

2. TOWARD THE IDENTIFICATION OF A NEW LANGUAGE

After this discussion of cuneiform writing in the ancient Near East we come to the hypotheses about the language of the Ebla texts that appeared plausible to me when I undertook the study of the 42 tablets unearthed during the 1974 campaign.

Here the statue of Ibbiṭ-Lim, king of Ebla, dating to circa 2000 B.C., comes into the picture again. Its inscription of 26 lines in cuneiform characters turned out to be recent Old Akkadian, but with some morphological peculiarities that suggested a new dialect of Akkadian, just as the dialect of the Mari tablets represents a new Akkadian dialect.[3]

Thus in 1974 the inscription on the statue, its paleographic aspect, and the archaeological context led me to expect to find only two languages: Sumerian and Old Akkadian. In a period so ancient no other languages were known to have been expressed by cuneiform signs.

As a matter of fact, the texts fully confirmed the use of Sumerian. A good percentage of the signs on each tablet represented for me a logogram which, read as Sumerian, yielded sense and gave rudimentary knowledge of the city's economy. But other signs read logographically resulted in no sense and, read as syllables, formed words which were not known in Akkadian. Hence it became necessary to think of a language different from Old Akkadian or East Semitic.

On the other hand, since the scribes passed with great ease from one language to another, it was nearly impossible to understand fully any one tablet in which words written in this other not yet comprehensible language alternated with Sumerian words.

But it was precisely the marked bilingualism of the scribes which offered the key to decipher the language of Ebla. Some tablets carry at the end the Sumerian annotation dub-gar, which means "tablet written" or "document composed"; in the same position on two other tablets appear two cuneiform characters with the Sumerian values gál and balag which, however, yield no sense. These two signs, though, have the well-attested syllabic values of *ig/k* and *d/túb* which, when put together, form the verb *ik-túb*. Putting these two syllables together and pronouncing them, I immediately thought of the West Semitic root *KTB*, "to write"; *iktub* then must be the Eblaite equivalent of dub-gar, it must have expressed the same idea.

Having identified a verbal root unknown to East Semitic, namely Akkadian, but proper to West Semitic, I concentrated all my efforts in this area, with the happy result that a Northwest Semitic language using cuneiform characters in a very ancient period emerged. This discovery takes its place alongside the decipherment of the Ugaritic texts in 1930 which revealed a Canaanite language employing a cuneiform alphabet but dating a millennium later.[4]

The 42 tablets found in 1974 began thus to yield their secrets gradually and the economy of the city to take form. The personal names of the inhabitants and of the gods venerated in the city slowly but steadily came to light. Though the administrative and technical terms were expressed in Sumerian, the personal names increasingly pointed to the Northwest Semitic area. As a matter of fact, composite names with Northwest Semitic elements such as *ṭù-bí,* "my good," *en-na,* "show favor," *eb-du,* "servant," etc., are attested in TM.74.G.120, a school tablet containing a series of names in vogue in the onomasticon of Ebla. In addition to personal names, many other substantives, verbs, and conjunctions deriving from Northwest Semitic were identified in the 1974 texts.

The tablets exhumed in 1975 and 1976 fully sustained the identification of the new Semitic language made on the basis of the 1974 discovery. This new Northwest Semitic language labeled "Eblaite" clearly manifests its autonomy of the languages nearest in time, namely Old Akkadian and Amorite, while demonstrating a close relationship with Ugaritic, Phoenician, and Hebrew. Its strict affinity with these three languages suggests that Eblaite be classified as Paleo or Old Canaanite. The occurrence of the term "Canaan" in these tablets forestalls the objection that to use the designation "Paleo Canaanite" for a third-millennium language would be anachronistic.

The bilingualism of the tablets is only apparent. Though 80 percent of the words are Sumerian and only 20 percent are Eblaite, all of them were read as Eblaite. The Sumerian terms are in reality logograms which the scribes translated without difficulty into their own language when they read them. The Sumerian verbs, in fact, such as the above-mentioned dub-gar, and gi$_4$, íla, etc., are used without conjugation prefixes; this would be inconceivable if the texts had been read in Sumerian. Even those verbal forms like ì-na-sum̃, "he has given to him," where we find the prefixes as well as the infixes, betray their nature of fossilized and stereotyped forms: precisely in the tablet attesting ì-na-sum there is lacking the complement of the term in the nominal phrase.[5] Hence it appears that the tablets were read in Eblaite.

The exceptional nature of the discovery of a Canaanite language in northwestern Syria of the third millennium justifies here a brief digression on the documentation of the Semitic languages known before the appearance of Eblaite.

In the Near East in the third millennium the languages documented till now are Sumerian, an agglutinative language, spoken in Mesopotamia, and Akkadian, an East Semitic language also spoken in Mesopotamia and at Mari. Only in the second millennium does the documentation of other Semitic languages begin, languages which, because of their geographical localization, receive names such as Northwest Semitic, which includes Amorite of Mari, Ugaritic, and the Canaanite glosses of the El Amarna tablets. Then, in the latter part of the second millennium in the area of Syria-Palestine, other Canaanite languages begin to emerge with their documentation: Biblical Hebrew, Phoenician, Punic, Moabite, Ammonite, and Edomite. The other Semitic languages which interest Arabia and Ethiopia begin their epigraphic life only in the first millennium; among these, Arabic and the Semitic languages of Ethiopia may be mentioned.

Thus the first attestations of Northwest Semitic languages went back to the second millennium; now Ebla weighs in with abundant testimony from the middle of the third millennium.[6]

Historical and linguistic speculations about Amorite led to hypotheses concerning a Semitic language (or eventually even several) spoken in the Syria-Palestine ambience before the penetration of the Amorites; in other words, one postulated a third-millennium Canaanite tongue and prayed that it would be found. Eblaite proves to be the answer to such a prayer.

3. STRUCTURE OF THE LANGUAGE OF EBLA

Under the cuneiform script is concealed a type of language which already bears those characteristics that will distinguish the tongues documented in succeeding millennia in that territory. But before describing the structure of Eblaite, it may not be amiss to outline briefly the structure of Semitic languages.[7]

They belong to an inflected type of language similar to the Indo-European tongues with which they share some general characteristics such as the distinction between masculine and feminine.

Typical of the Semitic languages is the basic structure consisting for the most part of three consonants which carry the meaning of the word. The position and the timbre of the vowels—only three in number, namely, a, i, and u—serve to modify the fundamental meaning of the words and to create the morphological variations. Thus from the Arabic root *ktb* (already witnessed in Ebla) derive *kitāb,* "book," *kutub,* "books," *kātib,* "scribe" (participial theme), *maktūb,* "a letter," *maktab,* "office," etc.

Though somewhat less evolved than the Indo-European languages, the Semitic tongues do manifest a considerable degree of development. The verb is well defined with respect to the noun and presents a quite complex inflection with one basic conjugation and numerous derived conjugations which specify the categories of "aspect" (opposition between action completed and action uncompleted), the arrangement "active and passive voice," the quality of the action (intensive, causative, reflexive, etc.).

The inflection of nouns is limited to but three cases: the *u* ending marks the case of the subject or nominative, the *i* ending attaches to those nouns governed by one of the numerous prepositions or by another noun in the so-called construct chain relationship, while the *a* ending indicates the object, or the accusative, and the adverbs.

The category of adjectives is very limited and the definite article comes into being only at a later period. There are, however, procedures for establishing whether a substantive is determinate or indeterminate.

The Semitic languages are very cohesive among themselves and constitute a sufficiently homogeneous group so that now and then it is difficult to recognize immediately to which of them an idiom belongs. Even to follow the characteristic features of their history constitutes a problem that has not been tackled with advanced methodology.

The documents of the language of Ebla collected and studied to date permit forming a sufficiently probable idea about its nature and its classification.

It should be stressed here that only linguistic considerations have been allowed to determine the kind of language present in Ebla. It would be tempting to integrate the data furnished by the texts with the archaeological material which effectively brings out the connections between Ebla and the Canaanite world, or to consider the pantheon of Ebla which houses many of the Canaanite gods such as Dagan, Baal, and Resheph, or to cite recurring personal names which have counterparts in the Old Testament.

All of these would sustain the Canaanite classification of Ebla, but only by linguistic elements must the new language be evaluated. During the past three years various linguistic elements important for the reconstruction of the grammar have come to light, and some of these will be set forth, but only in rough outline. Some readers may be discouraged by this prospect since for many the word "grammar" evokes images of boring paradigms drawn up by stodgy savants.

In the study of this language pride of place belongs to the grammar that can be reconstructed from the words; then personal names will be examined because they too are useful for determining grammar insofar as they contain verb forms, nouns, and pronouns.

Here follow some examples of forms that have been identified thus far in the Ebla tablets which fit into the framework of the Semitic languages and, more specifically, in that which later emerges as the Northwest Semitic group.[3]

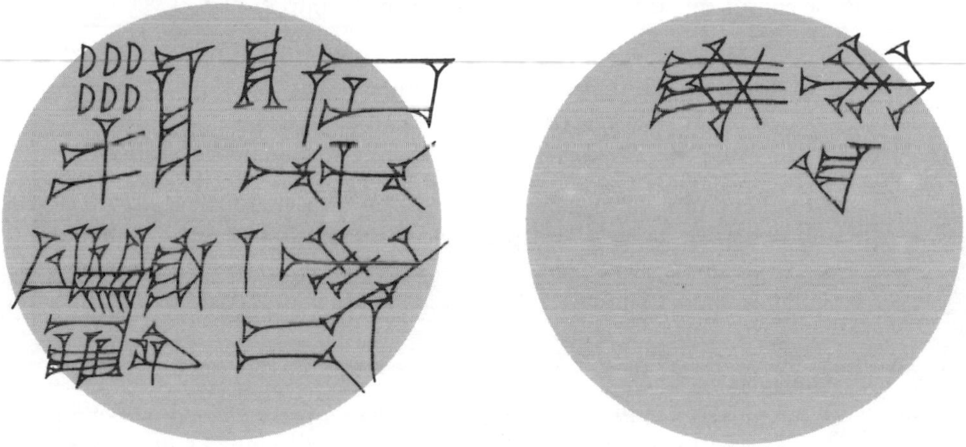

Figure IV, 1 Copy of a cuneiform text (TM.74.G.126)

3.1. WRITING AND PHONETICS

When interpreting the texts discovered in 1974, I based my work on the syllabary in use in Mesopotamia during the Sargonic period as it had been reconstructed by I. J. Gelb.

The subsequent study of the archives emerging in 1975 required a review of my position, and now it appears that the Eblaites used the Sumerian logograms more in a purely phonetic function. This is a rather simple procedure but one which at the same time reveals the precision of the scribes of Ebla who were able to adapt a writing system created for an agglutinative language to the expressive exigencies of an inflected language such as Eblaite happens to be.[9] To be sure, the time is not ripe for synthesizing all the phonetic phenomena of the new language, but some interesting data are ready for presentation.

W:

The consonant *w* is always preserved, be it at the beginning of a word as in *wa,* "and," *wa-ti-nu,* "giver," or in the midst of a word, as in *mu-wallidatum,* "she who gives birth," or at the end *qá-nu-wu,* "reed."

Y:

The consonant *y* is expressed by either *ì* (*ì-da*<*yd'*) or simply through *i* (*i-šar*<*yšr*) or even *i-i.*

', *ḥ,* and *h:*

These three consonants are expressed at the beginning of a word and in the middle by a graphic sign containing the vowel *e,* which suggests that these consonants influence the shift of *a* sound into *e:*

' : *eb-du* <*'abd,* "servant."
ḥ: *en-na* <*ḥanan*> ḥanna, "show favor."
h: ^{d}*é-da* <^{d}*had(d)a,* "the god Hadad."
ti-é-ma-tum <*tihamatum,* "the ocean waters."

At the end of a word there is no uniform treatment; the *a* vowel is generally preserved, as in *ì-da*<*iyda',* "he knows," *iš-má*<*išma',* "he knows." The last example shows that in choosing the sign *má* instead of *ma,* the Eblaites wanted to indicate the presence of a sound different from the *aleph* at the end of a word.

Sibilants:

As in all the Semitic languages, the sibilants present some serious problems also in Eblaite. A general treatment would be out of place here, but attention might be called to the consistency in the writing of the pronouns that is not found in Old Akkadian:

3rd masc. sing. independent pronoun:	SU-*wa*<*šuwa*
3rd masc. sing. possessive pronoun:	*-sù*<*šu*
3rd masc. sing. determinative:	*šu/ši*

Just the choice of three different graphic signs to express the sibilants shows how careful the Eblaites were in distinguishing between such sounds.

Alternation of consonants:

r/l: these two consonants are interchangeable, as in *ḫurmu/ḫul(u)mu,* month name, *bukaru/bukalu,* "firstborn," *barašu/balašu,* "cypress."

b/g: very interesting is the interchange *b/g* encountered in Canaanite dialects, as witnessed by *'agaragum/'abaragum,* "superintendent."

k/ḫ: examples occur in which *k* has been weakened to *ḫ,* such as *kapatu/ḫa'patu,* "the goddess Ḫepat," or *ik-su-up-da-mu/iḫ-su-up-da-mu,* the name of one of Ebrium's sons.

g/n: ba-la-gu-um/ba-la-núm as a translation of Sumerian NE.RU in the vocabularies.

Gemination:
to represent the doubled consonant, the Eblaites, at variance with the Mesopotamians, do not choose graphic signs like VC+CV as in *um-mu,* "mother," but prefer the unusual writing CV+CV, as in *ù-mu-mu,* "mother," or even *gu-ra-ra-kul* for *gurrakul,* the name of a city. Obviously there are cases where the gemination is not expressed at all, e.g., *gu-ra-kul*^{ki}.

This phenomenon must be distinguished clearly from epenthesis, for which the Eblaite generally saves the short vowels in post-tonic position, here differing from Akkadian practice; examples include *tihamatum* (Eblaite)/*ti'amtum* (Akkadian), *malikum/malkum.* An obvious exception is *ḫurmu* with respect to *ḫulumu.* However, the vowel in post-tonic position could fall out as in the case of *maliktum,* "queen," vis-à-vis Akkadian, *malkatum,* but this does not always happen.[10]

These few observations on the writing and phonetics give some idea of the novelty of the language of Ebla as well as of its archaic nature with respect to all the known Semitic languages.

3.2. THE NOUN AND THE NOMINAL FORMATION

The types attested can be represented by using three conventional consonants, *q t l,* and inserting between them the characteristic vowels. The following formatives already known from other Semitic languages have been identified at Ebla:

qal	*'ab*	(>*a-bù*)
qil	*yid*	(>*ì-dì-lum*)
qūl	*ṭwb*	(>*ṭù-bí*)
qull	*lupp*	(>*lu-pù*)
qatl	*'bd*	(>*eb-du*)
qutl	*puzur*	(>*puzur*$_4$*-ra-ìa*)
qātil	*mālik*	(>*ma-li-ku*$_8$*-um*)
qatīl	*parīs*	(>*pá-rí-su*$_{11}$)
qitīl	*'izīl*	(>*i-zi-lum*)
qutal	*kubar*	(>*gu-bar*)
qutil	*kutim*	(>*ku*$_8$*-tim*)
qutul	*dubuḫ*	(>*du-bù-ḫu*)

Among types with preformatives may be cited:

aqtul	*arkuḥ*	(>*ar-ku-ḫu*)
maqtāl	*maškānu*	
taqtil	*tá-da-bí-lu*	

As in all the Semitic languages the feminine is formed with the infix *-at-um* or *-t-um;* e.g., *maliktum,* "queen," alongside *mālikum,* "king," *iris-ātum,* "desire," *kalumatum,* "she-goat," *ti'amatum,* "ocean water," *nupu-štum,* "life." As afformatives *-ūtum* (in plural *na-bí-u-tum*), *an-um, ayy,* etc., are also documented.

As regards the inflection of the noun, the lack of cases is to be remarked; most of the nouns appear without endings, a good number end in *-u,* some in *-um* (that is, *-u* + letter *m* which constitutes the phenomenon of mimmation known in many Semitic languages), and a few nouns end in *-a* or in *-i.* It is growing steadily clearer that the scribes of Ebla were more concerned with reproducing the consonants than the vowels. Even if the cuneiform sign that they used to write their own language was to be read as a syllable of consonant plus vowel, they were much more interested in the consonant.

What is more, this phenomenon of consonantism is fundamental in the Northwest Semitic languages so that its appearance in the new member of the group should engender no surprise.

3.3. THE PRONOMINAL SYSTEM

3.3.1. INDEPENDENT PERSONAL PRONOUNS

Many forms of independent personal pronouns are now documented.

a) Nominative case:

1st pers. sing.	*an-na* in personal name *A-na-Ma-lik,* "I am Malik"
2nd pers. sing.	*an-tá,* "you"
3rd pers. sing.	*šu$_{11}$-wa,* "he"
2nd pers. plur.	*an-tá-nu,* "you"

b) Oblique case:

2nd pers. masc.	*ku-wa-ši*
3rd pers. masc.	*šu$_{11}$-wa-ši*

c) Accusative case:

2nd pers. masc.	*ku-wa-ti*
3rd pers. masc.	*šu$_{11}$-wa-ti*

3.3.2. SUFFIXES OF PERSONAL PRONOUNS

sing. 1 pers. *-i* attested in names and with prepositions, e.g. *ṭù-bí-Da-lu,* "Dalu is my good"
-ni attested with verbs; e.g., *I-bí-ni-Li-im,* "Lim has called me"

2nd pers. -ka: a m a - g a l - *kà,* "your mother"
kum in the verbs ì - n a - s u m - *kum*

3rd pers. masc. *-šu:* m a š k i m - *sù,* "his steward"

3.3.3. OTHER PRONOUNS

Of the determinatives are witnessed *šu* and *ši;* of the interrogatives *mi* in personal names like *mi-kà-il,* "who is like Il?" and also *mi-nu;* of the indefinites: *mi-nu-ma, me-na-ma-ma.*

3.4. PREPOSITIONS

The system of prepositions is both highly developed and complex. The following have turned up:

in, "in," locative
lí-na, "to, for" dative: *lí-na be-li-šù,* "to his master"
iš, "for, to" terminative
áš-tù, "from, with" ablative
ší-in, "to" motion to place
al, "above" motion to place
ka, "like" comparative as in *mi-kà-il,* "who is like Il?"
a-dè, "for" finality
iški "for"

3.5. CONJUNCTIONS AND ADVERBS

The common Semitic conjunction *wa,* "and," is frequently attested; one also finds *ù* and the enclitic *-ma.*

Adverbs: *en,* "thus"; *lam,* "truly"; *lu,* "I beg you!"

3.6. VERBAL SYSTEM

Like all the other Semitic languages, Ebla too knows diverse conjugations; those identified with some certainty are the following:

I Base: *qatal* (G)
II Intensive: *qittil* (D)
III Causative: *šiqtil* (Š)
IV Passive: *niqtal* (N)

To these fundamental conjugations are added others which are derived or composite; thus for conjugation I there is Gt with the insertion of the infix *t(a)*, as in *iš-tá-má,* "he heard." The DŠ conjugation is a convergence of II and III, while DŠt contains the *t(a)* infix; finally a passive conjugation IV/2 (*quttal*).

As regards the tenses, the situation appears complex. In the first place, under the formal aspect every conjugation has two fundamental forms of inflection; the first is effected by prefixes, the second with suffixes. From the analysis of personal names, the form with prefixes has the value of the past while the suffixed forms express the stative, i.e., a condition of being.[11]

The vowels of the prefix conjugation, in G or base, are, surprisingly, *i-* for the third person, as in East Semitic, where West Semitic tongues use *ya-,* while for the first person singular *a-* is used and for the second person singular *ta-*. A stunning surprise is contained in the masculine name of a scribe *ti-ra-il* which analyzes as third masculine singular with preformative *ti-;* hence the name signifies "Il sees."

The vowels of the suffix conjugation of G are for the third person *a-a,* as in the personal names *ba-qá-da-mu* and *kà-ra-ba-il.*

For the intensive or D conjugation with suffixes the vocalic sequence is *i-i* (*qittil*) and with prefixes, *u-a-i* (*uqattil*). The same obtains for the causative or Š: *šiqtil* and *ušaqtil,* while the N conjugation exhibits the sequence *i-i-a* (*ippiḫar*).

In addition to the past and stative forms, each conjugation also possessed participles, imperatives, and infinitives, as in other languages.

One must draw attention to a verb form which appears to be a hybrid of both prefixed and suffixed conjugations, namely, *iš-tá-má-a-tá,* "you listen," a hybrid conjugation well attested in the Canaanite dialect of the El Amarna letters.[12]

After this presentation, some general considerations which appear fundamental for the eventual reconstruction of Semitic, especially of Northwest Semitic in the third millennium, are in order. First, significant is the use of the prefix *i-* with the preterite, as attested in Akkadian and unlike Amorite which employs the prefix *ya-*. This means that Barth's law does not hold for Eblaite. Second, the prevalence of the vowel *i* in the *qittil* and *šiqtil* conjugations and the presence of the *š* in the causative form reflect the *š* of East Semitic and the vowel *i* of West Semitic. Third, the force of the prefixed form, rightly called the preterite, is in effect that of the past and not of present-future. Finally, the lack of the final *-a* in both *qatal* and *iqtul* forms upsets the attempts to reconstruct Proto-Semitic on an exclusively Arabic base.

3.7. SYNTAX AND STYLE

The construction of the sentence also sets the language of Ebla apart from Sumerian and Akkadian and aligns it with the West Semitic tongues. The verb, in fact, does not occupy the final position in the sentence, as can be deduced from the following examples: 10 ÉŠ $2^{giš}$ ašud-^{giš}-ÉŠ *i-bù-bu*$_6$ in-na-sum sukkal-du$_8$, "10 pieces of furniture and 2 knickknacks (I) Ibubu have given to the ambassador," where the sequence is object-subject-verb-oblique case.

Enlarging the discussion, one notes the interesting use of *wa* not only as the simple connecting word but also as the particle of emphasis in the example *wa* ì-na-'sum, "Indeed he gave." At present the use of the *waw* conversive in Eblaite cannot be supposed, though its existence should not be precluded a priori.

Rhyme and parallelism characterize the following jingle:[13]

u-šu la kà-la	a
u-šu la ti-li	b
gú-šu la kà-la	a
gú-šu la ti-li	b

where $_a$ corresponds to $_a$ and $_b$ to $_b$ in a very harmonious sequence.

4. THE POSITION OF EBLAITE AMONG THE SEMITIC LANGUAGES

The schematic presentation of the verbal, nominal, and pronominal systems warrants classifying Eblaite in the West Semitic group.

Some illustrious scholars such as Von Soden, Landsberger, and Bauer had advanced the hypothesis of the existence in Syria during the third millennium of a Semitic language that according to some must have been a particular dialect of Akkadian but according to others an Old Amorite dialect. But Old Amorite, as subsequently shown by Buccellati, is not much different from classical Amorite. Now we know, however, that in third-millennium northern Syria a Northwest Semitic language was spoken which is sharply distinguished both from Old Akkadian (lexically and in the verbal system) and from Amorite (because of the pronominal and verbal system). For this reason I prefer to classify Eblaite as a Canaanite language, thanks to its close relationship with Ugaritic, Phoenician, and Biblical Hebrew.

As the oldest Northwest Semitic language, Eblaite becomes a chronological companion of Old Akkadian of the East Semitic group. And Amorite gets reduced, as Giovanni Garbini correctly maintains, to its true dimensions as a later and innovating language.

The discovery of this new language will considerably facilitate the study of Ugaritic and permit a better explanation of some of its phenomena, without recurring to distant Akkadian. The same will hold true for Phoenician and Biblical Hebrew.[14]

Notes

1. See Chapter I, pp. 10ff.
2. A. Falkenstein, *ATU,* pp. 4ff.
3. See Chapter II.
4. *OrNS* 44 (1975), pp. 367ff.
5. In one text there is even the fossilized Sumerian verbal form with the possessive pronominal suffix of the second person singular attached, to wit, ì-na-sum-*kum,* "I/he has given to you" (TM.75.G.1766, obv II 4).
6. G. Garbini, *Le Lingue semitiche* (Naples 1972), pp. 66ff.
7. S. Moscati, *An Introduction to the Comparative Grammar of the Semitic Languages* (Wiesbaden 1962).
8. Many of the examples given here have already been discussed in my article in *OrNS* 44 (1975), pp. 367–374, with additions made in *BA* 39 (1976), p. 50, and *RBI* 25 (1977), p. 236f. Also consult I. J. Gelb, *SMS* I/1 (1977), pp. 3ff.; P. Fronzaroli in *Interferenza Linguistica* (Atti del Convegno della Società Italiana di Glottologia 1977; Pisa 1977), pp. 27ff.; G. Garbini, *AIUON* 38 (1978), pp. 41ff.
9. G. Pettinato, *RPARA* 48 (1975–1976), p. 56.
10. For this phenomenon consult P. Fronzaroli, *Interferenza Linguistica,* p. 39, and the observations of G. Garbini, *AIUON* 38 (1978), pp. 45–46.
11. One of the more interesting problems concerning the Eblaite verb is the presence or absence of the so-called present (alongside the prefixed preterite tense and the suffixed stative tense). Thus far no certain example of the present tense has been identified, but now it would appear that in the literary texts such a form was not unknown, namely, *i-pá-ḫur,* "he gathers." This obviously would complicate the discussion regarding the character of this new language.
12. Consult F. M. Th. Böhl, *LSS* V/2 (1909), p. 58f.
13. TM.75.G.2394.
14. For this concept cf. *OrNS* 44 (1975), pp. 373ff. In substantial agreement with my position are W. von Soden, G. Garbini, P. Fronzaroli, and M. Dahood, whereas I. J. Gelb underlines the close kinship with Old Akkadian. To be sure, the question cannot be decided until the literary texts and the pure Eblaite documents have been deciphered and read.

CHAPTER V

The Dynasty of Ebla and Its Historical Documents

1. Reconstruction of the dynasty and historical synchronisms. 2. The king, the queen, the queen mother, and the princes. 3. The "Elders" and the king. 4. International politics. 4.1. Alliances. 4.2. Wars. 4.3. Treaties. 4.4. The political expansion of Ebla.

When describing above[1] the types of texts in Ebla's royal archives, I stressed that so far as historical documents are concerned, no historical inscriptions celebrating the achievements of the kings in war or in peace had yet been found. Hence to reconstruct the events of the dynasty and the internal politics of Ebla at the time of the great archives one must rely almost exclusively on information furnished by the economic and administrative texts. But for foreign policy it is very difficult to give an adequate description of the history of Ebla in the third millennium B.C. because the tablets rarely connect an incident with a specific king.

An imaginative description would compare this situation to a marvelous mosaic which must be put together; the pieces are at hand and through painstaking labor must be fitted into a harmonious unity. It is a fascinating job—not exempt from errors and failings—which must be undertaken with the means available. Critics and perfectionists will, to be sure, look askance, but scientific research as such is always in a state of becoming and this condition lends it interest and fascination.

To expect a work of synthesis at this stage is to ask too much; the best one can hope for is that the data at hand will permit a deductive and inductive analysis. In this and the following chapters the Eblaites will be allowed to speak for themselves, in their own words, expressions, and in entire tablets tentatively translated and interpreted. The readers are invited to take a journey through the centuries to reach a remote world and a different society that flourished nearly five thousand years ago. With their own eyes they can watch the events of this ancient Near Eastern empire with all its intrigues, follow the succession of various kings of the dynasty, get an idea of its amazing wealth, learn about its political expansionism, its wars and alliances, its social and economic life.

1. RECONSTRUCTION OF THE DYNASTY AND HISTORICAL SYNCHRONISMS

To the first and obvious question about the structure of the state of Ebla circa 2500 B.C., the sufficiently certain reply is that it was based on the monarchy; the texts even permit the reconstruction of the dynasty with its succession of different kings. This problem has received considerable attention since the discovery of the tablets; during the preparation of the logical catalogue of the documents from the archives it kept coming to the fore[2] with this succession of kings emerging:

Igriš-Ḫalam
Ar-Ennum
Ebrium
Ibbi-Sipiš
Dubuḫu-Hada
Irkab-Damu

Further study based on photographs made available by the head of the mission required the cancellation of Dubuḫu-Hada from the earlier list where he appears as the crown prince, but never yet as king, and the advancing to the second position of Irkab-Damu who, attested only once and out of context, had been relegated to the last position.[3]

I had written that the kinship of the above-cited kings was not very clear with regard to numbers 1, 2, and 3, whereas 3, 4, and 5 were respectively father, son, and grandson. It was difficult to relate the sixth king to his predecessors.[4]

This paragraph will first present the data for the reconstruction of the dynasty and its sequence, then tackle the problem of dynastic succession, and finally mention historical synchronisms that will serve to give the dynasty a position in time.

That a certain person was a king of Ebla can most surely be inferred from the apposition e n-*eb-la*^{ki}, "king of Ebla," attached to his name. This prestigious title is attested for Igriš-Ḫalam[5] and Irkab-Damu[6] so that no doubt can be attached to the royal status of these two sovereigns.

Less telling is the simple epithet e n, "king," juxtaposed to a personage, since only the context can reveal if it refers to the kingship of Ebla or of another city. In any case the epithet "king" is borne in connection with Ebla by Irkab-Damu,[7] Ar-Ennum,[8] Ebrium,[9] and Ibbi-Sipiš.[10]

At the present moment of research the names of the kings in alphabetical order are: Ar-Ennum, Ebrium, Ibbi-Sipiš, Igriš-Ḫalam, and Irkab-Damu.

The order of succession cannot, however, be said to be definitively established. The sequence Ebrium–Ibbi-Sipiš can be considered certain since the latter is the son of Ebrium,[11] so that one may speak of dynastic succession. But the kinship and the sequence of Igriš-Ḫalam, Ar-Ennum, and Irkab-Damu presents a more complex problem. To resolve it we must have recourse to various clues in the economic texts that mention the different kings.

On the basis of the numerous available lists of functionaries, the sequence Igriš-Ḫalam, Ar-Ennum, and Ebrium appears probable. Moreover, Igriš-Ḫalam seems to have been the founder of the dynasty or at least the first and most ancient king of Ebla, an inference supported by the paleographic evidence. Thus far the sequence indicated by the first publications has undergone no changes; now, however, Irkab-Damu must be assigned the second place in the proposed list. Some tablets,[12] in fact, report the sequence:

ig-rí-iš-Ḫa-lam	Igriš-Ḫalam
wa	and
ìr-ib-Da-mu	Irib-Damu
ìr-kab-Da-mu	(and) Irkab-Damu

If now, in this text, Igriš-Ḫalam is the king of Ebla, it probably follows that both Irib-Damu and Irkab-Damu are high state officials, and the latter can be identified with Irkab-Damu the king. Another tablet[13] contains the sequence:

Igriš-Ḫalam
Irkab-Damu
Ebrium

which can only evoke the three kings of Ebla bearing the same names.

TM.75.G.2290 yields the further information that Irkab-Damu was not the son of Igriš-Ḫalam but rather of Iga-Lim,[14] permitting the inference that succession at Ebla was not hereditary. This element, not absolutely probative, warrants as plausible this sequence of kings at Ebla:

I	Igriš-Ḫalam
II	Irkab-Damu
III	Ar-Ennum
IV	Ebrium
V	Ibbi-Sipiš

While the sequence of the five kings of Ebla has been established with reasonable certainty, the principle of succession and the length of the reign of the individual kings and of the entire dynasty present some thorny problems. With regard to succession I recently had occasion to write, "One can no longer speak of dynastic succession; the other hypothesis that succession at Ebla was in a certain sense elective is gaining ground, sustained by a very important element recurrent in the tablets, namely, the ceremony of the king's anointing.[15] This obviously obtains for the first four kings, precisely because the fifth king, being the son of the fourth, ascended the throne by reason of hereditary succession.

With the question of dynastic succession at Ebla is tied up the problem of the length of each king's reign and of that of the whole dynasty. To put the question in clearer terms: Once seated on the throne, did the king remain for life? The most obvious reply would be "yes," but the reality of facts is quite other; kingship was not for life but only for a limited term.

The already cited text TM.75.G.1681 is very precise on this point. It mentions King Ebrium's five sons, described as d u m u - n i t a e n, "sons of the king"; Ebrium was already in office but at the same time Igriš-Ḫalam, Irib-Damu, and Irkab-Damu are mentioned in the same tablet. It could be objected that nothing suggests the identity of these personages with the first two kings of Ebla, but it is equally obvious that such an identity cannot be excluded a priori. This is not the only example that can be adduced; Ar-Ennum is still alive when Ebrium is already king. From these indications it would appear that the king at Ebla was a charismatic leader with functions for a fixed period.

Such a hypothesis appears to rule out the possibility of answering the question about the duration of each king's reign and that of the dynasty as a whole. But such pessimism may be uncalled for in view of some indications in monthly statements covering several years that can prove extremely useful for solving this important problem.

Text TM.75.G.427 which, as will be seen, permits the reconstruction of the new monthly calendar of Ebla, is a monthly account of barley rations, especially for palace functionaries, extending over a seven-year period. In my edition of this calendar I did not comment on this fact, but now the reader's attention should be drawn to the possible correspondence of a prima facie administrative phenomenon with the political reality. In other terms, is it possible that a king was elected for seven years, thereby explaining the tablet as the final adjustment of accounts of the royal mandate?

Nor is this the only element that can be adduced to give a positive answer to the question posed. In the preparation of the catalogue it was noticed with considerable surprise that the monthly accounts covering a longer period did not list the years progressively—from one up—but rather regressively, which means that there were fixed periods. One example may be cited, text TM.75.G.1376, which lists donations of precious metals for making a statue of a god with them. It ends with the clause:

dub-gar	tablet
lú nì-ba	of donations
mul	for the divinity
áš-tù	from
nidba$_x$	the feast
na-rú	of the stelas
7 mu	year 7
6 mu	year 6
5 mu	year 5
4 mu	year 4
3 mu	year 3
2 mu	year 2

To begin precisely with the seventh year suggests that the period or cycle lasted seven years, nor does the omission of year one cause any difficulty since that is the year the document was compiled.

These two examples in such agreement underscore the value of the fixed seven-year cycle which permitted the Eblaites to follow the downward order in dating the years. To link this cycle to the royal mandate is, to be sure, daring but not to be excluded presumptively.

If the king got elected for seven years and there was no ban on reelection, then one can explain how at the time of Ebrium's term the preceding en, "kings," were still alive, as text TM.75.G.1681 supposes. This hypothesis also helps explain two expressions recurring in the administrative texts listing rations; the first reads "measure of barley en *wa* en-en (for) the king and the kings (former)" (TM.75.G.344), and the second, en-*maliktum*-en-en, "the king, the queen, the kings," in TM.75.G.411 which, as will be seen presently, documents the highest offices of the Eblaite state at the time of Ibbi-Sipiš.

Since this hypothesis threatens to upset some revered theories regarding kingship in the ancient Near East, it should be understood as such and verified step by step.

One thing seems clear: the hypothesis which maintains that the dynasty of Ebla at the time of the great archives lasted some 150 years lacks a solid foundation. For this reason I have recently counseled caution when discussing the date of the archives: "Till now I have accepted as an approximate date that indicated in earlier publications, namely, the period between 2400 and 2250 B.C. As a result of studies on the texts the past year and especially this year, the ever closer paleographic[16] and cultural relationship between Ebla and Abu Salabikh convinces me that the dates proposed earlier for the royal archives of Ebla must be raised at least 100 years. Hence I propose dating our archives to circa 2500 B.C."[17]

This new dating runs counter to the archaeological data as interpreted by the archaeologists of the mission,[18] but it enjoys the support of the historical and commercial information emerging from the tablets.

The first important element consists of the fact that the only sure synchronism is that between Ar-Ennum, the third king of Ebla, and the king of Mari, Iblul-Il, who clearly lived before the Sargonic period.[19] The total absence of Akkad in the tablets constitutes the second important factor.[20] Instead, the city most frequently mentioned is Kish, followed by Adab. Hence the period of the royal archives appears to precede the rise of Akkad and to be contemporary with the first dynasty of Kish (2600–2500 B.C.). A further argument for this date is the recurrence in the literary texts of the god Zababa, who, as widely recognized, was the city-god of Kish.[21] Nor should it be overlooked that the professor of mathematics at Ebla hailed from Kish; the relations between the two cities must have been very close.

It is obvious that when in the commercial texts Kish and Adab occur side by side, the name of the great king Mesalim of Kish springs to mind; it was he who extended his dominion over Adab and this fact consequently warrants linking the dynasty of Ebla to that of Mesopotamia where Mesalim was a leading figure.

At this point it may be asked whether there are more convincing reasons for tying the dynasty of Ebla to that of Kish. A positive reply would come from those texts which speak not only of Kish but also of lugal-Kiš^{ki}, "the king of Kish,"[22] and from that tablet mentioning a personage with the unusual name *me-sà-li-ma,*[23] a name immediately recalling that of the king of Kish.

Hence the proposal to make the period of the great archives of Ebla contemporary with Mesalim in Mesopotamia deserves serious consideration, being based on paleographic as well as historical and cultural arguments furnished by the epigraphic material.

Other synchronisms in the texts of Ebla between the rulers of this center and those of other cities are not lacking, to be sure, but for the moment they are not probative since they treat of kings mentioned for the first time. This means that in the future Ebla will play an important role in determining the historical setting of these newly mentioned kings. Such will be the case for the kings of Byblos, Nagar, Ḫarran, Ḫamazi, etc., hitherto all unknown. In the future it will be possible to arrange entire dynasties using Ebla as the basis. Other sovereigns, such as Ṭudia of Ashur, till now considered as merely legendary figures,[24] have become, thanks to Ebla, historical realities.

These considerations point to the conclusion that the Ebla dynasty is contemporary with the dynasty of Mesalim of Kish in Mesopotamia and with the fourth dynasty in Egypt. A date around 2500 B.C. best accords with the data now available.

As regards the problem of its duration, a plausible hypothesis would be that the first three kings reigned seven years each, that Ebrium succeeded in being elected four times, while the reign of Ibbi-Sipiš lasted from ten to fifteen years. This means that the royal archives cover a period of sixty to seventy years at most.

2. THE KING, THE QUEEN, THE QUEEN MOTHER, AND THE PRINCES

A) The King

The king of Ebla bears the Sumerian title e n, "lord," which is rendered *malikum*, "king,"[25] in the bilingual vocabularies. This marks a new and unexpected development; in contemporary Mesopotamia, in fact, the king bears the Sumerian title l u g a l translated *šarrum* by East Semitic. Ebla therefore is clearly autonomous with respect to Mesopotamian traditions and possessed a different culture and organization of the state. This is confirmed by the fact that the term l u g a l is used at Ebla, but to designate the "governor" of the various provinces, not the autonomous sovereign, so long as it is not used with cities of Mesopotamian customs such as Kish and Mari.

The use of e n to indicate the king strikingly indicates a special relationship between Ebla and Uruk insofar as the kings of Uruk also carry the title e n, unlike the other Mesopotamian sovereigns, who are called l u g a l. At this point comes to mind the poem of Gilgamesh which describes the king of Uruk's trip into Syria to slay the monster Huwawa and to take possession of the cedars of Lebanon. Is Ebla a Sumerian foundation going back to the days of Gilgamesh? At the moment one cannot answer that question, but perhaps when the strata below the large archives are dug, a precise and sure reply will be forthcoming.

Of the figure and role of the king, however, a clear image has developed. He was the head of the state and ultimately responsible for domestic and foreign policy, insofar as he guided all administrative and political functions. To him in fact the various l u g a l, "governors," and the MI + ŠITA$_x$ itself, a kind of prime minister of the state, had to give an account; to him the generals sent in their war reports; he was the author of international treaties and, finally, at least at the time of Ebrium and Ibbi-Sipiš, it is the king who named the various state officials.

What has been said would point to absolute power in the hands of Ebla's king, but numerous elements counsel caution before concluding thus. The presence of the MI + ŠITA$_x$, of the elders, and of the numerous members of the royal family makes it quite clear that the king did not rule alone; he shared responsibilities with others. Here one example may suffice to illustrate the point. In text TM.75.G.1881 appears the expression igi-du$_8$ *eb-rí-um wa eb-la*^{ki}, "inspection of Ebrium and Ebla," which clearly suggests a dichotomy or division of power.

This is a far cry from the absolutist concepts documented for contemporary Mesopotamia and the following periods where the king was an absolute despot who exercised the right of life and death over his subjects. The search for parallels in other cultures brings us back to the epic poems about Gilgamesh, in particular the poem recording the struggle between Uruk and Kish for the supremacy over Sumer. Before engaging in the epic duel, Gilgamesh seeks the opinion first of the chamber of elders and then of the chamber of youths of Uruk; this proceeding has evoked numerous studies on the problem of primitive democracy[26] and on the bicameral or two-chamber system.[27]

Within the West Semitic ambience the situation of Ebla seems to correspond more to the fixed traditions of tribes in which those effectively responsible are the heads of families who together decide the fortunes of the tribe. The objection will immediately arise that during the period of the royal archives Ebla was a highly developed sedentary state and scarcely governable by principles better suited to a nomadic society. But the emerging facts point to the contrary; as will be seen in section 3, the decisive role of the elders at Ebla obliges an abandonment of current theories in favor of the newly acquired data.

B) The Queen and the Queen Mother

The queen is always designated by the noun *maliktum,* the feminine form of *malikum,* "king." She is often united to the king in the phrase en *wa maliktum,* "the king and the queen,"[28] and is also an integral part of the administration of the state since she carries out many transactions such as acknowledging "receipt" and "delivery" of goods.[29] The spinning mills of the kingdom which turned out fabrics, Ebla's chief industry, were under her direction so that her responsibilities were not insignificant.

These preliminary observations based on a cursory reading of the tablets put the Near Eastern woman in a new light. No longer relegated to the home, she participated in important decisions and bore considerable responsibility in certain sectors of the economy.

When a text from Ebrium's reign reports:

1 *é-da-um-*túg-2	1 Edaum fabric,
1 aktum-túg	1 Aktum fabric,
1 íb-túg ša$_6$-dar	1 fine multicolored Ib fabric
du-bù-ḫu-^{d}*'à-da*	to Dubuḫu-Hada,
1 dumu-nita	a son
i-bí-sí-piš	of Ibbi-Sipiš
ma-lik-tum	the queen
ì-na-sum	has given[30]

we appreciate the importance of this woman's role in the state as well as detect a note of human warmth; it is the grandmother, in fact, who gives, surely as a gift, three garments to her grandson.

In the discussion earlier of the king's powers, the phrase igu-du$_8$ *eb-rí-um wa eb-la*^{ki}, "inspection of Ebrium and Ebla," was cited to illustrate the limitations of royal authority. Another text may also be cited which mentions the queen together with the king and Ebla; it deals with a gift of silver for various divinities and includes the clause:

nì-du$_8$ en	gift of the king
ù	and
nì-du$_8$ *ma-lik-tum*	gift of the queen
ù	and
nì-du$_8$ *eb-la*^{ki}	gift of Ebla.[31]

The primary role of the queen in state affairs as well as a certain economic independence stand forth from this brief clause. As will be seen later, the queen herself was obliged to pay taxes to the state; the revenue authorities spared no one!

This modern role of responsibility of queen and woman is not peculiar to Ebla, but must correspond to a concept prevalent in Syria-Palestine. In the tablets recording commercial statements the deliveries are sometimes made to queens and not to kings so that one may rightly hold that certain states were governed by women. Here the most obvious parallel is that of the queen of Sheba. But to conclude that royal authority in some states was always in the hands of women would transgress the present evidence.

The queen mother is designated by the term ama-gal-en, "mother of the king." Precisely the fact that the Eblaites never use the Sumerian word for queen, nin, "lady," the companion of en, "lord," permits the inference that ama-gal corresponds in a certain measure to *maliktum* and hence simply signifies "queen," but the addition of en after ama-gal suggests rather that ama-gal defines the queen mother.

Her role in the state can readily be deduced from phrases such as en *wa* ama-gal-*sù,* "the king and his mother,"[32] and en *wa* ama-gal-en *wa eb-rí-um,* "the king and the mother of the king and Ebrium."[33] That the queen mother was the mind behind some important decisions is confirmed by TM.75.G.1444, the document by which Ebrium notifies, as will be seen, his son and successor Ibbi-Sipiš, of assigning some properties to three of his sons and which explicitly mentions that this allotment was decided by the queen mother (nam-tar ama-gal-*kà,* "decision of your [i.e., the king's] mother.").

These citations and facts concerning the queen mother recall other societies, such as the Hittite or Patriarchal societies, in which the queen mother and the wife of the patriarch, respectively, played a primary role in the social life and in the succession itself. The role of the Hittite Tawanannas in selecting the king is well known and the example of Rebecca in choosing the firstborn leads one to ask if something similar didn't take place in Ebla.

This applies to the last two kings in particular; there is no evidence that either Ibbi-Sipiš or Dubuḫu-Hada were firstborn sons, and their designation as successors to the throne may well have been due to the influence of the queen mother.

C) The Royal Princes

Here the question concerns only the period of the last two kings, Ebrium and Ibbi-Sipiš. The text simply designates the royal princes as d u m u - n i t a - e n, "son(s) of the king," or in the case of princesses, d u m u - m í - e n, "daughter(s) of the king."

The tablets supply ample information on their function in the administration of the state. In the case of Ibbi-Sipiš it is possible to trace each step of his career to his becoming co-regent and finally king of Ebla. Of the other princes too one can outline their curriculum which shows to what degree all were involved in the gigantic bureaucratic machine of Ebla.

Two examples concerning Ebrium, his sons, and Ibbi-Sipiš and his sons claim a word of comment, but first the concept of co-regency, an illustration of rare political sagacity, should be explained. This is expressed by the formula e n *wa* N P, "the king and so-and-so," attested for Ebrium,[34] in e n *wa* a m a - g a l - e n *wa eb-rí-um,* "the king and the queen mother and Ebrium," for Ibbi-Sipiš,[35] in the formula, e n *wa i-bi-si-piš,* "the king and Ibbi-Sipiš," and for Dubuḫu-Hada[36] who, however, did not mount the throne, e n *wa du-bù-ḫu-*^{d}*'à-da.* "the king and Dubuḫu-Hada."

Of course, the simple mention of the king together with a prince does not by itself signify a division of power, but mere chance will hardly explain that in two of the three cases cited the prince actually became king. Hence with due reserve one may advance the hypothesis that the prince selected for the succession—speaking only of the last two kings—at a certain time came to share the power of the king. That Ebrium was also co-regent of the preceding king can be accounted for by an institutional phenomenon of the Eblaite state which harmonizes with the theory proposed above that kingship was elective.

D) Relationships Between the Members of the Royal House

Two examples illustrate at one and the same time the relationships between members of the royal family and the structure of the top positions of the Eblaite state at a precise moment.

1) The structure of the state at the time of King Ibbi-Sipiš:
Text TM.75.G.411, a tablet of 11 columns dating to the reign of Ibbi-Sipiš, lists daily and monthly rations of "bread" for different persons and various purposes. It reads:[37]

5 ninda	5 loaves of bread,
2 ninda *ga-zi-tum*	2 loaves of bread . . .
en	for the king,
2 ninda	2 loaves of bread
ma-lik-tum	for the queen,
2 ninda *ga-zi*	2 loaves of bread . . .
en-en	for the (former) kings,
3 ninda	3 loaves of bread
dumu-nita-nita	for the sons
en-en	of the (former) kings,
4 ninda	4 loaves of bread
Du-bù-ḫ[u-^{d}*'à-d]a*	for Dubuḫu-Hada,
2 ninda	2 loaves of bread
ip-ṭù-ra	for Ipṭura,
íl-zi	the official Ilzi,
2 ninda	2 loaves of bread
dumu-nita-en	for the king's son,
2 ninda	2 loaves of bread
dumu-mí	for the daughter
en	of the king,
2 ninda *ga-zi*	2 loaves of bread . . .
x xx 1 ^{giš}šilig	. . . one axe
10 lá 2 ninda	8 loaves of bread
AB x ÁŠ	for the Elders,
4 ^{giš}šilig	4 axes
10 ninda	10 loaves of bread
ku-li-en-en	for the ambassadors of the kings
ar-mi^{ki}	of the (various) cities.

The text continues, listing rations first of bread, then of flour and barley, and finally of wine for the representatives of various cities, for divinities, and for some officials of Ebla to whom we shall return in Chapter VI.

The real interest lies in the hierarchy of the state at the time of Ibbi-Sipiš which the tablet presents. Prescinding from the order in which the various personalities are listed, the explicit reference to Dubuḫu-Hada and Ipṭura, two sons of the king as other texts clearly report, merits special attention, because the first was co-regent and responsible for foreign affairs and the second looked after domestic policy and headed its administration.[38] The presence of the en-en, "the former kings," suggests a situation in which the kings, after their term expired, formed a kind of senate and retained their title. Noteworthy is the appearance of the Elders, to be discussed presently, and of the ambassadors of the different kingdoms accredited to Ebla.

From the foregoing text the following list emerges:

I	king
II	queen
III	(former) kings and their children
IV	Dubuḫu-Hada
V	Ipṭura
VI	princes
VII	princesses
VIII	Elders
IX	accredited ambassadors

When the secondary elements are omitted, the structure of the state looks like this:

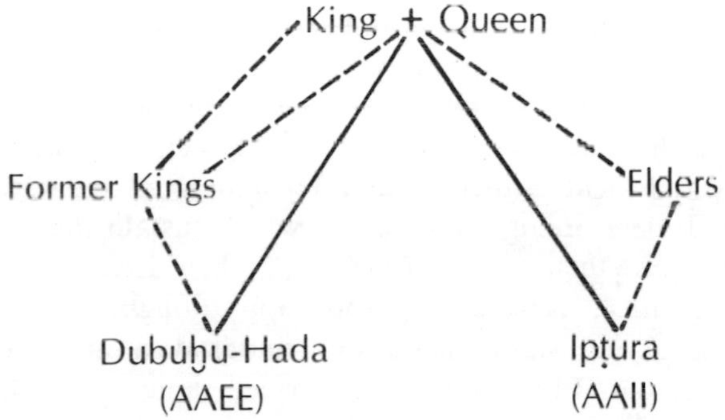

Figure V, 1 The greatest holders of power during the reign of Ibbi-Sipiš

Deduced from text TM.75.G.411, this structure is confirmed by many other tablets of the same period; one of these is TM.75.G.527:[39]

5 ninda	5 loaves of bread
en	for the king,
2 ninda	2 loaves of bread
en-en	for the (former) kings,
3 ninda	3 loaves of bread
dumu-nita	for the sons
en-en	of the kings,
2 ninda	2 loaves of bread
AB x ÁŠ	for the Elders,
2 ninda	2 loaves of bread
ma-lik-tum	for the queen,

2 ninda	2 loaves of bread
íl-zi	for the official Ilzi,
ip-ṭù-ra	Ipṭura,
2 ninda	2 loaves of bread
du-bù-ḫu-^{d}*'à-da*	for Dubuḫu-Hada.

Here the essential positions of the state of Ibbi-Sipiš are arranged in a slightly different order:

I	the king
II	former kings and their sons
III	Elders
IV	queen
V	Ipṭura
VI	Dubuḫu-Hada

With respect to the list drawn up from TM.75.G.411, the position occupied by the Elders is striking, namely, right after the former kings and their sons, and the dropping of the queen from the second to the fourth position in the new list is not less noteworthy. The essential structure as outlined in Fig. V, 2 does not, however, differ.

King Ibbi-Sipiš turned Eblaite sovereignty into a strictly family affair, having divided the executive power among his closest relatives. Nonetheless, two other elements which cannot be liquidated remain: the former kings and the Elders. Being the columns which sustain the structure, they continue to exercise their power of decision, albeit discreetly.

Under the political aspect, King Ibbi-Sipiš brought to completion the transformation of the state institutions undertaken and shrewdly conducted by his father, Ebrium. On the surface things look the same, but the reality has radically changed; it is precisely under Ibbi-Sipiš that the monarchy ceases to be elective and becomes hereditary. Ebrium was successful in getting himself elected king four times and in getting his son Ibbi-Sipiš, an able governor under all the preceding kings, chosen as his successor. Ibbi-Sipiš in turn entrusts to two of his sons the highest and most sought-after posts of the kingdom, those of co-regent and head of the administration. He also reforms the calendar, a reform bringing many ideological upheavals in its wake.[40]

How did the patrician families of Ebla react to these radical changes?

Mention was made above of the fact that Ibbi-Sipiš was the last king of the so-called dynasty of Ebla; with him, in fact, the written documents cease. Nothing concrete is known of the reasons that brought the dynasty to an end. The archaeologists of the mission link its downfall to the destruction of the palace wrought by Naram-Sin of Akkad,[41] but the date proposed above for the archives would preclude this possibility. It is much more likely that Ibbi-Sipiš' abuse of office to the detriment of the concept of the Eblaite state brought about its collapse.

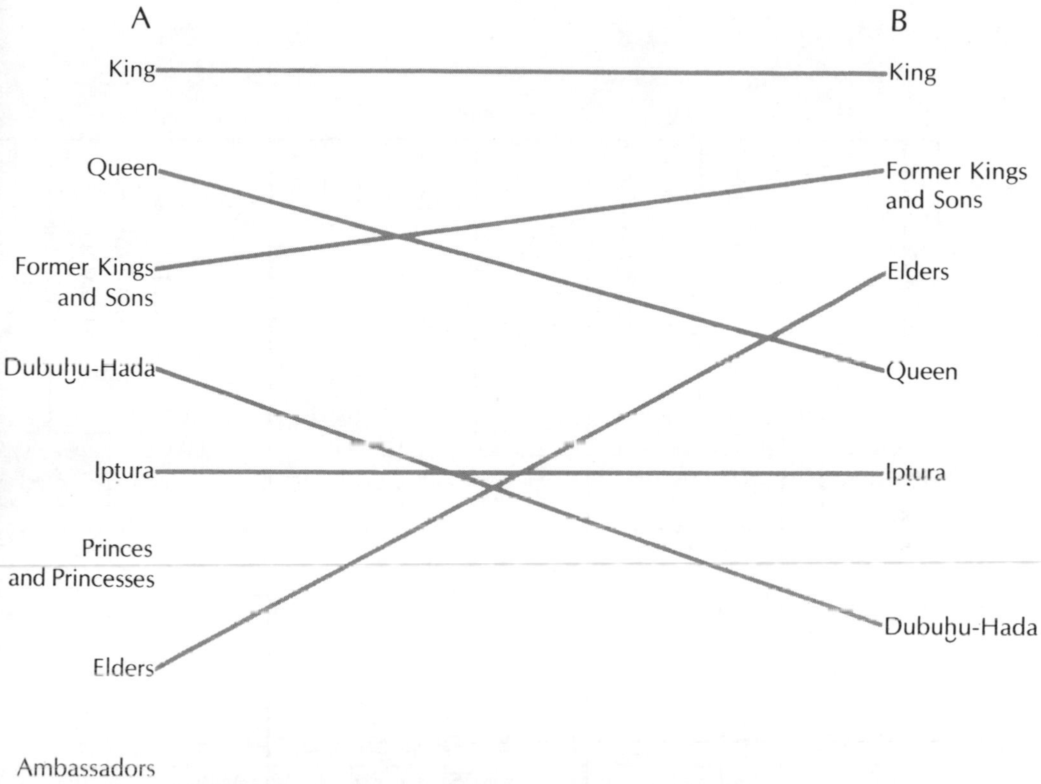

Figure V, 2 Diverse positions of the greatest extension of power in the texts TM.75.G.411 and TM.75.G.527

2) The offspring of King Ebrium:

The second example illustrating the relationships among the various members of the royal family concerns Ebrium and his children. The following table (3) shows that thus far 44 of his children have been identified, 24 princes and 20 princesses, all clearly designated either dumu-nita-en, "sons of the king,"[42] or dumu-mí-en, "daughters of the king."[43]

When Ebla studies are more advanced, it will be possible to write an entire book about Ebrium and his family, but one can already trace the main lines of his political policy, which consisted of investing the members of his family with the greater part of the executive powers of the state. Ebrium is without doubt the most prestigious of Ebla's kings, and not without reason was his mandate renewed at least four times.[44] His enlightened policy of transforming some institutions by action both tentacular and profound accounts in great measure for his reelection.

As regards the male offspring—the princes—Ibbi-Sipiš (no. 7) was

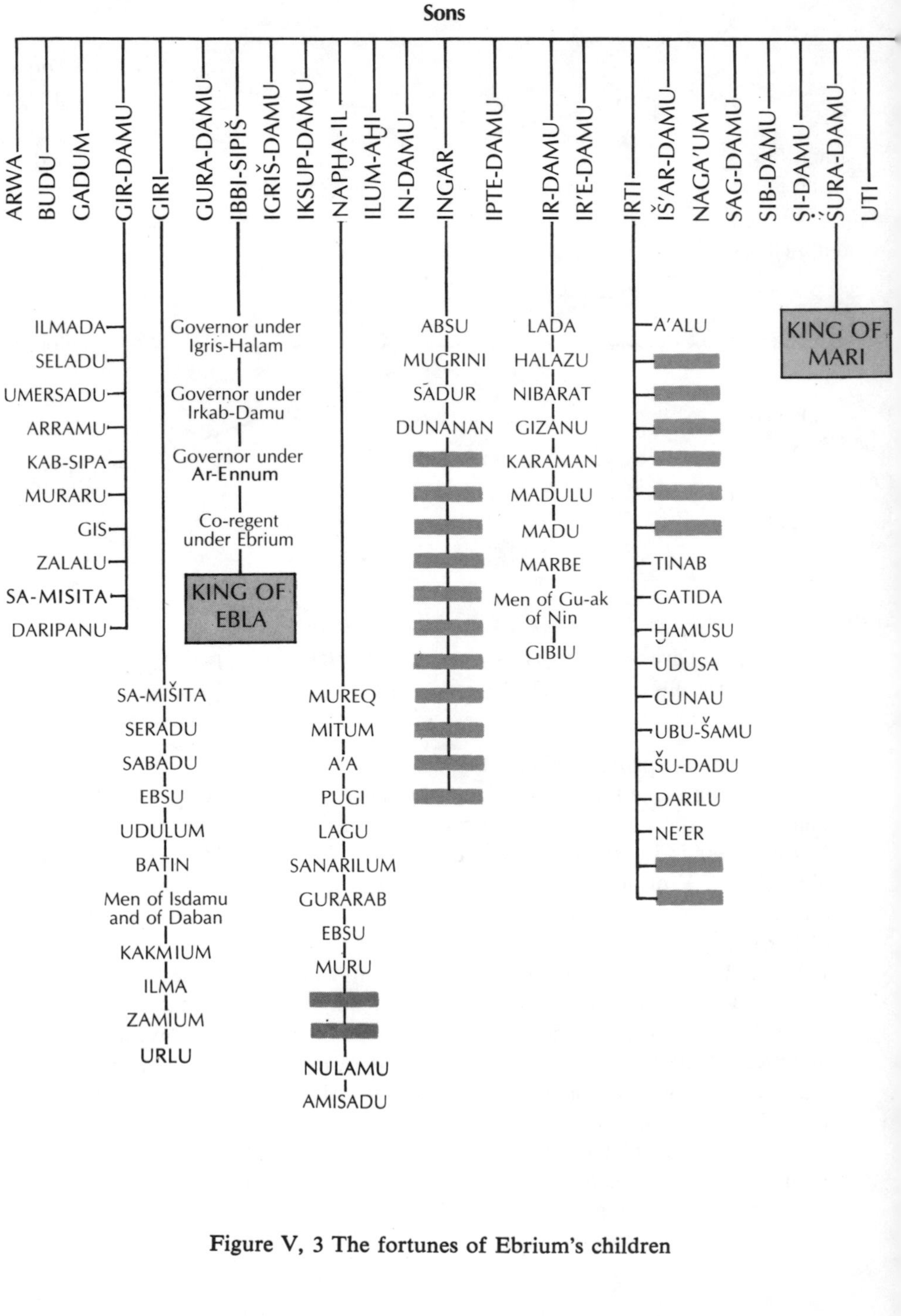

Figure V, 3 The fortunes of Ebrium's children

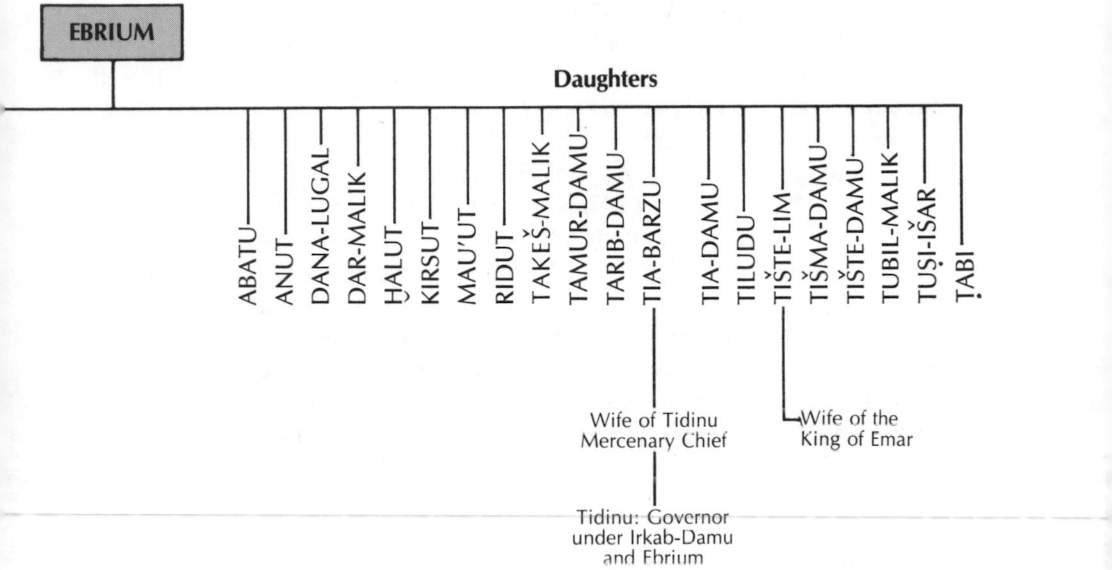

first co-regent with Ebrium and then his successor; Šura-Damu (no. 23) became king of that age-old rival city Mari, at this time under Ebla's dominion.[45]

As will be seen later, Mari was a thorn in Ebla's side, thwarting its plans of expansion to the east. Hence as the result of the military victory over Iblul-Il, king of Mari, the kings of Ebla decided to name themselves kings of Mari, an action perfected by Ebrium who named one of his own sons king of the rebel city. Ebrium coherently followed this nearly personalistic policy; Giri (no. 5), for example, received the governorship over six cities, as text TM.75.G.1470 reports:

sa-MI+ŠITA$_{x}$^{ki}	the governorate
šè-ra-du^{ki}	of the city Šeradu,
ša-ba-du^{ki}	of the city Šabadu,
eb-su^{ki}	of the city Ebsu,
ù-du-lum^{ki}	of the city Udulum,
ba-ti-in^{ki}	of the city Batin,
lú *iš-da-mu*	the men of Iš-Damu,
lú *da-ba-ù*	the men of Daba'u,
ì-na-sum	he has given
gi-rí	to Giri
dumu-nita	the son
eb-rí-um	of Ebrium.

According to text TM.75.G.1444, the same Giri receives in trust the cities of Kakmium, Ilma, Zamium, and Urlu together with their overseers. TM.75.G.6030 reports that 17 cities are assigned to Irti (no. 17), with the final clause uru^{ki}-uru^{ki} *ir-ti,* "the cities of Irti,"[46] information confirmed by another text specifying that Irti is a son of Ebrium. Seven cities, among them Absu, Mugrini, Sadur and Dunanan, are entrusted to Ingar (no. 13) and others to Napḫa-il (no. 10).[47]

Very interesting in this connection is text TM.75.G.1444 which deals with the Ebrium's division of real estate among his sons Gir-Damu (no. 4), Ir-Damu (no. 15), and Napḫa-il (no. 10). At the time of this distribution Ebrium, while retaining the title of en, "king," was no longer in office and informs his successor of this decision, if we interpret correctly, according to the formula *en-ma eb-ri-um ší-in* en, "thus Ebrium to the king." This tablet reveals not only the power of Ebrium but also his extraordinary wealth spread throughout the whole kingdom. To be sure, Ebrium is not assigning cities but "houses," but the meaning of this term in cuneiform sources suffices to give some idea of the power this former king continued to wield.

A complete list of the estates acquired by the three sons reads according to the order of the tablet:

a) Gir-Damu[48]

wa	and
i-na-sum	I have given
gi-ir-da-mu	to Gir-Damu
. . . . .	. . . . .
é	the house
ìl-ma-da^{ki}	of Ilmada (city),
é	the house
šè-la-du^{ki}	of Šeladu (city),
é	the house
ù-mer-sà-du^{ki}	of Umersadu (city),
é	the house
ar-ra-mu^{ki}	of Arramu (city),
é	the house
kab-sipa^{ki}	of Kab-sipa (city),
é	the house
mu-ra-ru$_x^{ki}$	of Muraru (city),
é	the house
giš^{ki}	of Giš (city),
é	the house
za-lu-lu^{ki}	of Zalulu (city),
é	the house
sa-MI+ŠITA$_x^{ki}$	of the governorate,

é	the house
da-ri-pa-nu^{ki}	of Daripanu (city).

b) Ir-Damu[49]

wa	and
ì-n a - s u m	I have given
ir-da-mu	to Ir-Damu
. . . . .	. . . . .
la-da$_5^{ki}$	the city of Lada,
é	the house
ḫa-la-zu^{ki}	Ḫalazu (city),
é	the house
ni-bu-ru-ut^{ki}	of Nibarat (city),
é	the house
gi-za-nu^{ki}	of Gizanu (city),
é	the house
kà-ra-ma-nu^{ki}	of Karaman (city),
é	the house
ma-du-lu^{ki}	of Madulu (city),
é	the house
ma-du^{ki}	of Madu (city),
g i š . n u . s a r	the gardeners
mar-be^{ki}	of Marbe (city),
l ú - g u - a k	the men-Gu.ak
n i n^{ki}	of Nin (city),
gi-bi-ù	the city of Gibiu
in	(situated) in
bar-ga-u$_9^{ki}$	Bargau

c) Napḫa-Il[50]

wa	and
í - n a - s u m	I have given
nap-ḫa-il	to Napḫa-il
. . . . .	. . . . .
é	the house
mu-rí-iq^{ki}	of Muriq (city),
é	the house
mi-tùm^{ki}	of Mitum (city),
é	the house
á-a^{ki}	of A'a (city),
é	the house
pù-gi^{ki}	of Pugi (city),
é	the house
la-gú^{ki}	of Lagu (city),

é	the house
sa-na-rí-lum^{ki}	of Sanarilum (city),
é	the house
gú-ra-ra-ab^{ki}	of Gurarab (city),
é	the house
eb-su^{ki}	of Ebsu (city).

Since these "houses" are scattered throughout the different villages of the kingdom, it becomes possible to reconstruct the geography of Ebla in smallest detail.

The catalogue of the fortunes of Ebrium's children could be protracted, but it seems wiser to select just one of the economic texts which permits the listing of Ebrium's numerous offspring which may not even be complete. This document mentions allotments of various kinds of stuffs and garments to different persons of Ebla and to messengers for trade. The first part reads:[51]

1 *é-da-um*-túg-2	1 Edaum fabric of second quality,
1 aktum-túg	1 Aktum fabric,
1 íb-túg-ša$_6$-dar	1 top quality Ib fabric multicolored
1 aktum-túg ti-túg	1 Aktum fabric, fabric . . .
1 íb-túg-sag	1 Ib fabric for head-cover,
1 gada-túg túg-mu	1 fabric of linen, fabric . . .
→ *ik-su-up-da-mu*	for Iksup-Damu
1 *é-da-um*-túg-2	1 Edaum fabric of second quality,
1 aktum-túg	1 Aktum fabric,
1 íb-túg sag-sal	1 Ib fabric for fine head-cover,
1 íb-túg ša$_6$-dar	1 top quality multicolored Ib fabric
5 aktum-túg ti-túg	5 Aktum fabrics, fabric . . .
1 gada-túg túg-mu	1 linen fabric, fabric . . .
→ *ṣi-da-mu*	for Ṣi-da-mu
1 aktum-túg túg-mu	1 Aktum fabric, fabric . . .
2 aktum-túg ti-túg	2 Aktum fabrics, fabric . . .
1 gada-túg túg-mu	1 linen fabric, fabric . . .
2 íb-túg ša$_6$-dar	2 top quality and multicolored Ib fabrics
→ *ga-du-um*	for Gadum
1 dùl-túg-ma-rí^{ki}	1 dul fabric of Mari
1 aktum-túg túg-mu	1 Aktum fabric, fabric . . .
2 aktum-túg ti-túg	2 Aktum fabrics, fabric
1 gada-túg túg-mu	1 linen fabric, fabric

2 íb-tug ša₆-dar	2 top quality, multicolored Ib fabrics
→ *ṣi-íb-da-mu*	for Ṣib-Damu
1 *é-da-um-*túg-2	1 Edaum fabric of second quality;
1 aktum=túg	1 Aktum fabric
1 íb-túg ša₆-dar	1 top quality multicolored Ib fabric
1 aktum-túg ti-túg	1 Aktum fabric, fabric
1 gada-túg túg-mu	1 linen fabric, fabric . . .
→ *sag-da-mu*	for Sag-Damu;
1 aktum-túg túg-mu	1 Aktum fabric, fabric . . .
1 aktum-túg ti-túg	1 Aktum fabric, fabric . . .
1 gada-túg túg-mu	1 linen fabric, fabric . . .
1 íb-túg ša₆-dar	1 top quality, multicolored Ib fabric
→ *ip-te-da-mu*	for Ipte-Damu
dumu-nita dumu nita	sons
en	of the king
. . . . .	. . . . .
1 gada-túg túg-mu	1 linen fabric, fabric . . .
→ *ìr-e̩-da-mu*	for Ir'e-Damu
dumu-nita	son
en[52]	of the king.

From this tablet alone the names of seven sons of Ebrium, all designated "sons of the king," come to light: Iksup-Damu (no. 9), Ṣi-Damu (no. 22), Gadum (no. 3), Ṣib-Damu (no. 21), Sag-Damu (no. 20), Ipte-Damu (no. 14), and Ir'e-Damu (no. 16).

To consolidate and extend his power, Ebrium dealt with his daughters no differently than with his sons. Tablet TM.75.G.2094 relates that one of his daughters, Tia-barzu (no. 12), was given in marriage to Tidinu, whom other texts describe as lugal-bar-an-bar-an, "chief of the mercenaries." This was a politically shrewd move on Ebrium's part; having no standing army, Ebla depended on foreign mercenaries so that the leader of the mercenaries was a key figure. Another princess, Tišelim (no. 15), became the wife of the friendly king of Emar and is called "the queen of Emar";[53] the practice of dynastic marriage as a tool of foreign policy obviously has a long history.

These few examples manifest the political genius of Ebrium, the real founder of the Ebla dynasty, who, however, committed the grave error of trying to change the fundamental concepts of Eblaite society, which could not remain passive in the face of this ideological revolution.

Just as with the princes, several economic texts permit drawing up a list of the princesses begotten by Ebrium. The citation of but one text should suffice for the present purpose:[54]

	13 zára-túg 26 bu-di	13 Zara fabrics, 26 pins
	20 (gín) kù: babbar	20 shekels of silver
→	*ti-a-bar-zu*	for Tia-Barzu,
→	*téš-ma-da-mu*	Tešma-Damu,
→	*tá-kéš-ma-lik*	Takeš-Malik,
→	*ri-du-ut*	Ridut,
→	*kir-sú-ut*	Kirsut,
→	*dar-^{d}ma-lik*	Dar-Malik,
→	*da-na-lugal*	Dana-Lugal,
→	*a-ba?-tù*	Abatu,
→	*tù-ṣí-i-šar*	Tuṣi-Išar,
→	*tù-bil-ma-lik*	Tubil-Malik,
	dumu-mí	daughters
	eb-rí-um	of Ebrium,
	. . . . .	. . . . .
→	*ti-iš-te-da-mu*	Tište-Damu
	dumu-mí-en	daughter of the king

This tablet alone mentions eleven daughters of Ebrium specified as either dumu-mí-*eb-ri-um,* "daughter of Ebrium" or dumi-mí-en, "daughter of the king." Following the numbering of the table on p. 82, they are no. 12, no. 16, no. 9, no. 8, no. 6, no. 4, no. 3, no. 1, no. 19, no. 18, and no. 17.

E) The Royal Palace and its Daily Life

With such a large family at hand, one wonders where and how they lived, how the king or queen or one of the royal offspring passed the normal day. The official character of available documents, alas, cannot satisfy this legitimate curiosity except by some indirect hints. What is more, the current state of research cannot paint a complete picture of everyday life at Ebla, so one must be content with some indicative citations.

From tablet TM.75.G.336, which will be examined in the next chapter, it appears that among the various palaces on the acropolis one was called é-en, "the king's house," which doubtless designates the residence of the royal family. This same text reports that "10 superintendents with 60 services" worked here, but it is difficult to say just what functions they performed.

As regards the topographical layout of the royal residence, within the space of palace G excavated at Ebla, P. Matthiae conjectures that the royal apartments could only have been on an upper floor of the palace whose front coincided with the east façade of the "audience court." The podium found in the "audience court" and the connected tower support this hypothesis. If extended investigations confirm this reconstruction, the palace, whose monumental gate opens on the east façade of the "audience court," would very likely be the "palace of the master" cited in TM.75.G.336.[55]

Unfortunately both the destruction of the palace and the structures built over it in subsequent centuries will never permit even an approximate reconstruction of the various quarters of the royal residence and it will be even less possible to write about the furnishings—beds, tables, chairs, to mention only the more obvious items—of the individual rooms.

When it comes, however, to the daily fare of the royal family or to what they wore, the tablets abound with detailed information.

The documents listing deliveries to the palace of foodstuffs already furnish at least indirect information about what was consumed by the royal family and their court. But given the amounts of certain consignments, it is obvious that not everything was used; even the royal house stored perishable goods, as can be inferred from TM.75.G.221:

1 *rí-ba*$_x$ 4 *li-im* 1[+x]*mi-at*	14,170 [+x]
70 zí *gú-bar*	Gubar measures of flour
mu-túm	delivered
é	to the palace
en	of the king

Other texts, however, are more specific; thus TM.75.G.220, for instance, lists the daily and monthly rations for the royal family and for the Elders, here juxtaposed to the royal family as if to underline their inseparable union:

4½ še-*bar*	4½ measures of barley
nì lu$_4$	daily ration
en	for the king
wa	and
ABxÁŠ	the Elder;
4 še-*bar*	4 measures
še+tin [ ]	of wine
[en]	[for the king]
[*wa*]	[and]
ABxÁŠ	for the Elder;
lú 1 itu 1 mi-at 25 še *bar*	in one month: 125 Gubar measures
še-*bar*-en-ABxÁŠ	ration of barley for the king and the Elder
1 itu	for one month;
1 *mi-at* 20 še-*bar*	120 Gubar measures
še+tin en-ABxÁŠ	wine for the king and the Elder
1 itu	for one month[56]

This document exemplarily gives the daily rations of cereals and fruits destined for "the king and the Elder" in relation to the monthly consumption of 30 days:

1 day	30 days
4½ Gubar of barley	125 Gubar of barley
4 Gubar of wine	120 Gubar of wine

The texts, however, normally cite the monthly or the daily requirement. TM.75.G.427 attests the allotment of grain flour for "the king" Ibbi-Sipiš for the seventh, ninth, and first month of the sixth year of his reign to the amount of 100 Gubar per month, and similarly for the ninth and eleventh months of the seventh year. The above-cited TM.75.G.411 records, on the other hand, the daily requirement of "bread" for each member of the royal family in the sequence:

7 loaves of bread	the king
2 loaves of bread	the queen
4 loaves of bread	Dubuḫu-Hada
2 loaves of bread	Ipṭura
2 loaves of bread	royal prince
2 loaves of bread	royal princess[57]

The last two entries reveal that the allotment of two loaves of bread counted as per person and should be considered as a fixed norm.

Thus far the discussion has focused mainly on rations of starches, but the royal table was also supplied with lamb and mutton. One tablet,[58] from the time of Ibbi-Sipiš, indicates the monthly supply of "81 sheep as food for the king," "16 sheep as food for the prince Ir'eak-Damu," "140 sheep as food for Dubuḫu-Hada," and "15 sheep as food for the dependents of the royal palace." Another text of an earlier period which records the delivery of sheep for various purposes, such as offerings to temples, food for the dependents, taxes, etc., informs us how much livestock was allotted as "food for the king," and, obviously, for his family, over a ten-month period. The precise figure is "1,382 sheep" subdivided as follows:

MONTHS:	I	II	III	IV	V	VI	VII	VIII	IX	X
SHEEP:	131	128	103	160	94	116	151	161	122	216

The fact that the sheep quota for the royal house is not fixed, instead of raising doubts, renders the document more credible; just as at certain times various situations arise in a family, such as a visit of friends or relatives, or a reception, that require a greater outlay, so the palace must have needed on special occasions a larger quantity of meat for the table.

It might be interesting to present in a synoptic table the heads of cattle assigned as "food for the king" together with those allotted or qualified in a different manner so that one can gain a clearer idea of the total requirement of meat for the city as well as the relationships between the different categories. The attributions encountered in this one text are in the order:

1)	é-mul	"house of the stars"
2)	kú-en	"food for the king"
3)	kú-guruš	"food for the dependents"
4)	kas$_4$	"(for) the messengers"
5)	šu-du$_8$-máš	"tax"
6)	al-du$_{11}$-ga	"request"
7)	ug$_6$	"slaughtered"

The first item certainly concerns temple offerings, items 2, 4, and 7 deal with the food for state functionaries and the population of Ebla, while 5 and 6 are administrative indications whose real meaning escapes us.

Table V, 1
Allocations of Sheep for Diverse Purposes in Various Months (TM.75. G.2096)

	MONTHS	é-mul	kú-en	kú-guruš	kas$_4$	šu-du$_8$-máš	al-du$_{11}$-ga	ug$_6$
1)	itu *ṣa-lul*	231	131	404	90	152	40	300
2)	itu *i-ba$_4$-sa*	194	128	289	81	74	36	300
3)	itu è	371	103	300	112	124	85	153
4)	itu kur$_6$	185	160	278	86	74	52	186
5)	itu *i-ší*	328	94	361	82	53	59	40
6)	itu *ig-za*	67	116	385	90[x]	99	17	—
7)	itu *ṣa-'à-tum*	363	151	220	112	35	30	200
8)	itu *kí-lí*	145	161	331	92	76	67	444
9)	itu *ḫa-li*	310	122	343	128	47	67	606
10)	itu *i-rí-sá*	413	216	201	100	61	59	303
	SUMS	2717	1382	3062	955	705	512	
	TOTAL				9423			2931

So long as these data have only relative value, generalizations are better avoided, but it might be noted that the quota allotted as "food for the king" corresponds to 9 percent of the total number of sheep (12,354) so accurately listed by the Eblaite scribe, a fact not to be passed over lightly.[59]

In addition to bread and starches in general and to meat, the royal table sparkled with exquisite drinks. As throughout the ancient Near East, the most common drink at Ebla was beer made from malt, but wine was not lacking; in fact, the documentation available shows that wine was the third essential ingredient of the royal board.

This information concerning wine consumption at Ebla is cordially welcome since it confirms what was known for later periods and more specifically for the second millennium; Syria has long been a center of outstanding viticulture and its wines were widely exported.[60]

This discussion of daily life in the palace would be incomplete without some mention of the garments and jewels with which the members of the royal family bedecked themselves. The sculptures and inlays discovered in the royal palace already offer some idea of the elegance of Eblaite garb in the third millennium B.C. Both the men and the women wore long, well-finished tunics, such as that of the prince "with the flounces of woolen tassels," or that of the lass with the "fringed" tunic,[61] but in this regard the texts are more detailed and precise.

As will be seen further on, Ebla was a most important center for the manufacture of textiles, which were exported in all directions. The materials were either wool or linen, the colors white, black, red, or many-colored. Some indications point to the existence of "damask," those fabrics with gold thread for which Syria became famous from the Middle Ages till today.

As was seen above, some texts mention the delivery of garments or fabrics for the members of the royal family; in fact, these are the tablets which yield the information about Ebrium's progeny. When research on the terms expressing the different kinds of stuff and the quality of the clothes is further advanced, it will be possible to write a chapter on fashion in Ebla, but even now one can affirm that the Eblaites were clothes-conscious.

Bound to the problem of the wardrobe is the more general one of the ornaments and jewels, about which the information is abundant; the texts very often mention the giving of gold or silver bracelets or golden earrings to the queen and the various princesses, while the king and the princes receive not only golden armlets but also "daggers of gold." Hence it would not be misleading to speak of royal pomp in connection with the palace and the lords of Ebla. The city was so rich in metals and textiles that it would be surprising not to find the ruling class making ample use of them.

3. THE "ELDERS" AND THE KING

When treating of the top echelons of the state, we noted the presence of the "Elders," called AB x ÁŠ or *abbū,* "fathers." Who were these "Elders"? In this simple question is concealed one of the many enigmas of the Eblaite state. The figure of the "Elder" or leader of the clan ill accords with the image of a state with a monarchical regime as depicted especially by the historical texts. The civilization of Ebla was highly developed and technological, while the Elders reflect a state structure of the tribal type.

Nonetheless the Elders are there at Ebla and form a kind of senate that controls the king in his exercise of power. When the texts are better understood, it will be possible to appreciate how the Eblaites succeeded in harmonizing the elements of the state structures so dissimilar—not to say opposed—but even now certain elements grant a glimpse of the role of the Elders in making the state function.

The administrative texts often attest the expression en *wa* ABxÁŠ, "the king and the Elders," a phrase revealing the bond between them, but the historical tablets really confirm the vital role of the Elders in the affairs of state. The crown prince Ibbi-Sipiš addresses his report[62] on a military campaign "to the king and to the Elders":

en-ma	Thus
i-bí-sí-piš	Ibbi-Sipiš
ší-in	to
en	the king
wa	and
ABxÁŠ ABxÁŠ	to the Elders.

This phrase manifests the interest and the vigilance exercised by the Elders over the fortunes of the kingdom.

A tablet cited earlier[63] suggests that in their organization the Elders appeared in pairs and that the symbol of their power was the axe:

10 lá-2 ninda	8 loaves of bread
ABxÁŠ	for the Elders
4 ^{giš}šilig	4 axes

Since the ration per person is two loaves of bread, the four axes indicate the number of the Elders represented, it would seem, by their symbol of authority. At this point it would be relevant to observe that the lovely wooden inlay of a male figure with an axe found at Ebla in 1974 probably represents not a king but an elder. Should this interpretation prove correct, we can form an idea of the majesty and solidarity of the Elders at Ebla, a real assembly of wise men.

In the treatment above of the kingship at the time of Ibbi-Sipiš,[64] it was noted that though he turned the sovereignty of Ebla into a family affair, neither the former kings nor the Elders, "the pilasters supporting the Eblaite state structure and, in the last analysis, the real decision-making body as imposing as it was discreet," were suppressed. An example of the discreet power of the Elders is forthcoming from a very sober letter but one charged with meaning sent by one of them or by the entire body to the crown prince responsible for foreign affairs under King Ibbi-Sipiš. The verb used in the document is in itself ambiguous: igi-du$_8$, in fact, means "to look" but with the particular connotation "be careful," "watch out," and lends to the letter a typically Oriental color:

en-ma	Thus
a-bu	the Elder
ší-in	to
du-bù-ḫu-^{d}'à-da	Dubuḫu-Hada:
i g i - d u 8	be careful
wa	and
da-na-lum	of Danalum,
lu-ma	for goodness' sake,
i g i - d u 8	be careful![65]

A few words, but filled with meaning; it is a very delicate and almost friendly warning, were the post occupied by Dubuḫu-Hada not known; but since it is known, the contents of the letter become deeply political.

To draw inferences at the present time would be premature, but it should not be overlooked that this crown prince never ascended the throne. This letter intimates that he was meeting opposition and prompts the surmise that the downfall of the dynasty was due to the struggle for power within the state of Ebla itself.

The tablet with the above-cited letter also contains another missive addressed to the same Dubuhu-Hada, this time by Šima-Kura, a state official; the tone and contents are the same as in the first letter:

en-ma	Thus
šì-ma-^{d}ku-ra	Šima-Kura
ší-in	to
du-bù-ḫu-^{d}'à-da	Dubuḫu-Hada:
i g i - d u 8	be careful,
wa	and
da-na-lum	of Danalum,
lu-ma	for goodness' sake,
i g i - d u 8	be careful;
wa	and
ti-kéš-ma-lik	of Tikeš-Malik,
lu-ma	for goodness' sake,
i g i - d u 8	be careful!

To the general warning "take heed" and to be careful of Danalum, the official Šima-Kura puts the crown prince on his guard against Tikeš Malik. These delicately worded documents are obviously of capital importance since they are dealing with the very reason of state.

What has been said thus far illustrates well the function of the Elders at Ebla. They are not to be looked on as a superseded body of a state organized on a tribal base but rather as an assembly very active and influential in the most important decisions. They are mentioned together with the king, they are listed among the high positions of the state immediately after the reigning king and before the former kings, they send letters to the prince heir warning him to take care—these all demonstrate both the limitations of the king's powers and the central role of the Elders in the hierarchy of the state.

4. INTERNATIONAL POLITICS

Before the discovery of the royal archives of Ebla, there was no reason to believe the existence of large states that were real world powers. Historians of the ancient Near East widely agree that the kings of the dynasty of Akkad that flourished circa 2350–2220 B.C. created the first world empire. This was a Semitic empire extending beyond the borders of Mesopotamia, reaching eastward as far as the western part of Iran and westward to Syria and the Mediterranean.[66]

The preceding period, on the other hand, was characterized by state structures that became city-states of Sumerian creation.[67] Though some Sumerian epic poems recount the epic wars conducted by the glorious kings of Uruk against Iran (Enmerkar and Lugalbanda) or against Syria, as in the case of Gilgamesh, the Mesopotamian hero par excellence, who first went to cut the cedars of Lebanon, the historical inscriptions of the entire Sumerian epoch narrate only the exploits concerning the struggle for supremacy of one city-state over another.[68]

Both the economic texts and, above all, the historical texts from Ebla now reveal that 200 years before the creation of the empire of Akkad the Near Eastern world was the center of state structures whose dominion extended for thousands of kilometers. Shortly after the discovery of Ebla, when the report of the geographical limits of Ebla's empire was first announced, there was an understandable skepticism. Further study of the tablets has gradually shown that the first report contained no exaggeration. With the steady unfolding of the expanse of Ebla's empire, other contemporary empires which played important parts in the history of the third millennium are coming to light in the tablets from Ebla. The known situation of the second millennium is verified for the third millennium as well; with Ebla the third pole alongside Egypt and Mesopotamia, Syria assumes the central role thanks to its marvelous geographical position. All the north-south (from Anatolia to Egypt) and east-west (from Iran and Mesopotamia to the Mediterranean Sea) commercial routes pass through Syria. Hence the agelong struggles, so well documented for the second millennium, to obtain control of Syria and the commercial routes passing through it. But there is a difference; during the second millennium Syria was divided into small states constantly at war among themselves, thus playing into the hands of the Hittite empire in the north and of Egypt to the south, but in the third millennium Ebla succeeded in winning control over the entire area and imposed itself as a first-rate power.

A state's efficiency can be measured and assessed by the sagacity of its political relationships with foreign powers. Ebla shows itself a world power by its peace treaties, alliances and, when necessary, by wars; through all of these it was able to predominate. While stressing that these studies are still in their initial stage, I would like to present some texts which underscore those aspects that permitted Ebla to control all of Syria-Palestine to the south, the Mediterranean as far as Cyprus to the west, a large part of Anatolia to the north, and to the east all of north-central Mesopotamia.

4.1. ALLIANCES

The kings of Ebla were aware that only respect for local autonomies could guarantee a secure and lasting alliance. Hence they took care to stipulate treaties which, while respecting the traditions of each state, assured themselves of the superiority necessary for the stability of the areas concerned.

As noted above, the kings of Ebla used dynastic marriages to strengthen friendly relationships with other states. King Ebrium gave his daughter Tišelim in marriage to the king of Emar, a city with a vital geographic position at the confluence of the Baliḫ with the Euphrates. Another princess became the bride of the king of Luban, a city still not located. These appear to be the first dynastic marriages on record and reveal how important the kings of Ebla considered ties of blood for obtaining or buttressing political alliances.

One text which deserves to be given in full as a fine example of diplomatic correspondence in the third millennium is the treaty between Ebla and the kingdom of Ḫamazi in northern Iran. The more than a thousand kilometers separating the two powers give some idea of how far-reaching were the diplomatic ties Ebla fostered with other states.

The tablet[69] bearing this diplomatic letter, surely a copy for the archive, contains the name of the scribe who drew up the document. The purely Near Eastern style with the recurring phrases "you are my brother, I am your brother" vividly recalls current modes of speech in that part of the world, showing the constancy of certain traditions in Syria down the centuries.

The letter was not written by the king of Ebla himself but rather by the superintendent of the royal palace; it was delivered to the ambassador of the king of Ḫamazi accredited to the court of Ebla. This item too underlines the modernity of the state of Ebla.

obverse

I	1)	*en-ma*	Thus
	2)	*i-bù-bu*$_6$	Ibubu,
	3)	agrig	the superintendent
	4)	é	of the palace
	5)	en	of the king,
	6)	*lí-na*	to the
	7)	sukkal-du$_8$ <*ší-má*>	messenger, <listen>:
	8)	*an-tá*	You
	9)	šeš	(are my) brother
	10)	*ù*	and
II	1)	*an-na*	I
	2)	šeš	(am your) brother;
	3)	lú-šeš	(to you) man-brother,
	4)	*mi-nu-ma*	whatever
	5)	al-du$_{11}$-ga	desire
	6)	*ṣi*	issuing
	7)	ka	from your mouth
	8)	*an-na*	I
	9)	in-na-sum	will grant
	10)	*ù*	and
III	1)	*an-tá*	you
	2)	al-du$_{11}$-ga	the desire
	3)	*ṣi*	issuing (from my mouth)
	4)	ì-na-sum	grant:
	5)	bar-an-ša$_6$	good soldiers
	6)	ḫi-mu-túm	send me, I pray:
	7)	*an-tá*	you
	8)	šeš	(are in fact my) brother
	9)	*ù*	and
	10)	*an-na*	I
	11)	šeš	(am your) brother.
IV	1)	10 ^{giš}ÉŠ	10 pieces of wooden furniture,
	2)	2 ^{giš}ašud-^{giš}ÉŠ	2 knickknacks,
	3)	*i-bù-bu*$_6$	I, Ibubu,
	4)	in-na-sum	have given
	5)	sukkal-du$_8$	to the messenger;
	6)	*ìr-kab-da-mu*	Irkab-Damu,
	7)	en	king
	8)	*eb-la*^{ki}	of Ebla
	9)	šeš	(is) brother
	10)	*zi-zi*	of Zizi,

V	1)	en	king
	2)	*ḫa-ma-zi-im*ki	of Ḫamazi;
	3)	*zi-zi*	Zizi,
	4)	en	king
	5)	*ḫa-ma-zi-im*ki	of Ḫamazi,
	6)	šeš	(is) brother
	7)	*ìr-kab-da-mu*	of Irkab-Damu,
	8)	en	king
VI	1)	*eb-la*ki	of Ebla.
	2)	*ù*	And
	3)	*en-ma*	thus
	4)	*ti-ra-il*	Tira-il,
	5)	dub-sar	the scribe
	6)	[*i*]*k-tub*	has written
	7)	*lí-na*	(and) to the
	8)	sukkal-du$_8$	messenger
	9)	(*zi-zi*)	of Zizi
reverse			
I	1)	ì-na-sum	has given (the letter).

Only a very close alliance between the two states will explain how the king of Ebla could turn to the king of Ḫamazi for some soldiers, in this case mercenaries. This document is important not only for the alliance it supposes but also for the revelation that Ebla had no standing army and was obliged to hire mercenaries. Thus the supreme interest of the Eblaites in commerce, not war, finds here further confirmation. Since the kings of Ebla were conscious of this dependence upon foreigners, King Ebrium, as noticed above, married off one of his daughters to the leader of the mercenaries.[70] Further study will serve to fill out the picture of Eblaite treaties with other states, but it is already possible to get a glimpse of diplomatic maneuvering in the third millennium.

Ebla's shrewd diplomacy is also reflected in a very interesting document reporting the alliance between the kingdom of Mari and the kingdom of Edu, a very tight alliance which Ebla succeeded in breaking by drawing Edu over to her side. The following complaints lodged by the king of Mari with the king of Edu are understandable:[71]

en-ma	Thus
*ma-rí*ki	Mari
lí-na	to the
en	king
*é-du*ki	of Edu:
guruš-guruš-*kà*	your men,
ša$_6$	good ones,
nu-ì-na-sum	you did not send

ší-in	to
eb-la^{ki}	Ebla
A B	to me you have given
g u r u š - g u r u š-*kà*	your men,
ḫ u l	inefficient ones,
ì - n a - s u m	you have sent me.

A pact between Mari and Edu clearly existed, but it is equally evident that Ebla was able to undermine it; in the reply of Edu's king to such expostulations it is affirmed that a new alliance has been sealed by the kings of Ebla and Edu with the gods as witnesses.

4.2. WARS

On more than one occasion we have stressed the peaceful nature of the Eblaites, but this does not mean that they did not resort to arms when need arose. Names of years and historical texts make it clear that Ebla was not unwilling to go into battle to impose its control.

The war between Ebla and Mari, its age-old rival, is particularly well documented by the report sent by the Eblaite general to the king of Ebla. Because of its structure this text might properly be termed a war bulletin or a camp diary. It gives the name of Mari's defeated and dethroned king as Iblul-Il, and describes the route followed by the Eblaite army to reach Ebla.[72] The letter begins with the following formula:

Introduction: Thus Enna-Dagan, king of Mari,
to the king of Ebla.

The continuation of the letter and other documents reveal that Enna-Dagan is the commander who directed the campaign against Mari and consequently became its king after his victory and deposition of the legitimate king Iblul-Il.

PHASE I. I set siege to the city of Aburu and the city of Ilgi, situated in the territory of Belan, and I defeated the king of Mari. In the land of Labanan I raised heaps of corpses.

As noticed above, the concise style resembles that of military bulletins and at the same time manifests the mentality of the warrior who when smiting hostile cities is conscious of smiting the king of Mari himself.

PHASE II. I set siege to the city of Tibalat and the city of Ilwi, and I defeated the king of Mari. In the land of Angai I raised heaps of corpses . . .

PHASE III. I set siege to the towns of Raeak and Irim and Ašaltu and Badul, and I defeated the king of Mari. Near the borders of Naḫal I raised heaps of corpses.

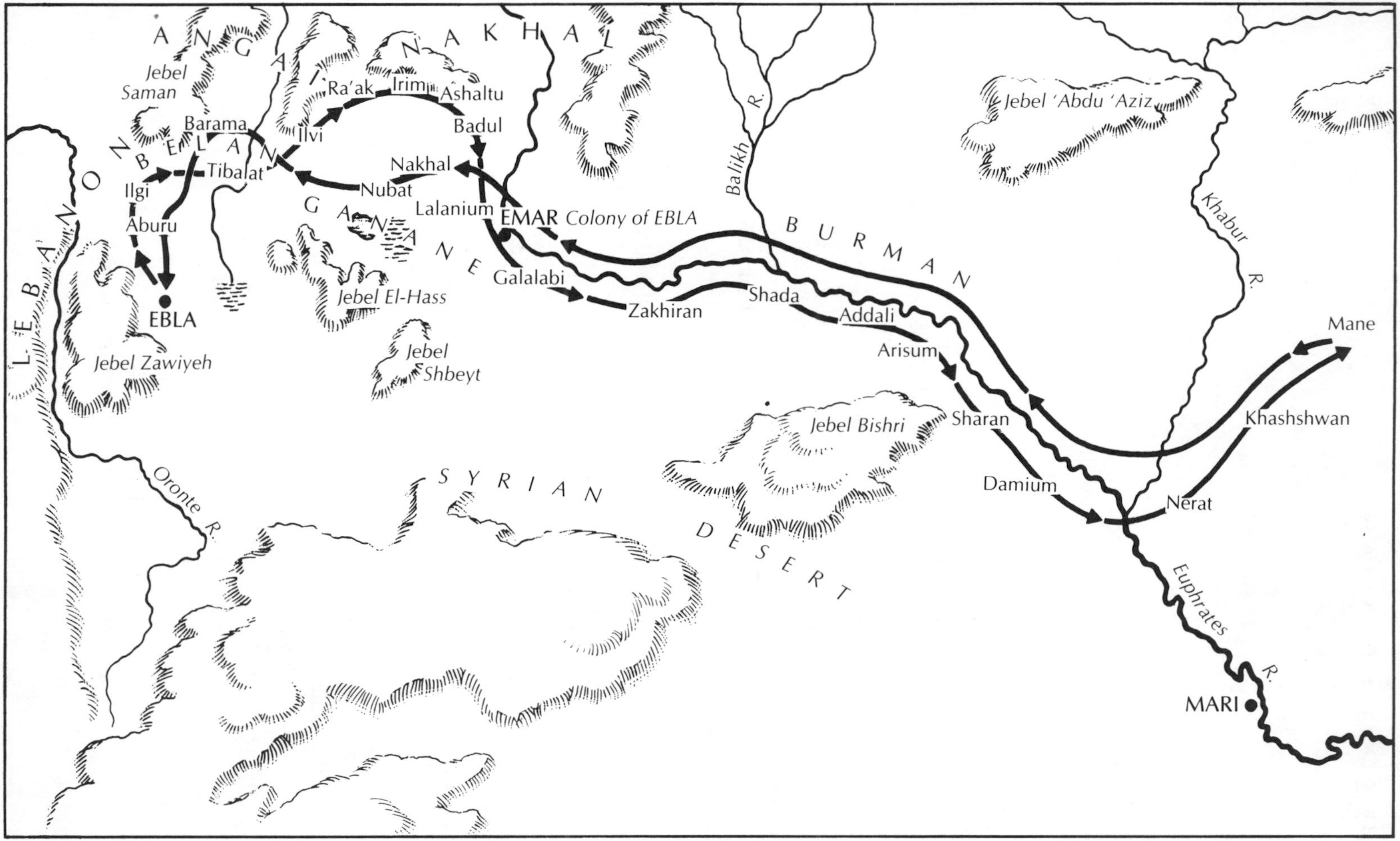

Figure V, 4 Military route of Enna-Dagan against Iblul-Il, king of Mari and Ashur

PHASE IV. And I defeated at Emar, and Lalanium and near the commercial colony of Ebla, Ištup-šar, the commander of Mari. In Emar and Lalanium I raised heaps of corpses.

In the first three phases Enna-Dagan reports in stereotyped phrases that he took rival cities and thus inflicted losses on Mari's king, but in the fourth phase he mentions the frontal encounter between the two armies in the neighborhood of Emar. Interesting is the reference to the commercial colony of Ebla which, as he reports, he liberated.

PHASE Va. And Galalabi and X and the commercial colony I liberated.

PHASE Vb. I defeated Iblul-Il, king of Mari and Ashur, in Zaḫiran, and raised seven heaps of corpses.

Precisely in the fifth phase there is mention for the first time of the king of Mari with the interesting and unexpected title "lord of Mari and Ashur," which suggests that the political bond between Ashur and Mari, till now considered the work of Šamši-Adad, already existed in the third millennium. Besides reporting this significant historical datum, phase Vb is structured differently from the first four: here the king is mentioned first and then the vanquished cities, whereas the opposite is true in the preceding phases. A reflection on the technical aspect of conducting the war suggests that the big encounter between the two armies took place in phase Vb. The encounter mentioned in phase IV was merely a skirmish in comparison to what was to happen later; Iblul-Il had sent ahead one of his generals while he himself held back with the strength of his army. After this defeat, the king of Mari retreats, but Enna-Dagan follows in hot pursuit and grants him no respite.

PHASE VI. I defeated Iblul-Il, king of Mari, and the cities of Šada, Addali, and Arisum, in the territory of Burman, together with the men of Sukurrim. I raised heaps of corpses.

PHASE VII. And I defeated Šaran and Dammium, together with Iblul-Il, king of Mari. I raised two heaps of corpses.

PHASE VIII. Iblul-Il, king of Mari, fled toward Nerad and to his house at Ḫašuwan, carrying with him to the city of Nema the tribute due Ebla.

At this point the military campaign takes an unexpected turn; instead of heading for Mari, Iblul-Il flees probably in the direction of Ḫabur. His intentions remain unclear to us, but he may have wanted to reach Ashur which was more strategically positioned and defensible than Mari. Iblul-Il's attempt proved unsuccessful because he was overtaken in the city Nema by the Eblaite general.

In the succeeding phases Enna-Dagan describes how on his return he consolidated the victories obtained when he went out from Ebla. He immediately set out for Emar where he had to intervene a second time:

PHASE IX. And I defeated Emar, raising heaps of corpses.

PHASE X. In Ganane I defeated Iblul-Il, king of Mari, and the cities of Naḫal and Šada of the territory of Gasur. I raised seven heaps of corpses.

PHASE XI. I, Enna-Dagan, king of Mari, defeated Iblul-Il, king of Mari, and the city of Barama, for the second time, and Aburu and Tibalat in the territory of Belan. I raised heaps of corpses.

The diagram attempts to trace on the basis of the indentifiable cities the routes followed by Enna-Dagan during the military campaign. The hypothetical character of the locations of the cities defeated by the Eblaite general must not, accordingly, be lost to sight. At any rate, it is evident that Enna-Dagan's return march was slightly different from his outward march; phases IX–XI mention both new cities and cities already known from the earlier phases. Two further phases follow, but the damaged text does not permit their complete reconstruction. In phase XII, however, Enna-Dagan boasts of having restored the scepter to various towns and phase XIII records an oath taken by Iblul-Il doubtless to signify total submission to Ebla. An economic text, TM.75.G.1953, unexpectedly reports the size of the tribute paid by the city of Mari to the king of Ebla, perhaps as a result of this military expedition. It comes to 2,193 minas of silver and 134 minas and 26 shekels of gold. Of these, 1,100 minas of silver and 93 minas of gold are specified as belonging to King Iblul-Il, while the rest of the sum was paid by the Ancients of Mari. It is noteworthy that the tablet specifies how much of the tribute will go to Enna-Dagan who conducted the expedition, namely, fifteen percent of the total tribute. These two texts dealing with the campaign and with the tribute raise a number of questions: What was Mari's attitude toward Ebla before the military incursion? How can one explain the enormous quantity of silver and gold paid to Ebla? For the moment no sure answers are forthcoming. What seems to have been the situation is the following: though independent, the kingdom of Mari was in a certain sense tributary to Ebla. Not only did King Iblul-Il refuse to pay the tribute due, he undertook an expansionist program, wresting control of cities either allied to Ebla or subject to it, as well as of Ebla's commercial colony situated near Emar. At this point Ebla reacted with energy. To the tribute due he added an exorbitant tax. We do not know if Iblul-Il was immediately dethroned (Enna-Dagan's affirmation seems to be military parlance) or whether Ebla waited awhile before sending its own governor, in this case Enna-Dagan himself. It is certain that a few decades later the kingdom of Mari was a vassal, precisely at the time of King Ibbi-Sipiš when Mari was governed by his brother Šura-Damu.

4.3. TREATIES

No one had suspected the existence of international treaties in the third millennium. Now Ebla comes forth with a number of treaties couched in terms bespeaking a very modern concept of the state as a royal entity. In none of the historical documents is the person of the king of Ebla ever mentioned but only the function of the king, as if to say that power was not attached to a specific person but that it was a function absolute in itself. With respect to the second-millennium treaties from Mesopotamia, Anatolia, and Egypt, in which the individual kings pledge themselves and their descendants and relatives, this is a new development: the Eblaites had no need for such formulas, for such pledges, for such assurances. The king of Ebla as such is the state of Ebla and hence there is no need for further guarantees.

Thus far ten treaties have been identified, but the most important seems to be that made between the king of Ebla and the king of Ashur,[73] a celebrated city of northern Mesopotamia. The text of the treaty begins with an introduction enumerating all the possessions of Ebla, then follows the body of the treaty divided into 19 paragraphs, and concludes with the formula of malediction.

In the introduction the king of Ebla lists all his possessions, not with the intention of humiliating the king of Ashur, but simply to present the real situation and the point of departure for the treaty itself.

In the Preface it was noted that the first text to emerge from the main library of Ebla was this treaty, and several of its passages were cited there. Here the complete translation of this part of the treaty is given:

> The city of Lagab is in the hands of the king of Ebla; Kablul and its fortresses are in the hands of the king of Ebla; Zaar and Uzilatu and their fortresses are in the hands of the king of Ebla; Gudadanum is in the hands of the king of Ebla; the men of all these fortresses of the king of Ebla are in the hands of the king of Ebla; the men of the king of Ashur are in the hands of the king of Ashur. Karkemiš is in the hands of the king of Ebla; Tinnu and its fortresses are in the hands of the king of Ebla; Arga is in the hands of the king of Ebla; Ladainu is in the hands of the king of Ebla; Dazaba is in the hands of the king of Ebla; Garamu is in the hands of the king of Ebla; Radda and its fortresses are in the hands of the king of Ebla; Elašune is in the hands of the king of Ebla; Raaš is in the hands of the king of Ebla; Edu is in the hands of the king of Ebla; Igi is in the hands of the king of Ebla; the men of all these fortresses of the king of Ebla are in the hands of the king of Ebla; the men of the king of Ashur are in the hands of the king of Ashur.[74]

The purpose of this list of possessions of the king of Ebla is very clear, namely, to establish the jurisdiction over the persons, be they Eblaites or Ashurites, in these cities. On the ground of the dispositions contained in this treaty, the Ashurites and the Eblaites preserved their citizenship and with it the liability to be tried in their land of origin. This is a new element, which may be termed modern, encountered for the first time in the third millennium.

After this long introduction follows the body of the treaty, which has as its subject the foundation of a commercial center in which both the kings of Ebla and Ashur are interested.

The various paragraphs enumerate the topics concerning commercial law, as well as subjects regarding the civil and penal fields. Thus, for example, they deal with the fixing of taxes for the use of this commercial center, the formalities of treatment of the messengers, the problem of slaves, judicial procedures for Eblaites and Ashurites, and even with cases of violence which can happen in such centers.

Since it is not possible to cite all the paragraphs here, I shall discuss the first paragraph, which deals with the toll to be paid for the use of such a commercial center:[75]

> A man of Ashur will pay the tax to Ebla, a man of Ashur will pay the tax to Ashur. A man of Ebla will pay the tax to Ashur, a man of Ebla will pay the tax to Ebla.

As readily appears from this paragraph, the merchants who wanted to take advantage of the new commercial center were subjected to double taxation; whether they were Eblaites or Ashurites, they had to pay the toll both to their city of origin and to the city signatory to the treaty. This paragraph cited as an example contains wording of the clauses that shows that the two contracting cities are on the level of parity.

In this treaty the king of Ebla is obviously requesting the king of Ashur to assume an important obligation, namely, to guarantee and facilitate Eblaite commerce in zones too distant from the fatherland. Hence the insertion of clauses in which the king of Ashur pledges to permit the sojourn of Eblaite merchants at Ashur and to assure them food and lodging, not to detain them beyond the established time, and not to use them for his own purposes. Any violations would result in the abrogation of the treaty and the subsequent abolition of Assyrian commerce in all the lands subject to Ebla.

This does not mean that Ebla refuses to offer a counterpart; in fact, it pledges to liberate eventual slaves of Ashur purchased by Eblaite merchants and assures the king of Ashur of the jurisdiction, already touched upon in the introduction to the treaty, over all his citizens; above all, capital trials must be held in the city of origin.

A number of other clauses invite commentary, but lack of space counsels turning at once to the curse formulas which conclude the treaty and reveal its real nature. Despite the generosity of the king of Ebla, the malediction addressed to the king of Ashur leaves no doubt about the superiority of one contracting party over the other. That Ebla has the upper hand appears from the following:[76]

kà-ma	Whenever
a-dè	(he)
ḫul-unken-aka	does wrong,
^d^utu ^d^'*à-da* ^d^mul igi	may the god sun, the god Hada, and the star who are witnesses,
du$_{11}$-ga-*sù*	his decision
in gána zàḫ	scatter in the steppe;
lí-na kas$_4$ kas$_4$	for the merchants
DU	who undertake
kaskal a nag	a journey, water
nu-gub	let there be none;
ma-in	may you have no
tuš	stable abode;
an-tá-ma	you,
kaskal-ḫul	a journey of perdition
DU	may you undertake,
ì-a-du-ud	O Tudia!

The tone of this malediction, so personal and adapted to the geographical reality of the ancient Near East, is something new within our ken; these are not phrases coined for the occasion but subjects which concern the daily life of people constantly traveling across the steppe and the desert. This treaty text furnishes, moreover, information of capital historical importance. Ashur has been known as a vital political center during the second and first millennium; now it turns out to have been a major power in the third millennium as well. Tudia, the king signing the contract, is famous as the founder of the great dynasty of Ashur, but nothing has been known about his historicity, and the Assyrian king list depicts him as a king living in a tent. Now, however, we are informed that Ashur under Tudia constitutes a center of power with which Ebla, choosing the peaceful route of a treaty, must come to terms.

4.4. THE POLITICAL EXPANSION OF EBLA

This chapter cannot conclude without a discussion, albeit brief, of what emerges indirectly in the preceding paragraphs, namely, the extraordinary political and commercial extension of the empire of Ebla. The historical texts, on the one hand, and the economic tablets, on the other, make it clear that Ebla dominated the entire area of the Fertile Crescent.

The first great Semitic empire of the Near East was not built by the kings of Akkad but rather by the Eblaites, not only by their sage and far-sighted policy of respecting local autonomies, but also by being firm with recalcitrant states like Mari.

Only the complete study of all the tablets will determine the exact extent of the empire of Ebla, but the boundaries traced above provide sure guidance to the amplitude of Ebla's supremacy. The citation of one historical text, alongside the treaty with Ashur discussed above, should meet present purposes.

It is a list of 17 countries subject to the king of Ebla, as the closing formula reveals. Most of these are still unknown, but the presence of the city of Kaniš in central Turkey gives a good idea of Ebla's political expansion in this period.

However, before citing this document in its entirety it may not be amiss to direct attention to a school text which contains the geographic gazetteer of the ancient Near East and corresponds, it would appear, to the zones of influence of the kingdom of Ebla.

The 289 cities included in the geographical gazetteer are, for the most part, located in Syria-Palestine, but cities of Mesopotamia and other areas of the ancient Near East are not lacking. Though a school text, this atlas seems faithfully to reproduce the immense geographical territory controlled to some degree by the state of Ebla.[77]

Here follows the document registering the 17 countries subject to Ebla:

obverse	
I 1) *šà*$^{?}$*-ni-ik-tù*^{ki}	Šaniktu
2) *lu*$_5$*-a-tum*^{ki}	Luatum
3) ⌜*x*⌝*-wa-ša*$_6$^{ki}	x-waša
II 1) *sí-rí-ba*^{ki}	Siriba
2) *ḫu-bù-ša-an*^{ki}	Ḫubušan
3) *ti-na-ma-zu*^{ki}	Tinamazu
4) *gi-za-nu*^{ki}	Gizanu
III 1) *NI-rí-bí*^{ki}	NI-ribi
2) *za-bur-rìm*^{ki}	Zaburrim
3) *ḫu-šu*^{ki}	Ḫušu
4) *bí-da-da-ar*^{ki}	Bidadar
IV 1) *kà-ni-šu*^{ki}	Kanišu
2) ⌜ ⌝	
3) *du-wu-um*^{ki}	Duwum
reverse	
III 1) *du-nu*^{ki}	Dunu
II 2) *al-šùm*^{ki}	Alsum

I	1)	*zú-mur*^{ki}	Zumur
	2)	an-šè-gú 17 kalam^{ki} kalam^{ki}	Total: 17 countries
	3)	*in* šu	in the hand
	4)	en	of the king
II	1)	*eb-la*^{ki}	of Ebla.[78]

The historical documents reviewed here cast a new light on the political situation of the ancient Near East in the third millennium B.C. Ebla does not rise alone from the death of the centuries but accompanied by a host of cities and states whose very existence was unknown. Though the material at hand does not complete the mosaic, a sufficiently clear outline is emerging.

Above[79] it was noted that the political situation of third-millennium Syria did not differ substantially from that of the later periods. To be sure, Ebla and its state existed, but alongside it coexisted a myriad of states and "statelets" whose independence was guaranteed by treaties and accords with the colossus, Ebla.

Extending the inquiry over the entire Fertile Crescent, we must emphasize that Ebla was not the only world power. In Egypt the glorious fourth dynasty of Cheops and Chephren, who built the great pyramids, flourished around 2500 B.C. In Mesopotamia the city of Kish united under its hegemony all the large Sumerian cities and thus was able to form a powerful state.

What were the relationships between these major powers? In other words, who was responsible for the decline and fall of Ebla's economic power?

The tablets from the royal archives are silent in this regard, but not a few indicators point to Kish as the destroyer of Ebla. One tablet studied above reports that Ebla had made a pact with Ḫamazi, a city of northern Iran.[80] Now, thanks to documents coming from Mesopotamia, we learn of a major conflict between Kish and Ḫamazi. With its customary conciseness the Sumerian King List reports that kingship passed from Kish directly to Ḫamazi;[81] what this surprising bit of information means is that Ḫamazi gained control over Sumer, at least for a certain time.

Though the Sumerian King List ascribes to Uruk the subsequent defeat of Ḫamazi, we possess some inscriptions of the kings of Kish, such as that of Uḫub,[82] which render it very likely that Kish definitively liquidated Ḫamazi.

Ebla, to be sure, is never mentioned, but it is not out of place to observe that a blood pact existed between Ḫamazi and Ebla, so that Ebla too got involved in this great encounter.

If, then, Ebla and Ḫamazi were both defeated by Kish around 2500 B.C., one begins to understand why the title "king of Kish" was always sought after and was borne by the Babylonian and Assyrian kings until

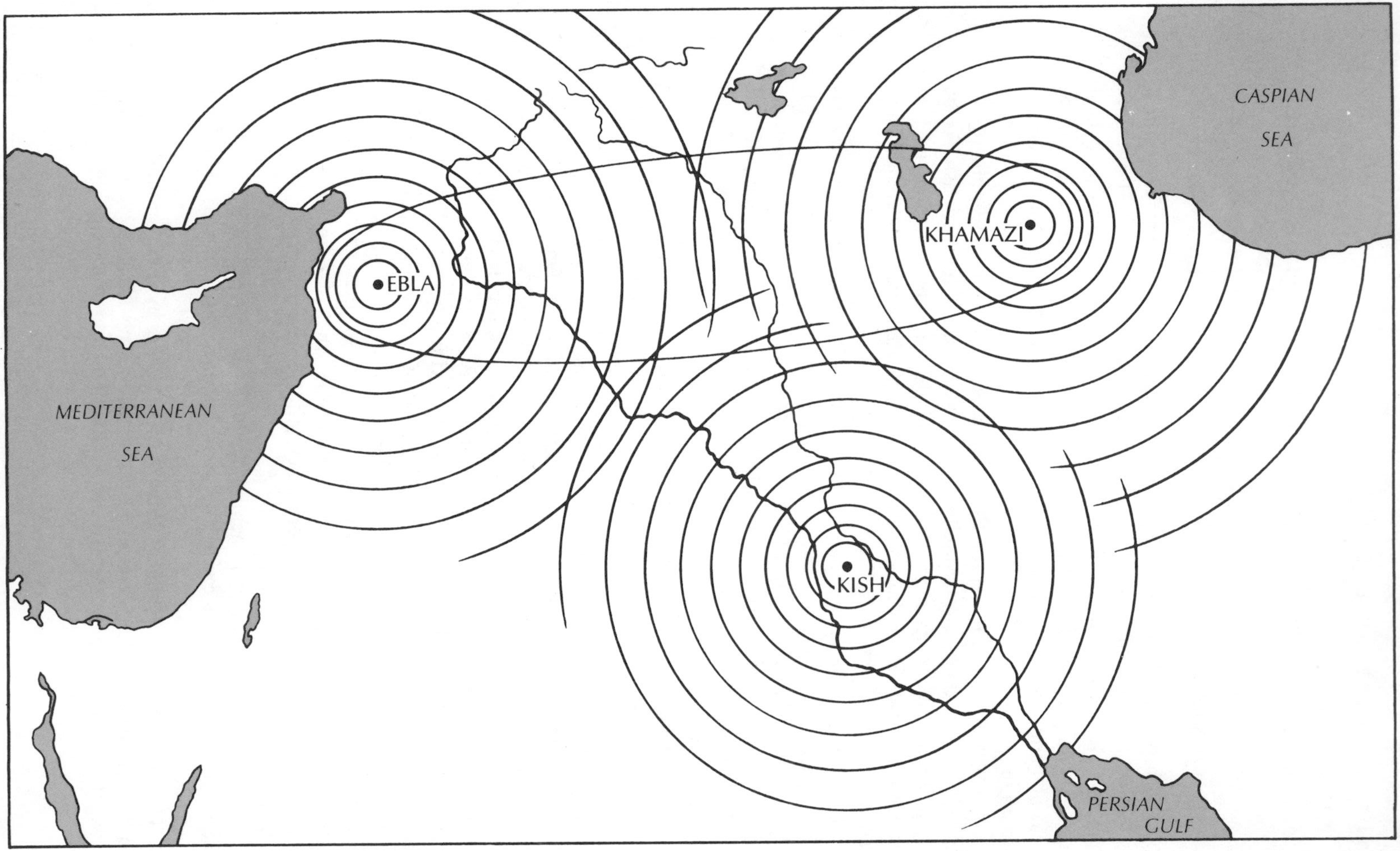

Figure V, 5 The great powers in the middle of the third millennium and their zones of influence

much later epochs.[83] Such a title recalled one of the greatest accomplishments ever of a Mesopotamian king, that of having destroyed the power of both Ebla and Ḫamazi which had threatened the very existence (Fig. V, 5) of the proud Sumerians.

Notes

1. See p. 46.
2. *BA* 39 (1976), pp. 46–47; *RlA* V, p. 12.
3. *RBI* 25 (1977), pp. 234–235.
4. *BA* 39 (1976), p. 43.
5. TM.75.G.1237; 1371.
6. TM.75.G.3242.
7. TM.75.G.1536.
8. TM.75.G.1358; 1881.
9. TM.75.G.1444.
10. TM.75.G.1443; 1525; 1591; 1691; 1812.
11. See the Table listing the family of Ebrium.
12. TM.75.G.1681; 1781.
13. TM.75.G.1335.
14. In another tablet, namely TM.75.G.1417, occurs the sequence Iga-Lim and Ebrium.
15. *RBI* 25 (1977), p. 235.
16. See Chapter I, p. 6.
17. *RBI* 25 (1977), p. 233.
18. P. Matthiae, *Ebla. Un impero ritrovato,* p. 182.
19. G. Pettinato, *Akkadica* 2 (1977), p. 28.
20. Early on I maintained that the city of Akkad was concealed in the writing A.EN.GA.DU^{ki}, but once it was established that the reading of the place name was *arugatu*^{ki}, as made clear by the geographical gazetteer of Ebla, I concluded that Akkad is definitely not mentioned in the texts of Ebla. In an economic tablet I had thought to read a personal name as *ša-ri-gi-nu* and, despite the odd spelling, to identify him with Sargon of Akkad. But a careful examination of the photograph of the tablet showed that the second sign should be read NAM and not RI, so that the name now reads *ša-NAM-gi-nu.* Thus the only epigraphic evidence for a low dating of the archives vanishes.
21. TM.75.G.2658.
22. TM.75.G.2236 rev.
23. TM.75.G.1435.
24. See below, p. 105.
25. To be more precise, the Sumerian equivalent of *malikum* is not e n, but rather n a m - e n which means "kingship." [Now one begins to understand why one of the words for "king" in Phoenician is the abstract form *mmlkt.* In Biblical Hebrew, too, *mamlākāh* means "king" in a number of texts such as I Sam. 10:18, Ps. 68:33. F. Zorell, *Lexicon Hebraicum* (Rome, 1955), p. 445a, is good on this point (M.D.)].
26. T. Jacobsen, *ZA,* 52 (1957), p. 91f.
27. S. N. Kramer, *The Sumerians,* p. 74.
28. TM.75.G.1688, and *passim.*
29. TM.75.G.427.

30. TM.75.G.1265, rev. I 10–15.
31. TM.75.G.1376.
32. TM.75.G.1688.
33. TM.75.G.1688.
34. TM.75.G.1681.
35. TM.75.G.1264; 1276.
36. TM.75.G.1414.
37. Obverse I 1 – III 9.
38. Ipṭura appears in other texts with the prestigious title of MI + ŠITA$_x$ of Ebla.
39. Obverse III 2 – IV 4.
40. See below, pp. 150ff.
41. *AfO* 25 (1974–1977), p. 1ff.
42. Here follow the names of the princes with a single attestation for each: Arwa (TM.75.G.1362); Budu (TM.75.G.1681); Gadum (TM.75.G.1643); Gir-Damu (TM.75.G.1444); Giri (TM.75.G.1470); Gura-Damu (TM.75.G.1681); Ibbi-Sipiš (TM.75.G.1643); Igriš-Damu (TM.75.G.1383); Iksup-Damu (TM.75.G.1446); Napḫa-Il (TM.75.G.1444); Ilum-aḫi (TM.75.G.1681); In-Damu (TM.75.G.1345); Ingar (TM.75.G.1643); Ipte-Damu (TM.75.G.1446); Ir-Damu (TM.75.G.1444); Ir'e-Damu (TM.75.G.1446); Irti (TM.75.G.1625); Iš'ar-Damu (TM.75.G.1345); Naga'um (TM.75.G.1643); Sag-Damu (TM.75.G.1413); Ṣib-Damu (TM.75.G.1389); Ṣi-Damu (TM.75.G.1436); Šura-Damu (TM.75.G.1362); Uti (TM.75.G.1743).
43. The following are the names of the princesses with an attestation for each: Abatu (TM.75.G.1443); Anut (TM.75.G.1648); Dana-Lugal (TM.75.G.1443); Dar-Malik (TM.75.G.1443); Ḫalut (TM.75.G.1444); Kirsut (TM.75.G.1443); Mau'ut (TM.75.G.1522); Ridut (TM.75.G.1663); Takeš-Malik (TM.75.G.1663); Tamur-Damu (TM.75.G.1444); Tarib-Damu (TM.75.G.2428); Tiabarzu (TM.75.G.1443); Tia-Damu (TM.75.G.1443); Tiludu (TM.75.G.1444); Tišma-Damu (TM.75.G.1443); Tište-Damu (TM.75.G.1442); Tubil-Malik (TM.75.G. 1443); Tuṣi-Išar (TM.75.G.1443); Ṭabi (TM.75.G.1393); Tiše-Lim (TM.75.G. 1436).
44. As deduced from TM.75.G.1749.
45. *OrNS* 44 (1975), pp. 366ff.
46. TM.75.G.6030, obv. III 6–7.
47. *Ibidem,* obv. III 8ff.
48. TM.75.G.1444, obv. V 17 – VII 4.
49. *Ibidem,* obv. VII 5 – VIII 12.
50. *Ibidem,* obv. VIII 13 – X 2.
51. TM.75.G.1446, obv. I 1 – III 10.
52. *Ibidem,* obv. IV 4–7.
53. TM.75.G.1264.
54. TM.75.G.1443, rev. VI 5–17; rev. IV 9–10.
55. P. Matthiae, *RSO* 50 (1975), pp. 26–27.
56. Obv. I 1 – III 1.
57. See above, p. 87.
58. TM.75.G.1764.
59. Cf. *OrAn* 16 (1977), pp. 263ff.
60. L. Milano, *Enologia nell'Asia Anteriore Antica dalle origini fino all'etá del bronzo* (doctoral dissertation, Rome 1974–1975).
61. *OrNS* 45 (1976), p. 354.
62. TM.75.G.247.
63. TM.75.G.411.
64. Page 15.

65. TM.76.G.89, rev. I 2 – II 5.
66. *Storia Universale Feltrinelli* I, 2 (Milano, 1968), pp. 100ff.
67. *Ibidem,* pp. 55ff.
68. This situation is also reflected in the "Sumerian King List," on which T. Jacobsen, *The Sumerian King List, AS* 11, (Chicago, 1939), should be consulted.
69. TM.75.G.2342, studied in *RBI* 25 (1977), pp. 238ff.
70. See above, p. 87.
71. TM.75.G.2561.
72. TM.75.G.2367, translated in *Akkadica* 2 (1977), pp. 24ff.
73. TM.75.G.2420.
74. TM.75.G.2420, obv. I 1 – VI 5.
75. *Ibidem,* obv. VI 12 – VII 13.
76. TM.75.G.2420, lower edge II 3′–18′.
77. TM.75.G.2321, published by G. Pettinato, *OrNS* 47 (1978), pp. 50–73.
78. TM.75.G.2136.
79. See pp. 85ff.
80. Pp. 86ff.
81. T. Jacobsen, *AS* 11, pp. 97–98.
82. *IRSA,* p. 39, IA2a.
83. *Storia Universale Feltrinelli* I/2, p. 68.

CHAPTER VI

Society

1. The division of power. 1.1. The social classes. 1.2. The administration. 2. The division of space. 2.1. Settlements and population. 2.2. Division of the city. 3. The division of time. 3.1. Systems of dating. 3.2. Calendars. 3.2.1. The old calendar. 3.2.2. The new calendar.

1. THE DIVISION OF POWER

1.1. THE SOCIAL CLASSES

A cursory reading of the archives[1] reveals at once two kinds of population quite different as regards rights and duties. First come the dumu-nita dumu-nita *eb-la*^{ki}, "the sons of Ebla,"[2] that is, the citizens whose share in all the rights and privileges recalls the *cives Romani,* "the citizens of Rome"; second come the bar-an bar-an, "the foreigners,"[3] living in Ebla for various reasons.

This first big distinction between the inhabitants cannot but have social consequences. Existing documents suggest the following subdivision of the citizens: a dense rank of state functionaries, to be discussed later,[4] and together with them, three large groups of citizens, to wit, the merchants, the artisans, and workers.

The terms indicating merchants or businessmen are lú-kar,[5] dam-gàr,[6] or ga-raš,[7] who are engaged in both land and maritime commerce. In contradistinction to Mesopotamian usage, the Ebla records use most frequently for "merchant" the first term lú-kar, literally, "the man of the commercial center," which underlines the way commerce was organized in the third millennium. Precisely to establish one such trade mart Ebla drew up a treaty with the kingdom of Ashur.[8] These were real cities with particular legislation and the lú-kar were precisely those who circulated throughout the Near East visiting the different trade centers. Another expression, kas_4 or also lú-kas_4 literally "messenger,"[9] was obviously used to indicate the category of merchant.

While the distinction between these kinds of merchants seems obvious, kas_4 appears to be a merchant of the state while lú-kar refers to the private businessman.

The second large component of citizens consists of the artisans.

Whether these were organized into corporations—given the great productivity of Ebla this seems quite plausible—cannot yet be made out. Among the terms referring to arts and crafts may be cited b a ḫ a r, "potters,"[10] š i t i m, "sculptors,"[11] n a g a r, "carpenters,"[12] s i m u g and k ù - d í m, "metal workers,"[13] t ú g - d u₈ and t ú g - n u - t a g, "textile workers."[14] Of less frequent occurrence are l ú - g i š - š i m, "perfumers,"[15] m u ḫ a l d i m, "bakers,"[16] k i k k e n, "millers."[17] This list gives only those terms which are easily translatable; the number of those not yielding to immediate translation runs close to 200.

Workers or laborers are designated by the generic terms l ú, "men," and d a m, "women." The kind of services they offer does not always appear from the texts, and only detailed examination of the tablets will produce satisfactory answers. Text TM.75.G.273, however, proves to be an exception in this regard, listing 385 women, all designated as "millers," 45 in the king's service and 340 working for others. This text tells not only for whom these women worked but also how much they earned each month; hence it should be quoted in full:

obverse

I	1)	3 d a m	3 women
	2)	6 š e -*bar*	6 Gubar measures of barley
	3)	20 d a m	20 women
	4)	20 š e -*bar* š u b a₄ - t i	received 20 Gubar;
	5)	22 d a m	22 women
	6)	11 š e -*bar*	11 Gubar
	7)	š u b a₄ - t i d a m - e n	received, women in the king's service;
	8)	30 d a m	30 women
	9)	6 š e -*bar* 1 g í n	6 Gubar at 1 *gin* each,
II	1)	A B x Á Š	in the service of the Elder;
	2)	2 š e -*bar*	2 Gubar
	3)	10 d a m NE.RA	10 women . . .
	4)	11 d a m	11 women
	5)	2; 1 g í n š e -*bar*	2 Gubar at 1 *gin*
	6)	g a : d u₈	in the service of Gadu;
	7)	34; 1 (g í n) d a m	34 women at 1 *gin*
	8)	6½ š e -*bar*	6½ Gubar
	9)	t ú g - n u - t a g	in the service of the weaver
	10)	*ma-na*	Mana;
	11)	55 d a m	55 women
	12)	11 š e -*bar*	11 Gubar

III	1)	t ú g - n u - t a g	in the service of the weaver
	2)	*bù-zu-ga*[ki]	(in) Buzuga;
	3)	25 d a m - k i k k e n	25 female millers
	4)	4 š e -*bar*	4 Gubar
	5)	*bù-zu-ga*[ki]	(in) Buzuga;
	6)	30 d a m	30 women
	7)	6 š e -*bar*	6 Gubar
	8)	pa_4 : š e š -*ma-lik-tum*	in the service of the queen's perfumer;
	9)	30 d a m	30 women
IV	1)	5 š e -*bar*	5 Gubar
	2)	*a-sí-piš*	in the service of Asipiš;
	3)	20 l á - 2 d a m	18 women
	4)	3 š e -*bar*	3 Gubar
	5)	*gú-zu-zi*	in the service of Guzuzi;
	6)	6 d a m	6 women
	7)	1 š e -*bar*	1 Gubar
	8)	*iš-lu-tù*	in the service of Išlutu;
	9)	3 d a m ½ š e + r a	3 women at ½ (Gubar)
	10)	*ga-du-we-du*	in the service of Gaduwedu;
V	1)	10 d a m	10 women
	2)	1½ 1 g í n š e -*bar*	1½ and 1 gin of Gubar
	3)	Z U . M A . N E	in the service of ZU.MA.NE;
	4)	6 d a m	6 women
	5)	1 š e -*bar*	1 Gubar
	6)	*ni-ba*	in the service of Niba
	7)	*wa ri-ga-ḫa-lu*	and Rigaḫalu;
	8)	12 d a m	12 women
	9)	2 š e -*bar*	2 Gubar
	10)	*SI-ba-tum*	in the service of Sibatum;

reverse

I	1)	6 dam	6 women
	2)	1 še-*bar*	1 Gubar
	3)	*ḫa-za-rí*	in the service of Ḫazari;
	4)	20 lá-2 dam	18 women
	5)	3 še-*bar*	3 Gubar
	6)	*lu-du-ù-na*	in the service of Luduna;
	7)	1 še-*bar* <6 dam>	1 Gubar <6 women>
	8)	íl-zi	in the service of official Ilzi;
	9)	6 dam	6 women
	10)	1 še-*bar*	1 Gubar
	11)	lú-ì-giš	in the service of "the sesame man";
II	1)	10 lá-1 dam	9 women
	2)	1½ še-*bar*	1½ Gubar
	3)	ú-a	in the service of the official Ua;
	4)	6 dam	6 women
	5)	1 še-*bar*	1 Gubar
	6)	UM-*lu-lu*	in the service of Umlulu;
	7)	4 dam	4 women
	8)	MU.SAL	bakers,
	9)	½ šik$_x$	½ (Gubar) of flour
	10)	*ì-lum-a-gàr-nu*	in the service of Ilumagarnu
	11)	*en-nu-ì-a*	(and) Ennu-ya;
	12)	1 še-*bar*	1 Gubar
III	1)	3 dam	3 women
	2)	lú-BAR.TUR	people . . .
	3)	*kí-núm*	in the service of Kinum;
	4)	1 (gín) dam	½ (Gubar), woman
	5)	*i-du-nu-na*	in the service of Idununa;
	6)	1 (gín) dam NE.RA	½ (Gubar), woman . . .
	7)	*en-nu-ì-a*	in the service of Ennuya;
	8)	1 še-*bar*	1 Gubar
	9)	šu ba$_4$-ti	have received;

IV	1)	an-šè-gú 40 lá-3 še-*bar*	sum: 37 Gubar
	2)	45 dam en	45 women in the king's service;
	3)	63 še-*bar*	63 Gubar
	4)	3 *mi-at* 40 dam	340 women
	5)	kikken	millers;
V	1)	dub-gar še-ba-dam	tablet listing rations of barley for the women,
	2)	itu ^{d}*a-dam-ma-um*	month: feast of Adamma.

The accompanying table shows that the monthly retribution averaged around 3 Eblaite silas reaching, but only for some women in the royal household, the quota of 2 Gubar per person. It might be pointed out that the women were paid in kind for their service, which is not novel or unusual; in the preceding chapter it was noted that the king himself received goods in kind.[18]

Thus far, among the classes of citizens of Ebla, no mention has been made of the farmers who are designated by the Sumerian term engar; they too enjoyed the full rights of citizens. When "the sons of Ebla" are discussed, this important category should not be overlooked. Though for obvious reasons they dwelt in villages surrounding Ebla, they were fully integrated into the social structure of Ebla. Greater Ebla with its 260,000 inhabitants includes both the city of Ebla and the encircling villages.[19]

By way of synthesis, five large groups forming the body politic of Ebla can be distinguished:

1. employees of the administration
2. merchants
3. artisans
4. peasants
5. laborers

A further subdivision into social groups does not appear advisable or possible at the present stage of research. To wish to speak of rich and poor, of classes more privileged than others, means applying some concepts which can scarcely be brought into focus at this point. For this reason it is necessary to insist on the initial affirmation that the dumu-nita dumu-nita *eb-la*^{ki} are the citizens of Ebla with all that this definition entails.

Unlike the foreigners, some of whom were slaves, all these citizens were completely free. It also appears highly probable that they could not be reduced to slavery because of the fundamental belief that an Eblaite was a privileged person in comparison with the mass of non-Eblaites.

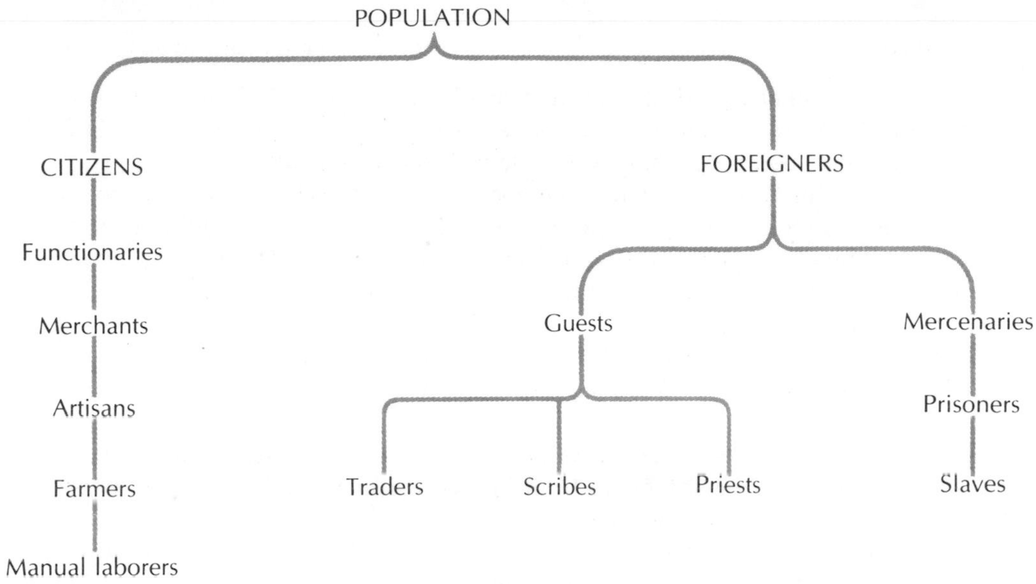

Figure VI, 1 The makeup of Eblaite society

This brings us to the second great component of the inhabitants of Ebla, the b a r - a n b a r - a n, "the foreigners."

Like every great metropolis Ebla offered hospitality to many strangers within its walls. It is reported that the city was visited by merchants, by scribes, singers, and also by priests coming from other centers.[20] These strangers certainly enjoyed the sacred right of Oriental hospitality and as guests were treated with respect. But if the presence of businessmen at Ebla is understandable, the arrival of scribes and priests requires some explanation. As for the scribes, Ebla was a famous cultural mecca and it is not surprising to read that scribes came from Mari to attend cuneiform courses offered at the academy of Ebla and, as will be seen in Chapter VIII, international symposia were held there. Ebla, moreover, took pains to increase its fame as a cultural center by inviting guest professors from different parts of the world; thus the professor of mathematics in Ebla came from distant Kish in Mesopotamia. The foreign priests belonged to the category of the *na-bí-ú-tum* the "prophets,"[21] holy men who traveled about the world.

But the foreigners who claim more detailed study are those who in some way have been integrated into the social context of the city.

First come the mercenaries, arriving from different cities and performing the work of soldiers. The omission of the army from the five groups of citizens mentioned above is explained by the fact that national defense was entrusted to mercenaries. The letter of the official Ibubu, cited in its entirety in the preceding chapter,[22] asks the king of Ḫamazi to send him some mercenary troops.

In the other historical document involving the triangle Mari, Edu, and Ebla,[23] Mari complains that the efficient soldiers were sent to Ebla while the good-for-nothing were held in reserve for Mari.

These mercenaries, whose number is unfortunately unknown, were under the command of lugal bar-an bar-an, "the one in charge of foreigners,"[24] a position so important that King Ebrium deemed it opportune to give one of his daughters in marriage to Tidinu, lugal bar-an bar-an.[25]

Little is known about the juridical status of these mercenaries but, given their important function, they must have enjoyed considerable privileges.

Prisoners of war form a second category of foreigners. Their juridical status was doubtless different from that of the mercenaries, but not much can be said of what work they did.

For the most part the tablets contain rolls of prisoners together with their provenience. This fact is significant because it sheds light on the power relationships in the ancient Near East. For example, text TM.75.G.309 lists 112 prisoners from the cities Ebal, Ḫarran, and Martu:

obverse

I	1)	30 lá-2 *na-si*$_{11}$ maḫ$_x$(=AL)	28 excellent persons,
	2)	54 *na-si*$_{11}$	54 persons,
II	1)	*šu-du*$_8$	prisoners
	2)	*ib-al*^{ki}	of the city of Ebal;
	3)	10 *na-si*$_{11}$	10 persons
	4)	*ḫar-ra-nu*^{ki}	of the city of Ḫarran;

reverse

I	1)	20 *na-si*$_{11}$	20 persons
	2)	MAR-TU^{ki}	of the city of Martu;
II	1)	an-šè-gú/1 *mi-at* 12 *na-si*$_{11}$	total: 112 persons
	2)	šu-du$_8$ *kà-ší*-en	prisoner under jurisdiction of Kaši, royal official.

Several such lists exist and when research is further along it may be possible to trace forced population shifts in remote antiquity.

The third category is that of slaves recruited, it would seem, among the foreign populations. The price of slaves was very high; according to TM.75.G.1402, 2 minas of silver were paid for a foreigner:

2 *ma-na* kù:babbar	two minas of silver
nì-šám	the price
1 bar-an	of one foreigner

This information is confirmed by another document reporting that two messengers set out for the city of Nagar to buy a male and paid the price of exactly two minas of silver.[26]

Since the first text dates to the reign of Ar-Ennum (second king of the dynasty) and the second to the time of Ibbi-Sipiš (fifth king of the dynasty), the price of slaves evidently remained unchanged.

In this connection, the pact signed by Ebla and Ashur contains the specific clause in which the king of Ebla pledges to liberate slaves in the event they were purchased in Ashur.[27]

Another example worthy of citation in full deals with children from the city of Ezan entrusted to two supervisors, and though their juridical condition is not evident, they could well be slaves, the offspring of slaves.

obverse

I	1)	80 igi-sal tu-da	80 newborn females
	2)	10 bar-an-nita 5, 4, 3 mu	10 foreign males of 5, 4, 3 years
	3)	14 bar-an-sal 5, 4, 3 mu	14 foreign females of 5, 4, 3 years
II	1)	4 bar-an-nita-tur	4 small foreign males
		5 bar-an-sal-tur 1 mu	5 small foreign females of 1 year
	2)	2 igi-nita 3 mu	2 males of 3 years
	3)	lú-1-šu	1 group (under)
	4)	*ba-du-lum*	Badulum
	5)	ugula-apin	superintendent of farms;
III	1)	72 igi-sal tu-da	72 newborn females
	2)	11 bar-an-nita 5, 4, 3 mu	11 male foreigners of 5, 4, 3 years
	3)	5 bar-an-sal- 5, 4, 3 mu	5 female foreigners of 5, 4, 3 years

reverse

I	1)	2 bar-an-sal-tur 1 mu	2 small foreign girls of 1 year
	2)	lú-2-šu	second group (under)
	3)	*in-gàr*	Ingar
	4)	ugula bar-an-bar-an	superintendent of foreigners
II	1)	igi. ḪI-du$_8$	"addition"
	2)	*é-za-an*^{ki}	of the city of Ezan
	3)	itu *ṣa-'à-tum*	month: Ṣâtum

The exact difference between the Sumerian terms bar-an and igi-sal/nita cannot be made out so that the ultimate meaning of this list must for the present remain hidden.

To end this discussion about the social classes of Ebla, we conclude that there are certainly some elements at hand to identify the two fundamental components of the social structure, namely, the freemen and the slaves. But the above inquiry permits further subdivisions, such as that made at the outset between citizens of Ebla and foreigners.

The attached table offers in synthetic fashion the various classes of residents at Ebla subdivided into the categories that can be identified.

1.2. THE ADMINISTRATION

The various grades of the state hierarchy and the names of the functionaries themselves have come into clear focus. It was noted above that the supreme head of Ebla was the king who was responsible for the destiny of Ebla. But the real head of the administration of the kingdom is called in Sumerian MI + ŠITA$_x$ whose reading still eludes us but whose Eblaite translation is *adānu,* "lord."[28] The "lords" who held this office under the five kings of the dynasty of Ebla are known, so that the post of the MI + ŠITA$_x$ can justly be said to be somehow connected with the position of king.

A synoptic list of the lords and the kings under whom they served would read as follows:

King	*"lord"*
Igriš-Ḫalam	Irkab-dulum[29]
Irkab-Damu	Ya-ramu[30]
Ar-Ennum	Aḫa-ar[31]
Ebrium	Giri
Ibbi-Sipiš	Ipṭura[32]

Only in the last two cases—those of Ebrium and Ibbi-Sipiš—did a bond of kinship exist between the king and the lord.[33] In all the other cases there is no kinship between the persons holding the highest offices of the state, so that the hypothesis advanced above seems correct; namely, that the Eblaites wanted these offices kept distinct, as if to guarantee the security of the state.[34]

The fact that with each king there is a different MI + ŠITA$_x$ suggests that the MI + ŠITA$_x$ was elected at the same time as the king.

The terms indicating the civil servants are diverse and go from the simple guruš, "man," all the way to lugal, a term which in Mesopotamia designates the king but which at Ebla indicates the official hierarchically inferior to the MI + ŠITA$_x$. Dependent upon the lugal were the di-ku$_5$, "judges," the maškim, "commissars," the sukkal, "ambassadors," the ku-li, "spokesmen," the ugula, "superintendents," and numerous other personages such as the eb, the ú-a, the a-am, the íl-zi whose specific functions will doubtless come into clearer focus as the study of the tablets progresses.

To return to the lugal, which henceforth will be rendered "governors," we possess several texts which suggest how the administration was subdivided.

From the fixed number of 14 lugal of the state of Ebla one can deduce that the kingdom was subdivided into 14 departments, two of which included the four quarters of the city, and hence were within the capital city, and 12 assembled the entire territory of the state.

The texts presently to be cited give the names of the various lugal under the kings Igriš-Ḫalam, Irkab-Damu, Ar-Ennum, and Ebrium, and it is noteworthy that of the 14 attested under King Igriš-Ḫalam, 11 are still in office under Irkab-Damu and 9 under Ebrium.

The transcription and translation of just one tablet, TM.75.G.1359, which lists the lugal at the time of King Igriš-Ḫalam along with the tribute paid to the Treasury, will give an idea of the state structure:

obverse

I	1)	gur$_8$ gín-dilmun guškin	20 Dilmun shekels of gold
	2)	mu-túm	tribute
	3)	*ar-en-núm*	of Ar-Ennum;
	4)	gur$_8$ gín-dilmun guškin	20 Dilmun shekels of gold
II	1)	mu-túm	tribute
	2)	*gi-gi*	of Gigi;
	3)	gur$_8$ gín-dilmun guškin	20 Dilmun shekels of gold
	4)	mu-túm	tribute
	5)	*i-bí-sí-piš*	of Ibbi-Sipiš;
III	1)	15 gín-dilmun guškin	15 Dilmun shekels of gold
	2)	mu-túm	tribute
	3)	*ib-u$_9$-mu-ut*	of Ibumut;
	4)	15 gín-dilmun guškin	15 Dilmun shekels of gold
	5)	mu-túm	tribute
IV	1)	íl-zi	of Ilzi;
	2)	10 gín-dilmun guškin	10 Dilmun shekels of gold
	3)	*la-da-ad*	(tribute) of Ladad;
	4)	10 gín-dilmun guškin	10 Dilmun shekels of gold
	5)	mu-túm	tribute
V	1)	*en-àr-ía*	of Enarya;
	2)	10 gín-dilmun guškin	10 Dilmun shekels of gold
	3)	mu-túm	tribute
	4)	*a-da-mu*	of Adamu;
	5)	10 gín-dilmun guškin	10 Dilmun shekels of gold
	6)	mu-túm	tribute

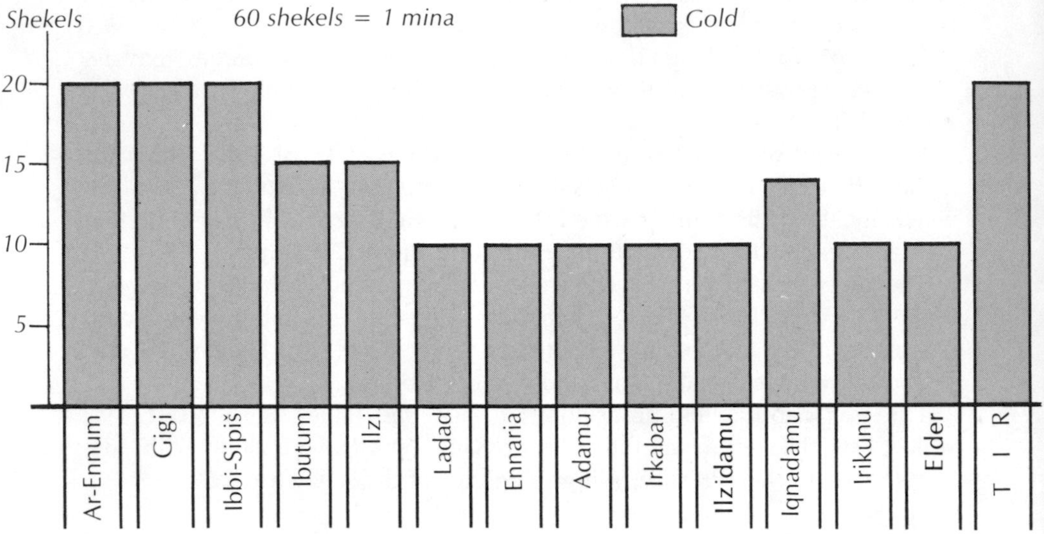

Figure VI, 2 Gold tribute paid by the royal governors

VI	1)	*ìr-kab-ar*	of Irkabar;
	2)	10 gín-dilmun guškin	10 Dilmun shekels of gold
	3)	mu-túm	tribute
	4)	*íl-zi-da-mu*	of Ilzidamu;
	5)	14 gín-dilmun guškin	14 Dilmun shekels of gold
reverse			
I	1)	mu-túm	tribute
	2)	*iq-na-da-mu*	of Iqna-Damu
	3)	10 gín-dilmun guškin	10 Dilmun shekels of gold
	4)	mu-túm	tribute
	5)	*i-rí-gú-nu*	of Irigunu;
II	1)	10 gín-dilmun guškin	10 Dilmun shekels of gold
	2)	mu-túm	tribute
	3)	*a-bu*	of the Elder;
	4)	gur$_8$ gín-dilmun guškin	20 Dilmun shekels of gold
	5)	mu-túm	tribute
	6)	*ti-ir*	of the official Tir;
III	1)	an-šè-gú 3 *ma-na*	total; 3 minas
		13 gín-dilmun guškin	13 Dilmun shekels of gold
	2)	mu-túm	tribute
	3)	lugal-lugal	of the governors
	4)	MI+ŠITA$_x$	"lord"
	5)	*ir$_x$-kab-du-lum*	Irkab-Dulum.

Just the last two lines of the text confirm that the governors mentioned in the tablet are those in office at the time of the first king of Ebla, Igriš-Ḫalam. The tribute paid to the Treasury is in gold and the varying sums encountered in the text are an indication of the relative wealth of the departments of the kingdom.

To afford the possibility of verifying what was said above, namely that the governors did not follow the fortunes of the king and of the "lord" but that they remained in office for life, we present a synoptic table of the names of the governors under the kings Igriš-Ḫalam, Irkab-Damu, Ar-Ennum, and Ebrium just as they are given in texts TM.75.G.1359, 1357, 1296, and 1655.

Figure VI, 3 lends itself to a quantitative analysis which yields some precious information about the political trends that matured during the nearly 50 years when Igriš-Ḫalam, Irkab-Damu, Ar-Ennum, and Ebrium reigned. Giving numbers to the four periods of ruling (Igriš-Ḫalam=I; Irkab-Damu=II; Ar-Ennum=III, Ebrium IV) and to the major governors (from 1 to 14, as indicated by Fig. VI, 3) who succeeded one another, we can compare the political patterns which alternated under the four kings. In this manner one can see if there was, and to what degree, an element of continuity throughout this period. Juxtaposing the 14 governors present under Igriš-Ḫalam with those who came after him reveals these sequences:

I → II = 1–2–3–4–5–6–9–10–11–12–14 = 11
I → III = 3–8–9–12–13–14 = 6
I → IV = 2–3–4–5–9–10–11–13–14 = 9

In synthesis, the 14 major governors under Igriš-Ḫalam register this continuity:

I		II		III		IV
14	—	11	—	6	—	9

The figures reveal that a high percentage of Igriš-Ḫalam's governors remained in office under the kings who succeeded him. Performing the same operation with the governors under Irkab-Damu and Ar-Ennum and then under Ar-Ennum and Ebrium, we observe the following development:

Under Irkab-Damu and Ar-Ennum:

II — III = 1–6–8–12 = 4
II — IV = 1–2–5–7–8–9–10–11–12–13 = 10

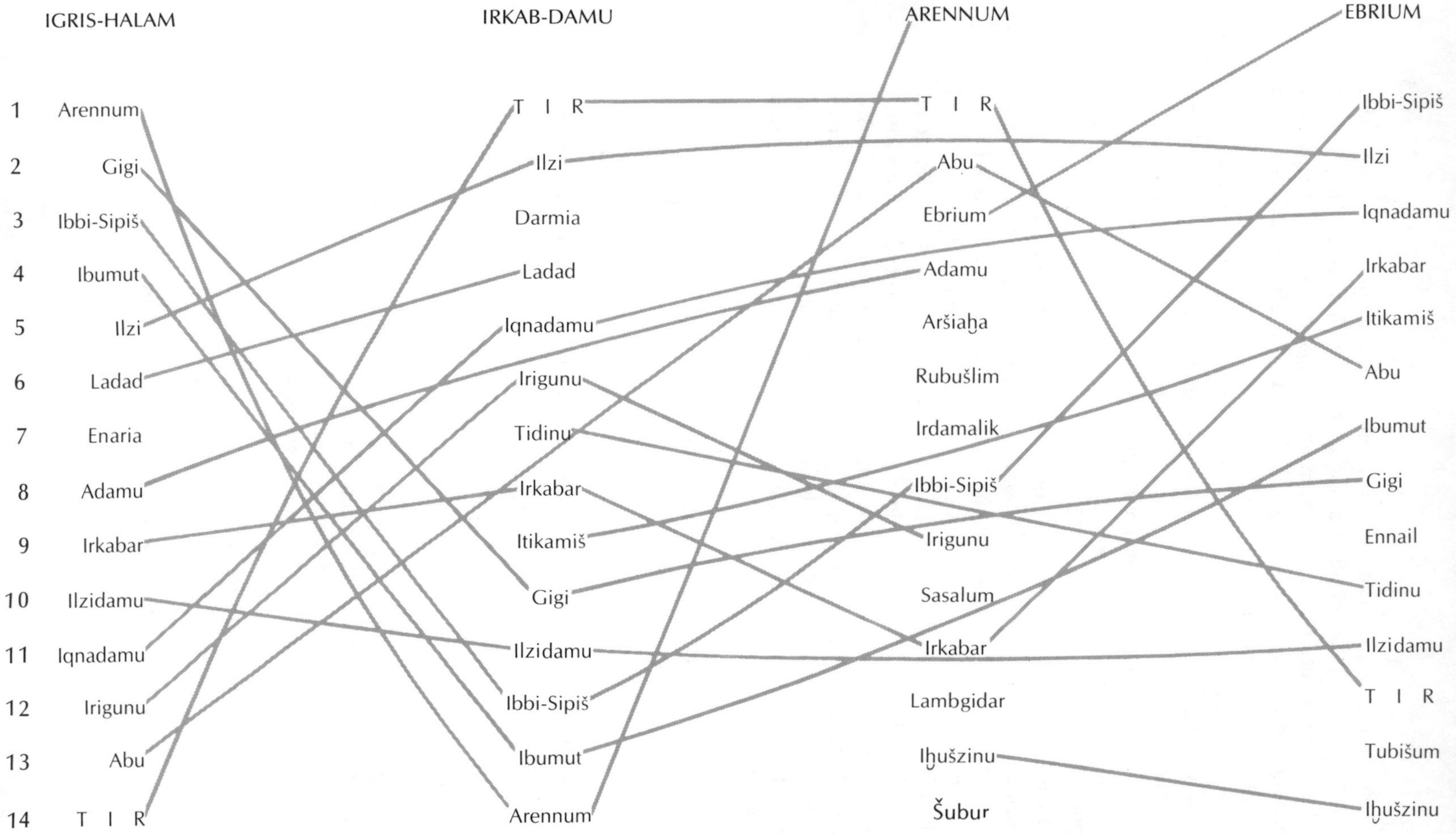

Figure VI, 3 The governors of state under the first four kings of the dynasty

In synthesis:

$$\begin{array}{ccccc} II & & III & & IV \\ 14 & — & 4 & — & 10 \end{array}$$

Under Ar-Ennum and Ebrium:

$$III — IV = 1–2–8–11–13 = 5$$

In synthesis:

$$\begin{array}{ccc} III & & IV \\ 14 & — & 5 \end{array}$$

Juxtaposing the relationships between the sovereigns as reflected by the presence of the governors we note an interesting succession:

$$\begin{array}{l} I : II = 14 : 11 \\ I : III = 14 : 6 \\ I : IV = 14 : 9 \\ II : III = 14 : 4 \\ II : IV = 14 : 10 \\ III : IV = 14 : 5 \end{array}$$

In synthesis:

$$\begin{array}{l} I : II = 14 : 11 \\ II : III = 14 : 4 \\ III : IV = 14 : 5 \end{array}$$

It appears evident that there was a certain break in the political framework before and after the ascent to the throne by Ar-Ennum, the third of the kings considered here. A clearer picture perhaps emerges when the hierarchical positions of the various governors under the four kings are considered; this is the real content of Fig. VI, 3. In this connection the following should be noted: the term *tir* is a title which designates a function, hence a kind of official, just as obtains for the term *abu* (elder). The other terms, on the other hand, are personal names. Finally, the position in the classification (from 1 to 14) is in relation to the precedence with which each term occurs in the texts considered in turn. A glance at Fig. VI, 3 reveals that the governors change positions hierarchically under different kings and that some governors are confirmed though changing their position in rank and others disappear temporarily or definitively. A closer look at this phenomenon of confirmation and substitution regroups the divers governors according to the number of times they appear in the tablets:

Appearances	*Governors*	*Position under the 4 kings* I →	II →	III →	IV	*Total Partial* / *Total General*
4	tir	14→	1→	1→	12	3 governors of 56 are always present, totaling 3×4=12 appearances out of 56
4	Irkab-Ar	9→	8→	11→	4	
4	Ibbi-Sipiš	3→	12→	8→	1	
3	abu	13→	→	2→	6	7 governors of 56 are present 3 times, making a total of 7×3=21 appearances out of 56
3	Irigunu	12→	6→	9		
3	Iqna-Damu	11→	5→	→	3	
3	Ilzi-Damu	10→	11→	→	11	
3	Ilzi	5→	2→	→	2	
3	Ibumut	4→	13→	→	7	
3	Gigi	2→	10→	→	8	
2	Adamu	8→	→	4		6 governors out of 56 are present twice, making a total of 6×2=12 appearances out of 56
2	Ar-Ennum	1→	14→	King		
2	Ladad	6→	4			
2	Tidinu		7→	→	10	
2	Iti-Kamiš		9→	→	5	
2	Iḫušzinu			13→	14	
1	Enarya	7				11 governors out of 56 are present only once (but one of them, Ebrium, later becomes king) making a total of 11 appearances out of 56
1	Darmia		3			
1	Ebrium			3→	King	
1	Aršiaḫa			5		
1	Rupušlim			6		
1	Irda-Malik			7		
1	Sasalum			10		
1	Išgidar			12		
1	Šubur			14		
1	Enna-Il				9	
1	Ṭubi-Šum				13	

From these figures emerges a series of indicative data. First and foremost, the *tir* in his capacity as an official must have been extremely important since he appears always: Fig. 21, 28, and 29 unexceptionably show his economic power. Of the other two governors who were always reconfirmed, Irkab-Ar must have belonged to an influential family which sustained him since he pays as tax only one plaque of gold more (see Fig. 29). Ibbi-Sipiš, however, is the son of Ebrium, whom he succeeds on the throne. The other sequences or changes also have their interest, but it is necessary to refine two points: What is the significance of citing one or other of the governors before or after according to the reigning king? Do these hierarchical positions shown in Fig. VI, 3 have an effective political control or not? Does the list of governors who appear but once have any meaning? We notice that the majority of them (6 out of 10 when one excludes Ebrium, who was not new to the political scene for reasons to be discussed later) appear under the same king, Ar-Ennum, who is the ruler under whom a break in the political continuity is seen. The governors named only once can be schematically presented with the kings under whom they served as follows:

under Igriš-Ḫalam	1 new governor
under Irkab-Damu	1 new governor
under Ar-Ennum	6 new governors
under Ebrium	2 new governors
under 4 kings	10 new governors

Ar-Ennum left a personal mark on his period of reign, changing the political framework by 60 percent, a 60 percent that Ebrium will take care to confirm later on.

The figures show that under Ar-Ennum something must have happened which we must try to explain. Toward this end it may be useful to add one item. As can be seen from Fig. VI, 3 and the corresponding Tables, the fifth king of the dynasty, Ibbi-Sipiš, is already an official under the preceding kings. The same is true of Ar-Ennum and Ebrium, so that the hypothesis touched upon in the foregoing chapter of the 60-year duration of the dynasty acquires a certain consistency. In this span of time the majority of governors managed to keep their posts under several kings, but Ar-Ennum changed 6 of them. Is this changing of the guard due mainly to a change of political orientation or merely to the shifting of the political equilibrium of the great families? The war against Mari, it will be recalled, was waged during the mandate of Ar-Ennum, and Enna-Dagan, the victorious general, was named king of Mari. Not much is known of how Ar-Ennum's decision was received, but it is clear that as soon as he ascended the throne, Ebrium changed course. He removed 6 of the governors and recalled 7 who had served under Irkab-Damu, the predecessor of Ar-Ennum. It is also significant that Enna-Dagan is no longer on the throne of Mari but rather Iku-šar, a local king. Did Enna-Dagan die a natural death or was he eliminated? Ebrium in fact lays the necessary bases for those institutional changes that will lead to the hereditary monarchy. The restoration of 7 governors is perhaps to be explained by Ebrium's need to have a wide consensus so as to be repeatedly reelected "king of Ebla" and to so consolidate his power as to impose the nomination of his son Ibbi-Sipiš as his successor on the throne. Nor should it be overlooked that TM.75.G.1296, a tablet from the time of Ebrium, mentions a 15th lugal,[35] which means an extension of the kingdom under this monarch and the consequent erection of new departments.

To return to Ar-Ennum's 7-year term and to the political implications it gave rise to, we can put forth two hypotheses. First, Ar-Ennum mounted the throne by supplanting Ebrium who already held an important position as co-regent under Irkab-Damu and hence the most powerful figure after the king; in fact, Ar-Ennum reduces the rank of Ebrium to that of governor (see Fig. VI, 3). Ar-Ennum's intervention obviously required the support of reliable persons if his undertaking is to be successful; this will explain the large number of new governors, who were subsequently removed by Ebrium. The second hypothesis envisions Ar-Ennum ascending the throne firmly resolved to enact substantial changes, in reality the same changes successfully implemented by Ebrium; but things went badly despite the precautions taken such as the appointment of 6 new governors. Ar-Ennum's failure obliged Ebrium to change many of the trusted officials and to bring back skilled supervisors. These two hypotheses must await the verdict of future research.

Passing mention was made above of the 2 governors responsible for the administration of the four quarters of the lower city. This information follows from the appearance of Ilzi in another tablet, to be treated later, as head of one of the two departments of the lower city.[36]

Under the lugals or governors there was a host of civil servants whose number varied according to the needs. But the archives have yielded a text which, in addition to recording the names of governors, contains the number of dependents who rendered service throughout the kingdom at the time of Ar-Ennum. It tells us that the entire personnel of the state totaled 11,700 functionaries, of whom 4,700 worked in the palace of the MI+ŠITA$_x$ and 7,000 were assigned to the various departments but always under the direction of the sa-MI+ŠITA$_x$:

obverse

I	1)	8 *mi-at* guruš-guruš	800 dependents
	2)	*ti-ir*	under Tir;
	3)	6 *mi-at* guruš-guruš	600 dependents
	4)	*a-bu*	under the Elder;
	5)	4 *mi-at* guruš-guruš	400 dependents
II	1)	*eb-rí-um*	under Ebrium;
	2)	6 *mi-at* guruš-guruš	600 dependents
	3)	*a-da-mu*	under Adamu;
	4)	4 *mi-at* guruš-guruš	400 dependents
	5)	*ar-ši-a-ḫa*	under Aršiaḫa;
	6)	4 *mi-at* guruš-guruš	400 dependents

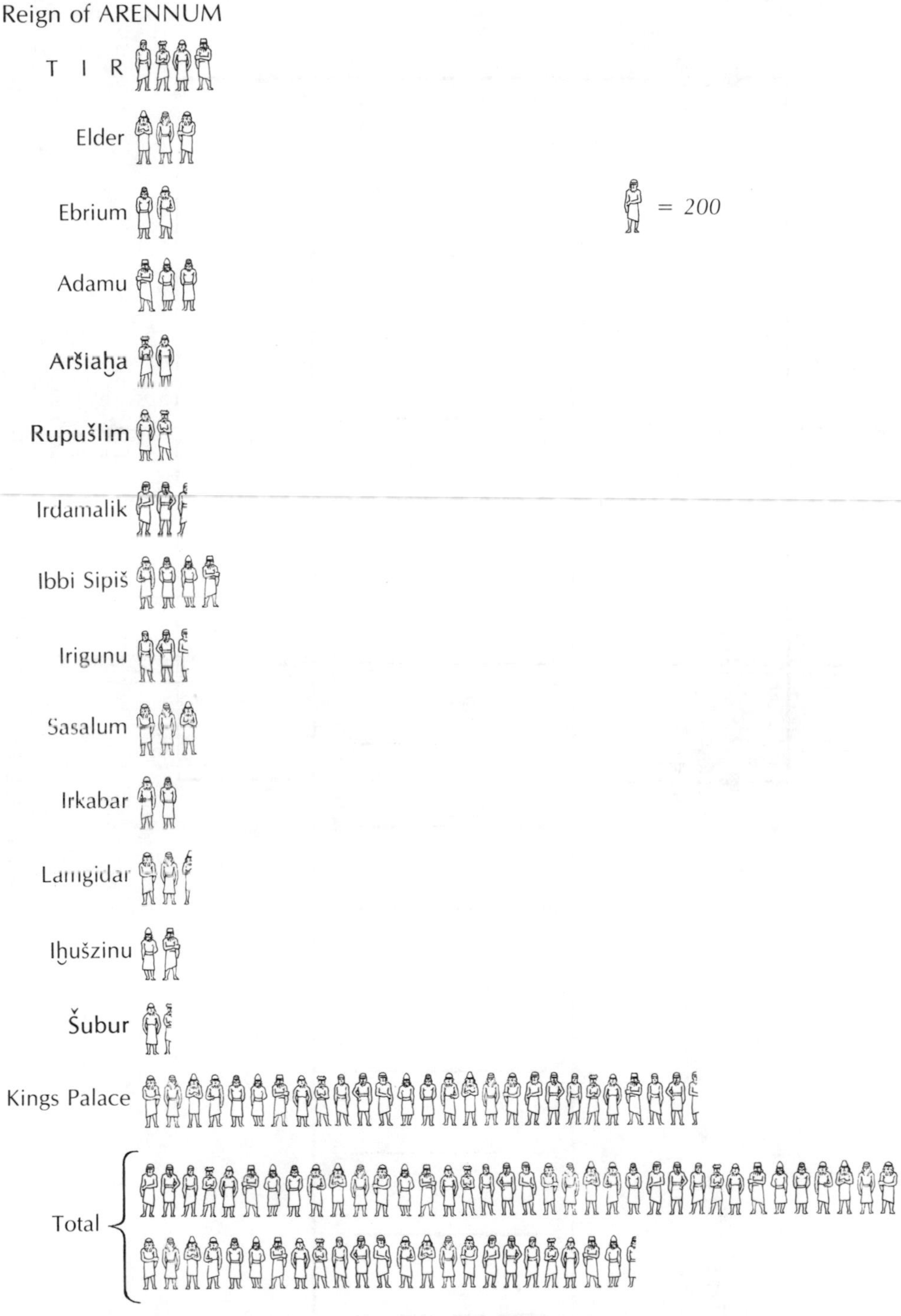

Figure VI, 4 The governors and the overseers at the time of Arennum

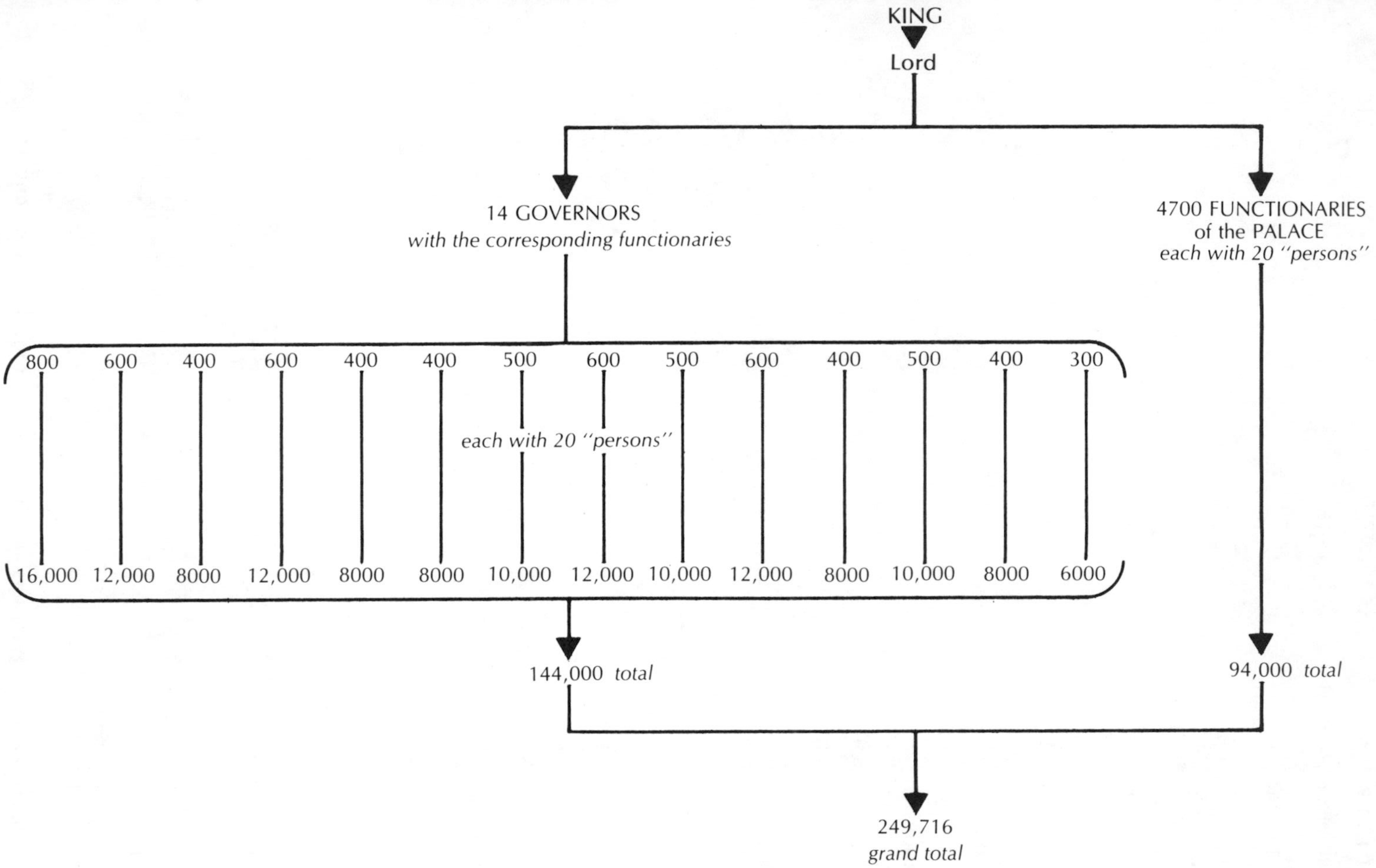

Figure VI, 5 The administrative cadres of Ebla

III	1)	*ru*$_{x}$*-pù-uš-li-im*	under Rupušlim;
	2)	5 *mi-at* guruš-guruš	500 dependents
	3)	*ìr-da-ma-lik*	under Irda-Malik;
	4)	6 *mi-at* guruš-guruš	600 dependents
	5)	*i-bí-sí-piš*	under Ibbi-Sipiš;
IV	1)	5 *mi-at* guruš-guruš	500 dependents
	2)	*i-rí-gú-nu*	under Irigunu;
	3)	6 *mi-at* guruš-guruš	600 dependents
	4)	*sà-sà-lum*	under Sasalum;
	5)	4 *mi-at* guruš-guruš	400 dependents
	6)	*ìr-kab-ar*	under Irkabar;
V	1)	5 *mi-at* guruš-guruš	500 dependents
	2)	*iš*$_{x}$*-gi-da-ar*	under Išgidar;
	3)	4 *mi-at* guruš-guruš	400 dependents
	4)	*i-ḫuš-zi-nu*	under Iḫušzinu;
	5)	3 *mi-at* guruš-guruš	300 dependents
reverse			
I	1)	šubur	under the Šubur,
	2)	4 *li-im* 7 *mi-at* guruš-guruš	4,700 dependents
	3)	sa-MI+ŠITA$_{x}$	of the palace of the "lord";
II	1)	an-šè-gú 1 *rí-ba*$_{x}$ 1 *li-im* 7 *mi-at* guruš-guruš	total: 11,700 dependents
	2)	KU	who render service
	3)	*áš-ti*	ordered
	4)	*ti-in*^{ki}	by the city of Tin;
	5)	itu *i-rí-sá*	month of Irisa.

The dependents qualified in this text by the generic term guruš appear elsewhere with the title ugula, "superintendent," which means that other dependents stood under their jurisdiction. From the texts emerges the information that under each ugula there were about 20 persons, who might also be called a "maniple," but whom the Eblaites surprisingly class as é-duru$_{5}$, "village," which corresponds here to the smallest administrative unit. This is borne out by an administrative document of rations for personnel numbering 7,000 grouped into 350 villages.[37]

The outline on p. 132 gives a visual image of the data discussed in this section on the administrative division:

2. THE DIVISION OF SPACE

2.1. SETTLEMENTS AND POPULATION

How many cities belonged to the kingdom of Ebla and how many were its inhabitants? The first question cannot yet be answered, but a reply to the second is happily forthcoming.

The indications given in the texts cited above, to wit, that each superintendent had 20 persons under him and that the roll of superintendents reached the number of 11,700, suggests that the population of Ebla exceeded 200,000. This purely theoretical datum is sustained by text 1392, an economic document of barley rations for 260,000 persons:

an-šè-gú 7 *li* 8 *mi* 80 lá-1 še *gú-bar*	Total: 7,879 Gubar measures
lú 2 *ma-i-ḫu* 6 *rí-ba*$_x$	for 260,000 persons.

This text does not flatly state that it is dealing with all the inhabitants of Ebla, but the nearly perfect correspondence between this figure and that theoretically deduced from the number of superintendents of Ebla renders plausible the hypothesis that Ebla numbered at least 260,000 permanent residents.

Obviously all these did not dwell in Ebla itself—it could accommodate 40,000 inhabitants at most—but in the towns and villages that formed Greater Ebla.

Of the same character as the preceding, another text, while not mentioning the number of people receiving the barley rations, is to the point because it names some of the towns forming part of the kingdom as well as the supervisors of the distribution of barley. The quantity of cereals mentioned here—precisely 95,160 Gubar—not only renders the number of persons mentioned in the preceding text credible, but points to an even higher number.

obverse

I	1)	[ ] 1 *rí-ba*$_x$ 3 *li-im* 2 *mi-at* še *gú-bar*	[X +) 13,200 Gubar of barley
	2)	kú	food
	3)	*na-si*$_{11}$ *na-si*$_{11}$	for people;
	4)	10 ugula še-*sù*	10 supervisors for this barley
	5)	*ik-du-lu*^{ki}	of the town of Ikdulu;
	6)	1 *rí-ba*$_x$ [ ] *li*-[ ]	10,000 [+ X +]
		broken	broken

II	1)	60 še *gú-bar*	60 Gubar of barley,
	2)	15 ugula še-*sù*	15 supervisors for this barley
	3)	*nu-ga-mu*^{ki}	of the town of Nugamu
	4)	1 *rí-ba*$_x$ 6 *li-im* 2 *mi-at* 20 še *gú-bar* 20 lá-3 ugula še-*sû*	16,220 Gubar of barley; 17 supervisors for this barley
	5)	*dag-ba-al*^{ki}	of the town of Dagbaal;
III	1)	2 *mi* še *gú-bar*	200 Gubar of barley,
	2)	1 ugula še-*sù*	1 supervisor for this barley
	3)	NE.NE-*du*^{ki}	of the town of Nenedu;
	4)	2 *rí-ba*$_x$ 5 *li* 6 *mi* 40 še *gú-bar*	25,640 Gubar of barley;
	5)	20 ugula še-*sù*	20 supervisors for this barley
	6)	*a-ru*$_x$*-lu*^{ki}-šè	of the town of Arulu;
	7)	1 *rí-ba*$_x$ 1 *li* 6 *mi* še *gú-bar*	11,600 Gubar of barley,
IV	1)	12 ugula še-*sù*	12 supervisors for this barley
	2)	*kul-ba-an*^{ki}	of the town of Kulban;
	3)	3 *li-im* še *gú-bar*	3,000 Gubar of barley,
	4)	2 ugula še	2 supervisors for the barley
	5)	sa-MI+ŠITA$_x$^{ki}	(from) the governate
	6)	uru-bar	(for) the cities;
	7)	5 *li* 2 *mi-at* 60 še *gú-bar*	5,260 Gubar of barley
	8)	6 ugula še	6 supervisors for the barley
	9)	*a-da-áš*^{ki}	of the town of Adaš
	10)	6 *mi* 80 še	680 (Gubar of barley)
V	1)	2 ugula še	2 supervisors for the barley,
	2)	ká	"gate"
	3)	*ba-ẓa-a*	of Baza;
	4)	an-šè-gú 9 *rí-ba*$_x$ 5 *li-im* 1 *mi-at* 60 še *gú-bar*	total: 95,160 Gubar of barley
	5)	94 ugula še	94 supervisors for the barley
	6)	*ip-ṭur-i-šar*	Ipṭur-Išar
		verse not written	verse not written

But this is not the only text which furnishes information about the towns and villages in the environs of Ebla. The numerous agricultural texts mention some 50 prevalently agricultural villages forming a circle around Ebla which supplied the grain essential for the capital of the kingdom.

The tablets with historical-administrative contents are also informative in this regard. One might mention TM.75.G.1444, cited above,[38] which records Ebrium's assigning for three of his sons houses located in various towns surrounding the capital.

Thus far it has been possible to count 250 towns and villages that constitute Greater Ebla, but their number cannot yet be fixed with any accuracy.

2.2. DIVISION OF THE CITY

That the city of Ebla was administratively subdivided into two departments which included the four quarters of the city received passing mention earlier. But thanks to a splendid tablet from the time of Ibbi-Sipiš, one can describe in considerable detail the topography of Ebla and know all its administrative centers. In fact, tablet TM.75.G.336 organically and fully gives not only the list of barley rations for the supervisors of the various administrative centers of the city of Ebla, but also mentions by name the officials and those under them, as well as the administration of which they form a part; hence it is possible to know the civil administrative structures and to deduce their topographic location. This text may then be classed as a register of the public land property and constitutes a unique document in all of the cuneiform literature known to date.

Here follows the complete transcription with the elaboration of those items pertinent to the administration of Ebla.

obverse

I	1)	*ì-lum*-bala	1
	2)	*en-na-ìa*	2
	3)	*da-sí-ma-ad*	3
	4)	*ti-dì-nu*	4
	5)	*ip-ṭur-iš-lu*	5
	6)	ugula 5	superintendents: 5
	7)	*puzur*$_4$-URU	1
	8)	lú-PÚ	
	9)	*iš-la-ìa*	2
	10)	lú-an-šè-gú	
	11)	*sí-piš-a-ḫu*	3
	12)	*iš-la-ìa*	4
	13)	nagar	

Group		Text	Functionaries	Dependents	Administration	Administrative Units	Topography
A	a)	r. I 1–III 2	20 ugula	100 ir$_{11}$–ir$_{11}$	é-duru$_5$^{ki}-maḫ	a)–c) → 50 na-se$_{11}$ maškim íl.zi	Lower City
A	b)	r. III 3–V 2	20 ugula	98 ir$_{11}$–ir$_{11}$	é-duru$_5$^{ki}-2		Lower City
A	c)	r. V 3–VI 3	10 ugula	30 ir$_{11}$–ir$_{11}$	é-duru$_5$^{ki}-3		Lower City
A		r. VI 4–7				50 na-se$_{11}$ maškim íl.zi	Lower City
A	d)	r. VI 8–v. I 8	20 + 1 ugula	50 ir$_{11}$–ir$_{11}$	é-duru$_5$^{ki} -4	→ 21 na-se$_{11}$ maškim Ida-Palil	Lower City
		v. I 9–12				21 na-se$_{11}$ maškim Ida-Palil	Lower City
B	e)	v. II 1–III 2	10 ugula (e–f: a.am)	60 ir$_{11}$–ir$_{11}$	é-en	e)–h) → (SA-MI + SITA$_x$^{ki})	Acropolis
B	f)	v. III 3–VI 4	10 ugula (e–f: a.am)	55 ir$_{11}$–ir$_{11}$	é-maḫ		Acropolis
B	g)	v. IV–V 5	63 (ugula) (g–h: ú-a)	60 ir$_{11}$–ir$_{11}$	gigir^{II}		Acropolis
B	h)	v. V 6–VII 4	20 ugula (g–h: ú-a)	35 ir$_{11}$–ir$_{11}$	é-am		Acropolis
			: na-se$_{11}$:				

Table VI, 2
The City of Ebla at the Time of King Ibbi-Sipiš

	14)	*puzur*$_4$*-ra-ma-lik*	5
	15)	ugula 5	superintendents: 5
II	1)	*mi-kà-ìa*	1
	2)	*bu-da-ìa*	2
	3)	lú-gigir^{ki}	
	4)	*a:píl-ma-lik*	3
	5)	*puzur*$_4$*-ra-be*	4
	6)	*i-šar*	5
	7)	ugula 5	superintendents: 5
	8)	*puzur*$_4$-URU	1
	9)	šeš-mu	
	10)	*we-du-lum*	
	11)	*ì-lum*-bala	2
	12)	lú-gigir^{ki}	
	13)	*en-na-ni-il*	3
	14)	*ni-ba-ìa*	4
	15)	*en-na-be*	5
	16)	ugula 5	superintendents: 5
	17)	é-duru$_5$^{ki}-maḫ$_x$	principal quarter
III	1)	100 ir$_{11}$-ir$_{11}$	100 dependents
	2)	é-duru$_5$^{ki}-maḫ$_x$	principal quarter
	3)	*wa-na*	1
	4)	*be-du-núm*	2
	5)	*qur-da-núm*	3
	6)	*be-du-núm*	4
	7)	lú-*i-da-núm*	
	8)	*ì-lum*-bala	5
	9)	lú[ ]	
	10)	ugu[la 5]	superintendents: 5
	11)	*mi*-[ ]	1
	12)	AL.DA.BÀD.KI	2
	13)	*a-bù-*^{d}*gu*$_5$*-ra*	3
	14)	*puzur*$_4$*-ra-ìa*	4
	15)	*be-du-núm*	5
	16)	lú-*ru*$_x$*-ba-nu*	
IV	1)	ugula 5	superintendents: 5
	2)	*é-da-ša*	1
	3)	*ti-la-ìa*	2
	4)	lú-PÚ	
	5)	*en-na-ìa*	3
	6)	IB.ZI	
	7)	*kà-za-na*	4

	8)	*ti-dì-nu*	5
	9)	ugula 5	superintendents: 5
	10)	*a-bù-*^{d}*gu*$_5$*-ra*	1
	11)	lú-[ ]	
	12)	*ti-[la]-ìa*	2
	13)	*ni-qì*	3
	14)	*mi-kà-ìa*	4
	15)	lú *lu-a-ìa*	
	16)	*sí-mi-na-ìa*	5
	17)	ugula 5	superintendents: 5
	18)	é-duru$_5^{ki}$-2	second quarter
V	1)	98 ir$_{11}$-ir$_{11}$	98 dependents
	2)	é-duru$_5^{ki}$-2	second quarter
	3)	*aḫ-ḫa-lum*	1
	4)	*mi-kà-ìa*	2
	5)	*wa-da-la-NI-mu*	3
	6)	*en-na-ìa*	4
	7)	lú *qú-ti-núm*	
	8)	*šu-ì-lum*	5
	9)	ugula 5	superintendents: 5
	10)	*ip-ṭù-ra*	1
	11)	*en-na-ma-lik*	2
	12)	*ḫa-ba-rí*	3
	13)	*a-lum*	4
	14)	*a-bù-*^{d}*gu*$_5$*-ra*	5
	15)	lú*-qú-ti-núm*	
VI	1)	ugula 5	superintendents: 5
	2)	30 ir$_{11}$-ir$_{11}$	30 dependents,
	3)	lú-é-duru$_5$-3	personnel of third quarter.
	4)	25 še *gú-bar*	25 Gubar of barley
	5)	50 *na-se*$_{11}$	(for) 50 prefects:
	6)	maškim	Inspector,
	7)	íl-zi	the official Ilzi
	8)	*ma-gal-lu*	1
	9)	*ip-ḫur-ìa*	2
	10)	*ba-ṣa-a*	3
	11)	*da-sí-ma-ad*	4
	12)	*a-kà-al-ma-lik*	5
	13)	ugula 5	superintendents: 5
	14)	*ar-šè-a-ḫu*	1

VII	1)	ìr-MI+ŠITA$_x$-ni	2
	2)	*ìr-ì-ba*	3
	3)	*i-i-da-du*	4
	4)	*a-ba-šu*	5
	5)	ugula 5	superintendents: 5
	6)	*ṭù-bí-sí-piš*	1
	7)	*en-na-*^{d}*ra-sa-ap*	2
	8)	NI*-é-ì-lu*	3
	9)	*ar-šè*	4
	10)	*puzur*$_4$*-ra-ma-lik*	5
	11)	ugula 5	superintendents: 5

reverse

I	1)	*áš-ba-ìa*	1
	2)	*ar-ra-sí-piš*	2
	3)	NI*-ṣa-ra-nu*	3
	4)	*en-na-ma-ni*	4
	5)	*da-ni-lum*	5
	6)	ugula 5	superintendents: 5
	7)	*a-lu-a-ḫu*	1
	8)	50 ir$_{11}$-ir$_{11}$-é-duru$_5$^{ki} <4>	50 dependents fourth quarter
	9)	10 še*-gú-bar*	10 Gubar of barley
	10)	21 *na-se*$_{11}$	(for) 21 prefects:
	11)	maškim	Inspector,
	12)	*ì-da-palil*	Ida-Palil
II	1)	*eb-du-ìa*	1
	2)	*ḫa-zu-ru*$_x$	2
	3)	*sí-ma-*^{d}*gu*$_5$*-ra*	3
	4)	ìr-^{d}*na-im*	4
	5)	*puzur*$_4$*-ra-a-gú*	5
	6)	UR.PI	6
	7)	*é-da-ša*	7
	8)	DU-GÚ	8
	9)	*i-da-nu*	9
	10)	*puzur*$_4$*-ra-ìa*	10
	11)	ugula 10 *na-se*$_{11}$	superintendents: 10 prefects,
	12)	60 ir$_{11}$ir$_{11}$	60 dependents,
III	1)	10 *na-se*$_{11}$	10 prefects
	2)	a-am é-en	officials a-am, royal palace
	3)	*é-da-ša*	1

	4)	*i-ti-kà-mi-iš*	2
	5)	*en-na-*^{d}*ra-sa-ap*	3
	6)	*a-a-bù-ìr-ku*$_{8}$	4
	7)	*ar-šè-a-ḫu*	5
	8)	*é-gi-a-lum*	6
	9)	*ar-šè*	7
	10)	lú-*ki-ni-lum*	
	11)	*a-la-sa-*GÚ	8
	12)	*ti-la-ìa*	9
IV	1)	*ar-šè*	10
	2)	ugula 10 *na-se*$_{11}$	superintendents: 10 prefects
	3)	55 ir$_{11}$ ir$_{11}$	55 dependents
	4)	10 *na-se*$_{11}$ a-am é-maḫ$_{x}$	10 prefects, officials a-am principal palace
	5)	10 še-*gú-bar*	10 Gubar of barley
	6)	20 *na-se*$_{11}$ a-am-am	(for) 20 prefects, officials a-am.
	7)	16,50 še-*gú-bar*	16.5 Gubar of barley
	8)	33 *na-se*$_{11}$	(for) 33 prefects,
	9)	1 še-*gú-bar*	1 Gubar of barley
	10)	3 *na-se*$_{11}$ ú-a	(for) 3 prefects, officials ú-a
	11)	*ìr-ì-ba*	(under) Iriba,
	12)	10 še-*gú-bar*	10 Gubar of barley
	13)	20 *na-se*$_{11}$ ú-a	20 prefects, officials ú-a
	14)	*ar-šè-a-ḫu*	(under) Arše-Aḫu
V	1)	3,50 še-*gú-bar*	3.5 Gubar of barley
	2)	10 lá-3 *na-se*$_{11}$ ú-a	(for) 7 prefects, officials ú-a
	3)	gigir^{ki}	stables
	4)	60 ir$_{11}$-ir$_{11}$	60 dependents,
	5)	ú-a	official ú-a
	6)	*ip-ṭur-ìa*	1
	7)	*ti-la-ìa*	2
	8)	*eb-du-*^{d}*ra-sa-ap*	3
	9)	*ip-ḫur-*^{d}*gu*$_{5}$*-ra*	4
	10)	*bu-da-ìa*	5
	11)	ugula 5	superintendents: 5
	12)	*ḫa-bil*	1

	13)	*i-da-*N I	2
	14)	*a-bù-sí*	3
	15)	*pù-tá-be*	4
VI	1)	*en-na-ni-il*	5
	2)	u g u l a 5	superintendents: 5
	3)	*gú-ra-sí*	1
	4)	*en-na-ìa*	2
	5)	*sí-piš-ar*	3
	6)	*ḫa-ra-ìa*	4
	7)	*eb-du-ìa*	5
	8)	u g u l a 5	superintendents: 5
	9)	[ ]-*ti-ni*	1
	10)	[ ]-*be*	2
	11)	[-*t*]*i*	3
	12)	[ ]-*zi-na-IM*	4
	13)	*a-bù-*d*gu₅-ra*	5
	14)	u g u l a 5	superintendents: 5
VII	1)	10 š e -*bar*	10 Gubar of barley
	2)	20 *na-se₁₁*	(for) 20 prefects,
	3)	35 i r₁₁-i r₁₁	35 dependents,
	4)	l ú - é - a m	personnel of the
			people's palace
	5')	n u š u b a₄-t i	have not received
	6')	l ú - i r₁₁-i r₁₁	the dependents
VIII	1)	a n - š è - g ú 85 š e *gú-bar*	total: 85 Gubar
			of barley
	2)	1 *mi-at* 70 *na-se₁₁*	170 prefects,
	3)	š e - x [ ]	barley . . .
	4)	š[u b a₄-t i]	received
	5)	i[t u] d[ ]	month: . . .

To form an idea of the structure of the text, it is necessary to divide it into two large sections, the first from obverse I 1 to reverse I 12, the second from reverse II 1 to VII 4. Each of these sections contains four subsections indicated by the letters of the alphabet a)–d) and e)–h).

As regards the structure of each subsection, observe that the officials, the dependents, and the administration of belongings are listed. As regards the officials, they are grouped into units of five superintendents in a)–d) and h) and are, moreover, with the exception of g), listed by name.

In the first section a)–d), the first three subsections constitute an administrative unit (obverse VII 4–7), while the fourth stands apart, forming another unit.

Following the structure of the text, we can sort out at least eight administrative units of the city, of which four are termed é-duru$_5^{ki}$, "village," and the others é, "house, palace." The first group may be called "ward districts" and the second "administrative palace."

2.2.1. POLITICAL DIVISIONS

WARD DISTRICTS

The first four administrations bear the name é-duru$_5^{ki}$-maḫ$_x$, é-duru$_5^{ki}$-2, é-duru$_5^{ki}$-3, and é-duru$_5^{ki}$ <-4>. The Sumerian term é-duru$_5$ normally signifies "rural village" as opposed to uru, "city." In our text, however, é-duru$_5^{ki}$ clearly refers to a part of the city, hence the translation "quarter" or "ward." This meaning of the term is confirmed by the alternation of é-duru$_5^{ki}$ with ká, "gate" in the larger signification of "quarter, ward."

If this interpretation is sound, the first section of text TM.75.G.336 enumerates the four quarters of the city with its functionaries and dependents.

THE QUARTERS OR WARDS

a) é-duru$_5^{ki}$-maḫ$_x$ "principal quarter." The first quarter named "principal quarter" is presented as an organic whole of 20 superintendents and 100 dependents. The superintendents (ugula) are subdivided into four groups of 5, but it is not possible to determine the rationale behind such grouping or their specific functions.

b) é-duru$_5^{ki}$-2, "second quarter." The second ward numbers 20 superintendents, again subdivided into groups of 5, with 98 dependents.

c) é-duru$_5^{ki}$-3, "third quarter." This ward constitutes an administrative unit smaller than the first two, counting only 10 superintendents divided into two groups of 5, and but 30 dependents.

d) é-duru$_5^{ki}$<-4>, "fourth quarter." This last ward of the city has an organic whole of 20 superintendents, subdivided into four groups of 5, with the addition of Alu-aḫu, whose function escapes us, and 50 dependents.

THE QUARTERS AND THE GATES

While the present text mentions only the é-duru$_5^{ki}$, "the quarters," other documents mention ká, "the gate." Each of these four gates bears the name of a god: ká-^{d}ra-sa-ap, "Gate of Rasap," ká-^{d}UTU, "Gate of Sipiš," ká-^{d}dagan, "Gate of Dagan," and ká-ba-al, "Gate of Baal."

ADMINISTRATIVE UNITS OF THE QUARTERS

The four quarters are grouped into two units headed by the officials with the title m a š k i m, "inspector." On the basis of obverse VI 4–7 the superintendents of the first three wards—exactly 50 prefects—are dependent upon the inspector, the official Ilzi. The fourth quarter, on the other hand, with its 20 + 1 prefects, is on the evidence of reverse I 9–12 under the authority of the inspector Ida-Palil.

While the superintendents are indicated earlier by the term u g u l a, in obverse VI 5 and reverse I 10 they are called *na-se*$_{11}$, "prefects."

The Palaces

The last four sections of the table on page 137, precisely e)–h), refer to houses or palaces with administrative functions:

é - e n, "palace of the king." In the first palace, which at the same time serves as the royal residence, 10 superintendents with 60 dependents are employed.

é - m a ḫ, "principal palace." Here 10 superintendents with 55 dependents are stationed. The role of this palace or management center cannot be made out clearly. Worthy of note is how the superintendents (u g u l a), still *na-se*$_{11}$ like those of the ward district, belong to the category of officials a - a m. Frequently attested in the documents, this type of official cannot be better identified, even though the term a - a m is very probably Sumerian.

g i g i r^{ki}, "stables." To this administrative center, which nicely accentuates the commercial character of Ebla, are attached 63 prefects with 60 dependents. Arše-aḫu heads 20 prefects, while three are under Iriba.

é - a m, "house . . ." The fourth administrative headquarters embraces 20 superintendents, subdivided into four groups of 5, with 35 dependents. The definition of *am* is not readily arrived at; if the root is Semitic, the root of *amtu,* "handmaid," springs to mind, but far better is the connection with *'am,* "people."

The prefects of the stables and of the é - a m belong to the category of ú - a officials, well attested both in our documents and in Mesopotamian lexical list.

s a - M I + Š I T A$_x$^{ki} *wa eb-la*^{ki}. Before drawing conclusions about Ebla's bureaucracy and proposing hypotheses about the city's topography, it might be good to examine the expression s a - M I + Š I T A$_x$^{ki} *wa eb-la*^{ki}. It is surprising, in fact, that this tablet does not mention s a - M I + Š I T A$_x$^{ki}, the administrative center of Ebla which might be rendered "governor's headquarters." The M I + Š I T A$_x$ was in reality the head of the city and its viceroy. But, with due reserve, it may be proposed that the four administrative centers (é - e n, é - m a ḫ$_x$, g i g i r^{ki}, and é - a m) correspond to the s a - M I + Š I T A$_x$, the great administrative complex of Ebla. If this holds true, then *wa eb-la*^{ki} must refer to the four ward districts of our text. The phrase sa-MI+ŠITA$_x$ *wa eb-la*^{ki} would thus embrace the eight administrative units of the city; this does not conflict with what was said above but seems rather to confirm it and to give it shape.

2.2.2. TOPOGRAPHY OF EBLA ACCORDING TO TM.75.G.336

The purpose of the text examined was not to describe the topography of Ebla but to enumerate the administrative centers of the capital. Hence it is not strange that of the many temples in the city not one is mentioned by this document. Nonetheless, it does furnish some useful hints as to the topographical layout of the above-mentioned administrative centers:

a) Acropolis. It would seem that, at least as a working hypothesis, the four administrative units, namely the é-en, é-maḫ, gigir^{ki}, and é-am indicated altogether as sa-MI+ŠITA$_x$^{ki}, are to be located on the acropolis of the city of Ebla.

b) Lower city. The first four administrative units, to wit, é-duru$_5$^{ki}-maḫ$_x$, é-duru$_5$^{ki}-2, é-duru$_5$^{ki}-3, é-duru$_5$^{ki}-4, according to the present supposition, stand for the four sectors of lower city which contrasted, so to speak, with the acropolis. They would, furthermore, correspond to the four above-mentioned gates of the city. Presented by a Table, the topographical data on Ebla's administration would look like that on p. 137.

3. THE DIVISION OF TIME

A civilization as sophisticated as that of Ebla, which had divided power and space according to the criteria of maximum administrative efficiency, could not neglect the third great aspect, time. The Eblaites actually subdivided time into years and months. The following paragraphs treat of this subdivision so indispensable for administrative maturity.

3.1. SYSTEMS OF DATING

Many of the economic tablets carry at the end of the text a clause referring to the year in which the document was drafted. The formula encountered most often indicates the year preceded by a number, such as, 3 mu, "third year," 5 mu, "fifth year."[39]

This type of dating, obviously not absolute but with a particular reference to the reign of each king of the dynasty, helps not a bit to determine the chronological sequence of the economic and historical events happening during the period of the royal archives of Ebla.

More useful for this scope are perhaps those texts witnessing several dates. In the preceding chapter the hypothesis was advanced, mainly on the strength of TM.75.G.1376, that the Eblaites must have had a fixed and recurring periodic cycle; in this document are recorded administrative facts that go from the seventh to the first year. The seventh year is indicated as that of the "feast of the stelae."[40]

The system of dating events and administrative acts in a regressive and not progressive manner clearly points to a fixed cycle. Above it was also conjectured that such a fixed cycle coincided with the normal reigning period of the individual kings.

The regressive system was in use until King Ibbi-Sipiš' ascent to the throne; as text TM.75.G.427 reveals, this king introduced the progressive system of dating the years, namely, 1, 2, 3, etc., which is certainly more consonant with our way of thinking.

This radical change in the manner of dating was doubtless bound up with the concept of kingship, at first elective and for a fixed period, and later hereditary and, in practice, for life.

But together with the method of indicating the years by numbers there also existed another mode, witnessed for the first time at Ebla and then transmitted in the historical periods to neighboring Mesopotamia. This consisted of indicating the years by important events touching the religious, civil, or military life of the state of Ebla. Not all dates have been collected or are, as they are termed in specialist jargon, year-names, but those assembled clearly reveal Ebla's priority to all the contemporary cultures.

Here are several examples of year-names which refer to political and economic relationships of Ebla with the city of Mari:

DIŠ mu nì-kas$_4$ Ma-rí^{ki}	"year of the campaign against Mari"
DIŠ mu til Ma-rí^{ki}	"year of Mari's defeat"
DIŠ mu lugal-Ma-rí^{ki} ug$_6$	"year in which Mari's king died"
DIŠ mu *ib-lul-il* lugal ug$_6$	"year in which King Iblul-Il died"
DIŠ mu šu-ra-da-mu lugal Ma-rí^{ki}	"year in which Šura-Damu became king of Mari"
DIŠ nidba$_x$ ì-giš Ma-rí^{ki}	"year of the feast of anointing at Mari"

A quick glance at these dates suffices to show how important this system of dating can be for the reconstruction of the history of the kingdom of Ebla during the period of the royal archives.

The names of the years are like pieces of a mosaic which permit us to visualize the most important happenings of the kingdom. From these can be deduced the specific character and the primary interests of Eblaite civilization; most of the year-names refer, in fact, to commercial journeys to important centers.[41]

3.2. CALENDARS

The Eblaite year was, like today, a solar year divided into twelve months. From some of the texts it has been possible to reconstruct completely the two calendars used at Ebla.

The old calendar was employed during the reigns of Igriš-Ḫalam and Ebrium, while the new calendar was introduced by King Ibbi-Sipiš. The difference between the two calendars is profound; the first is of an agricultural nature, but the second is more adapted to the technological civilization of Ebla. Nor are these the only differences; the old calendar is prevailingly Semitic, whereas the new one is surprisingly more Sumerian than Semitic. Both calendars are, however, lunar and hence have an intercalary month to synchronize the calendar with the solar year.

3.2.1. THE OLD CALENDAR

My term for the first calendar from Ebla was "the Semitic calendar of the third millennium";[42] this designation took rise from the names of the months which are Semitic and for the most part West Semitic, and from the diffusion of this calendar throughout the whole Near East during the period from circa 2600 to 2200 B.C.

The reconstruction of this calendar is based on texts TM.75.G.1629, 1630, and 2096, three economic tablets recording the delivery of livestock for various purposes.

The month-names are the following:

I	itu	*ḫa-li-tù*	month of the phoenix
II	itu	*i-rí-sá*	month of sowing
III	itu	*ga-šúm*	month of the rains
IV	itu	ì-num	month of oil
V	itu	*ṣa-lul*	month of processions
VI	itu	*i-*ba_4*-sa*	———
VII	itu	M Ax*ganatenû*-sag	———
VIII	itu	M Ax*ganatenû*-$gudu_4$	———
IX	itu	*i-ší*	month of fires
X	itu	*ig-za*	month of harvest
X_2	itu	*ig-za*-mìn	month of second harvest
XI	itu	*ṣa-'à-tum*	month of flocks
XII	itu	*kí-lí*	month of measuring

Though the meaning of the month-names are not all evident, those that are intelligible are agricultural, so that the whole calendar would appear to be the product of a farming community or culture.

This calendar, so ill adapted to the culture of Ebla during the period of the royal archives, enjoyed notable success, being attested at Mari and Gasur, in northern Mesopotamia, at Abu-Salabikh and in the Diyala, and as far as Lagash in southern Mesopotamia. This diffusion strikingly illustrates the cultural unity of the Near East in the third millennium, while the West Semitic names of the months indicate Ebla as the likely center of its radiation.

To illustrate how the names of various months appear in the economic tablets, a transcription and translation of TM.75.G.1630 may prove helpful. It reports on small livestock, more precisely, on 36,892 sheep destined as offering for the temples and as food for the population during the twelve months of the year.

obverse

I	1)	6 *mi* 92 udu nidba$_x$	1) 692 sheep (as sacrificial) offering,
	2)	2 *li* 3 *mi* udu ug$_6$	2) 2,300 "dead" sheep,
	3)	itu *ṣa-lul*	3) month: Salul;
	4)	9 *mi* 23 udu nidba$_x$	4) 923 sheep (as sacrificial) offering,
II	1)	1 *li* 6 *mi* udu ug$_6$	1) 1,600 "dead" sheep,
	2)	itu *i-ba$_4$-sa*	2) month: Ibasa;
	3)	4 *li* 3 *mi* 60 udu nidba$_x$	3) 4,360 sheep (as sacrificial) offering,
	4)	8 *mi* udu ug$_6$	4) 800 "dead" sheep,
	5)	7 *li* udu tùn-šè	5) 7,000 slaughtered sheep,
III	1)	itu MAx*ganatenû*-sag	1) month: MAxganatenû-sag;
	2)	2 *li-im* 5 *mi* 60 udu nidba$_x$	2) 2,560 sheep (as sacrificial) offering,
	3)	6 *mi* 50 udu ug$_6$	3) 650 "dead" sheep,
	4)	itu MAx*ganatenû*-gudu$_4$	4) month: MAxganatenû-gudu$_4$;
	5)	1 *li* 5 *mi* 80 udu nidba$_x$	5) 1,580 sheep (as sacrificial) offering,
	6)	5 *mi* udu ug$_6$	6) 500 "dead" sheep,

IV	1) itu *i-ší*	1)	month: Iši;
	2) 8 *mi* 33 udu nidba$_x$	2)	833 sheep (as sacrificial) offering,
	3) 4 *mi-at* udu ug$_6$	3)	400 "dead" sheep,
	4) itu *ig-za*	4)	month: Igza;
	5) 6 *mi-at* 98 udu nidba$_x$	5)	698 sheep (as sacrificial) offering,
	6) 4 *mi* udu ug$_6$	6)	400 "dead" sheep,
V	1) itu *ig-za*-mìn	1)	month: second Igza;
	2) 9 *mi* 22 udu nidba$_x$	2)	922 sheep (as sacrificial) offering,
	3) 5 *mi* 30 udu ug$_6$	3)	530 "dead" sheep,
	4) itu *ṣa-'à-tum*	4)	month: Ṣa'àtum;
	5) 8 *mi* 72 udu	5)	872 sheep

Table VI, 3
Allotments of Sheep for Various Purposes in the Twelve Months of the Year According to TM.75.G.1630

MONTHS	nidba$_x$	ug$_6$	tùn-šè
1) itu *ṣa-lul*	692	2300	—
2) itu *i-ba$_4$-sa*	923	1600	—
3) itu M Ax*ganatenû*-sag	4360	800	7000
4) itu M Ax*ganatenû*-gudu$_4$	2560	650	—
5) itu *i-ší*	1580	500	—
6) itu *ig-za*	833	400	—
7) itu *ig-za*-mìn	698	400	—
8) itu *ṣa-'à-tum*	922	530	—
9) itu *kí-lí*	872	444	—
10) itu *ḫu-li-tù*	1051	610	—
11) itu *i-rí-sá*	1051	600	—
12) itu *ga-šúm*	4910	606	—
SUMS	20452	9440	7000
TOTAL		36892	

reverse

I	1) nidba$_x$	1)	(as sacrificial) offering,
	2) 4 *mi* 44 udu ug$_6$	2)	444 "dead" sheep,
	3) itu *kí-lí*	3)	month: Qili;
	4) 1 *li-im* 51 udu nidba$_x$	4)	1,051 sheep (as sacrificial) offering,
	5) 6 *mi* 10 udu ug$_6$	5)	610 "dead" sheep,

II	1)	itu *ḫa-li-tù*	1) month: Ḫalitu;
	2)	1 *li* 51 udu nidba$_x$	2) 1,051 sheep (as sacrificial) offering,
	3)	6 *mi* udu ug$_6$	3) 600 "dead" sheep,
	4)	itu *i-rí-sá*	4) month: Irisa;
	5)	4 *li* 9 *mi* 10 udu nidba$_x$	5) 4,910 sheep (as sacrificial) offering,
III	1)	6 *mi* 6 udu ug$_6$	1) 606 "dead" sheep,
	2)	itu *ga-šúm*	2) month: Gašum;
IV	1)	an-šè-gú 2 *rí-ba*$_x$ 4 *mi* 52 udu nidba$_x$	1) total: 20,452 sheep (as sacrificial) offering,
	2)	9 *li* 4 *mi* 40 udu ug$_6$	2) 9,440 "dead" sheep,
	3)	7 *li* udu tùn-šè	3) 7,000 slaughtered sheep,
V	1)	šu-nigín 3 *rí-ba*$_x$ 6 *li* 8 *mi* 92 udu	1) total: 36,892 sheep.

3.2.2. THE NEW CALENDAR

Among the various reforms effected by King Ibbi-Sipiš, reforms which radically changed Ebla's appearance and its basic traditions, must be numbered that of the calendar. Under Ibbi-Sipiš a new calendar was in use, profoundly differing from its predecessor and which may be described as cultural.

This new calendar emerges from TM.75.G.427, a seven-year report on rations of barley and flour for the different months of each year.[43] Here in succession is the list of the months with their English translation:

I	itu *be-li*	month of the lord
II	itu nidba$_x$-^{d}*aš-tá-pi*$_5$	month of the feast of Aštabi
III	itu ì-túm	month of the taxes
IV	itu nidba$_x$-^{d}*'à-da*	month of feast of Hada
V	itu *er-me*	month of the cities
VI	itu *ḫur-mu*	month of the fires
VII	itu è	month of the expenses
VIII	itu kur$_6$	month of the provisions
IX	itu ^{d}*a-dam-ma-um*	month of the feast of Adamma
X	itu še-gur$_{10}$-ku$_5$	month of the harvest
Xbis	itu še-gur$_{10}$-ku$_5$-mìn	month of the second harvest
XI	itu ^{d}AMA-*ra*	month of Ištar
XII	itu nidba$_x$-^{d}*kà-mi-iš*	month of the feast of Kamiš

As was done for the old calendar, a text may be cited here in its entirety to permit the reader to see in context the month-names of the new calendar.

obverse

I 1) è-en
2) itu *ì-la-mu*
3) *wa*
4) itu izi-gar
5) itu è
6) itu kur$_6$
7) *ì-dì*

II 1) *ar-mi*^{ki}
2) *ší-in*
3) sa-MI+ŠITA$_x$^{ki}
4) itu ^{d}*a-dam-ma-um*
5) 3 mu
6) itu še-gur$_{10}$-ku$_5$
7) DU
8) *wa*
9) itu ^{d}AMA-*ra*

III 1) DU
2) uru^{ki}-uru^{ki}
3) IB.RA
4) itu nidba$_x$-^{d}*kà-mi-iš*
5) uru^{ki}
6) šu mu-gur$_4$
7) *wa*
8) *gu*-KU

IV 1) itu *be-li*
2) itu ^{d}*aš-tá-pi*$_5$
3) DU
4) *ar-mi*^{ki}
5) *wa*
6) è
7) en
8) *ší-in*

reverse

I 1) uru^{ki}
2) itu ì-túm
3) itu nidba$_x$-^{d}*'à-da*
4) itu *ì-la-mu*

5) itu *ḫur-mu*
6) itu è
7) itu kur$_6$
8) itu ^{d}*a-dam-ma-um*

II 1) itu še-gur$_{10}$-ku$_5$
2) ^{d}*ì a-ra-mu*
3) *ar-mi*^{ki}
4) *ší-in*
5) uru^{ki}
6) itu še-gur$_{10}$-ku$_5$-mìn
7) itu ^{d}AMA-*ra*

III 1) itu nidba$_x$-^{d}*kà-mi-iš*
2) itu *be-li*
3) itu ^{d}*aš-tá-pi*$_5$
4) itu ì-túm
5) itu nidba$_x$-^{d}*'à-da*
6) itu *ì-la-mu*
7) itu *ḫur-mu*
8) itu è

IV 1) itu kur$_6$
2) 2 mu 5 itu
3) *ì-dì*
4) *ar-mi*^{ki}
5) *ší-in*
6) sa-MI+ŠITA$_x$^{ki}

An examination of the intrinsic nature of this calendar shows that eight month-names refer to religious feasts and four to administrative acts. The calendar of Ibbi-Sipiš thus presents some distinct characteristics which place it among those types of calendars used in socially developed countries. Most of what has been discussed in this chapter serves to confirm that Ebla's culture was very mature and its technology at the apex of its development.

But the value of the new calendar does not end here; the presence of the Hurrian divinities Aštabi and Adamma together with the Semitic gods Dagan, Beli, Hadad, Ištar, and Kamiš permits the identification of the two ethnic components of Eblaite society at this period, the Semites and the Hurrians. This is one of the most precious items issuing from the archives. The dominant Semitic element appears as sedentary and its culture so urbanized as to be able to compete with the city cultures of contemporary Mesopotamia. But alongside the Semites the Hurrians already appear in these parts in the mid-third millennium; the two month-names commemorating Hurrian divinities assure us of this.

Both the old and new calendars are lunar in character, so that at recurring periods an intercalary month was added, in both a second harvest month to align the lunar with the solar year.

As evidenced by tablets registering daily and monthly rations, the month consisted of 30 days,[44] so that the year was not perfectly lunar but already a blend of two systems. Twelve multiplied by 30 equals 360 days, a bit less than the 365 of the solar year, but certainly more than those of the lunar year. The second harvest month inserted at recurring but not fixed periods served to fill this gap.

Little is yet known about the division of the month into weeks, though a quadruple subdivision on the basis of the quarters of the moon corresponding to the first, seventh, fourteenth, and twenty-first days of the month does not appear unreasonable.

On the other hand, the reply to the question of a weekly day of rest would be negative; in the texts no indication can be found that there was a day on which all operations ceased.

Notes

1. The richest sources for the problem discussed here are the administrative documents and those of an economic character.
2. See, for example, TM.75.G.1285; 1344; 1366; 1735.
3. TM.75.G.1402; 1414; 1559; 11126.
4. Pp. 130ff.
5. TM.75.G.1263; 1289; 1317; 1319; 1680; 2121, and *passim.*
6. TM.75.G.1286.
7. TM.75.G.1264; 1293.
8. See above on pp. 103ff.
9. TM.75.G.400; 441; 520.
10. TM.76.G.199.
11. TM.75.G.308.
12. TM.75.G.336; 408, and *passim.*
13. TM.75.G.1608; 1659.
14. TM.75.G.1513; 1817.
15. TM.75.G.519.
16. TM.75.G.273.
17. TM.75.G.427.
18. See pp. 78ff.
19. See below on pp. 157ff.
20. For the merchants see Chapter VII, 4.4.
21. TM.75.G.454.
22. Pp. 97ff.
23. Pp. 98f.
24. TM.75.G.1375 and *passim.*
25. See p. 87.
26. TM.75.G.2133.

27. TM.75.G.2420.
28. TM.75.G.2000.
29. TM.75.G.1359; 1373.
30. TM.75.G.1357.
31. TM.75.G.1366; 1402.
32. TM.75.G.411; 527, and *passim.*
33. Ipṭura.
34. See above on p. 93.
35. The subject is Gugiwan who pays 4 minas of gold (rev. III 2–4).
36. TM.75.G.336.
37. TM.75.G.245.
38. Pp. 84f.
39. TM.75.G.1299; 1371; 1374, and *passim.*
40. TM.75.G.1376. See p. 72.
41. TM.75.G.1817; 2086.
42. *OrAn* 16 (1977), pp. 257ff.
43. *AfO* 25 (1978), pp. 1ff.
44. TM.75.G.220; see above on p. 89.

CHAPTER VII

The Economy

1. Economic resources. 1.1. Agriculture. 1.2. Cattle breeding. 1.3. Industry. 1.4. Alloys of metals: an example of advanced technology. 2. Models of production. 3. Units of measure. 3.1. Dry and liquid measures. 3.2. Weights. 3.3. Surfaces. 3.4. Numbering systems. 4. Commerce. 4.1. Models of exchange. 4.1.1. Barter. 4.1.2. Purchase and sale. 4.1.3. "Tributes." 4.2. Value of exchange: prices and currency. 4.2.1. The value of goods and the dynamics of prices. 4.3. Commercial goods; import-export. 4.4. Commercial empire.

Anticipating what might be evident only at the end of the chapter, we should acknowledge that this new Semitic people knew how to invest all its resources and to create a true economic empire respected and feared throughout the Near East in the middle of the third millennium. The Eblaites seem to have been called to commerce by nature; this was their prime and all-embracing activity. But commerce cannot exist without the riches which constitute the basis for preferred relationships with the other states mentioned by the royal archives of Ebla.

1. ECONOMIC RESOURCES

TM.75.G.1392, cited above, contains information about the quantity of barley, precisely 7,879 Gubar measures, needed for 260,000 persons.[1] Another text was also quoted in which the quantity of barley reached 95,160 Gubar measures, meaning that Ebla could feed a much greater number of people.

The treatment of Ebla's economic resources can nicely be introduced by TM.75.G.1474 where one reads at the end:

1)	an-še-gú 5 *ma-i-at* 4 *rí-ba*$_x$ 8 *li-im* 5 *mi-at* še-*gú-bar*	1)	total: 548,500 Gubar measures of barley
2)	sa-MI+ŠITA$_x$	2)	for the "lord's" palace;
3)	*ṭù-bí-šúm*	3)	Ṭubišum is the official—
4)	íl-zi	4)	Ilzi.

It follows from a simple, theoretical comparison of the quantity of barley here reported as stored in the state granaries with the 7,879 Gubar sufficient to feed 260,000 persons that Ebla was in condition, according to this new text, to assure the sustenance of more than 18 million people.[2] At this point it becomes evident that the basic wealth of the kingdom of Ebla lay in farm products seconded by a flourishing breeding of livestock.

Ebla, therefore, did not start from scratch, so to speak, to create its economic might essentially centered on industry and consequent international commerce.

1.1. AGRICULTURE

The geographical situation of Ebla renders agriculture not only possible but also highly profitable. The countryside around Tell Mardikh is flat and abundantly watered,[3] and the data emerging from the tablets show that the Eblaites appreciated the natural potential of their territory.

The metropolitan area was, as a matter of fact, completely encircled by countless towns and villages dedicated to agriculture. When we learn that 17 kinds of wheat were raised, then we understand how rationally they exploited the soil. But before passing on to the various crops, one question should be raised: What area was utilized by agriculture?

A reply to this query will become possible only when all the tablets dealing with work in the field have been studied together, but even now one can safely assert that a vast area was available for farming purposes.

One cadastral text dealing with the farming territory of but 10 villages mentions an area of more than 57 kilometers squared; hence to infer that the farming area of Ebla must have covered hundreds, if not actually thousands, of kilometers squared would not be unwarranted.

The principal crop was that of grains, especially barley and wheat. Numerous are the tablets which describe both the surface and the annual harvest. To give an example, TM.76.G.188 records in the first part the amount of barley needed for sowing, and in the second mentions the agricultural terrain of the 10 villages mentioned above.

obverse

I	1)	[ ]+26 še-numun	[x +] 26 (Gubar) of barley for sowing
	2)	1 *m*[*i*] 30 [ ]	130 . . .
	3)	*al na-si*$_{11}$ *na-si*$_{11}$	due to the people
	4)	*da-gu*^{ki}	of the village Dagu;
	5)	66 še-mumum	66 (Gubar) of barley for sowing
	6)	⌜x?⌝ *gú-bar* mug?-šim	⌜x⌝ Gubar . . . šim

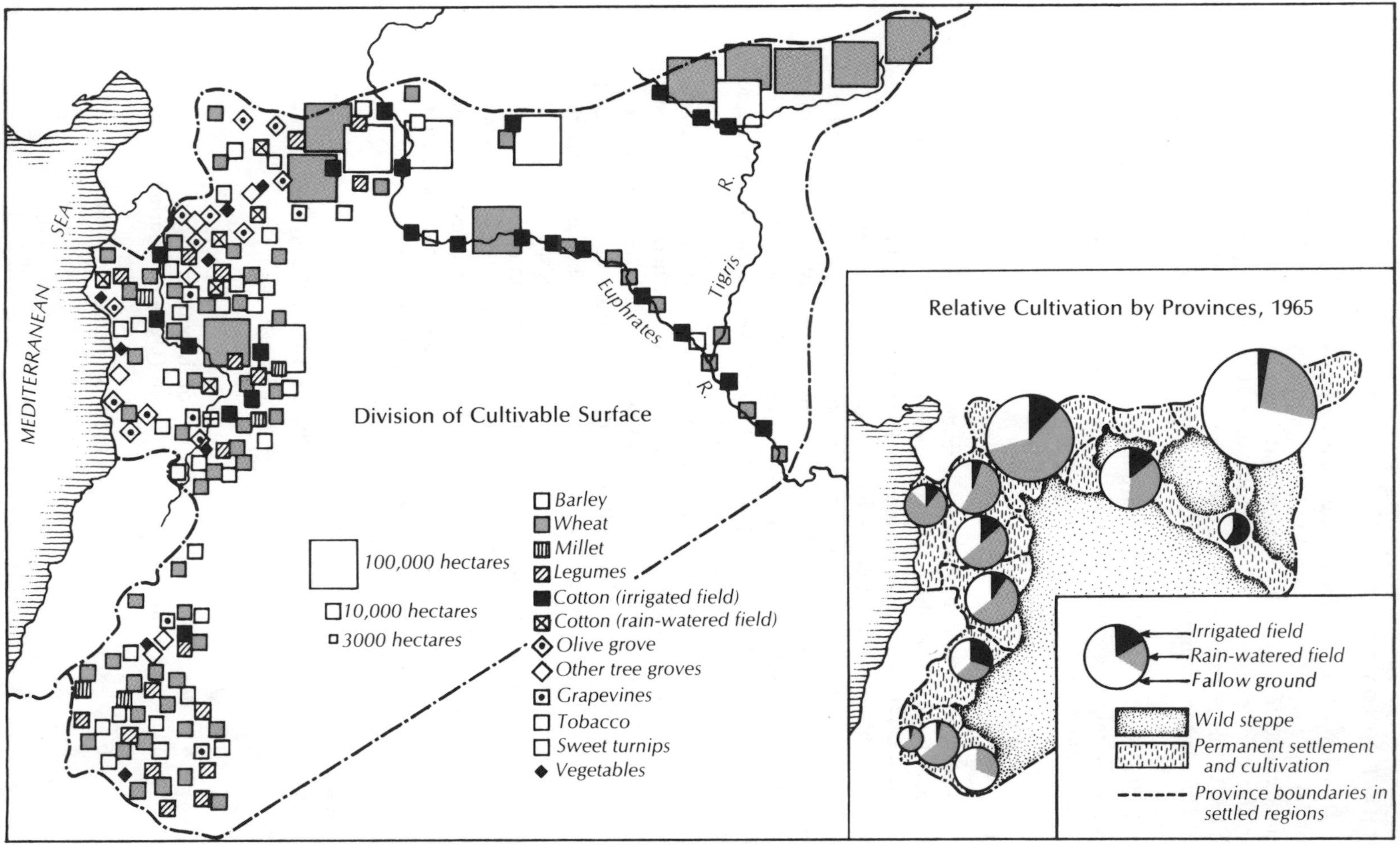

Figure VII, 1 Geography of the agricultural crops of present-day Syria (from E. Wirth, *Syrien*)

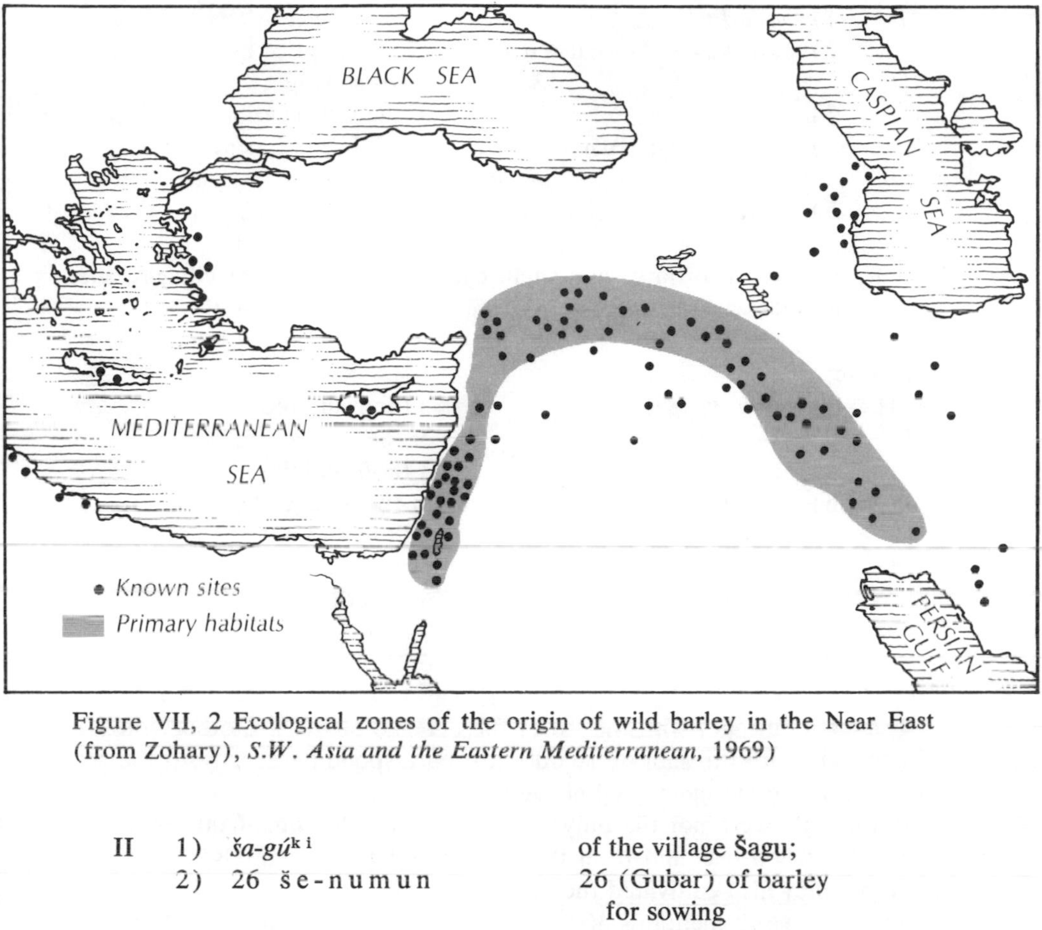

Figure VII, 2 Ecological zones of the origin of wild barley in the Near East (from Zohary), *S.W. Asia and the Eastern Mediterranean,* 1969)

II	1)	*ša-gú*^{ki}	of the village Šagu;
	2)	26 še-numun	26 (Gubar) of barley for sowing
	3)	*za-ba-tù*^{ki}	of the village Zabatu;
	4)	30 še-numun	30 (Gubar) of barley for sowing
	5)	30 še KAxX-^{d}mul	30 (Gubar) of barley . . .
	6)	*ur-lum*^{ki}	of the village Urlum;
	7)	70 še-numun	70 (Gubar) of barley for sowing
III	1)	1 *m*[*i*] 26 [ ]^{d}mul	126 [Gubar] . . .
	2)	*i-ti-*^{d}*'à-da*	for Iti-Hada;
	3)	20 še-numun	20 (Gubar) of barley for sowing
	4)	*gú-wa-lu*^{ki}	of the village Guwalu;
	5)	20 še-numun	20 (Gubar) of barley for sowing

IV	1)	*a-a-da*ki	of the village A'ada;
	2)	20 lá-3 še-numun	17 (Gubar) of barley for sowing
	3)	*gi-du*ki	of the village Gidu;
	4)	15 še-numun	15 Gubar of barley for sowing
	5)	*ì-zu*ki	of the village Izu;

After a short list of large and small cattle present in these villages, the tablet continues with the indication of the agricultural acreage:

reverse

II	2)	3 *li ki*	3 thousand iku
	3)	*ša-gu*ki	of the village Šagu;
	4)	3 *li ki*	3 thousand iku
	5)	*da-gu*ki	of the village Dagu;
	6)	1 *li ki*	a thousand iku
	7)	*a-a-da*ki	of the village A'ada.
	8)	*gi-du*ki	and Gidu
	9)	7 *mi ki*	7 hundred iku
	10)	*gú-wa-lu*ki	of the village Guwalu.

The text continues with the list of the acreage of the five other villages to conclude with the sum of 16,000 iku, corresponding exactly to the 57 kilometers squared mentioned above.[4]

But cereals were not the only crops raised by the inhabitants of Ebla. From the ration lists and from the agricultural texts themselves it is evident that they also cultivated the vine.

Thus text 1847 mentions 300 tuns of wine which the man in charge of viticulture consigned to the governor of the kingdom. Though this is a sporadic bit of information, one may assume that, like the cereals, the vintage must have been abundant.

In the third position belongs the cultivation of olives for the production of olive oil. TM.76.G.281 registers the casks of olive oil delivered by eight villages; it specifies 341 casks of oil described as "of the hillside."[5] Text TM.75.G.1767 records the acreage and the number of olive trees thereon. These olive groves are located in various villages, and the scope of the text is to indicate those charged with their care:

obverse

I	1)	2 *li* 2 *mi* 60 gána-kešdaki	2,260 iku of cultivated ground
	2)	1 *li* giš-ì-giš	1,000 olive trees
	3)	lú-al-KU	in charge of

II	1)	*zú-ba-lum*	Zubalum
	2)	lú-*ḫu-ba-ra*	the man of Ḫubara
	3)	šu-ba₄-ti	has received;
	4)	1 *li* 1 *mi* gána-kešda[ki]	1,100 iku of cultivated ground
	5)	5 *mi* giš-ì-giš	500 olive trees
	6)	al-KU	in charge of
III	1)	*ip-ṭù-*⌜*la*⌝	Ipṭula
	2)	lú-*en-na-il*	the man of Enna-Il
	3)	šu-ba₄-ti	has received;
	4)	6 *mi* gána-kešda[ki]	600 iku of cultivated ground,
	5)	5 *mi* giš-ì-giš dil-dil	500 olive trees . . .
IV	1)	ga-sa[ki]	from the town of Gasa.

Then follow the areas of various other villages which have Gasa as the chief town, without, however, any indications of the olive trees. The oil of Ebla was surely much sought after if it constitutes an article of export, as witnessed by several texts, of which one may be quoted:

obverse

I	1)	3 sìla ì-giš-du₁₀	3 sila of excellent oil
	2)	*ḫa-ra-yà*	Ḫara-Ya
	3)	šu-ba₄-ti	has received
	4)	4 sìla i-giš-du₁₀	4 sila of excellent oil
	5)	*ší-in*	for
	6)	*du-bù-ḫu-ma-lik*	Dubuḫu-Malik;
II	1)	2 sìla	2 sila
	2)	*ra-é-ak*[ki]	(for the city of) Raeak
	3)	2 sìla	2 sila
	4)	*ì-mar*[ki]	(for the city of) Emar,
	5)	2 sìla	2 sila
	6)	*tù-ub*[ki]	(for the city of) Tub,
	7)	1 sìla	1 sila
	8)	*bur-ma-an*[ki]	(for the city of) Burman,

reverse

I	1)	1 sìla	1 sila
	2)	*gàr-mu*[ki]	(for the city of) Garmu,
	3)	1 sìla	1 sila
	4)	*lum-na-nu*[ki]	(for the city of) Lumnanu,
	5)	1 sìla	1 sila
	6)	*i-*NE*-bu-ni*[ki]	(for the city of) Inebuni,

II	1)	1 sìla	1 sila
	2)	*gú-da-da-núm*^{ki}	(for the city of) Gudadanum,
	3)	2 sìla	2 sila
	4)	*ur-sá-um*^{ki}	(for the city of) Ursa'um.[6]

Not all of the nine cities mentioned here are identifiable, but the appearance among them of Emar, present-day Meskene on the Euphrates, suggests that Ebla's olive oil reached other kingdoms.

In addition to the growing of cereals, grapes, and olives, which doubtless form the nucleus of the agricultural wealth of Ebla's kingdom, the texts point to the existence of a very diversified production.

Malt, for instance, was intensely cultivated for brewing beer, surely the most common drink at Ebla as well as in the entire ancient Near East. Among the fruits figure the fig and the pomegranate, together with other species which have not yet been identified.

From this brief catalogue it appears that the crops raised are those proper to the Mediterranean regions. This accords with the westward extension of its kingdom, nor does the almost complete lack of date palms, so characteristic of the Mesopotamian belt, engender surprise.

This discussion would be incomplete without mention of plants raised for industrial purposes, such as the flax used by the highly developed textile industry of Ebla; linen was doubtless the number one article of export.

1.2. CATTLE BREEDING

When speaking of the royal table in Chapter V and of the old calendar[7] in Chapter VI, we had occasion to mention quantities of small cattle. What is more, Ebla had need for small cattle, especially sheep, not only to feed its population, but also for the wool, a basic element of the textile industry.

The breeding of cattle, whether large or small, was intensely developed throughout the kingdom and the figures given by the texts are truly impressive. In three homogeneous texts, for example, the numbers of sheep destined as offerings to the gods and for other purposes are 10,796, 12,354, and 36,892.[8]

Even more impressive are the figures gathered from those tablets dealing with the period inspection of cattle in the kingdom. TM.75.G.1846 registers 79,300 sheep of the king of Ebla, while TM.75.G.1582 records more than 80,000 sheep.[9]

The following tablet records the number of sheep counted during the inspection carried out in the month of Iši as 72,240.

obverse				
I	1)	[2] *rí-ba*$_x$ 2 *li-im* 1 *mi-at* 60 udu-udu igi-du$_8$	1)	22,160 sheep inspected,
II	1)	[3] *rí-ba*$_x$ 1 *li-im* 1 *mi-at* 40 sila$_4$-sila$_4$	1)	31,140 lambs
	2)	3 *li-im* udu-udu	2)	3,000 sheep
	3)	šu-du$_8$	3)	tax
III	1)	kur^{ki}	1)	of the mountain town
	2)	*i-ḫuš-zi-nu*	2)	Iḫušzinu,
	3)	2 *mi-at* udu-udu-niga	3)	200 fat sheep
	4)	2 *mi-at* udu-udu	4)	200 sheep
	5)	PA.USAN PA.USAN	5)	superin-tendent . . .
IV	1)	1 *mi-at* 50 udu-udu	1)	150 sheep
	2)	*iš-tá-al*	2)	Išta'al,
	3)	1 *mi-at* 50 udu-udu	3)	150 sheep
reverse				
I	1)	mu-túm	1)	mutum taxes
	2)	1 *rí-ba*$_x$ 3 *li-im* 2 *mi-at* udu-udu igi-du$_8$	2)	13,200 sheep inspected,
	3)	*dar-mi-a*	3)	Darmia,
II	1)	1 *li-im* 6 *mi-at* 10 udu-udu	1)	1,610 sheep
	2)	PA.USAN PA.USAN	2)	superin-tendent . . .
	3)	4 *mi-at* 30 udu-udu	3)	430 sheep
	4)	GIBIL.ZA-*il*	4)	GIBIL.ZA-*il,*
III	1)	en	1)	for the king
	2)	2 mu	2)	second year,
IV	1)	an-šè-gú 7 *rí-ba*$_x$ 2 *li-im* 2 *mi-at* 40 udu-udu igi-du$_8$	1)	total: 72,240 sheep inspected,
	2)	[it] u *i-ší*	2)	month of Iši.

This text[10] proves all the more interesting when mentioning Iḫušzinu and Darmia, two provincial governors of the kingdom,[11] whose administrative role becomes so evident. Besides sheep, rams, and ewes, it explicitly lists 31,140 lambs, thus giving a good idea of the amount of sheep breeding practiced.

Other tablets are more explicit in distinguishing various species of small livestock; the following records goats and pigs alongside the sheep:

16 u_8	16 sheep
14 udu-nita	14 rams
23 megida	23 pigs
81 ùz-sal máš-sal máš-nita ti-la	81 she-goats with he-goats and kids.[12]

For the destination of the small livestock, see the Table on p. 91, where for 12,354 sheep there are seven precise assignments corresponding to their current uses.

But if the small livestock is preponderant, the large cattle are surely not lacking; text TM.75.G.2033, which lists 417 bull calves, proves the existence of large herds of oxen. Another tablet mentions 273 cattle coming from various districts of the kingdom.[13]

Greater numbers of large livestock are documented as imports, such as that from the city Luatim:

1 *li-im* 3 *mi-at* gu_4-gu_4	1,300 oxen
en	of the king,
gàr-ra	(delivered by) Garra
lu-a-tim^{ki}	of the city Luatim.[14]

Another document yields information about the delivery of heads of large cattle to the palace from some villages situated around Ebla:

1 áb	1 cow
ri-du^{ki}	from the village Ridu,
2 áb	2 cows
za-ba-tù^{ki}	from the village Zabatu,
2 gu_4 2 áb	2 oxen, 2 cows
ur-lum^{ki}	from the village Urlum,
1 gu_4	1 ox
gú-wa-lu^{ki}	from the village Guwalu,
2 áb	2 cows
ni-zi-mu^{ki}	from the village Nizimu,
2 gu_4	2 oxen
da-'à-wa^{ki}	from the village Da'awa,
2 gu_4 [ ] áb	2 oxen [ ] cows
zu-ra-mu^{ki}	from the village Zuramu.[15]

Some bovids were destined for slaughter or as offerings to the gods, but for the most part they served for work in the fields, an activity which, curiously enough, has found no documentation in the archives. Equally surprising is the lack of references to beasts of burden. The tablets frequently talk about messengers traversing the whole Near East and we know they traveled on carts,[16] but thus far no mention of beasts of burden has come to our knowledge.

1.3. INDUSTRY

The third source of wealth for the state of Ebla was the industry which may be considered the chief activity of this newly discovered people. To be sure, it was more a question of transforming raw materials imported from outside the country, but once exported through the complex commercial network, these transformed materials formed the true wealth of Ebla.

The textile industry must be mentioned first. This consisted of working the wool and the flax to produce fabrics in the state spinning mills. Since the most significant texts will be quoted in connection with commerce (section 4), it will suffice here to cite some brief pieces which will give an idea of the extraordinary production of cloths in Ebla:

2 *li-im* 4 *mi-at* 50 lá-3 túg-túg	2,447 fabrics;
30 *é-da-um*-túg-2	30 Edaum fabrics of second quality,
2 *mi-at* 30 lá-3 íb-túg-ša$_6$-dar	227 Ib fabrics of top quality and multicolored;
61 íb-túg-dar	61 multicolored Ib fabrics
al-gál	present
é-síg	in the spinning mill.

This brief but clear inventory tablet confirms the existence in the city of a spinning mill[17] called "house of wool," where materials of various colors and qualities were produced. Very similar to the preceding is this tablet, which reports more substantial quantities of fabrics:

5 *li* 8 *mi* 91 túg-túg	5,891 fabrics;
70 lá-1 *é-da-um*-túg-2	69 Edaum fabrics of second quality;
4 *mi-at* 80 íb-túg-ša$_6$-dar	480 fabrics of top quality and multicolored;
2 *li* 2 *mi* 34 íb-túg-dar al-gál	2,234 Ib fabrics, multicolored, present.[18]

The different quantities documented in the examples previously cited confirm the character of simple inventory of the material existing at a given moment, which does not mean to include the entire production or to detail all the kinds of cloth manufactured in Ebla.

As a matter of fact, the series of kinds of cloth that Ebla exported to all the world is much more variegated, and one must note with satisfaction that medieval and contemporary Syria has kept alive a millennia-old tradition.

Among the kinds of material produced in Ebla is damask. Linen or woolen fabrics intertwined with threads of gold, these have become so famous that they take their name from the present capital of Syria, Damascus. This tradition is ancient indeed, and though its populations have changed, Syria has faithfully preserved and transmitted for several millennia some techniques of workmanship that may have originated with Ebla.

Though the textile industry employed the largest percentage of workers, it was not the only enterprise at Ebla. The metal industry was no less impressive. When a tiny tablet reads "1,740 *ma-na* guškin al-gál," that is, "1,740 minas of gold present" (= circa 870 kilograms),[19] then one begins to form an idea of Ebla's wealth and the modernity of its concepts.

The gold was not only crafted and reexported but also served, as will be shown presently, as a commodity of international exchange. The first notice of this practice in the third millennium comes from these archives.

The texts mention not only enormous quantities of gold and numberless precious objects made from this metal but also indicate that the Eblaites appreciated diverse kinds of gold, more or less pure, which we today classify by carats. An example may be cited from TM.75.G.1479:

an-še-gú 1 *mi* 22 *ma-na* guškin-4	total: 122 minas of gold at 4
1 *li* 3 *mi* 36 *ma-na* 5 guškin 1½	1,136 minas and 5 shekels of gold at 1½,
bù-la-ù	Bulau.[20]

It is still too early to determine the grade of purification of the gold and the signification of "at 4" and "one and a half," but it would appear that carats are intended.[21]

Gold was the most precious metal, but silver was the most common among the precious metals; tons of it were on hand in Ebla. The reader may well suspect exaggeration, but the texts speak for themselves. After its defeat Mari had to pay Ebla tribute amounting to 2,193 minas of silver and 134 minas and 26 shekels of gold, which correspond to a ton of silver and 60 kilograms of gold.[22] Someone might ironically reply that this is typical Oriental rhetoric, but similar data crop up in economic texts where falsification cannot readily be admitted.

Moreover, Ebla must have been very rich in silver if it could afford "annual outlays" approaching tons as may be gathered from TM.75.G.1841 dealing with three years of King Ebrium's reign:[23]

3 *li-im* 7 *mi-at* 96 *ma-na* 10 (gín) kù:babbar	3,796 minas and 10 shekels of silver
è	outlay
3 mu	of the third year;
1 *li-im* 7 *mi-at* 80 *ma-na* 50 (gín) kù:babbar	1,780 minas and 50 shekels of silver
2 mu	(outlay) of the second year;
2 *li* 6 *mi* 36 *ma-na* kù:babbar	2,636 minas of silver
wa	and
1 *mi-at* 1 *ma-na* kù:babbar	101 minas of silver
kaskal	(for) the voyage;
10 *ma-na* kù:babbar	10 minas of silver
bar-za-ma-ù	(for) Barzamau;
6 *ma-na* kù:babbar	6 minas of silver
du-bù-ḫu-^{d}*'à-da*	(for) Dubuḫu-Hada
an-šè-gú 2 *li* 8 *mi-at* 6 *ma-na* kù:babbar	Sum: 2,806 minas of silver
è	outlay
1 mu	of the first year.
šu-nigín 8 *li* 3 *mi* 90 lá-1 kù:babbar	Total: 8,389 minas of silver.

On the strength of this text alone, Ebla's outlays in just three years exceeded four tons of silver subdivided thus:

3rd year	3,796 minas 10 shekels	=	circa 2,000 kg.
2nd year	1,780 minas 50 shekels	=	circa 900 kg.
1st year	2,806 minas	=	circa 1,400 kg.

We do not know if the text furnishes information about all the outlays of silver by the state of Ebla or whether it treats of some specific budgets of only one department, but even then the wealth of this state exceeds all expectations. The same text goes on to list the expenditures of gold for six years of the reign, and it will serve a purpose to cite the second part of the document so that a comparison of the two outlays may permit a verification of how much the Eblaites appreciated gold:[24]

10 lá-1 *ma-na* 30 (gín) guškin	9 minas and 30 shekels of gold (at 4)
10 lá-1 *ma-na* 10 (gín) guškin-2½	9 minas and 10 shekels of gold at 2½,
è	outlay
6 mu	of the sixth year;
30 *ma-na* guškin-4	30 minas of gold at 4,

⌜65 *ma*⌝*-na*	65 minas and
50 (gín) guškin	50 shekels of gold (at 2½),
5 mu	(outlay) of the fifth year;
1 *ma-na*	1 mina and
5 (gín) guškin-4	5 shekels of gold at 4,
70 lá-1 *ma-na*	69 minas and
ša-pi guškin-2½	40 shekels of gold at 2½
4 mu	(outlay) of the fourth year,
1 *ma-na*	1 mina and
52 (gín) guškin-4	52 shekels of gold at 4,
46 *ma-na*	46 minas and
35 (gín) guškin	35 shekels of gold (at 2½),
3 mu	(outlay) of the third year;
56 *ma-na*	56 minas and
25 (gín) guškin-4	25 shekels of gold at 4,
1 *mi-at* 64 *ma-na*	164 minas and
30 (gín) guškin-2½	30 shekels of gold at 2½,
è	outlay
2 mu	of the second year;
an-šè-gú 96 *ma-na*	sum: 96 minas and
5 (gín) guškin-4	5 shekels of gold at 4,
4 *mi* 5 *ma-na ša-pi*	405 minas and
7 (gín) guškin-2½	47 shekels of gold at 2½,
è	outlay.

From this text it appears that the outlays of silver with respect to gold are, for the same stretch of time, 16 times superior; this shows that gold was certainly considered more valuable than silver. This tablet is also important for revealing a degree of purity of gold unknown till now, namely, 2½.

Among the other precious metals, copper, tin, lead, and bronze also figure. Text 1656 mentions 209 minas of bronze received by the "metal worker."[25]

The third type of industry deals with precious stones. Two kinds deserve attention, as they are frequently encountered in the texts: carnelian and lapis lazuli. The discovery at Ebla of an undressed block of lapis lazuli brings to mind TM.75.G.1599 which reads:

obverse

I	1)	1 *ma-na* 10 (gín) za:gìn	1 mina and 10 shekels of lapis lazuli
	2)	*a-du-lum*	Adulum
	3)	nagar	the smith
	4)	šu-ba$_4$-ti	has received;

II	1)	13½ (gín) za:gìn	13 and a half shekels of lapis lazuli
	2)	*a-bù-ma-lik*	Abu-Malik
	3)	šu-ba_4-ti	has received.

The very small quantities received by the two smiths underline how precious must have been this stone which, according to current opinion, was imported from Afghanistan.

Before concluding this discussion, it may be instructive to cite a text dealing with silver and gold and their utilization. Only thus will a clearer idea of the Eblaites and their activities take shape. As the final clause reveals, 56 minas and 50 shekels of silver were used as purchase and sale, exchange, donation, and taxes of governors.[26]

obv.

I	1)	8 *ma-na* kù:babbar	8 minas of silver
	2)	UNKEN-aka	to make
	3)	an-dùl	a statue;
	4)	15 *ma-na* kù:babbar	15 minas of silver
	5)	šu-bala-aka	to be converted
	6)	3 *ma-na* guškin	into 3 minas of gold
	7)	UNKEN-aka	to make
II	1)	an-dùl	a statue,
	2)	ni-du_8	a gift
	3)	en	of the king
	4)	é	for the temple
	5)	^{d}*'à-da*	of Hada;
	6)	1 *ma-na* kù:babbar	1 mina of silver
	7)	šu-bala-aka	to be converted
	8)	6 2-NI gín-dilmun guškin	into 6 and ⅔ shekels of gold
	9)	2 *gú-li-lum*	(for) two bracelets
III	1)	^{d}*ku-ra*	of the god Kura,
	2)	5 3-NI gín-dilmun guškin	(and) into 5 and ⅓ shekels of gold
	3)	UNKEN-aka	to make
	4)	gír-gír-dingir	daggers of the divinity;

	5)	1 *ma-na ša-pi* gín-dilmun kù:babbar	1 mina and 40 shekels of silver
	6)	ní-šam$_x$	price
	7)	1 *mi-at* na$_4$:síg-ša$_6$	of 100 "threads" of fine wool
	8)	6 gín-dilmun kù:babbar	6 shekels of silver
IV	1)	šu-bala-aka	to be converted
	2)	3 gín-dilmun MI+ŠITA$_x$-gul za:gìn-si$_4$-si$_4$	into 2 shekels of . . . clear reddish lapis lazuli;
	3)	4 *ma-na* kù:babbar	4 minas of silver
	4)	nì-šam$_x$	price
	5)	10 zára-túg	of 10 Zar fabrics
		2 aktum-túg	2 Aktum fabrics
		2 íb+3-babbar-túg	of white Ib,
		1 nì-lá-sag	and 10 foulards;
	6)	10 gín-dilmun kù:babbar	10 shekels of silver,
	7)	nì-šam$_x$	price
V	1)	udu:nita:ša$_6$	of excellent rams
	2)	*áš-ti*	from
	3)	*kab-lu$_5$-ul*^{ki}	the city of Kablul;
	4)	4 *ma-na* 50 gín-dilmun kù:babbar	4 minas and 50 shekels of silver
	5)	ní-šam$_x$	price
	6)	1 *mi-at* 45 sal-túg	of 145 fine fabrics
	7)	*iš$_x$-ki*	for
	8)	*ìr-ra-ku*^{ki}	the city of Irraku;
VI	1)	2(+x) *ma-na* 7 gín-dilmun kù:babbar	2(+x) minas and 7 shekels of silver,

	2)	ní-šam$_x$	price
	3)	1 gír-mar-tu guškin-ša$_6$	of one Martu dagger of fine gold;
	4)	ku$_5$ 6 gín-dilmun kù:babbar	36 shekels of silver
	5)	UNKEN-aka	to make
	6)	^{giš}ban-^{giš}ban	bows
	7)	guruš-guruš	of the officials;
VII	1)	5 gín-dilmun kù-babbar	5 shekels of silver
	2)	kešda	"alloy"
	3)	gír-mar-tu zú-^{d}a-ama	of point of Martu dagger of A'ama
	4)	nin-uš-ḫu	Ninušḫu
	5)	šu-ba$_4$-ti	has received
	6)	3 gín-dilmun kù:babbar	3 shekels of silver;
	7)	1 šu ba$_4$-ti	first receipt
	8)	3 gín-dilmun kù:babbar	3 shekels of silver;
VIII	1)	2 šu ba$_4$-ti	second receipt
	2)	1 gín-dilmun kù:babbar	one shekel of silver;
	3)	3 šu ba$_4$ti	third receipt
	4)	*a-na-ma-lik*	Ana-Malik
	5)	šu-ba$_4$-ti	has received
	6)	5 gín-dilmun kù:babbar	5 shekels of silver;
	7)	*íl-tá-gàr*	Iltagar
	8)	lú *i-gi*	the man of Tgi.

reverse

I	1)	šu ba$_4$-ti	has received
	2)	⌜3⌝gín-dilmun kù:babbar	3 shekels of silver;
	3)	2 BU.DI	2 Budi pins
	4)	⌜x⌝-ti	. . . -ti
	5)	ÉxPAP	house . . .

	6)	ama	the mother
	7)	*i-⌜ti⌝-da-ši-⌜in⌝*	of Iti-Dašin,
	8)	15 *ma-na* kù:babbar	15 minas of silver
	9)	1 nì-gú	1 Nigu object
II	1)	al-gál	present
	2)	é	in the palace
	3)	en	of the king;
	4)	5 *ma-na* kù:babbar	5 minas of silver
	5)	šu-bala-aka	to be converted
	6)	ku_5 guškin	into 30 shekels of gold
	7)	2 *gú-li-lum*	for 2 bracelets
	8)	*zàr-i-iq-da-mu*	of Zariq-Damu;
III	1)	gur_8 4 gín-dilmun guškin	24 shekels of gold
	2)	giš-PI-lá	for . . .
	3)	*ir_x-kab-du-lum*	of Irkab-Dulum;
			———
			———
IV	1)	an-šè-gú 56 *ma-na* 50 gín- -dilmun kù:babbar	total: 56 minas, 50 shekels of silver;
	2)	dub-gar	tablet concerning
	3)	nì-$šam_x$	purchase sale,
	4)	šu-bala-aka	exchange,
	5)	nì-ba	gift
	6)	mul	for the divinity;
	7)	mu-túm	tax
V	1)	lugal-lugal	of the governors,
	2)	2 mu	second year,
	3)	itu M A*xganatenû*-sag	month: M Axganatenû-sag.

1.4. ALLOYS OF METALS: AN EXAMPLE OF ADVANCED TECHNOLOGY

Among the texts speaking specifically about metals, those that deal with the state's distribution of quantities of copper, tin, and gold for fusion into the alloys needed to make various objects deserve special attention. Text TM.75.G.2505, written during the reign of Ebrium, and text

TM.75.G.2429 (first part of the reign), 1860 and 1918, from the reign of his son Ibbi-Sipiš, furnish the most ample and detailed information. The data relative to the shipment of the metals are always given according to this formula:

> so many shekels of tin to fuse with so many shekels of copper[27] to obtain so many x objects for such and such a city.

Reasons of space preclude a discussion of the numerous operations recorded; instead we give a table showing all the data concerning the bronze alloys mentioned in the four tablets. It focuses attention on the percentage of tin, which is costlier than copper, used for the manufacture of various objects grouped by categories.

Table VII, 1

Percentages of Tin in the Bronze Alloys

Type of objects	*Percentages of tin* TM.75. G.2505	TM.75. G.2429	TM.75. G.1860	TM.75. G.1918
A. Vases				
vases "anzam"	9.09			
vases "zakirratum"		10.00		
B. Art objects				
heads of statues		10.00		
C. Arms				
arms "šita"	10.00			
small axes			9.50	
			10.80	
lances	13.46			
maces			7.21	
			7.03	
"martu" daggers	11.11	12.69	10.52	12.50
D. Utensils				
"nails" (chisels?)			11.85	
			15.09	
			15.00	
"teeth" (plowshares?)				13.97
				13.33
maces (mallets?)		12.48		
"green eyes"			16.60	
plaques "dub"				13.33
razors	16.66	20.00	14.28	
pins ("budi")				14.28
wagon tongues	12.50			
hoes			13.04	

By obtaining an average percentage of the words occurring more than once in the same or several texts, we can at this point report by means of a graph the quantities of tin used as an alloy of copper. This graph shows the data relative to the physical characteristics of the different bronze alloys (Fig. VII, 3).

The gradual adding of tin to copper effects a series of physical changes in the bronze that makes the resultant alloy more suitable for the functions of the object to be made. When the tin content is increased the alloy becomes harder and harder and the color of the alloy changes; less than 5 percent of tin results in copper-red which, however, becomes golden-yellow when the tin reaches between 5 and 10 percent, and when the percentage hits 20 the alloy becomes pale yellow. So long as the content of tin remains under 12 percent, the alloy assumes the form of a "solid solution" and is hence workable when cold (malleable alloys). When the tin content rises to 12 to 20 percent, the bronze can be worked only when heated to between 590 and 790 degrees centigrade. Bronze with only 4 to 11 percent of tin is extremely fluid and hence is used for fusing statues, etc. (foundry bronze) because it easily fills all the cavities of the mold.

A look at Fig. VII, 3 reveals that these characteristics of bronze alloys were perfectly understood at Ebla.

The categories A, B, and C shown in Table VII, 1 belong to the foundry alloys, namely, those used for vases, art objects and, with the exception of the "martu" daggers, arms. All the utensils (category D), on the other hand, are made of hard alloys.

For the vases a malleable alloy was needed to permit their being worked in a cold state while the objects were being hammered. The heads of statues similarly required fluid alloys (less than 11 percent of tin) if they were to conform to real life, and the vases and other art objects did not necessitate particularly hard alloys.

What is at first surprising is to find the position of arms on the chart among the malleable alloys. But, then again, this does not seem unreasonable if the weapons were intended more for ceremonial use than for war; for example, the *šita*$_x$ arms, well known as an attribute of the gods in the iconographic repertory; the axes which were the symbol of the senior members of the government, and the ax of the "god" in wood.

In view of their function, the "martu" daggers were made of a harder metal, and the utensils without exception were made of an alloy with a high tin content. This is obviously true of razors which, if they were to be effective in removing the beard, had to be made of a very hard alloy.

These facts give some idea of the level of civilization reached at Ebla in the "Early Bronze" period. The development of a civilization corresponds to the development of its technology insofar as the technology demonstrates the capacity of its members to meet their needs in their given am-

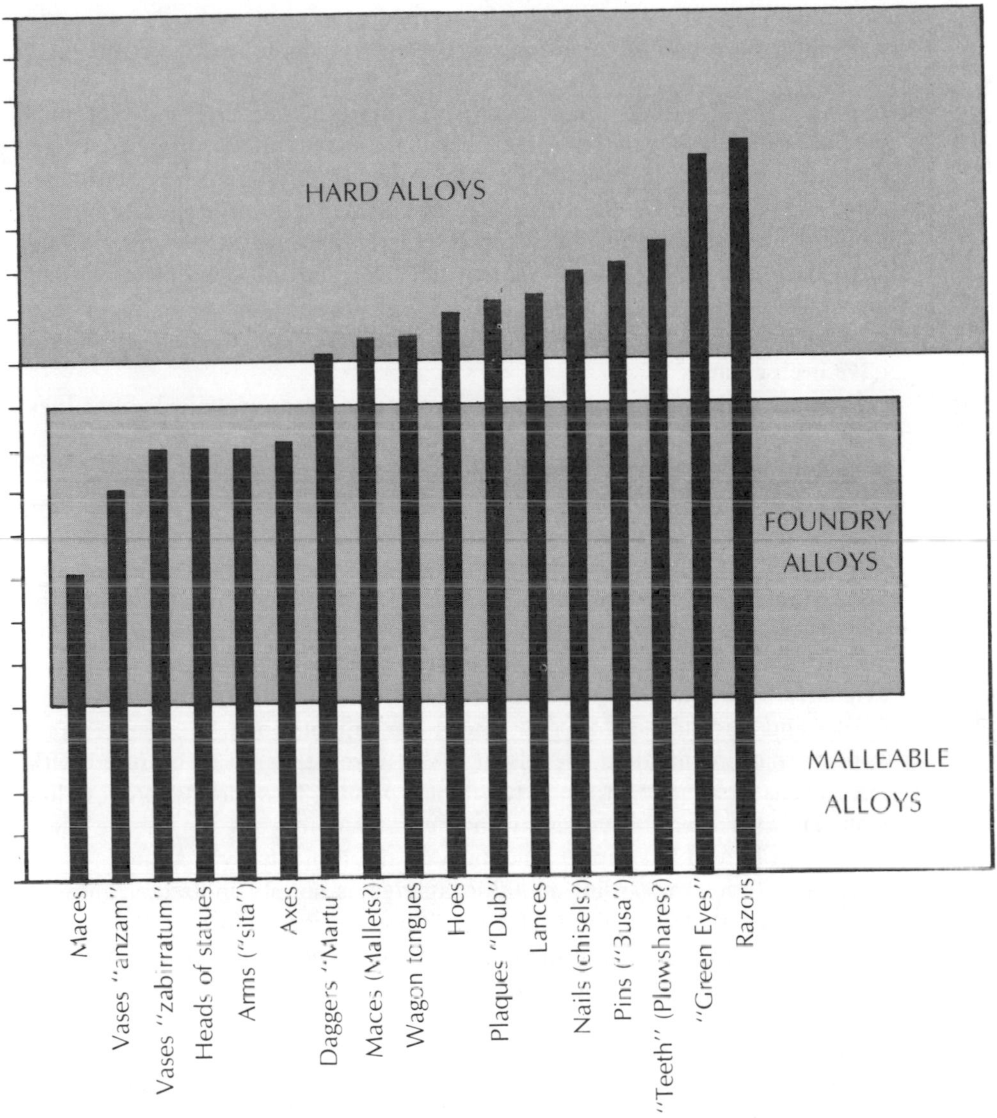

Figure VII, 3 Percentages of tin in relation to the physical characteristics of the bronze alloys

bience once they have defined them with a certain precision. Once these needs were spelled out, they overcame the technical difficulties in the way. At Ebla the difficulties of the environment were solved admirably.

We have seen that in one case particular hardness and resistance were not needed in a metallurgical product. With relative ease this condition was met by adding just a small quantity of tin to the alloy, thus guaranteeing a good fusion suited for molds, easy working of the unheated alloy, and a lower cost of the alloy. But when greater hardness and resistance were required of the bronze, the real difficulties began. The first and most immediate difficulty stems from the need to discover that the greater concentration of tin with the copper would result in a different physical characteristic of the alloy. Once this was established, the processes of fusion would have become more difficult especially because the casting would have been less suited to the molds. The working of the objects would have always had to be done at high temperatures and, finally—not a negligible factor—the cost of the alloy with the high tin content would have been greater.

Proof is at hand that the Eblaites overcame these technical difficulties and succeeded in turning out sets of utensils in hard metals that were indispensable for their process of economic and social growth.

In addition to the bronze alloys, text TM.75.G.1860 contains two passages—the first is an act of purchase and sale and the second an act of shipment of metals—that witness the existence of the alloy of silver and gold. It relates that one mina and ten shekels of gold are needed to obtain one mina and eighteen shekels of gold for making one bracelet. This means that an x quantity of gold served to obtain a greater y quantity, evidently by the addition of another metal that would result in an alloy harder and less ductile than gold and more suitable for a bracelet. It also appears that one hundred shekels of silver were delivered to be fused with ten shekels of gold to produce two lance points. This clearly proves that Ebla knew of a gold-silver alloy in the ratio of one to ten, hence electrum, well known later and particularly in the Minoan civilization.

These citations regarding metallic amalgams supply indirectly another string of data that are quite useful for filling out the picture of Ebla's material culture. By specifying the quantities of elements necessary for forming the alloys, the texts also indicate in shekels the weights of the individual objects which often help to identify the objects whose identification cannot be established on philological grounds alone.

The outline is interesting because the weights listed contribute to the definition of objects rarely found in archaeological contexts. For instance, we learned that the vase "a n z a m" was much larger than the vase *"zakirratum";* that there were two distinct kinds of "martu" daggers, one of which was at least twice as heavy as the other. The same pertains for razors. The importance of the weight data is further illustrated by the light weight of the so-called "budi" object which, with the help of the citation of another text, has served to understand a gloss.

The following chart summarizes the weights obtained from the four texts:

Table VII, 2

Summary Outline of Unitary Weights of the Bronze Objects

Objects	*Weight in shekels* TM.75. G.2505	TM.75. G.2429	TM.75. G.1860	TM.75. G.1918
A. Vases				
vases "anzam"	82.5			
vases "zakirratum"		20.0		
B. Art objects				
heads of statues		60.0		
C. Arms				
arms "šita"	120.0			
smaller axes			24.6	
			22.1	
lances	20.8			
maces			120.2	
			119.4	
"martu" daggers	40.5	40.0	19.0	40.0
	20.8	20.0	18.6	
	20.2		20.8	
D. Utensils				
"nails" (chisels?)			10.3	
			10.6	
			10.0	
"teeth" (plowshares?)			30.0	23.2
				30.0
maces (mallets?)		745.0		
"green eyes"			36.0	
plaques "dub"				10.0
razors	6.0	12.5	14.0	
pins ("budi")				1.2
wagon tongues	40.0			
hoes			23.0	

It might be helpful here to translate the average weights of the objects from ancient shekels into the modern decimal metrical system, bearing in mind that the so-called light shekels exactly correspond to 8.37 grams.

Table VII, 3

Mean Weight Measures of the Bronze Objects

	Shekels	*Grams*
Pin	1.2	10.0
Small razor	6.0	50.2
Plaque "dub"	10.0	83.7
Nail (chisel?)	10.3	86.2
Large razor	13.2	110.4
Light "martu" dagger	19.9	166.5
Vase "zakirratum"	20.0	167.4
Lance head	20.8	174.0
Hoe	23.0	192.5
Small ax	23.3	195.0
"Tooth" (plowshare?)	27.7	231.8
"Green eye"	36.0	301.3
Wagon tongue	40.0	334.8
Heavy "martu" dagger	40.1	335.6
Head of statue	60.0	502.2
Vase "anzam"	82.5	690.5
Mace head	119.8	1002.7
Weapon "šita"	120.0	1004.4
Club (mallet?)	745.0	6235.6

One should not overlook the fact the figures obtained do not correspond to the real weights of the object found in the archaeological levels. Prescinding from the obvious loss of metal due to oxidization, the weight of an object must have been less than that of the metal needed to make it either because of the loss during the smelting process or during the course of shaping the object.

Text TM.75.G.1860 handsomely illustrates this point; two of its passages deal with the smelting of axes:

> 40 shekels of tin to fuse with 5 minas and 30 shekels of copper to make 15 small axes, each weighing 20 shekels.
>
> 42 shekels of tin to fuse with 6 minas and 40 shekels of copper to make 20 small axes, each weighing 20 shekels.

As can be seen on the chart and, if one wishes, directly deduced from the passages cited, in the first text the weight of each ax would be 24.6 shekels instead of 20, and in the second passage 22.1 shekels. The foreseen weight of 20 shekels evidently took into account the loss of metal during the process of smelting and subsequent manufacture. The average percentage of losses, some 16.9 percent, should not be considered excessive; while admitting that a minimal amount was lost in smelting, one should remember that the manufacture of the axes was done, as shown by the arrangement of such objects among the foundry alloys (Fig. VII, 3), by pouring the molten metal into mono- or bi-valve molds. Such molds frequently recovered in Near Eastern excavations, not permitting a perfect sealing, created a series of protuberances that had to be subsequently removed by refining the product. From this it follows that for an approximately correct calculation of the weight of the object containing from 4 to 11 percent of tin (foundry bronze), one must subtract between 15 and 20 percent from the estimated weight of the component elements.

These data regarding the percentage of tin used in the alloys of bronze and concerning the weights of the objects obtained have been presented to bring out the precise mentality of a people so intent on preparing and programming the entire process of technological development. They also serve in the assessment of the material culture of the social group in question.

In this case philological research puts two items at the disposition of the archaeologist in his effort to identify as precisely as possible the objects which he finds. He may now be able to file his bronze finds, once analyzed, in apposite compartments guided by at least two identifying norms: percentage of the composition and the weights of the objects. Should the archaeologist accept or reject these two norms, they will still offer useful elements for a new historical-philological inquiry and classification.

Though only two of the many qualities that characterize manufactured objects, they sharply limit the field of hypotheses of identification. They enable the philologist to understand what was meant by "green eye" and the archaeologist to find out what it was for, for whom it was destined, and by whom that vase was made which he may now call *"zakirratum."*

2. MODELS OF PRODUCTION

Having reviewed what we consider the economic resources of Ebla and still deeply impressed by its unexpected wealth, we must nonetheless pause for a moment's reflection. Who is the creator of this wealth?

The reply to this question hinges on the examination of so many factors, for the most part not yet explored, that what is said here will need further verification. On the other hand, the sudden burst of discoveries found scholars so unprepared to evaluate them that first impressions were not always subjected to necessary controls. To reply that Ebla's economy was a state economy, not unlike that of the Sumerians in contemporary Mesopotamia, means not facing the problems thrown up by the new finds.

It is true that the state in Ebla is felt to such a degree as to seem depersonalized, but at the same time a bureaucratic apparatus so complex and ramified exists that no one can elude its control. Add to this that the records found are the archives of state, and it will be difficult to deny the exactness of the first impression, namely, that the economy described by the texts is the economy of state.

All sectors of production, from agriculture to industry, stand subject to an iron-handed administration which, guided by the "lord" and passing through the "governors" and "superintendents," not only controls and registers every phase of the work, but also plans and promotes it.

That Ebla's economy is essentially a state economy is confirmed by the fact that all the Eblaites, beginning with the king down to the simple hod carrier, receive rations in kind and that all, the king included, pay taxes to the state treasury. Hence to answer that the artificer of Ebla's wealth is the state would not be wide of the mark.

But then the second question immediately arises: "Was there no private economy in Ebla?" The great novelty of Ebla lies precisely in the fact that in it coexist in a perfect symbiosis the public and the private economy. To be sure, one runs a risk when using in connection with a culture so distant in time a terminology which today has some very specific meanings.

Above all in economic studies on the ancient Near East one notes the somewhat conformist tendency to square everything with the preconstituted conceptions of certain great thinkers. But it seems quite clear that the Mesopotamian cultures in particular do not readily lend themselves to framing within evolutionistic schemes of the world economy. And that of Ebla seems even more to elude such schemes.

In fact, there can be little doubt that free enterprise had ample space in which to operate, above all in commerce, the chief activity of the Eblaites. Alongside official carriers there are certainly private merchants, not less active or affluent than the official representatives of the state.

It is moreover ascertained that in Ebla there was private property in the form of real estate and personal property: earlier was cited a list of estates which Ebrium bequeaths to his son and presently we shall see how individual citizens hoarded gold, obvious signs of wealth.

What has been said thus far points to the conclusion that Ebla's economy was both public and private. But as remarked above, the reality was much more complex; the type of economy reflected by the texts would seem to be that of a patrician economy. The great families of Ebla are, in the last analysis, the true creators of the economic miracle worked at Ebla in the third millennium.

3. UNITS OF MEASURE

In the discussion both of agriculture and of metals there was obvious need to mention dry measures and weights which, together with surface measures, complete the picture of a society truly autonomous with respect to Mesopotamian civilizations from which the Eblaites borrowed the system of writing. To have units of measure different from those known and to use them when keeping records reflects the degree of autonomy attained by the civilization of Ebla.

Here the systems of units of measure will be briefly discussed to permit the reader to understand and interpret for himself the data emanating from the tablets.

3.1. DRY AND LIQUID MEASURES

The highest unit of measure for the dry substances is the *gubar,* which may provisionally be rendered "full measure," doubtless corresponding to a kind of jar of well defined size. The next measure is the *parīsu,* signifying "half" and equaling half the *gubar.* Under the *parīsu* there is the sila, improperly translated "liter," and equaling one tenth of the *parīsu.* The smallest measure is the anzam which corresponds to one sixth of the sila.

The relationship between the various units of measure is thus clear, but at this point of research their absolute value eludes fixing.[28] The foregoing data may schematically be presented thus:

gubar	parīsu	sagšu sila	anzam
1	2	20	120
	1	10	60
		1	6

3.2. WEIGHTS

In the Ebla texts at least two systems of measure regarding the weights are recognizable. One is the classic system known throughout the Near East which has the mina as its base, the other is peculiar to Ebla, where in place of weights are found some standardized jars and the like used with the value of the weights.

To this system of units of measure for domestic use belong the giš-gigir, "the cart," the *luppu,* "wine—or oil—skin," and the *sal,* "jar." The *luppu* seems to equal half the giš-gigir[29] and the *sal* one fourth.

But the system used most widely in the international commercial texts is that based on the *mina.* The largest unit among the weights, the *mina* corresponds, as in Mesopotamia, to 60 shekels. In the writing occur submultiples of the *mina* and precisely of some particular names to indicate 40, 30, and 20 shekels respectively. The shekel in turn is divisible into five parts.

Table VII, 4

Units of Measure of the Weights

MINA	SHEKEL*	—NI
1	60	360
	1	6

*Specific names: 20 Shekels=GUR_8
30 Shekels=KU_5
40 Shekels=ŠA.PI

What surprises in the tablets is the absence of gú, "talent," corresponding to 60 minas. We do not know to what to ascribe this omission, surely not to the lack of conspicuous quantities which, as has been seen, sometimes ran into tons.

The shekel, always written with the Sumerian term gín, is usually accompanied by the addition Dilmun, which may be parsed either as a noun or as an adjective. Should the first hypothesis be accepted, then "Dilmun" would contain a forceful indication that this unit of weight originated in Dilmun, the present-day Islands of Bahrein, famous in antiquity as the source of precious metals.[30] If, however, the second hypothesis is adopted, it means "noble shekel" or a measure standardized by international agreements.

3.3. SURFACES

Another surprise springing from these archives is the new system of measuring surfaces. Throughout Mesopotamia surfaces were measured on the basis of the bùr equivalent to 6.48 hectares of land. Submultiples of the bùr were the iku equal to 3,600 meters squared and which constituted one eighteenth of the normal measure bùr.

At Ebla the bùr never appears, the normal unit of measure being the iku. Here too one should note that the absence of the bùr is not due to a lack of large surfaces; the texts often speak of thousands of iku.

3.4. NUMBERING SYSTEMS

This chapter would be incomplete without a discussion, albeit brief, of the systems followed by the Eblaites to indicate the numbers.

The Sumerians from whom the Eblaites borrowed their manner of writing expressed numbers according to the sexagesimal system, having invented some corresponding cuneiform signs valid for all units of measure.

Thus, for example, the gur, the unit of measure for dry and liquid substances, has as submultiple the sila which, according to the period, corresponds to $1/300$, $1/240$, $1/144$ of a gur, and the multiple gur_7 equivalent to 3,600 gur. For the units of measure as well as of surfaces the system followed is the sexagesimal. That the system is not purely sexagesimal may be deduced from the fact that cuneiform Sumerian has a sign to indicate ten; this points to a somewhat mixed system.

Having borrowed Sumerian writing, the Eblaites knew all the cuneiform signs expressing numbers, but they still prefer a system with a decimal base. This appears most clearly in the numbers above 100 which are always expressed by this system and not by the sexagesimal prevalent in Mesopotamia.

The cuneiform signs which indicate the numbers from one to nine are the horizontal or vertical half-moons.

The 10 is indicated by a small circle *o,* the 20 by two small circles, etc. . . . up to 50 by five small circles. The Eblaites very curiously preserved the sign for 60 formed by a large half-moon D, a progeny of the sexagesimal system, and kept it for all the higher numbers to 100, so that 70 is written 60+10, that is, a large half-moon+a small half-moon, etc. From 100 up the decimal system takes over again and the numbers have precise names:

100 = 1 *mi-at*
1,000 = 1 *li-im*
10,000 = 1 *rí-*ba_x
100,000 = 1 *ma-i-at/ma-i-ḫu*

Rather interesting is how 100,000 is expressed by the plural of a hundred. Names of numbers higher than 100,000 have not yet been identified.

To indicate the submultiples of both the *mina* and the *gubar,* the Eblaites had another series of numbers formed by vertical cuneiform signs for 1 to 9 and by rhombuses for the 10:

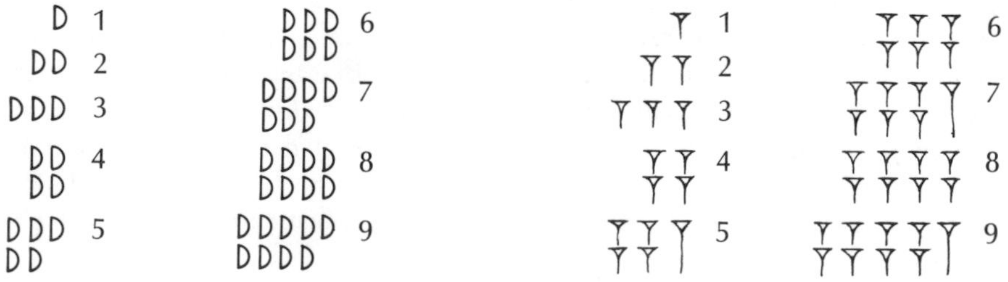

This way they avoided all confusion with the numbers indicating the basic units. This second series of numbers was also used to mark the regnal years of the kings in the economic tablets.

In conclusion it may be said that the Eblaites preferred the decimal system even though they did not disown the sexagesimal scheme prevailing in contemporary Mesopotamia, thanks to the Sumerian cuneiform writing.

4. COMMERCE

As frequently observed above, the chief activity of the Eblaites was commercial and the majority of tablets economic. Among the texts that scholars desire to have most are commercial statements.[31] Though Ebla now holds the primacy in bestowing first this genre of document, there is every reason to believe that other tells conceal copies of this new genre.

The value of these documents is both historical and economic; they aid in reconstructing the geographic map of the ancient Near East because they mention so many foreign cities in outlining the first history of the kingdoms and dynasties of the third millennium B.C.

Under the economic aspect the commercial texts prove most useful in that they permit a good view of the skill with which this Semitic people dealt with other countries and show the economic equilibrium throughout the Near East in the third millennium. It would even seem that their great economists were at work to create a Common Market that was both functional and stable. This may look like an exaggeration, but when prices are stable and all are related to gold in the fixed ratio of 5 to 1 with silver, it becomes evident that this economic equilibrium must have been based on very modern concepts.

If, as will be seen later, Ebla succeeded in monopolizing this important sector of the economy, it was due to the political sagacity of her rulers who made pacts with other sovereigns, as in the case of the treaty between Ebla and Ashur, to regulate the bilateral relationships with the individual states and to guarantee the safety of the commercial routes. The fruit of the "pax Eblaitica," the safety of the commercial routes, enabled merchants to move around without running unusual risks.

The prevailing concepts regarding Oriental empires are colored by those of Mesopotamia, which were founded on military force and the subjugation of other peoples, but these should not be allowed to prejudice the present discussion because the Ebla empire does not fit into this canon. What emerges from the tablets is a markedly economic-commercial empire, not a political-military complex, and this new reality promises to upset the preconceived notions of Oriental despotism rampant in the preclassical period. The quotation of an entire text with translation will permit the reader to see how refined and sophisticated were the techniques of exchange developed by Ebla.

4.1. MODELS OF EXCHANGE

In studies dedicated to models of exchange, two fundamental types are usually distinguished, the barter and the purchase and sale which represent two historical phases of commerce where barter characterizes the primitive and more archaic stage and purchase and sale the more advanced phase. To our surprise Ebla exhibits both these forms of commerce, to which a third must be added, that of "tributes," secondary, to be sure, with respect to the first two but not to be underestimated for that.

4.1.1. BARTER

The Ebla texts not only witness this type of commerce but also furnish for the first time the term expressing it: šu-bala-aka which literally translates "to effect the passage of hand," that is, to barter one thing for another or, better, goods for goods.

Barter at Ebla involves the exchange of the basic metal silver for various goods. That it is not a question of purchase and sale can be inferred from the existence of the term nì-šam, "price" besides the more proper term for barter, but obviously this is no longer the primitive form of barter but a practice well on the way to giving the metal the value of price and money. In the final clauses text TM.75.G.1406 reports the barter of silver for other metals:

šu-bala-aka zabar	barter for bronze,
šu-bala-aka	barter
urudu	for copper,
šu-bala-aka	barter
nagga	for tin.

But the barter more commonly took place between silver and gold in the fixed ratio of one to five, which reflects a solid and non-inflationary world economy.

Here are some examples taken from various texts:

10 *ma-na ša-pi* 5 gín-dilmun kù:babbar	10 minas and 45 Dilmunite shekels of silver
šu-bala-aka	barter
2 *ma-na* 9 gín-dilmun guškin	for 2 minas and 9 Dilmunite shekels of gold.[32]
5 *ma-na* kù:babbar	5 minas of silver
šu-bala-aka	barter
1 *ma-na* guškin	for 1 mina of gold.[33]

an-šè-gú 25 *ma-na* kù:babbar	total: 25 minas of silver
šu-bala-aka	barter
5 *ma-na* guškin	for 5 minas of gold
lugal-lugal	the governors
in-na-sum	have given.[34]

Though the kind of barter most attested concerns that of silver for other metals, gold in particular, some texts witness more diversified barters. The following passage reports the exchange of silver for lapis lazuli:

1 *ma-na ša-pi* gín-dilmun kù:babbar	1 mina and 40 Dilmunite shekels of silver
šu-bala-aka	barter for
5 *ma-na* 10 gín-dilmun za:gìn	5 minas and 10 Dilmunite shekels of lapis lazuli
UNKEN-aka	to make
an-dùl	a statue
zi-da-lu^{ki}	for the city Zidalu.[35]

The ratio between lapis lazuli and silver is 3.1 to 1, hence inferior to that between gold and silver. The text also specifies the destination of the lapis lazuli, namely, to decorate a statue, certainly of a god.

Another expression for barter in this developed form is encountered in TM.76.G.523, reverse VI 21 and following:

22 gín kù:babbar	22 shekels of silver
a-dè gu-mug-túg	for Gumug fabric:
22 sal-túg	22 fine fabrics and
22 íb-túg-dar	22 Ib multicolored fabrics

where *a-dè*, "for," expresses purpose, hence "whence to obtain." One immediately thinks of the price of the materials, but the Eblaites did not wish with this formula to express the concept of purchase and sale.

4.1.2. PURCHASE AND SALE

The second form of commerce is signified by the term nì-šám, "price," which surely implies purchase and sale by means of payment of an internationally recognized payment. One can easily deduce from the tablets that this means of payment was silver which, as has been seen above, was not lacking in Ebla.

Here again citations prove the most instructive manner of proceeding:

13 gín-dilmun kù:babbar	10 Dilmunite shekels of silver
nì-šám$_x$	price

10 gada-ḫul	of 10 (measures) of inferior linen,
16 gín-dilmun kù:babbar	16 Dilmunite shekels of silver
nì-šám$_x$	price
3 túg-*ì-lí*	of 3 excellent materials
áš-ti	from the part
gul-la	of Gulla
ma-rí^{ki}	of Mari;
15 gín-dilmun kù:babbar	15 Dilmunite shekels of silver
nì-šám$_x$	price
5 gada-ša$_6$	of 5 (measures) of the best linen;
5 gín-dilmun kù:babbar	5 Dilmunite shekels of silver
nì-šám$_x$	price
udu-nita *ma-rí*^{ki}	of rams of the city Mari;[36]
20 gín-dilmun kù:babbar	20 Dilmunite shekels of silver
nì-šám$_x$	price
esir	of bitumen.[37]

This example informs that with silver the Eblaites bought textiles from other cities, livestock and bitumen, and in some cases it is even possible to draw up a chart of current prices.

Gold is likewise used as means of payment in transactions involving objects of value such as bracelets, daggers, earrings, vases, etc., and especially plaques and precious sheets. The last evoke the modern gold bars since they served as an element in hoarding wealth. The plaques or sheets had the weight of the gold with which they were acquired and were carefully preserved either by the palace or by the individual families.

Text TM.75.G.1696 speaks of 8 minas and 3 shekels of gold converted into "plaques or sheets" for divers persons; here are three examples:

a)	1 gín-dilmun guškin	1 Dilmunite shekel of gold
	ni-zi-mu	ornament
	1 díb *ṭù-bí-sí-piš*	of 1 sheet for Ṭubi-Sipiš
	lú *áš-ba-il*	the man of Ašba-Il.[38]
b)	2 gín-dilmun guškin	2 Dilmunite shekels of gold
	ni-zi-mu	ornament
	1 díb *i-ib-ma-lik*	of one sheet for Ib-Malik
	šeš	brother
	du-ší-gú	of Dušigu.[39]
c)	2 gín-dilmun guškin	2 Dilmunite shekels of gold
	ni-zi-mu	ornament
	1 díb *i-bí-sí-piš*	of one sheet for Ibbi-Sipiš,
	dumu-nita	son
	eb-rí-um	of Ebrium.[40]

The same text records more substantial quantities such as the following which refers to a donation to Hada's temple in Ḫalam:

2 *ma-na* 23 gín-dilmun	2 minas and 23 Dilminute shekels
guškin 1 díb-maḫ$_x$	of gold in the form of a "large" sheet
lú-^{giš}gidri-^{giš}gidri	the men of the scepter
in-na-sum	have given
^{d}*'à-da*	to Hada
ḫa-lam^{ki}	of Ḫalam
in AMA-*ra*	in the month of Amara;
en	the king
šu mu-dúb	has delivered.[41]

In the first examples the quantities were small but here the sheet exceeds a kilogram in weight.

4.1.3. "TRIBUTES"

Commercial transactions in the form of barter or purchase and sale were carried out with the two precious metals silver and gold. A text was also cited reporting the outlay of silver in three years and of gold in six years and giving some idea of the city's wealth. How did Ebla obtain all the silver and gold cramming its vaults? No texts studied thus far answer this question, but surely these metals must have been imported. This situation leaves one perplexed.

Numerous, on the other hand, are the records in which these two metals appear as tribute of the governors of the realm and of other cities. This fact creates a problem in that tributes have been subsumed under forms of commerce; tribute, in fact, is something coercive which ill fits the liberal character of commerce. But it does appear that "tribute" which usually translates the term mu-túm does not adequately render the gamut of meanings hidden in the Sumerian term, which is more literally reproduced by "contribution, income" and which includes therefore the profits and the surplus that converge on the central palace from all the disparate seats.

In the available documents are lacking telling passages on how administrative and economic deeds were performed. On debits and credits the information is good, but the variations of these transactions cannot always be made out.

Returning to "tributes" in the broad sense, we learn of payments made to the central seats, but not of titles under which they were made. It is significant, however, that these tributes have to do mainly with silver and gold, though other goods such as textiles are not lacking.

Text TM.75.G.1359, cited earlier, reports that the tribute brought by the governors amounted to 3 minas and 13 shekels of gold;[42] another

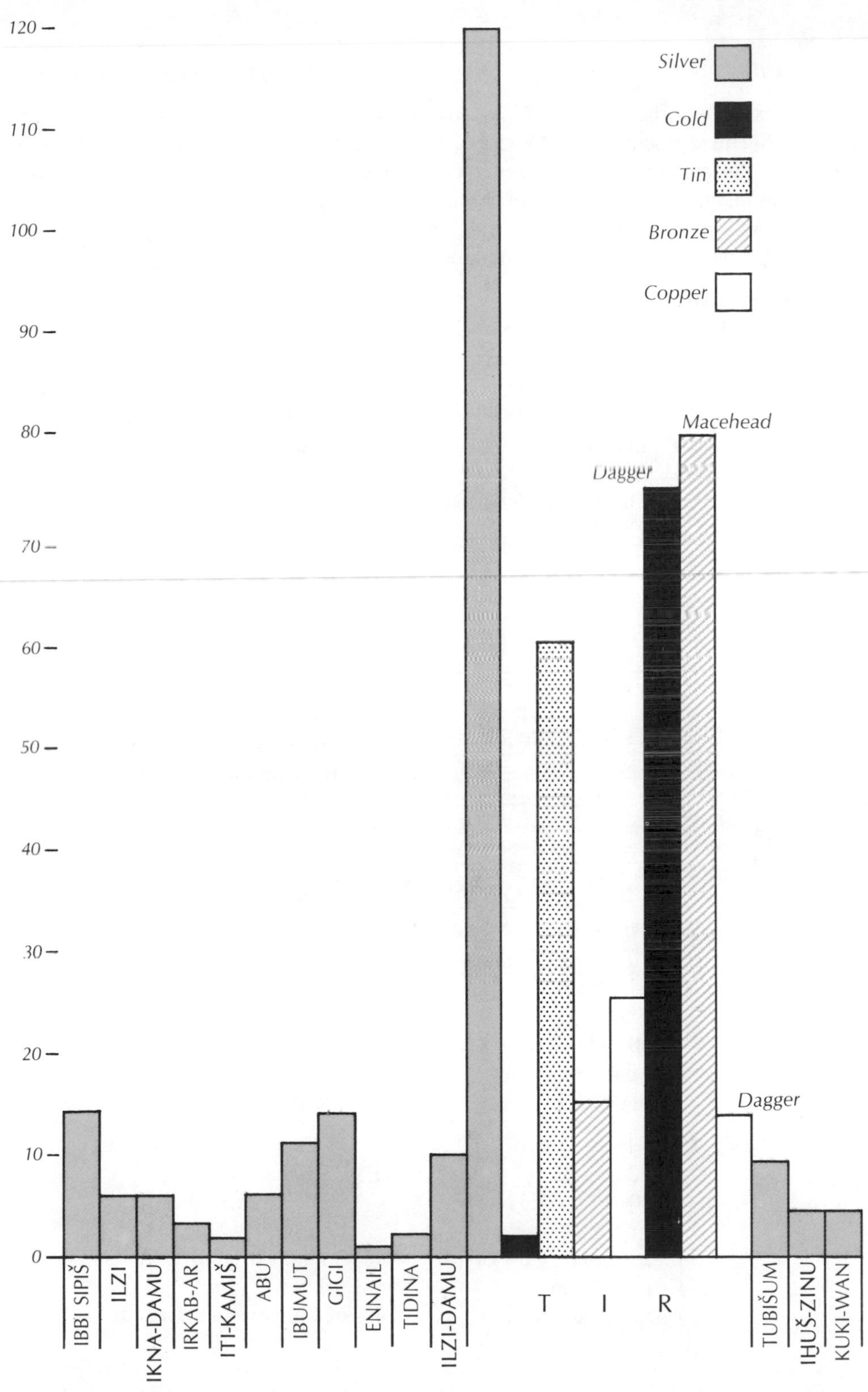

Figure VII, 4 Tribute paid by the governors and the king to the state treasury according to TM.75.G.1296

text[43] puts the figure at 203 minas of silver. Here, however, will be cited an entire document, TM.75.G.1357, which registers not only the tribute of the governors but also that of some cities and, if the text is correctly understood, of the king of Ebla himself. This surprising element of the king's paying taxes to the state treasury underscores the depersonalizing of government offices and the abstract concept of the state.

obverse

I	1)	1 *mi-at* 31 *ma-na* 53 gín-dilmun kù:babbar	1)	131 minas and 53 Dilmunite shekels of silver
	2)	1 *ma-na* guškin	2)	1 mina of gold,
	3)	mu-túm	3)	tribute
	4)	*ti-ir*	4)	of the governor Tir;
	5)	10 *ma-na* kù:babbar	5)	10 minas of silver,
II	1)	mu-túm	1)	tribute
	2)	íl-zi	2)	of the governor Ilzi;
	3)	33 *ma-na ša-pi* gín-dilmun kù:babbar	3)	33 minas, 40 Dilmunite shekels of silver,
	4)	TAR.TAR	4)	———
	5)	33 *ma-na* ku_5 kù:babbar	5)	33 minas, 30 Dilmunite shekels of silver,
	6)	*zi-du*	6)	———
III	1)	4 ^{giš}*ṣe* kù:babbar	1)	4 vases of silver,
	2)	šu-nigín 57 *ma-na* 10 gín-dilmun kù:babbar	2)	sum: 57 minas and 10 Dilmunite shekels of silver;
	3)	5 *ma-na* 50 gín-dilmun guškin	3)	5 minas and 50 Dilmunite shekels of gold,
	4)	mu-túm	4)	tribute
IV	1)	*dar-mi-a*	1)	of the governor Darmia;
	2)	23 *ma-na* 50 gín-dilmun kù:babbar	2)	23 minas and 50 Dilmunite shekels of silver,
	3)	2 *ma-na* guškin	3)	2 minas of gold,
	4)	mu-túm	4)	tribute
	5)	*la-da-ad*	5)	of the governor Ladad;

	6)	*en-na-ìa*	6)	Enna-Ya
	7)	di-ku$_5$	7)	judge.
V	1)	9 *ma-na* gur$_8$ gín-dilmun kù:babbar	1)	9 minas, 20 Dilmunite shekels of silver
	2)	mu-túm	2)	tribute
	3)	*iq-na-da-mu*	3)	of the governor Iqna-Damu
	4)	ul^{ki}	4)	of the city of Ul;
	5)	4 *ma-na* 55 gín-dilmun kù:babbar	5)	4 minas and 55 shekels of silver,
	6)	mu-túm	6)	tribute
VI	1)	*i-rí-gú-nu*	1)	of the governor Irigunu;
	2)	2 *ma-na* kù:babbar	2)	2 minas of silver,
	3)	mu-túm	3)	tribute
	4)	*ti dì nu*	4)	of Tidinu,
	5)	lugal	5)	governor
	6)	bar-an-bar-an	6)	of the mercenaries;
	7)	3 *ma-na* 55 gín-dilmun kù:babbar	7)	3 minas and 55 Dilmunite shekels of silver,
	8)	1 ^{giš}banšur guškin	8)	1 table of gold
VII	1)	mu-túm	1)	tribute
	2)	*ìr-kab-ar*	2)	of the governor Irkab-Ar;
	3)	4 *ma-na* ku$_5$ kù:babbar	3)	4 minas, 30 shekels of silver
	4)	mu-túm	4)	tribute
	5)	*i-ti-*^{d}*kà-mi-iš*	5)	of the governor Iti-Kamiš;
	6)	11 *ma-na ša-pi* gín-dilmun kù:babbar	6)	11 minas, 40 Dilmunite shekels of silver
	7)	mu-túm	7)	tribute
VIII	1)	*gi-gi*	1)	of the governor Gigi;
	2)	4 *ma-na* 50 gín-dilmun kù:babbar	2)	4 minas and 50 Dilmunite shekels of silver
	3)	mu-túm	3)	tribute
	4)	íl-zi-*da-mu*	4)	of the governor Ilzi-Damu;

	5)	⌜14⌝ *ma-na*	5)	14 minas
		kù : babbar		of silver,
	6)	mu-túm	6)	tribute
reverse				
I	1)	*i-bí-sí-piš*	1)	of the governor Ibbi-Sipiš;
	2)	10 *ma-na* ku$_5$	2)	10 minas and 30 shekels
		kù : babbar		of silver,
	3)	mu-túm	3)	tribute
	4)	*ib-*u_9*-mu-ut*	4)	of the governor Ibumut;
	5)	2 *ma-na* ku$_5$	5)	2 minas, 30 shekels
		guškin		of gold,
	6)	mu-túm	6)	tribute
	7)	*ar-en-núm*	7)	of the governor Ar-Ennum;
II	1)	8 gín-dilmun	1)	8 Dilmunite shekels
		kù : babbar		of silver,
	2)	mu-túm	2)	tribute
	3)	*gàr-maš-da-ni-um*^{ki}	3)	of the commercial center of Mašdanium;
	4)	1 *ma-na*	4)	1 mina
		kù : babbar		of silver,
	5)	mu-túm	5)	tribute
	6)	ambar.ambar^{ki}	6)	of the city Ambar.Ambar;
	7)	*ša-pi* gín-dilmun	7)	40 Dilmunite shekels
		kù : babbar		of silver
	8)	mu-túm	8)	tribute
III	1)	*en-na-il*	1)	of Enna-Il
	2)	lugal	2)	governor
	3)	igi-nita-igi-nita	3)	of the men Igi-nita;
	4)	*ša-pi* gín-dilmun	4)	40 Dilmunite shekels
		kù : babbar		of silver,
	5)	mu-túm	5)	tribute
	6)	*dar-áb*^{ki}	6)	of the city Darab;
	7)	gur$_8$ gín-dilmun	7)	20 Dilmunite shekels
		kù : babbar		of silver,
	8)	mu-túm	8)	tribute
IV	1)	NI*-du-úr*^{ki}	1)	of the city Nidur;
	2)	1 *ma-na*	2)	1 mina
		kù : babbar		of silver,
	3)	mu-túm	3)	tribute

Figure VII, 5 Tribute paid by the governors according to TM.75.G.1357

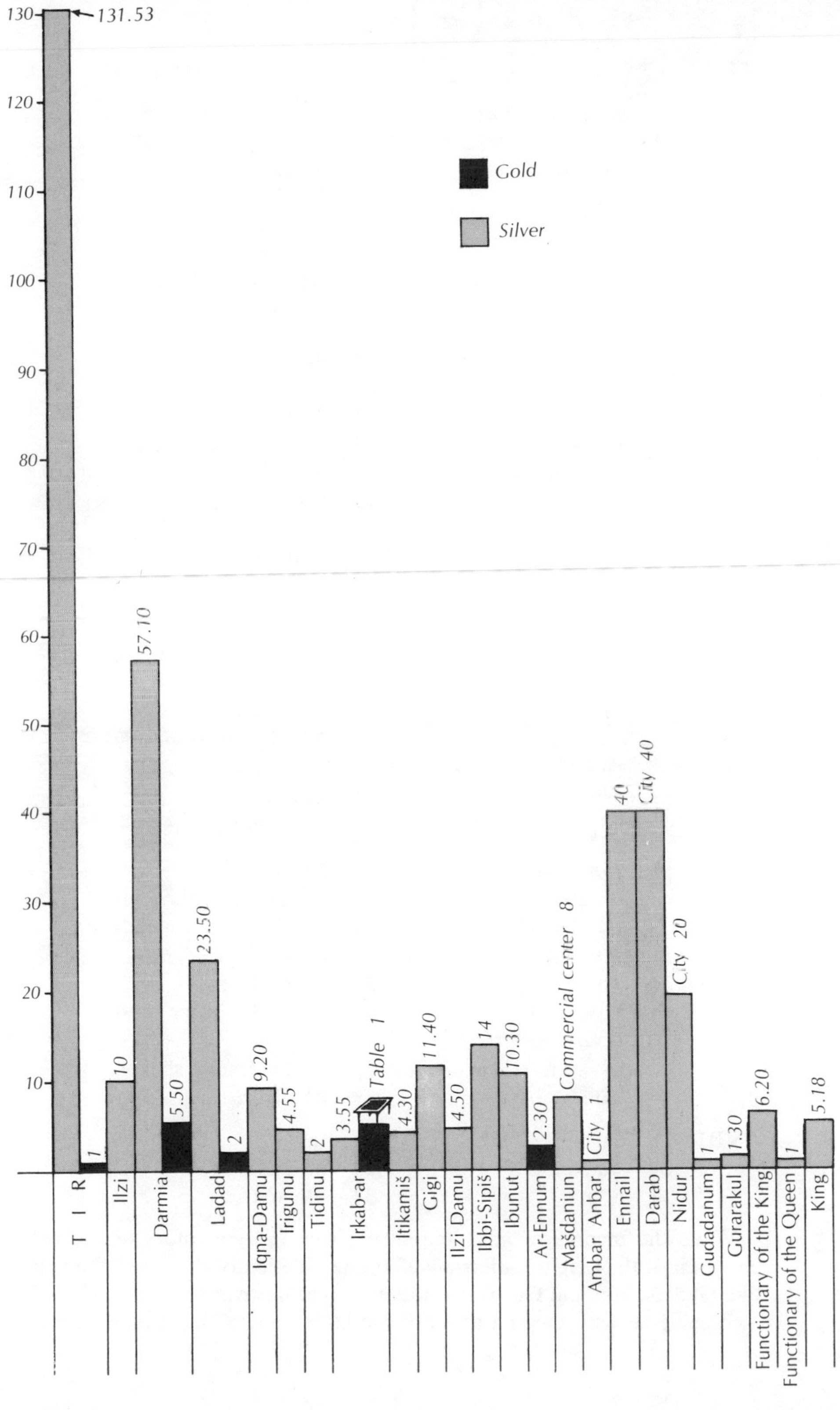

Gold
Silver
130
120
110
100
90
80
70
60
50
40
30
20
10
131.53
1
10
57.10
5.50
23.50
2
9.20
4.55
2
3.55
Table 1
4.30
11.40
4.50
14
10.30
2.30
Commercial center 8
City 1
40
City 40
City 20
1
1.30
6.20
1
5.18
T I R
Ilzi
Darmia
Ladad
Iqna-Damu
Irigunu
Tidinu
Irkab-ar
Itikamiš
Gigi
Ilzi Damu
Ibbi-Sipiš
Ibunut
Ar-Ennum
Mašdaniun
Ambar Anbar
Ennail
Darab
Nidur
Gudadanum
Gurarakul
Functionary of the King
Functionary of the Queen
King

	4)	*gú-da-da-núm*^{ki}	4)	of the city Gudadanum;
	5)	1 *ma-na* ku$_{5}$	5)	1 mina, 30 shekels
		kù : babbar		of silver,
	6)	mu-túm	6)	tribute
	7)	*gú-ra-ra-kul*^{ki}	7)	of the city Gurarakul;
	8)	6 *ma-na*	8)	6 minas and
		gur$_{8}$ gín-dilmun		20 Dilmunite shekels
		kù : babbar		of silver,
V	1)	mu-túm	1)	tribute
	2)	*qá-da-mu*	2)	in favor
	3)	en	3)	of the king;
	4)	1 *ma-na*	4)	1 mina
		kù : babbar		of silver,
	5)	mu-túm	5)	tribute
	6)	*qá-da-mu*	6)	in favor
	7)	*ma-lik-tum*	7)	of the queen;
VI	1)	an-šè-gú 3 *mi-at*	1)	total: 315 minas
		15 *ma-na*		
		56 gín-dilmun		and 56 Dilmunite shekels
		kù : babbar		of silver;
	2)	11 *ma-na*	2)	11 minas and
		gur$_{8}$ gín-dilmun		20 Dilmunite shekels
		guškin		of gold,
	3)	mu-túm	3)	tribute
	4)	lugal-lugal	4)	of the governors;
VII	1)	5 *ma-na*	1)	5 minas and
		18 gín-dilmun		18 Dilmunite shekels
		kù : babbar		of silver,
	2)	mu-túm	2)	tribute
	3)	en	3)	of the king;
	4)	šu-nígin 3 *mi-at*	4)	total: 321 minas and
		21 *ma-na*		
		14 gín-dilmun		14 Dilmunite shekels
		kù : babbar		of silver;
VIII	1)	dub	1)	tablet
	2)	^{d}*ìa-ra-mu*	2)	of Yaramu,
	3)	6 *mu*	3)	6th year.

While the income of gold and silver from the governors of the realm and even of the king is understandable, the mention of "tribute" from cities like Gudadanum and Gurukal without further motivation is surprising. But a comparison with the text that will presently be cited in its entirety makes is quite clear that not a little effort will be required to comprehend the technique of the exchanges used by Ebla and their registration in the master records of the state. In column IV 9ff. of TM.76.G.523 a shipment of textiles for Gudadanum is recorded without a counter-item. This leads one to suppose that there were some separate registrations for incoming and outgoing goods, and scholars will have to collect much more information before they can disentangle all the items which at first blush look inexplicable.

4.2. VALUE OF EXCHANGE: PRICES AND CURRENCY

Commerce, even in the form of barter, was based on silver. Did the concept of "money" come into play at the time of Ebla? It would be premature to hazard an answer, even though everything would lead us to believe that "money" as understood today could not have existed then.

It is certain, however, that Ebla manifests a highly developed economic system which, once it outgrew the phase of pure barter, moved toward more complex and nuanced economic paradigms. All goods are put in relationship to the principal good which is silver; this means that they already had an idea of abstract value which entails the formulation of very exact prices.

But how was the stability of market prices achieved? The Eblaites were most affluent in silver and yet the signs of debasing inflation cannot be detected. There appear to have been two deterrents to this plague which would have debilitated the state. The first deterrent was the very close network of commercial relationships which required huge investments to control a very lively budget.

The second deterrent appears more interesting: the fixed and relatively low ratio with the precious metal, gold. This ratio of 1 to 5 discussed above is an indicator of considerable prosperity and at the same time of economic stability. Throughout the seventy years of the dynasty of Ebla the silver/gold ratio remained unchanged; hence the economic situation must have fluctuated very little.[44]

It may well be an exaggeration to hold that gold alone was the official international price-list, but it does appear that the economic tenets of the Eblaites differed but slightly from modern practice where strict laws regulate the possession of the most precious metal.

Gold was, as a matter of fact, stored in the coffers of the state, as the beginning of a tablet reports:

4 *mi-at ma-na* guškin	400 minas of gold
40 *zi-ru*$_x$	40 jars
2 *mi-at ma-na* guškin	200 minas of gold
40 dug	40 vases.[45]

In all there are 300 kilograms of gold preserved at Ebla perhaps in the form of precious vessels, surely not intended for commerce but as non-invested wealth.

4.2.1. THE VALUE OF GOODS AND THE DYNAMICS OF PRICES

Goods and work are valued according to the prices and salaries that they receive. This intrinsic value is the primary factor in an economy. So-called primitive economies depend almost entirely on their capacity for exploitation and strict control. Here the primary factor means whatever is cultivated: it is everything that is necessary for sustenance and derives from farming, animal husbandry, fishing, hunting, and gardening. In such a society the largest percentage of the workers is assigned to this primary production. This was true for the neolithic villages as well as the preclassic cities of the Near East. It created a cycle of work-food-work. Agriculture produced something that could be distributed among the workers; this in turn guaranteed that there would be more work and more product. This cycle was the fulcrum of social equilibrium; and, as the studies of Deimel and Falkenstein showed, the fundamental function of the temple was that of distribution so as to insure the continuation of the cycle. Since land was the chief means of production, control meant ownership of the land and storage of produce by those who would distribute it.

In ancient times the harvest varied because those climactic and social factors on which it so heavily depended could not be controlled by the means that the age possessed. Prices and salaries would also be affected by these conditions. But Ebla was a city, the capital of a fertile territory that extended over the whole of the Aleppo basin. Presumably, a large percentage of the agricultural force lived in farm villages and was in immediate contact with the earth.

Almost by antonomasia (Childe), urban population means craftsmen who are specialists, and persons who coordinate the services that a society needs. And, as is known, the civil authorities had more or less direct control over the production of many tools and of almost all luxury items. The native and imported materials necessary for this industry were delivered to the city. Thus, by controlling, amassing, and redistributing goods, the city could to some extent stabilize the system of prices and salaries.

It must not be forgotten that money was unknown in protohistoric cities. Most payments were made in kind. This most commonly meant allotments of food, but it also took the form of goods such as textiles, tools, etc. The control of essential production by the state was all the more decisive in that, to guarantee at least minimal levels of production, the state could 1) cultivate a variety of crops; 2) stockpile produce; and 3) practice intense animal husbandry.

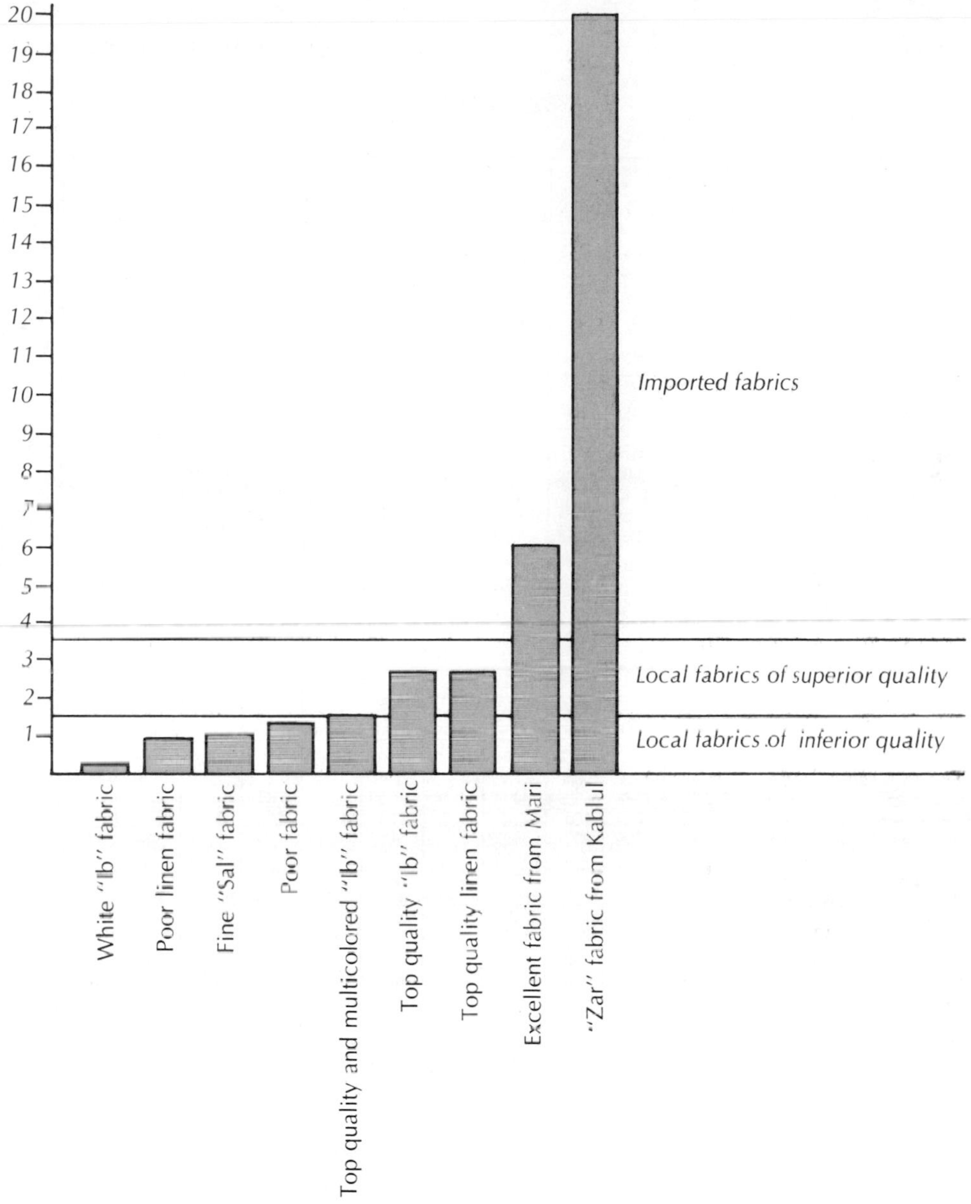

Figure VII, 6 Value of textiles in silver shekels

In the first case, optimum cultivation was assured by planting those crops that were most suited to the land and to the seasons.[46] In the second, a stockpile of goods came about through the storage of all the crops in the capital and in peripheral centers. All of the crops were then distributed with the exception of what was kept for seed and tribute. All the system of storage was regulated by a bureaucracy for which cylinder seals

Table VII, 7

Slb 1 Silver shekel	Silver shekels	Gold shekels	Tin shekels	Copper shekels	Shekels of lapis lazuli	Shekels of mixed stone	Shekels of bitumen	Oxen	Sheep	Skins	Turtles	''Long'' figs	Mercenaries from Nagar	Slaves (male)
Minerals														
1 Silver shekel	1	0.21	1.51	50	3.10	0.5	3.03	0.03	0.85	1	7.14	3.03	0.01	0.07
1 Gold shekel	4.75	1	7.19	237.5	14.84	2.37	14.39	0.15	4.05	4.75	33.92	14.39	0.05	0.36
1 Tin shekel	0.66	0.13	1	33	2.06	0.33	2	0.02	0.56	0.66	4.71	2	0.007	0.05
1 Copper shekel	0.02	0.004	0.03	1	0.06	0.01	0.06	0.0006	0.017	0.02	0.14	0.06	0.0002	0.001
1 Shekel of lapis lazuli	0.32	0.06	0.48	16	1	0.13	0.96	0.01	0.27	0.32	2.28	0.96	0.003	0.02
1 Shekel of mixed stone	2	0.42	3.03	100	6.25	1	6.06	0.06	1.70	2	14.28	6.06	0.02	0.15
1 Shekel of bitumen	0.33	0.08	0.5	16.5	1.03	0.16	1	0.01	0.26	0.33	2.35	1	0.003	0.02
Livestock														
1 Ox	30.0	6.31	45.45	1500	93.75	15.0	90.9	1	33.33	30	214.28	90.9	0.33	2.30
1 Sheep	1.17	0.24	1.77	58.5	3.65	0.58	3.54	0.03	1	1.17	8.35	3.54	0.013	0.09
1 Skin	1	0.21	1.51	50	3.12	0.50	3.03	0.03	0.85	1	7.14	3.03	0.01	0.07
1 Turtle	0.14	0.02	0.21	7	0.43	0.07	0.42	0.004	0.11	0.14	1	0.42	0.001	0.01
Agricultural product														
1 ''Long'' fig	0.33	0.08	0.5	16.5	1.03	0.16	1	0.01	0.28	0.33	2.35	1	0.003	0.02
Men														
1 Mercenary of Nagar	90	18.94	136.3	4500	281.2	45	272.7	3	76.9	90	642.8	272.7	1	6.92
1 Slave (male)	13	2.73	19.69	650	40.62	7.50	39.39	0.43	11.11	13	92.85	39.39	0.14	1
1 Slave (female)	8	1.68	12.12	400	25	4	24.24	0.26	6.83	8	57.14	24.24	0.08	0.61
1 Slave (child)	18	3.78	27.27	900	56.25	9	54.54	0.6	15.38	18	128.5	54.54	0.2	1.38
Metal Products														
1 Gold ''Martu'' dagger	33.75	7.10	51.13	1687	105.46	16.87	102.2	1.12	28.84	33.75	241.07	102.2	0.37	2.59
1 Bronze ''Martu'' dagger	15.43	3.24	23.37	771.5	48.21	7.71	46.75	0.51	13.18	15.43	110.2	46.75	0.17	1.18
1 Bronze lance	10	2.10	15.15	500	31.25	5	30.3	0.33	8,54	10	71.42	30.3	0.11	0.76
1 Bronze arrow	0.60	0.12	0.9	30	1.87	0.3	1.81	0.02	0.51	0.60	4.28	1.81	0.006	0.04
1 Gold bracelet	5.40	1.13	8.18	270	16.87	2.70	16.36	0.18	4.61	5.40	38.57	16.36	0.06	0.41
1 Bronze razor	0.5	0.10	0.75	25	1.56	0.25	1.51	0.016	0.42	0.5	3.57	1.51	0.005	0.03
Wooden Products														
1 Bow	1.40	0.29	2.12	70	4.37	0.70	4.24	0.04	1.19	1.40	10	4.24	0.015	0.10
Textiles														
1 measure of top-grade wool	1	0.21	1.51	50	3.12	0.50	3.03	0.03	0.85	1	7.14	3.03	0.01	0.07
1 measure of white ''1B'' material	0.25	0.05	0.37	12.5	0.78	0.12	0.25	0.008	0.21	0.25	1.78	0.25	0.002	0.019
1 measure of low-grade linen	1	0.21	1.51	50	3.12	0.50	3.03	0.03	0.85	1	7.14	3.03	0.01	0.07
1 measure of fine ''SAL'' material	1.17	0.24	1.77	58.5	3.65	0.58	3.54	0.04	1	1.17	8.35	3.54	0.013	0.09
1 measure of low-grade material	1.30	0.27	1.96	65	4.06	0.65	3.93	0.04	1.11	1.30	9.28	3.93	0.014	0.1
1 measure of excellent and multi-colored material	1.58	0.33	2.39	79	4.93	0.79	4.78	0.05	1.35	1.58	11.28	4.78	0.017	0.12
1 measure of excellent ''1B'' material	3	0.63	4.54	150	9.37	1.50	9.09	0.1	2.56	3	21.42	9.09	0.03	0.23
1 measure of excellent linen material	3	0.63	4.54	150	9.37	1.50	9.09	0.1	2.56	3	21.42	9.09	0.03	0.23
1 measure of excellent material from Mari	5.90	1.24	8.93	295	18.43	2.95	17.8	0.19	5.04	5.90	42.14	17.8	0.06	0.45

Relationship of Prices Among the Various Products

Slaves (female)	Slaves (children)	Gold "Martu" daggers	Bronze "Martu" daggers	Bronze lances	Bronze arrows	Gold bracelets	Bronze razors	Bows	Measures of top-grade wool	Measures of white "1B" material	Measures of low-grade linen material	Measures of fine "SAL" material	Measures of low-grade material	Measures of excellent and multi-colored "1B" material	Measures of excellent "1B" material	Measures of excellent linen material	Measures of top grade material from Mari
0.12	0.05	0.02	0.06	0.1	1.66	0.18	2	0.71	1.00	4.00	1.00	0.85	0.76	0.63	0.33	0.33	0.16
0.59	0.26	0.14	0.04	0.47	7.91	0.87	9.5	3.39	4.75	19.0	4.75	4.05	3.65	3.00	1.58	1.58	0.80
0.08	0.03	0.019	0.04	0.06	1.1	0.12	1.32	0.47	0.66	2.54	0.66	0.56	0.50	0.41	0.22	0.22	0.11
0.002	0.001	0.0005	0.001	0.002	0.03	0.003	0.04	0.014	0.02	0.08	0.02	0.017	0.015	0.012	0.006	0.006	0.003
0.04	0.017	0.009	0.03	0.03	0.53	0.06	0.61	0.22	0.30	1.20	0.30	0.27	0.24	0.20	0.10	0.10	0.05
0.25	0.11	0.05	0.12	0.2	3.33	0.37	4	1.42	2.0	8.0	2.0	1.7	1.53	1.26	0.66	0.66	0.33
0.04	0.018	0.009	0.021	0.03	0.56	0.061	0.66	0.23	0.33	1.32	0.33	0.28	0.25	0.20	0.11	0.11	0.06
3.75	1.66	0.88	1.94	3	50	5.55	60	21.42	30.0	120	30.0	25.64	23.07	18.98	10.0	10.0	5.08
0.14	0.06	0.03	0.07	1.11	1.95	0.21	2.34	0.83	1.17	4.68	1.17	1.0	0.90	0.74	0.39	0.39	0.19
0.12	0.05	0.02	0.06	0.1	1.66	0.18	2	0.71	1	4	1	0.85	0.76	0.63	0.33	0.33	0.16
0.01	0.007	0.004	0.009	0.01	0.23	0.02	0.28	0.01	0.14	0.56	0.14	0.119	0.10	0.08	0.04	0.04	0.02
0.04	0.018	0.009	0.021	0.03	0.56	0.061	0.66	0.23	0.33	1.32	0.33	0.28	0.25	0.20	0.11	0.11	0.05
1.25	5	2.66	5.83	9	150	16.6	180	64.2	90	360	90	76.9	69.2	56.9	30	30	15.2
1.62	0.72	0.38	0.84	1.3	21.6	2.40	26	9.28	13	52	13	11.11	10	8.22	4.33	4.33	2.20
1	0.44	0.23	0.51	0.8	13.3	1.48	16	5.7	8	32	8	6.83	6.15	5.06	2.66	2.66	1.35
2.25	1	0.53	1.16	1.8	30	3.33	36	12.8	18	72	18	15.3	13.8	11.3	8	8	3.05
4.21	1.87	1	2.18	3.37	56.2	6.25	67.5	24.1	33.75	135	33.75	28.84	25.9	21.36	11.25	11.25	5.72
1.92	0.85	0.45	1	1.54	25.7	2.85	30.8	11.02	15.43	61.7	15.43	13.18	11.8	9.76	5.14	5.14	2.61
1.25	0.55	0.29	0.64	1	16.6	1.85	20	7.14	10	40	10	8.54	7.69	6.32	3.33	3.33	1.69
0.07	0.03	0.017	0.038	0.06	1	0.11	1.2	0.4	0.60	2.4	0.60	0.51	0.46	0.37	0.2	0.2	0.10
0.67	0.3	0.16	0.34	0.54	9	1	10.8	3.85	5.40	21.6	5.40	4.61	4.15	3.41	1.8	1.8	0.91
0.06	0.02	0.01	0.03	0.05	0.83	0.09	1	0.35	0.5	2	0.5	0.42	0.38	0.31	0.16	0.16	0.08
0.17	0.07	0.04	0.09	0.14	2.33	0.25	2.8	1	1.40	5.6	1.40	1.19	1.3	0.88	0.46	0.46	0.23
0.12	0.06	0.02	0.06	0.1	1.66	0.18	2	0.71	1	4.0	1	0.85	0.76	0.63	0.33	0.33	0.16
0.03	0.01	0.007	0.01	0.02	0.41	0.04	0.5	0.17	0.25	1	0.25	0.21	0.19	0.15	0.08	0.08	0.04
0.12	0.05	0.02	0.06	0.1	1.66	0.18	2	0.71	1	4.0	1	0.85	0.76	0.63	0.33	0.33	0.16
0.14	0.06	0.03	0.07	0.11	1.95	0.21	2.34	0.83	1.17	4.68	1.17	1	0.90	0.74	0.39	0.39	0.19
0.16	0.07	0.03	0.08	0.13	2.16	0.24	2.6	0.92	1.30	5.2	1.30	1.11	1	0.82	0.43	0.43	0.22
0.19	0.08	0.04	0.1	0.15	2.63	0.29	3.16	1.12	1.58	6.32	1.58	1.35	1.21	1	0.52	0.52	0.26
0.37	0.16	0.08	0.19	0.3	5	0.55	6	2.14	3	12	3	2.56	2.3	1.89	1	1	0.50
0.37	0.16	0.08	0.19	0.3	5	0.55	6	2.14	3	12	3	2.56	2.3	1.89	1	1	0.50
1.96	0.32	0.17	0.38	0.59	9.8	1.09	11.8	4.21	5.9	23.6	5.9	5.04	4.53	3.73	1.96	1.96	1

and tablets were the indispensable means of control and regulation. In the third case, there was intense animal husbandry and selective breeding. This guaranteed the best possible use of the land and was also a form of storage. Parcels of land were set aside as either year-long or seasonal pasture—in this latter case, usually between the time of the harvest and that of sowing. Surplus crops and plant parts unfit for human consumption were used as forage, thus transforming them into energy and storing them in the muscles of domestic animals.

The relation between production and urban economy can easily be imagined: one determined the other, so that the cycle of work-food-work was really a complex network of relations between the capital and the outlying regions; the city and the country; the administration and the workers; and the craftsmen and the peasants. The tablets of Ebla minutely reflect this chain of interdependence; but, at the same time, they reveal that, in addition to the cycle of productivity, there were also prices based on gold and silver.

The ratio of these two metals seems to have been a constant 4 or 5 to 1,[47] just as it was in Egypt during the Old Kingdom. A scale of values for all goods can be constructed by determining their value in silver as seen in the shekel of the light Oriental mina whose weight was 8.37 grams.

Using two coordinates, we can discover the value of any commodity in reference to all other commodities. With this goal in mind, we have studied the texts TM.75.G.1289, 1390, 1406, 1806, 1918, 2428, 2429, and 2505. These texts list in measures of area and capacity the prices of 34 kinds of goods (cf. Table VII, 7). The goods are divided into 7 categories: minerals, animal products, crops, persons, metal objects, wooden objects, and textiles. What results is a first sketch of the goods and services whose study will permit a critical analysis of the economy of Ebla.

The information obtained from the texts will provide the data for understanding the economy. The texts have been treated as if they were contemporary to each other. But only when we possess all of the information and can make use of a computer will we be able to see the fluctuation of values. Only in this way will it be possible to see the impact of a particular variable on the economy.[48] At the same time, we will understand the role played in third millennium social development by such factors as the city, political classes, long-distance commerce, and the control of landed property by a small group.

The following conclusions can be drawn from the diagram:

1) The consistency of the relation between gold and silver shows how little an effect the abundance or scarcity of these metals—which in any case were imported from outside the plain of Aleppo—had on an agriculture whose production varied from year to year. Gold and silver had a

special and separate role in the economy. They were amassed either to buy goods from abroad, or to make up for agricultural insufficiency. In this way it was possible to have dealings with the surrounding countries, and, more importantly, with distant places whose climate was different. The Aleppo basin is quite different from the delta plains of central Asia, such places as Sistan and the lower Turkoman, where the proto-urban economy developed during the third millennium, for these places were islands of agriculture surrounded by a vast desert. But Ebla was surrounded by states to which it was related by trade and its necessary bureaucracy. According to our hypothesis, gold and silver were the means by which Ebla became part of the world of international trade.[49] The texts suggest that the city, owing to its geographic position, coordinated the flow of goods among lands that were remote from each other: Egypt, Cyprus, Mesopotamia, and the Western Zagros.

2) That the value of labor differed according to what was produced is seen by comparing the cost of a golden *martu* dagger to that of worked gold; or by comparing the cost of a given measure of raw wool to that of quality cloth, such as *ib* cloth of the finest type. A comparison of the work of the goldsmith with that of the weaver shows that the former was more valued. This is not surprising, since metallurgy demanded a more complex technology and more expensive tools than did the work of the weaver. All this information will permit an exact determination of the different prices attached to different kinds of work.

3) Another cost comparison that can be made is that of high-grade and low-grade local textiles with that of local and imported textiles. Four kinds of texts have an average price of less than 1.3 shekels of silver: white *ib* cloth; linen cloth of poor quality; fine *sal* cloth; and poor cloth. But high-quality products, such as the best *ib* cloth, best linen, and the best multicolored *ib* cloth, always had a stable higher price that varied between 1.6 and 3 shekels. Imported goods, such as fine cloth from Mari and *zar* cloth from Kablul, show extreme differences in price; but this price is always greater than that of local products.

These are only a few of the many conclusions that an initial study of the texts has achieved. They give some idea of the range of the texts, and of the importance of the economic texts as a prodigious source of information. All of this information is located within space and time; but it is also located within those factors—such as technology, economy, and society—that give a culture its actual shape. Although non-economic texts have already given some information, it is precisely the information contained in the economic texts that will slowly reveal the motives of the civilization of Ebla, the factors that gave impetus and direction to commerce, alliances, wars, and political and religious relations.

4.3. COMMERCIAL GOODS: IMPORT-EXPORT

From the examination above of Ebla's economic resources it was concluded that the bases of her economy were agriculture and industry. Though the exports of agricultural products, especially olive oil, were considerable, they were surpassed by industrial goods.

First come the textiles produced in enormous quantities. To the data given above may be added those forthcoming from TM.75.G.2070:

an-šè-gú 5 *li-im* 9 *mi-at* 80 lá-3 túg-túg	total: 5,977 fabrics
5 *mi-at* 98 *é-da-um*-túg-2	598 Edaum fabrics of second quality
5 *mi-at* 63 íb-túg-ša$_6$-dar	563 Ib fabrics, top quality and multicolored
2 *li* 1 *mi* 10 íb-túg-dar	2,110 multicolored Ib fabrics
3 *mi-at* gu-súr-túg	300 Gusur fabrics

When the sum of 9,548 fabrics of different kinds is added to the preceding 6,474 materials mentioned in the same text, one realizes that one is dealing with the chief industry of Ebla.

Second come the products turned out by the industries of precious metals in the form of jewels, precious stones, and prized wooden objects.

As for imports, in addition to silver and gold serving more as the price of the goods sold, there are raw materials such as precious stones, among which lapis lazuli and carnelian figure prominently, as well as large and small livestock, the latter being essential for the huge quantities of wool needed to produce cloths for export.

Thus a text [50] reports that 17,000 head of sheep were imported from divers cities, following this pattern:

2 *li-im* 1 *mi-at* udu-udu	2,100 sheep
áb-ru$_y$-um^{ki}	from Abrum,
1 *li-im* 3 *mi-at* udu-udu	1,300 sheep
ti-gi-NI^{ki}	from Tigini,
3 *li-im* 7 *mi-at* udu-udu	3,700 sheep
ne-er^{ki}	from Neer,
3 *li-im* 5 *mi-at* udu-udu	3,500 sheep
ne-er^{ki} mìn	from Neer, a second time,
2 *li-im* 2 *mi-at* udu-udu	2,200 sheep
la-da-bi-ì^{ki}	from Ladabi,
4 *li-im* 8 *mi-at* udu-udu	4,800 sheep
x-ra-ad^{ki}	from X-rad.

In practice Ebla imported and exported every kind of goods ever with an eye to profit that made it a real economic power on an international level.

As mentioned above, a tablet is going to be cited in full here because it will convey to the reader a clear description of Ebla's relationships with other states, and will give an idea of the precision and the volume of transactions carried out within the span of only one month. To facilitate its reading, the text has been subdivided into paragraphs which find a faithful collating in the accompanying chart.

obverse

§1

I	1)	3 *é-da-um-túg*-2	1)	3 Edaum fabrics of second quality,
		3 aktum-túg		3 Aktum fabrics,
		3 íb-túg-ša$_6$-dar		3 Ib fabrics, top quality and multicolored,
	2)	1 gu-kak-šub-gíd-urudu	2)	1 "scepter" of copper,
		1 giš-šilig		1 axe, and
		1 ⌜gír⌝-mar-[t]u?		1 Martu dagger
	3)	*é-mi-šum*	3)	(for) Emišum,
	4)	lú-*iš-má-da-ba-an*	4)	the man of Išma-Daban,
	5)	*i-ti-*^{d}*aš-tár*	5)	(for) Iti-Aštar,
	6)	lú-*en-na-ni-il*	6)	the man of Ennani-Il
	7)	*eb-du-ìa*	7)	(for) Ebdu-Ya
	8)	*á-lu*^{ki}	8)	of the city Alu,
	9)	šeš-2-eb	9)	officials
	10)	*in*	10)	in the
	11)	*ir-mi*	11)	cities of the kingdom;

§2

12)	1 *é-da-um*-túg-2	12)	1 Edaum fabric of second quality,
	1 aktum-túg		1 Aktum fabric,
	1 íb-túg-ša$_6$-dar		1 Ib fabric, top quality and multicolored
13)	en	13)	for the king
14)	*bur-ma-an*^{ki}	14)	of the city of Burman;
15)	1 *é-da-um*-túg-2	15)	1 Edaum fabric of second quality,
	1 *é-da-um*-túg-1		1 Edaum fabric of first quality,
	1 aktum-túg		1 Aktum fabric,
	1 sal-túg		1 fine fabric,

		1 íb-túg ša$_6$-dar		1 Ib fabric, top quality and multicolored,
		1 íb-túg-dar		1 multicolored Ib fabric
II	1)	ABxAŠ-*sù*	1)	for his "Elders";
§3				
	2)	1 *é-da-um*-túg-2	2)	1 Edaum fabric of second quality,
		1 aktum-túg		1 Aktum fabric,
		1 íb-túg-ša$_6$-dar		1 Ib fabric, top quality and multicolored
	3)	en	3)	for the king
	4)	*tù-ub*^{ki}	4)	of the city Tub;
	5)	10 lá-2 *é-da-um*-túg-2	5)	8 Edaum fabrics of second quality,
		6 *é-da-um*-túg-1		6 Edaum fabrics of first quality,
		10 lá-2 aktum-túg		8 Aktum fabrics,
		6 sal-tug		6 fine fabrics,
		10 lá-2 íb-túg-ša$_6$-dar		8 Ib fabrics, top quality and multicolored;
		6 íb-túg-dar		6 Ib fabrics, multicolored,
	6)	a-mu-*sù*	6)	for his father,
	7)	šeš-šeš-*sù*	7)	for his brothers,
	8)	dumu-nita-dumu--nita-*sù*	8)	and for his sons;
§4				
	9)	*al*	9)	credit
	10)	5 aktum-túg	10)	of 5 Aktum fabrics
	11)	šeš-šeš-*sù*	11)	for his brothers,
	12)	20 gu-súr-túg	12)	20 Gusur fabrics,
		20 sal-túg		20 fine fabrics,
		20 íb-túg-dar		20 multicolored Ib fabrics
	13)	ABxÁŠ-*sù*	13)	for his "Elders,"
	14)	1 sal-túg	14)	1 fine fabric,
		1 íb-túg-dar		1 multicolored Ib fabric
	15)	*ma-za-lum-sù*	15)	for his general,
III	1)	1 zára-túg	1)	1 Zara fabric
	2)	*ma-lik-tum*	2)	for the queen
	3)	3 zára-túg	3)	3 Zara fabrics

	4)	dumu-mí-*sù*	4)	for her daughters,
	5)	13 túg-*ì-lí*	5)	13 excellent fabrics
	6)	dam	6)	for the women,
	7)	10 lá-2 sal-tug	7)	8 fine fabrics
	8)	dumu-mí-tur	8)	for the girls
	9)	*tù-ub*^{ki}	9)	of the city Tub;
§5				
	10)	1 *é-da-um-*túg-2	10)	1 Edaum fabric of second quality,
		1 aktum-túg		1 Aktum fabric,
		1 íb-túg-ša$_6$-dar		1 Ib fabric, top quality and multicolored,
	11)	en	11)	for the king
	12)	*i-BU-tum*^{ki}	12)	of the city Ibutum;
	13)	3 *é-da-um-*túg-2	13)	3 Edaum fabrics of second quality,
		2 *é-da-um-*túg-1		2 Edaum fabrics of first quality,
		3 aktum-túg		3 Aktum fabrics,
		2 sal-túg		2 fine fabrics,
		3 íb-túg-ša$_6$-dar		3 Ib fabrics, top quality and multicolored,
		2 íb-túg-dar		2 multicolored Ib fabrics
	14)	ABxÁŠ-*sù*	14)	for his "Elders";
§6				
	15)	1 *é-da-um-*túg-2	15)	1 Edaum fabric of second quality,
		1 aktum-túg		1 Aktum fabric,
		1 íb-túg-ša$_6$-dar		1 Ib fabric, top quality and multicolored,
	16)	en	16)	for the king
	17)	*ur-sá-um*^{ki}	17)	of the city Ursa'um;
	18)	4 *é-da-um-*túg-2	18)	4 Edaum fabrics of second quality,
IV	1)	4 *é-da-um-*túg-1	1)	4 Edaum fabrics of first quality,
		4 aktum-túg		4 Aktum fabrics,
		4 sal-túg		4 fine fabrics,
		4 íb-túg-ša$_6$-dar		4 Ib fabrics, top quality and multicolored;
		4 íb-túg-dar		4 Ib fabrics, multicolored,
	2)	ABxÁŠ-*sù*	2)	for his "Elders";

§7				
	3)	1 *é-da-um*-túg-2 1 aktum-túg 1 íb-túg-ša$_{6}$-dar	3)	1 Edaum fabric of second quality, 1 Aktum fabric, 1 Ib fabric, top quality and multicolored
	4)	*ḫu-ti-mu*^{ki}	4)	for the city Ḫutimu
	5)	1 *é-da-um*-túg-2 1 aktum-túg 1 íb-túg-ša$_{6}$-dar	5)	1 Edaum fabric of second quality, 1 Aktum fabric, 1 Ib fabric, top quality and multicolored
	6)	ABxÁŠ-*sù*	6)	for his elder;
	7)	10 lá-2 gu-súr-túg 10 lá-2 sal-túg 10 lá-2 íb-túg-dar	7)	8 Gusur fabrics, 8 fine fabrics, 8 multicolored Ib fabrics
	8)	guruš-*sù*	8)	for his officials;
	9)	1 *é-da-um*-túg-2 1 aktum-túg 1 íb-túg-ša$_{6}$-dar	9)	1 Edaum fabric of second quality, 1 Aktum fabric, 1 Ib fabric, top quality and multicolored
	10)	*gú-da-da-núm*^{ki}	10)	for the city Gudadanum;
	11)	1 sal-túg 1 íb-túg-dar	11)	1 fine fabric, 1 multicolored Ib fabric
	12)	*ma-za-lum-sù*	12)	for his general;
§8				
	13)	1 *é-da-um*-túg-2 1 aktum-túg 1 íb-túg-ša$_{6}$	13)	1 Edaum fabric of second quality, 1 Aktum-fabric, 1 top quality Ib fabric
	14)	⌜en⌝	14)	for the king;
§9				
V	1)	1 *é-da-um*-túg-2 1 aktum-túg 1 íb-túg-ša$_{6}$-dar	1)	1 Edaum fabric of second quality, 1 Aktum-fabric, 1 Ib fabric, top quality and multicolored
	2)	en	2)	for the king

	3)	*kak-mi-um*^{ki}	3)	of the city Kakmium,
	4)	*ší-in*	4)	for
	5)	É x P A P	5)	the house . . . ;
§10				
	6)	1 *é-da-um-* t ú g - 2	6)	1 Edaum fabric of second quality,
		1 aktum-túg		1 Aktum fabric,
		1 íb-túg-ša$_6$		1 top quality Ib fabric,
		1 díb-16 (gín)		1 thin sheet of 16 shekels
	7)	*ì-lum-* bala	7)	for Ilum-bala
	8)	maškim	8)	the official
	9)	*i-bí-sí-piš*	9)	of Ibbi-Sipiš
	10)	lú:tuš	10)	the resident
	11)	*gú-da-da-núm*^{ki}	11)	of Gudadanum
§11				
	12)	2 *é-da-um-* t ú g - 1	12)	2 Edaum fabrics of first quality,
		2 aktum-túg		2 Aktum fabrics,
		2 íb-túg-dar		2 multicolored Ib fabrics,
		2 *gú-li-lum* a-gar$_5$-guškin *sa-ḫa-*P I-2		2 copper bracelets double-coated with gold
	13)	*ap-rí-a-ḫu*	13)	for Apri-Aḫu
	14)	*gú-za-ma-lik*	14)	and Guza-Malik;
	15)	2 gu-mug-túg	15)	2 Gumug fabrics,
		2 sal-túg		2 fine fabrics,
		2 *gú-li-lum* a-gar$_5$ guškin AB.SI-2		2 copper bracelets double-coated with gold
	16)	*mi-*N E	16)	for MI-NE
	17)	[*a*]*-da-zu*	17)	and [A] dazu;
§12				
VI	1)	21 sal-túg	1)	21 fine fabrics,
		21 íb-túg-dar		21 multicolored Ib fabrics
	2)	*gú-da-da-núm*^{ki}	2)	for the city of Gudadanum,
	3)	maškim	3)	the official
	4)	*i-lum-* bala	4)	of Ilumbala;

§13

5)	1 *é-da-um-*túg-1 1 aktum-túg 1 íb-túg-dar 1 *gú-li-lum sa-ḫa-*PI-2	5)	1 Edaum fabric, 1 Aktum fabric, 1 multicolored Ib fabric, 1 double-coated bracelet,
6)	*ip-qà-ìa*	6)	for Ipqa-Ya;
7)	1 gu-mug-túg 1 sal-túg 1 íb-túg-dar 1 *gú-li-lum* AB.SI-2	7)	1 Gumug fabric, 1 fine fabric, 1 multicolored Ib fabric, 1 double-coated bracelet,
8)	maškim-*sù*	8)	for his supervisor,
9)	maškim	9)	supervisor
10)	*en-zi-ma-lik*	10)	of Enzi-Malik
11)	šu-du$_8$	11)	as tribute

§14

12)	1 dùl-túg-*ma-rí*^{ki}	12)	1 Dul fabric of Mari
13)	*kéš-du-ut*	13)	for Kešdut;
14)	1 *é-da-um-*túg-2 1 aktum-túg 1 íb-túg-ša$_6$ 1 díb gur$_8$	14)	1 Edaum fabric of second quality, 1 Aktum fabric, 1 top quality Ib fabric, 1 thin sheet of 20 shekels
15)	*mi-na-lí*	15)	for Minali,
16)	lú-*sà-sà-lum*	16)	the man of Sasalum,
17)	*da-ra-um*^{ki}	17)	of the city Dara'um,
18)	šu-du$_8$	18)	tax
19)	*a-la*^{ki}	19)	of the city Ala;

§15

20)	1 *é-da-um-*túg-2 1 aktum-túg 1 íb-túg-ša$_6$ 1 díb ku$_5$-5	20)	1 Edaum fabric of second quality, 1 Aktum fabric, 1 top quality Ib fabric, 1 thin sheet of 35 shekels
21)	⌜*i-ti*⌝ - [ ]	21)	for Iti [ ]

VII	1)	*ar-ga*^{ki}	1)	of the city Arga;
	2)	2 *é-da-um-* t ú g - 2	2)	2 Edaum fabrics of second quality,
		2 a k t u m - t ú g		2 Aktum fabrics,
		2 í b - t ú g - š a$_6$		2 top quality Ib fabrics
	3)	*ar-ší-a-ḫu*	3)	for Arši-Aḫu
	4)	*gàr-kà-mi-iš*^{ki}	4)	of Karkamiš,
	5)	m a š k i m	5)	supervisor
	6)	*en-zi-ma-lik*	6)	of Enzi-Malik
	7)	*a-si-ma-lik*	7)	and for Asi-Malik
	8)	*gub-lu*^{ki}	8)	of the city Byblos
	9)	s u - d u$_8$ - m á š	9)	as tribute;
§16				
	10)	1 g u - m u g - t ú g	10)	1 Gumug fabric,
		1 s a l - t ú g		1 fine fabric,
		1 í b - t ú g - d a r		1 multicolored fabric
	11)	*a-šu-ur-ìa*	11)	for Ashur-Ya
	12)	*a-zi-du*^{ki}	12)	of the city Azidu,
	13)	n ì - ^{d}m u l	13)	property of the "Star"
	14)	ì - g i š	14)	(feast of the) anointing
	15)	e d e n^{ki}	15)	at Eden,
	16)	n i d b a$_x$	16)	as an offering;
§17				
	17)	2 *é-da-um-* t ú g - 2	17)	2 Edaum fabrics of second quality,
		2 a k t u m - t ú g		2 Aktum fabrics,
		2 í b - t ú g - d a r		2 multicolored Ib fabrics,
		2 *gú-li-lum* a - g a r$_5$ - g u š k i n AB.SI-2		2 copper bracelets double-coated with gold
	18)	*iš*$_x$*-gi-bar-zú*	18)	for Išgi-Barzu
	19)	*ù-nu-ub*^{ki}	19)	of the city Unub,
	20)	l ú : t u š	20)	who resides
	21)	*a-la*^{ki}	21)	in Ala,
	22)	*ba-ti-lum*	22)	and for Batilum
	23)	*ba-ti-nu*^{ki}	23)	of the city Batinu,
	24)	m a š k i m	24)	supervisor
	25)	*ki-ti-ir*	25)	of Kitir
	26)	š u - d u$_8$	26)	tribute
	27)	*ì-a-pí-nu*^{ki}	27)	of the city Yapinu;

§18				
	28)	1 dùl-túg *ma-rí*^{ki}	28)	1 Dul fabric of Mari
VIII	1)	*i-bí-sí-piš*	1)	for Ibbi-Sipiš,
	2)	2 gu-mug-túg	2)	2 Gumug fabrics
	3)	2 dumu-mí	3)	for two daughters
	4)	lú-é-mul	4)	attached to the temple of the "Star";
	5)	1 gu-mug-túg	5)	1 Gumug fabric,
		1 sal-túg		1 fine fabric,
		1 íb-túg-dar		1 multicolored Ib fabric,
		1 *gú-li-lum*		1 copper bracelet
		a-gar$_5$-guškin AB.SI-2		double-coated with gold
	6)	*i-ti-ma-lik*	6)	for Iti-Malik
	7)	IGI^{ki}	7)	of the city Igi;
	8)	šu-du$_8$	8)	tribute
	9)	*tù-ub*^{ki}	9)	of the city Tub;
§19				
	10)	2 íb-túg-ša$_6$	10)	2 Ib fabrics of top quality
	11)	*i-ni-lum*	11)	for Inilum
	12)	*mu-ší-lu*^{ki}	12)	of the city Mušilu,
	13)	*iš-má-da-ba-an*	13)	and for Išma-Daban
	14)	mar-tum^{ki}	14)	of the city Martu;
	15)	šeš-2-eb	15)	officials-šeš-2-eb
	16)	kéš-da	16)	under control;
§20				
	17)	1 *é-da-um-*túg-2	17)	1 Edaum fabric of second quality,
		1 aktum-túg		1 Aktum fabric,
		1 íb-túg-ša$_6$		1 top quality Ib fabric,
		1 gír-mar-tu guškin		1 dagger of Amorite gold,
	18)	1 *ma-na* kù:babbar	18)	1 mina of silver
	19)	en	19)	for (?) the king
	20)	*i-*BU*-tum*^{ki}	20)	of the city Ibutum,
§21				
	21)	20 gu-mug-túg	21)	20 Gumug fabrics,
		20 íb-túg-babbar		2 white Ib fabrics
	22)	1 é-duru$_5$^{ki}	22)	for 1 "village"
	23)	*šu-ti-gú*^{ki}	23)	of the city Šutigu;

	24)	*iš-má-šum*	24)	Išma-Šum,
	25)	ugula-ká	25)	the inspector of the gate,
	26)	šu ba_4-ti	26)	has received
§22				
	27)	1 aktum-túg	27)	1 Aktum fabric,
IX	1)	2 sal-túg	1)	2 fine fabrics
	2)	*ti-a*	2)	for Tia,
	3)	1 dam	3)	1 woman
	4)	*ṣi-íb-da-mu*	4)	of Ṣib-Damu;
§23				
	5)	2 aktum-túg *ti-a*	5)	2 Aktum fabrics for Tia
	6)	1 dumu-mí-en	6)	1 daughter of the king
	7)	*a-ru$_x$-ga-tù*^{ki}	7)	at Arugatu;
§24				
	8)	1 *é-da-um-*túg-2	8)	1 Edaum fabric of second quality,
		1 aktum-túg		1 Aktum fabric,
		1 íb-túg-sal		1 fine Ib fabric,
	9)	*ḫa-ba*	9)	Ḫaba,
	10)	dumu-nita-en	10)	the son of the king,
	11)	nì-^{d}mul	11)	(as) possession of the "Star"
	12)	*da-pi$_5$-nu*^{ki}	12)	of the city Dapinu
	13)	šu-ba_4-ti	13)	has received;
§25				
	14)	2 gu-mug-túg	14)	2 Gumug fabrics,
		2 sal-túg		2 fine fabrics,
		2 íb-túg-dar		2 multicolored fabrics
	15)	2 dumu-nita	15)	for two sons
	16)	*bù-GAN*	16)	of Bugan
	17)	šu-du_8-maš	17)	(as) tribute;
§26				
	18)	4 *é-da-um-*túg-1	18)	4 Edaum fabrics of first quality,
		4 sal-túg		4 fine fabrics,
		4 íb-túg-dar		4 multicolored Ib fabrics
	19)	*iš$_x$-gú-lu*	19)	for Išqulu,
	20)	*ip-qá-iš-lu*	20)	Ipqa-Išlu,
	21)	*ip-ḫur-ìa*	21)	Ipḫur-Ya,

	22)	N E-*a-a*	22) NE-A’a,
	23)	l ú - k a r	23) the merchants
	24)	*ti-šúm*^{ki}	24) of the city Tišum;
§27			
	25)	2 *é-da-um-* t ú g - 2	25) 2 Edaum fabrics of second quality,
		2 a k t u m - t ú g	2 Aktum fabrics,
		2 í b - t ú g - š a$_6$	2 top quality Ib fabrics
	26)	*a-zu-ba-da*	26) for Azubada
	27)	*mi-kà-ìa*	27) and for Mika-Ya;
§28			
	28)	2 *é-da-um-* t ú g - 1	28) 2 Edaum fabrics of first quality,
		2 a k t u m - t ú g	2 Aktum fabrics,
X	1)	2 í b - t ú g - d a r	1) 2 multicolored Ib fabrics
	2)	*é-wa-ra*	2) for Ewara
	3)	*a-lum*	3) and Alum
	4)	*ḫu-ti-mu*^{ki}	4) of the city Ḫutimu
	5)	š u - d u$_8$	5) tribute
	6)	i n . m a	6) ———
	7)	*ḫu-ti-mu*^{ki}	7) of the city Ḫutimu;
§29			
	8)	1 g a d a - t ú g	8) 1 linen fabric
	9)	*ga-da*	9) for Gada,
	10)	l ú *na-*^{d}ì - g i š	10) the man of Na-Igiš;
	11)	1 g a d a - t ú g - M U	11) 1 MU fabric of linen,
		2 g a d a - t ú g T I N . K A S K A L^{ki}	2 fabrics of Tinkaskal linen,
		2 g a d a - t ú g š u - é	2 ŠU-É fabrics of linen,
		4 g a d a - t ú g - š u	4 ŠU fabrics of linen
	12)	e n	12) for the king;
	13)	4 *é-da-um-* t ú g - 2	13) 4 Edaum fabrics of second quality,
		4 a k t u m - t ú g	4 Aktum fabrics,
		4 í b - t ú g - š a$_6$	4 top quality Ib fabrics
	14)	l u g a l *-a-ba*$_4$	14) for Lugal-Aba
	15)	*ma-rí*^{ki}	15) of the city Mari,
	16)	š u - d u$_8$	16) tribute
	17)	*ma-nu-wa-at*^{ki}	17) of the city Manuwat;

	18)	*ša-ma*	18)	for Šama
	19)	*ir-i-tum*^{ki}	19)	of the city Iritum,
	20)	*en-zú-we-rum*	20)	and for Enzuwerum
	21)	lú *a-na-ba*	21)	the man of Anaba,
	22)	šu-du$_8$	22)	tribute
	23)	*ší-zú-gú*^{ki}	23)	of the city Šizugu,
	24)	*mi-na-lí*	24)	for Minali
	25)	*da-ra-um*^{ki}	25)	of the city Daraum,
	26)	šu-du$_8$	26)	tribute
	27)	*gur-da-bí-du*^{ki}	27)	of the city Gurdabidu;
§30				
XI	1)	1 *é-da-um*-túg-1	1)	1 Edaum fabric of first quality,
		1 aktum-túg		1 Aktum fabric,
		1 íb-túg-dar		1 multicolored Ib fabric,
		1 *gú-li-lum* a-gar$_5$ guškin *sa-ḫa*-PI-2		1 copper bracelet double-coated with gold
	2)	*ìr-íb-a-ḫu*	2)	for Irib-Aḫu
	3)	*a-ru*$_x$*-ga-tù*^{ki}	3)	of the city Arugatu;
§31				
	4)	1 *é-da-um*-túg-1	4)	1 Edaum fabric of first quality,
		1 sal-túg		1 fine fabric,
		1 íb-túg-dar		1 multicolored Ib fabric,
		1 *gú-li-lum* a-gar$_5$ guškin AB.SI-2		1 copper bracelet double-coated with gold
	5)	*i-da*-NE	5)	for Ida-NE
	6)	*gal-tum*-x	6)	———
	7)	maškim	7)	supervisor
	8)	⌜x⌝-*na* [ ]	8)	———
§32				
	9)	1 *é-da-um*-túg-1	9)	1 Edaum fabric of first quality,
		1 aktum-túg		1 Aktum fabric,
		1 íb-túg-ša$_6$-dar		1 top quality and multicolored Ib fabric
		1 díb-10 (gín)		1 thin sheet of 10 shekels
	10)	*é-wa-ra*	10)	for Ewara;

	11)	1 díb-10 (gín)	11)	1 thin sheet of 10 shekels
	12)	KA-*ba-nu*	12)	for KA-banu
	13)	*ḫu-ti-mu*^{ki}	13)	of the city Ḫutimu;
§33				
	14)	1 *é-da-um*-túg-2	14)	1 Edaum fabric of second quality,
		1 aktum-túg		1 Aktum fabric
		1 íb-túg-ša$_6$		1 top quality Ib fabric
	15)	ugula *šu-ti-gú*^{ki}	15)	for the inspector of the city Šutigu;
reverse				
I	1)	1 *é-da-um*-túg-1	1)	1 Edaum fabric of first quality,
		1 sal-túg		1 fine fabric,
		1 íb-túg-dar		1 multicolored Ib fabric
	2)	maškim-*sù*	2)	for his supervisor;
§34				
	3)	2 *é-da-um*-túg-1	3)	2 Edaum fabrics of first quality,
		2 sal-túg		2 fine fabrics,
		2 íb-túg-dar		2 multicolored Ib fabrics
	4)	*ù-nu*-NI^{ki}	4)	for the city of Unu-NI,
	5)	šu-du$_8$	5)	tribute
	6)	*iš-má-ìa*	6)	of Išma-Ya,
	7)	lú-kar	7)	the merchant
	8)	*ma-rí*^{ki}	8)	of the city Mari;
§35				
	9)	1 *é-da-um*-túg-2	9)	1 Edaum fabric of second quality,
		1 aktum-túg		1 Aktum fabric,
		1 íb-túg-ša$_6$-dar		1 top quality, multicolored Ib fabric,
		1 gada-túg		1 linen fabric,
		2 nì-lá-du		2 Niladu objects
	10)	en	10)	for the king
	11)	*ir-i-tum*^{ki}	11)	of the city Iritum;
	12)	1 *é-da-um*-túg-1	12)	1 Edaum fabric of first quality,

		1 aktum-túg		1 Aktum fabric,
		1 gada-túg		1 linen fabric
	13)	dumu-nita-*sù*	13)	for his son;
§36				
	14)	1 aktum-túg	14)	1 Aktum fabric,
		1 gír-ma-tu		1 Amorite dagger with
		KA-ak		blade
	15)	^{d}*ni-da-kul*	15)	for the divinity Nidakul
	16)	*é-ma-tù*^{ki}	16)	of the city Ḥama;
§37				
	17)	1 aktum-túg	17)	1 Aktum fabric,
		1 íb-túg-ša$_6$-dar		1 top quality and multicolored Ib fabric
	18)	ì-giš-sag	18)	for the anointing of the head
II	1)	*en-na-ìa*	1)	of Enna-Ya,
	2)	lú *a-du-lu*	2)	the man of Adulu;
	3)	1 *é-da-um-*túg-2	3)	1 Edaum fabric of second quality,
		1 aktum-túg		1 Aktum fabric,
		1 íb-túg-ša$_6$		1 top quality Ib fabric,
		1 díb-10 (gín)		1 thin sheet of 10 shekels
	4)	*é-da-ša*	4)	for Edaša,
	5)	lú *a-mu-du*	5)	the man of Amudu,
	6)	*zu-ša-ga-bù*^{ki}	6)	in Zušagabu
	7)	lú:tuš	7)	residing;
§38				
	8)	5 *é-da-um-*túg-1	8)	5 Edaum fabrics of first quality,
		5 aktum-túg		5 Aktum fabrics,
		5 íb-túg-ša$_6$		5 top quality Ib fabrics,
		5 *gú-li-lum*		5 copper bracelets
		a-gar$_5$-guškin		double-coated with gold
		AB-SI-2		
	9)	*é-da-ša*	9)	for Edaša
	10)	*a-bu$_x$-gú-ra*	10)	and Abu-Gura
	11)	*ti-in*^{ki}	11)	of the city Tin,
	12)	*iq-na-um*	12)	Iqna'um
	13)	*zu-ša-ga-bù*^{ki}	13)	of the city Zušagabu,
	14)	*ga-du-um*	14)	Gadum

	15)	*i-rí-sa*	15)	and Irisa
	16)	NI-*ší-gú*^{ki}	16)	of the city NI-šigu;
§39				
	17)	3 *é-da-um*-túg-1	17)	3 Edaum fabrics of first quality,
		3 aktum-túg		3 Aktum fabrics,
		3 íb-túg-ša$_6$		3 top quality Ib fabrics
	18)	*a-na*-lugal	18)	for Analugal
	19)	*ma-rí*^{ki}	19)	of the city Mari,
	20)	nì-^{d}mul	20)	possession of the "Star"
	21)	*ma-nu-wa-at*^{ki}	21)	of the city Manuwat
	22)	til	22)	etc. . . .
III	1)	*gú-la*	1)	for Gula
	2)	*gàr-mu*^{ki}	2)	of the city Garmu,
	3)	*en-na-Be*	3)	and for Enna-Be
	4)	*ší-zú*^{ki}	4)	of the city Šizu,
	5)	šu-du$_8$	5)	tribute
	6)	*i-li-bí*^{ki}	6)	of the city Ilibi;
§40				
	7)	1 *é-da-um*-túg-2	7)	1 Edaum fabric of second quality,
		1 aktum-túg		1 Aktum fabric,
		1 íb-túg-ša$_6$		1 top quality Ib fabric
	8)	*i-ti-*^{d}*ni-da-kul*	8)	for Iti-Nidakul
	9)	*ir-i-bí-tù*^{ki}	9)	in Iribidu
	10)	lú:tuš	10)	residing;
	11)	1 aktum-túg	11)	1 Aktum fabric,
		1 íb-túg-dar		1 multicolored Ib fabric
	12)	*en-na-ì̀a*	12)	for Enna-Ya,
	13)	maškim-*sù*	13)	his supervisor,
	14)	*šu-bù-gú*^{ki}	14)	of the city Šubugu
	15)	lú *kak-mi-um*^{ki}	15)	in the region of Kakmium;
§41				
	16)	4 *é-da-um*-túg-1	16)	4 Edaum fabrics of first quality,
		4 sal-túg		4 fine fabrics,
		4 íb-túg-dar		4 multicolored fabrics,
		2 *gú-li-lum sa-ḫa*-PI-1		2 bracelets once-coated,

		2 *gú-li-lum* AB-SI-2		2 bracelets twice-coated,
	17)	*en-na-ìa*	17)	for Enna-Ya
	18)	IGI^{ki}	18)	of the city Igi,
	19)	šu-du$_8$	19)	tribute
	20)	*ar-'à-mu*^{ki}	20)	of the city Aramu,
	21)	*gú-gi-a-nu*	21)	for Gugianu
	22)	*ti-in*^{ki}	22)	of the city Tin,
	23)	šu-du$_8$	23)	tribute
	24)	*ar-ga*^{ki}	24)	of the city Arga,
	25)	*pù-ḫi*	25)	for Puḫi
IV	1)	*mu-ru*$_x^{ki}$	1)	of the city Muru,
	2)	šu-du$_8$	2)	tribute
	3)	*é-du*^{ki}	3)	of the city Edu,
	4)	*ip-ḫur-ìa*	4)	for Ipḫur-Ya
	5)	IGI^{ki}	5)	of the city Igi,
	6)	šu-du$_8$	6)	tribute
	7)	SAG^{ki}	7)	of the city Sag;
§42				
	8)	3 gu-mug-túg 3 íb-túg-dar	8)	3 Gumug fabrics, 3 multicolored fabrics
	9)	lú-kar	9)	for the merchants
	10)	*kak-mi-um*^{ki}	10)	of the city Kakmium
	11)	*gu-da-da-núm*^{ki}	11)	and of the city Gudadanum
	12)	DU.DU	12)	who undertake
	13)	kaskal	13)	a journey,
	14)	*en-na-ía*	14)	and for Enna-Ya,
	15)	lú *pù-wu*	15)	the man of Puwu;
§43				
	16)	1 dùl-túg *ma-rí*^{ki} 1 aktum-túg	16)	1 Dul fabric of Mari, 1 Aktum fabric
	17)	*du-bù-ḫu-*^{d}*'à-da*	17)	for Dubuḫu-Hada,
§44				
	18)	1 gu-súr-túg	18)	1 Gusur fabric
	19)	1 dam	19)	for 1 woman
	20)	en	20)	of the king
	21)	*ìr-ra-*DI*-mu*	21)	Irra-Dimu
	22)	šu-ba$_4$-ti	22)	has received;

§45				
	23)	3 íb-túg-sal	23)	3 fine Ib fabrics
	24)	*ga-du-um*	24)	for Gadum,
	25)	SAG-*da-mu*	25)	Sag-Damu,
	26)	*ip-te-da-mu*	26)	and Ipte-Damu,
	27)	dumu-nita-en	27)	sons of the king;
§46				
	28)	1 gada-túg	28)	1 linen fabric
	29)	*íl-e-i-šar*	29)	for Ile-Išar,
	30)	lú *ag-ga*	30)	the man of Agga
§47				
	31)	2 gu-mug-túg 2 sal-túg 2 íb-túg	31)	2 Gumug fabrics, 2 fine fabrics, 2 Ib fabrics
	32)	*da-sí-ma-ad*	32)	for Dasi-Maad
	33)	maškim	33)	supervisor
	34)	*ki-ti-ir*	34)	of Kitir,
	35)	šu-du_8	35)	tribute
V	1)	*u_9-na-gu*[ki]	1)	of the city Unagu;
	2)	*ṭù-bí-sí-piš*	2)	and for Ṭubi-Sipiš
	3)	maškim	3)	supervisor
	4)	*e-zi*	4)	of Ezi,
	5)	šu-du_8	5)	tribute
	6)	*za-mi-da-nu*[ki]	6)	of the city Zamidanu,
§48				
	7)	2 aktum-túg	7)	2 Aktum fabrics
	8)	*ip-te-da-mu*	8)	for Ipte-Damu
	9)	SAG-*da-mu*	9)	and Sag-Damu;
§49				
	10)	2 aktum-túg 2 íb-túg-$ša_6$-dar	10)	2 Aktum fabrics, 2 top quality, multicolored Ib fabrics
	11)	*é-mu-ru_x-gú*	11)	for Emurugu
	12)	*za-ma-'à-ru_x*	12)	for Zama' aru;
§50				
	13)	4 sal-túg 4 íb-túg-$ša_6$	13)	4 fine fabrics, 4 top quality Ib fabrics
	14)	*dur-é-*NE*-zu*	14)	for Durenezu,
	15)	*wa-da-é*	15)	Wada'e,
	16)	*bar-i*	16)	Bari,
	17)	*pù-šu*	17)	and Pušu;

§51				
	18)	15 s a l - t ú g 15 í b - t ú g - d a r	18)	15 fine fabrics and 15 multicolored Ib fabrics
	19)	*gú-ba*	19)	for Guba,
	20)	*u_9-bil-lum*	20)	Ubillum,
	21)	*en-na-ìa*	21)	Enna-Ya,
	22)	*ga-da-na*	22)	Gadana,
	23)	*na-zi*	23)	Nazi,
	24)	*su-lum*	24)	Sulum,
	25)	*a-wa-i-šar*	25)	Awa-Isar,
	26)	*bù-da-ya*	26)	Buda-Ya,
	27)	*a-bù-^{d}ku-ra*	27)	Abu-Kura,
	28)	*Ni-ba-ìa*	28)	Niba-Ya,
	29)	*zu-zu-ga-mu*	29)	Zuzugamu,
	30)	*zi-ru_x-šu*	30)	Zirušu,
	31)	*gú-li-lu*	31)	Gulilu,
	32)	*ù-rí-ḫa-mu*	32)	Uriḫamu,
VI	1)	Ḫ Ú B	1)	of the city of Ḫub;
§52				
	2)	1 *é-da-um-* t ú g - 2 1 a k t u m - t ú g 1 í b - t ú g - $ša_6$	2)	1 Edaum fabric of second quality, 1 Aktum fabric, 1 top quality Ib fabric
	3)	*$iš_x$-GA*	3)	for Išga
	4)	*na gàr^{ki}*	4)	of the city Nagar;
§53				
	5)	2 g a d a - t ú g	5)	2 linen fabrics
	6)	2 d a m - e n	6)	for two women of the king
	7)	*gú-ba-lum*	7)	Gubalum
	8)	š u - ba_4 t i	8)	has received;
§54				
	9)	1 *é-da-um-* t ú g - 1 1 a k t u m - t ú g 1 í b - t ú g - d a r 1 *gú-li-lum* a - g a r_5 g u š k i n A B - S I - 2	9)	1 Edaum fabric of first quality, 1 Aktum fabric, 1 multicolored Ib fabric, 1 copper bracelet double-coated with gold
	10)	*ìr-ì-ba*	10)	for Iriba

	11)	*gàr-ru*$_x$^{ki}	11)	of the city of Garru;
	12)	šu-du$_8$	12)	tribute
	13)	*a-ḫa-da-mu*^{ki}	13)	of the city Aḫa-Damu;
§55				
	14)	23 sal-túg 23 íb-túg-dar	14)	23 fine fabrics, 23 multicolored Ib fabrics
	15)	2 nar-maḫ$_x$ (=AL)	15)	for 2 older singers,
	16)	21 nar-tur	16)	for 21 younger singers,
	17)	*ma-rí*^{ki}	17)	of the city Mari;
§56				
	18)	1 *é-da-um-*túg-1 1 aktum-túg	18)	1 Edaum fabric of first quality, 1 Aktum fabric
	19)	*BU-ra-kam*$_x$	19)	for Bura-Kam
	20)	*ur-sá-um*^{ki}	20)	of the city Ursa'um;
§57				
	21)	gur$_8$-2 (gín) kù:babbar	21)	22 shekels of silver
	22)	*a-dè* gu-mug-túg	22)	for Gumug fabric,
	23)	22 sal-túg 22 íb-túg-dar	23)	22 fine fabrics and 22 multicolored Ib fabrics
	24)	22 nar	24)	for 22 singers
	25)	sa-MI+ŠITA$_x$^{ki}	25)	of the lord's palace;
§58				
	26)	10 (gín) kù:babbar	26)	10 shekels of silver
	27)	*a-dè*	27)	for
VII	1)	⌜2⌝ *é-da-um-*túg-2 1 aktum-túg	1)	2 Edaum fabrics of second quality, 1 Aktum fabric,
	2)	1 íb-túg-ša$_6$	2)	1 top quality Ib fabric
	3)	*é-mu-ru*$_x$*-gú*	3)	for Emurugu;
	4)	7 (gín) kù:babbar	4)	7 shekels of silver
	5)	*a-dè* 2 gu-súr-túg	5)	for 2 Gusur fabrics;
	6)	1 íb-túg-ša$_6$	6)	1 top quality Ib fabric
	7)	*za-ma-à-ru*$_x$	7)	for Zama'aru;
	8)	8 (gín) kù:babbar	8)	8 shekels of silver
	9)	*a-dè* 4 *é-da-um-*túg-1	9)	for 4 Edaum fabrics of first quality;

	10)	4 (gín) kù:babbar	10)	4 shekels of silver
	11)	*a-dè* 4 sal-túg	11)	for 4 fine fabrics,
	12)	4 íb-túg-ša$_6$	12)	4 top quality Ib fabrics
	13)	*dur-é-NE-zu*	13)	for Durenezu,
	14)	*wa-da-é*	14)	Wada'e,
	15)	*bar-i*	15)	Bari,
	16)	*pù-šu*	16)	and Pušu;
	17)	gur$_8$ kù:babbar	17)	20 shekels of silver
	18)	*a-dè* 15 gu-mug-túg	18)	for 15 Gumug fabrics
	19)	15 íb-túg-dar	19)	and 15 multicolored Ib fabrics
	20)	*gú-ba*	20)	for Guba,
	21)	*u$_9$-bil-lum*	21)	Ubillum,
	22)	*en-na-ìa*	22)	Enna-Ya,
	23)	*en-na-ìa* 2	23)	Enna-Ya, second time,
	24)	*ga-da-na*	24)	Gadana,
	25)	*na-zi*	25)	Nazi,
	26)	*su-lum*	26)	Sulum,
	27)	*a-wa-i-šar*	27)	Awa-Išar,
	28)	*bù-da-yà*	28)	Buda-Ya,
	29)	*a-bù-^{d}ku-ra*	29)	Abu-Kura,
	30)	*Ni-ba-ìa*	30)	Niba-Ya,
	31)	*zu-zu-ga-mu*	31)	Zuzugamu,
	32)	*zi-ru$_x$-šu*	32)	Zirušu,
VIII	1)	[*gu-li*]-*lu-nu*	1)	[Guli]lunu,
	2)	*ù-ri-ḫa-mu*	2)	Uriḫamu,
	3)	ḪÚB^{ki}	3)	of the city Ḫub,
	4)	6 (gín) kù:babbar	4)	6 shekels of silver
	5)	*a-dè* 2 gu-súr-túg 2 sal-túg	5)	for 2 Gusur fabrics, 2 fine fabrics;
	6)	2 íb-túg-dar	6)	2 multicolored Ib fabrics
	7)	nar-maḫ$_x$ (=AL)	7)	for older singers;
	8)	gur$_8$-8 kù:babbar	8)	28 shekels of silver
	9)	*a-dè* 21 sal-túg	9)	for 21 fine fabrics,
	10)	gur$_8$-4 kù:babbar	10)	21 shekels of silver
	11)	*a-dè* 21 gu-mug-túg	11)	for 21 Gumug fabrics;
	12)	21 íb-túg-dar	12)	21 multicolored Ib fabrics
	13)	21 nar-tur	13)	for 21 younger singers
	14)	*ma-rí*^{ki}	14)	of the city Mari;

§59				
	15)	2 *é-da-um-*túg-2	15)	2 Edaum fabrics of second quality,
		2 aktum-túg		2 Aktum fabrics,
		2 íb-túg-ša$_6$		2 top quality Ib fabrics
	16)	*i-ti-*^{d}*ni-da-kul*	16)	for Iti-Nidakul
	17)	*ir-i-bí-tù*^{ki}	17)	of the city Iribitu;
	18)	lú:tuš	18)	and for the resident
	19)	*na-i*^{ki}	19)	of Nai,
	20)	ìr-^{d}*ma-lik*	20)	Ir-Malik,
	21)	maškim	21)	the supervisor
	22)	*é-zi*	22)	of Ezi;
§60				
	23)	1 *é-da-um-*túg-2	23)	1 Edaum fabric of second quality,
		1 aktum-túg		1 Aktum fabric,
		1 íb-túg-ša$_6$		1 top quality Ib fabric,
		1 *gú-li-lum* a-gar$_5$ guškin-2		1 copper bracelet double-coated with gold
	24)	*gú-ba-ù*	24)	for Gubau
	25)	*ir-i-bí-tù*^{ki}	25)	of the city Iribitu
	26)	lú:tuš	26)	residing
	27)	*ša-ra-*NE^{ki}	27)	in Šarane;
§61				
	28)	1 *sal-túg*	28)	1 fine fabric
IX	1)	[ ]	1)	[ ]
	2)	*iš-la-ìa*	2)	Išla-Ya,
	3)	*puzur*$_4$*-ra-ìa*	3)	Puzur-Ya,
	4)	nì-^{d}mul	4)	possession of the "Star"
	5)	*du-bù-ḫu-*^{d}*'à-da*	5)	(from) Dubuḫu-Hada
	6)	lú:tuš	6)	residing
	7)	*ma-nu-wa-at*^{ki}	7)	in Manuwat;
§62				
	8)	1 *é-da-um-*túg-1	8)	1 Edaum fabric of first quality,
		1 sal-túg		1 fine fabric,
		1 íb-túg-dar		1 multicolored Ib fabric,

	1 *gú-li-lum*		1 copper bracelet
	a-gar$_5$ guškin		double-coated with
	AB-SI-2		gold
9)	lú-kar	9)	for the merchant
10)	*ší-zu*^{ki}	10)	of the city Šizu;
11)	šu-du$_8$	11)	tribute
12)	*a-zu*^{ki}	12)	of the city Azu;

§63

13)	1 gu-mug-túg	13)	1 Gumug fabric,
	1 sal-túg		1 fine fabric,
	1 íb-túg-dar		1 multicolored fabric
14)	maškim	14)	for the supervisor
15)	*ki-ti-ir*	15)	of Kitir;
16)	1 *é-da-um*-túg-1	16)	1 Edaum fabric of first quality,
	1 aktum-túg		1 Aktum fabric,
	1 íb-túg-ša$_6$		1 top quality Ib fabric
17)	*Da-ni*	17)	for Dani,
18)	ugula kur-bar+an	18)	inspector of the foreign land,
19)	*eb-du-lu*	19)	Ebdulu
20)	*in*	20)	in
21)	*ì-ti-ba*^{ki}	21)	Litiba
22)	šu ba$_4$-ti	22)	has received;

§64

23)	1 *é-da-um*-túg-2	23)	1 Edaum fabric of second quality,
	1 aktum-túg		1 Aktum fabric,
	1 íb-túg-ša$_6$		1 top quality Ib fabric,
	1 *gú-li-lum*		1 copper bracelet
	a-gar$_5$ guškin		double-coated with
	AB-SI-2		gold
24)	*gú-gi-a-an*	24)	for Gugian
25)	*gú-ra-kul*^{ki}	25)	of the city Gurakul;
26)	1 *é-da-um*-túg-2	26)	1 Edaum fabric of second quality,
	1 aktum-túg		1 Aktum fabric,
	1 íb-túg-ša$_6$		1 top quality Ib fabric
27)	*šu-ì-lum*	27)	for Šuilum
28)	*ti-in*^{ki}	28)	of the city of Tin;

§65

X	1)	2 aktum-túg 1 dam-TI	1)	1 Aktum fabric for 1 woman . . .
	2)	*iḫ-su-up-da-mu*	2)	of Iḫsup-Damu;

§ 66

	3)	3 *é-da-um-*túg-1	3)	3 Edaum fabrics of first quality,
		3 sal-túg		3 fine fabrics,
		3 íb-túg-dar		3 multicolored Ib fabrics
	4)	*ì-lum-*bala	4)	for Ilum-Bala,
	5)	maškim	5)	the inspector
	6)	*da*$_5$*-da-'ar*	6)	of Dada-Ar,
	7)	*ip-pi*$_5$ (=NE)*-ḫir*$_x$ (=HAR)	7)	for Ippiḫir
	8)	*ir-i-bí-tù*^{ki}	8)	of the city Iribitu
	9)	lú:tuš	9)	residing
	10)	*a-ra*^{ki}	10)	in Ara,
	11)	*ṭù-bí-sí-piš*	11)	and for Ṭubi-Sipiš
	12)	*ar-ra*^{ki}	12)	of the city Arra,
	13)	šu-du$_8$	13)	tribute
	14)	*ba-na-na-a-tù*^{ki}	14)	of the city Bananatu

§67

	15)	22½ kin-síg	15)	22½ (measures) of unbleached wool
	16)	*iš*$_x$*-a-ma-lik*	16)	for Isa-Malik,
	17)	*a-da-a-du*	17)	Adadu,
	18)	*i-du-na-nu-ni*	18)	Idunanuni
	19)	ŠUM.URU^{ki}	19)	of the city ŠUM.URU,
	20)	*i-ti-yà*	20)	Iti-Ya,
	21)	[*ìr*]*-ì-ba*	21)	[Ir]iba,
XI	1)	*sí-piš-ìa*	1)	Sipiš-Ya,
	2)	*ip-ṭur-ìa*	2)	Ipṭur-Ya,
	3)	*en-na-ìa*	3)	Enna-Ya,
	4)	*wa-ti-lu*	4)	Watilu,
	5)	*ma-é-ù*	5)	Ma'e'u,
	6)	*ší-a-um*	6)	Ši'aum
	7)	*za-mi-lu*	7)	Zamilu
	8)	*bù-da-ma-lik*	8)	Buda-Malik
	9)	UR$_4$	9)	———
	10)	1 *zi-rí* síg	10)	1 (measure) of choice wool

	11)	du$_{11}$-ga	11)	ordered
	12)	nidba$_{x}$	12)	as offering
	13)	^{d}*ra-sa-ap gú-nu*	13)	to Rasap (of the city) Gunu
	14)	50 kin-síg	14)	50 (measures) of unbleached wool
	15)	1 *mi-at* ìr-dumu-zi	15)	100 (measures of unbleached wool) for (?) Ir-Dumuzi,
	16)	20 lá-3 kin-síg	16)	17 (measures) of unbleached wool
	17)	íb-túg	17)	for Ib fabrics,
	18)	ú-a	18)	the official Ua;
XII		empty		empty
XIII	1)	an-šè-gú 55 *é-da-um*-túg-2	1)	total: 55 Edaum fabrics of second quality,
	2)	90 aktum-túg	2)	90 Aktum fabrics,
	3)	80 lá-2 gu-súr-túg *é-da-um*-túg-1	3)	78 Gusur fabrics, (1) Edaum fabric of first quality,
	4)	1 *mi-at* 66 sal-túg	4)	166 fine fabrics,
	5)	4 zára-túg- 13 túg-*ì-lí*	5)	4 Zara fabrics, 13 top quality fabrics,
	6)	80 lá-1 íb-túg ša$_{6}$-dar	6)	79 Ib fabrics, top quality and multicolored,
	7)	2 *mi-at* 24 íb-túg-dar	7)	224 multicolored Ib fabrics,
	8)	šu-nigín 4 *mi-at* 6 túg-túg	8)	total: 406 fabrics,
	9)	35 gu-mug-túg	9)	35 Gumug fabrics,
	10)	15 gada-túg	10)	15 linen fabrics,
	11)	itu *ṣa-lul*	11)	month: Ṣalul.

4.4. COMMERCIAL EMPIRE

In the preceding pages it was often stressed that Ebla's economic zone of influence was most extensive and covered most of the Fertile Crescent. It was also noted that the term "empire" applied to Ebla was misleading since its power was more economic than military. Nonetheless, the emergence before our eyes of an economic-commercial colossus in the middle of the third millennium elicits wonder and surprise even when lacking military might.

For the present most of the cities mentioned in the bills of lading as commercial partners of Ebla cannot be located, but those known from contemporary and posterior documentation do allow a tracing of the ideal boundaries of such an economic empire.

To the south the range of influence extended through all of Syria and Palestine as far as Sinai. The coastal cities of Lebanon and Palestine occur with frequency, Byblos being preeminent; it must have been the seaport where Egyptian ships carrying gold for Ebla docked. Of the cities to the south may be mentioned Ašdod, Jaffa, Akko, Sidon, Beirut, Alalakh on the coast, and Megiddo, Lachiš, Damascus, Ḥoms, and Ḥama inland.

To the west Ebla certainly traded with the island of Cyprus and, in this regard, the term employed at Ebla to signify copper is *kaparum* whose root clearly relates it to Cyprus.[51]

Northward, the geographic borders embraced most of modern Turkey; it will be recalled that Kaniš in central Turkey was subject to Ebla.

But it was to the east that Ebla's commercial activity flourished most. It controlled the Euphrates region with the cities of Karkemiš, Emar, and Mari and the entire zone coinciding with the modern Gezira and northern Mesopotamia. This area, which must have been heavily populated in the third millennium, can be included in the triangle Ḫarran-Ashur-Gasur (or Erbilum). Ebla's zone of influence even transgressed the frontiers of Mesopotamia to reach Ḫamazi in northern Iran.

To the southeast its sway was felt in the heart of central and southern Mesopotamia, as can be inferred from the frequent references to Kish and Adab and with these all of Sumer.

The geographical map accompanying this chapter will help to visualize the immense zone controlled by Ebla, the dynamic promoter of lively commercial exchanges at a time when such seemed inconceivable.

Notes

1. TM.75.G.1474.
2. Since the texts do not specify the length of time the barley was supposed to last, this last datum is purely theoretical.
3. Consult E. Wirth, *Syrien,* p. 72.
4. Reverse IV 1, šu-nigín 1 *rí-ba*$_x$ 6 *li* ki, "total: 16,000 iku." On the surface measures, see Chapter VII 3.3.
5. The Sumerian term used is ì-giš-du$_6$, literally, vegetable oil of the hillside." That it deals with olive oil is a hypothesis put forward here for the first time.
6. TM.75.G.217.
7. See pp. 147–53.
8. TM.75.G.1629; 1630; 2096.
9. TM.75.G.1582.

10. TM.75.G.2112.
11. See p. 128.
12. TM.76.G.151, rev. I-4.
13. TM.75.G.1570.
14. TM.75.G.1852.
15. TM.76.G.189.
16. One of the four palaces, it will be recalled, is called g i g i r[ki], translated "stable," but which literally signifies "wagon-barn"; see p. 144.
17. TM.75.G.2068.
18. TM.75.G.2065.
19. TM.76.G.187.
20. TM.75.G.1479, rev. III 1–3.
21. It is quite possible that the addition "at 4," "at 2½," etc. indicates the percentage of gold in the metal alloy; cf. CAD B, under *balālu* (courtesy of K. Butz).
22. See p. 102.
23. TM.75.G.1841, obv. I 1 – IV 3.
24. *Ibidem,* rev. I 1 – IV 3.
25. TM.75.G.1656.
26. TM.75.G.1377.
27. In these texts the word employed for "copper" is a - g a r_5 which is translated into East Semitic *abāru* and interpreted as "lead" by Assyriologists. Our texts indicate that it refers rather to copper.
28. See *AfO* 25 (1974–1977), p. 26.
29. This is the system commonly used in the tablets found in 1974.
30. Cf. *Mesopotamia* 7 (1972–1973), p. 109.
31. See above on p. 45.
32. TM.75.G.1860, obv. VI 1–3.
33. *Ibidem,* obv. VI 12–14.
34. TM.75.G.1267, rev. V 1 – VI 1.
35. TM.75.G.1860, obv. VI 6–11.
36. TM.75.G.1390, obv. II 4 – III 8.
37. *Ibidem,* rev. II 1–3.
38. Obv. V 9 – VI 1.
39. Rev. V 9 – VI 2.
40. Rev. VI 3–7.
41. Obv. I 1 – II 2.
42. See p. 123, 125.
43. TM.75.G.1296.
44. Only toward the end of Ibbi-Sipiš' reign is the gold-silver relationship at 4 to 1, which means a 20 percent revaluation of silver. This fact points to a certain amount of speculation.
45. TM.75.G.528, obv. I 1–4.
46. The introduction of fallow land was a corollary of multicropping.
47. Cf. pp. 195–96.
48. Cf. W. W. Leontief, "Input-Output Economics," *Scientific American,* 185 (1951), pp. 15–21.
49. It is difficult to assume that one system was superior to the other, in that the two complemented each other. Cf. T. F. Barth, "Circuiti economici in Darfur," in E. Grandi, *L'antropologia economica,* Torino, 1972, p. 246f.
50. TM.75.G.1558.
51. TM.75.G.1678.

CHAPTER VIII

Culture

1. The school. 1.1. Structure and curriculum. 1.2. Documents of the school. 2. Higher culture. 2.1. Lists of cuneiform signs. 2.2. Syllabaries. 2.3. Dictionaries and vocabularies. 2.4. Encyclopedias. 2.5. Literary texts. 3. Scientific congresses and cultural exchanges.

What has been said thus far delineates ever more clearly a great metropolis, rich and developed, with commercial and cultural contacts over an area reaching from modern Egypt to Iran. In the first half of the third millennium Ebla was already a major cultural center fruitfully interchanging with the neighboring countries, and some of its specifically cultural institutions claim here a word of comment.[1]

1. THE SCHOOL

By "school" is meant that institution which in the ancient Near East was generally charged with preparing and drilling the scribes in the art of writing to enable them to look after the affairs of state and to draft its documents. In this very broad sense one can admit that there was a school wherever inscribed tablets have been found in quantity.

In the Mesopotamian centers, however, which, chronologically according to their floruit, are Uruk, Ur, Fara, Abu-Salabikh, Kish, Adab, and Nippur, the school not only prepared the scribes to draft administrative texts, but was also the place where the cultural patrimony was preserved. Here the myths and poems transmitted by tradition were put into writing, literary and religious compositions were created, and knowledge was catalogued in lexical texts.

In these creative cultural centers the school appeared as a complex and many-faceted institution of a high cultural level; it may properly be termed an "academy."

It should be noted, though, that throughout the third millennium the only documented academies were situated in the heart of southern Mesopotamia. Still, with the recovery of the first 42 tablets in 1974 the hope of recovering an academy at Ebla began to grow.

Among these tablets there was one in particular, TM.74.G.120, with a peculiar content. It consisted of a list of popular personal names arranged by the scribe on the basis of the formative elements of the name itself. It could be classified as a "school text," that is, a tablet written by a student for practice.[2]

The discovery of a schoolboy exercise and the more significant fact that the Eblaites employed the Sumerian cuneiform script to express their own language prompted the supposition that a scribal school and a cultural center existed at Ebla in the third millennium. This supposition was fully confirmed in 1975 by the unearthing of impressive archives which showed that Ebla could enter the ranks of those few cities boasting academies.

The tablets generously furnish information about the structure and functioning of the academy, the curriculum of studies pursued by the scribes, the sundry fields of knowledge entered by these third-millennium students and professors.

Early on it was remarked that of the three locales of the ancient palace of Ebla, room L.2769 turned out to be a real library in which the tablets were arranged on wooden shelves according to the most modern archival standards, demonstrating with what care cuneiform records of every type were preserved.[3]

In fact, 70 percent of the texts preserved are economic-administrative, and so their careful conservation by the bureaucratic apparatus is readily understandable. Another 10 percent are historical and, containing important international treaties, were jealously to be guarded. A good 20 percent are literary and the care shown for the grouping and preserving of these demonstrates that the academy was responsible for the safeguarding and diffusion of the cultural patrimony, now open, as will be presently seen, to cultural exchange with nearby lands.

The most evident products of this exchange are the lexical texts and the vocabularies to be discussed below.

1.1. STRUCTURE AND CURRICULUM

Some texts preserve the legible signature of their scribe; certain scribes also specify after their name the post they hold in the school administration. This enables us to retrieve the ranks of authority in the school and to plot the course of studies the students had to follow. The scholastic career of several of them can even be traced; they can be seen to draw good grades in their studies and in turn become professors.

The tablets with the signature, which is called the colophon, must have had an official character about them and so were composed with great care and signed. For example, the lexical text TM.75.G.1398 is doubtless an official document of the school since it is the examination of a young scribe who signs it at the end and also mentions his superiors and probable examiners.

The colophon reads:

a-zi	Azi
dub mu-sar	has written the tablet,
ip-ṭur-i-šar	Ipṭur-Išar
dub-zu-zu	(being) the teacher,
AB.BA	the Elder
tám-tá-il	Tamta-Il,
um-mi-a	the dean
a-zi	Azi.

This colophon informs us that the hierarchical ranks of the school are, starting from the top, indicated by the three Sumerian terms um-mi-a, "the expert," dub-zu-zu, "one who knows the tablets," and dub-sar, "the scribe."

The official nature of the document can be inferred from the mention of Tamta-Il, the Elder, the "dean" or "prefect" of the academy, who by his authority ratifies the validity of what is written on the tablet. This tablet most probably constitutes one of the numerous tests to which young Azi was subjected in order to acquire the title of dub-sar, "scribe." To all appearances young Azi emerged with flying colors because later on he receives the title dub-zu-zu, "teacher," and then again a higher grade; his brilliant career is crowned when he becomes the top administrator of Ebla.

The colophon presently to be cited already puts him in a higher category and documents the official character of this tablet; Enna-Il, who must have been the "dean," is presented as the king's representative:

ti-ra-il	Tira-Il
dub mu-sar	has written the tablet,
a-zi	Azi
dub-zu-zu	(being) the teacher,
en-na-il	Enna-Il
zi-lugal-da	by the life of the king.[4]

From other colophons, where at least 10 scribes are mentioned, one may deduce that certain documents were surely composed in a seminar and then written by one scribe alone.

1.2. DOCUMENTS OF THE SCHOOL

Such documents can be divided into two large groups: the first includes scholastic texts properly speaking, that is, those written by the students, the second group embraces those written by the professors, some for a pedagogical purpose, others for cataloguing knowledge or for preservation of the oral traditions. Needless to say, from this latter group the very high cultural level reached by the Ebla school shines forth.

A good segment of texts belonging to the school are really scholastic exercises. Cuneiform is a highly complex writing and requires much practice; for this reason the young students had to practice for years to attain the proficiency of their masters.

Some of the tablets preserved are clearly the efforts of fledglings in first contact with cuneiform script; the unsteady hand, the slight familiarity with complex signs, and finally the little patience revealed by tablets uncompleted, halfway finished. Some bear signs of erasure, and one contains a large X put there by the master who obliged the student to redo the lesson so badly accomplished. Other tablets, however, manifest the hard work of the beginner eager to turn in a good assignment.

Of these well-executed exercises may be cited TM.75.G.2200, a tablet of 10 lines. In the first four lines are written words consisting of only one cuneiform sign; in the following, words comprised of several signs. In front of each word there is a circle which at this period serves as an "indicating element" or "marker," that is, it indicates that after it begins a new word or phrase:

1)	○	ki	earth
2)	○	gal	large
3)	○	é	house
4)	○	gur_8	boat
5)	○	an-ki-bi-da	heaven and earth
6)	○	u_4-ni-gi-tar	day . . .
7)	○	nin-bará-kú	lady/throne/food
8)	○	u_4-u_4-u_4	day, day, day
9)	○○	a-si	excellent
10)	○	šu nu-gi_4	has not given back

In this school exercise, which was either dictated or which he copied, the student has written substantives, adjectives, particular expressions, verbal forms with no criterion of a typological order, but apparently only for mere practice.

Other scholastic exercises deserving mention are the "note tablets" containing only one word and the "pocket vocabularies," tiny tablets with a single word written in two languages, Sumerian and Eblaite. One of these reads nam-mí=*ù-nu-šum,* "femininity";[5] one pictures the lads diligently doing their homework in a cultured, developed, and refined city.

2. HIGHER CULTURE

The vitality of the school of Ebla is better gauged by the documents which may be termed "textbooks," because they served as the basis for the lessons. Among these may be distinguished the lists of cuneiform signs, the syllabaries, and the vocabularies, both monolingual and bilingual. To these may be added texts which were surely used for the advanced grades, but in which the element of pure culture prevails over the practical and pedagogical function; the encyclopedias and the literary texts belong in this class.

2.1. LISTS OF CUNEIFORM SIGNS

These lists belong to the category of basic textbooks, indispensable tools for learning the syllabaries and other more complex texts. The principles, though, on which these lists of signs are arranged grant them the right to be classed among the "academic" texts.

To exemplify this type of text one may cite tablet TM.75.G.2260, written with a firm and expert hand by a precise and organized scribe. It contains a list of cuneiform signs ordered either on the basis of the external shape of the signs or on the principle of homophony and also of sets of words expressed by several cuneiform signs.

Here are some interesting sequences:

in-na-sum	I have given,
ì-na-sum	he has given,
nu-ì-na-sum	he has not given,
ḫi-na-sum	may he give,
ba-til	it is finished,
nu-til	it is not finished,
in-til	he has finished,
ḫi-til	may he finish.[6]

2.2. SYLLABARIES

Among the "textbooks" the syllabaries come in the second position. Though very close to those of the first group, they form a separate category for the fact that in these the cuneiform sign follows the reading furnished by the splitting-up of the word into syllables.

Here it may be helpful to recall that originally every cuneiform sign represented a word so that such writing could be called logographic. But the Sumerian words expressed by only one sign could consist of one, two, or more syllables. For example, é, "house," is a one-syllable word, bará, "altar," consists of two syllables. What then did the scribes of Ebla do? They first wrote the Sumerian sign and immediately added the pronunciation. For example:

gána	=	*ga-na-um*
dim	=	*dì-mu-um*
ašgab	=	*áš-ga-bù*
suḫur	=	*šu-ḫ̬u-ru-um*([7])

Hence the Ebla syllabaries are extremely important not only for the knowledge of teaching techniques but also because they reveal the pronunciation of the Sumerian words. It should be noted moreover that the oldest syllabaries known heretofore date to 1800 B.C., to a period, that is, when Sumerian was no longer spoken.

These are not the only merits of the syllabaries. Some Sumerian signs whose reading and hence whose phonetic value were unknown now appear for the first time with their pronunciation.

2.3. DICTIONARIES AND VOCABULARIES

The most pleasant surprise of the 1975 campaign was the discovery of the monolingual and bilingual vocabularies. Without doubt they may be considered the oldest on record, the earliest known till now dating to 1800 B.C. Studies conducted thus far reveal that 114 tablets contain vocabularies and reflect in divers copies three master vocabularies composed on the basis of monolingual Sumerian lists with a total of some 3,000 words.

The modernity of their formulation can only elicit admiration. Just as our vocabularies are ordered according to the alphabet, so at Ebla the principle of arranging the words is very similar. The scribes adopted the principle of homography, ordering the words according to the initial formative elements, just as would happen in Mesopotamia many centuries later. Thus they contain different sections clearly divided one from the other by the initial elements.

As an example the list TM.75.G.2422 will serve handsomely; it is a monolingual Sumerian dictionary, a basis for the composition of bilingual dictionaries. It divides into 50 sections. The first includes the words beginning with the term nì, then follow words beginning with ka, then sag, ú, sa, é, šu, á, šà, etc. At the end of each section, moreover, as a dividing device and as a mark of reference, the formative element is repeated.

Such monolingual lists are called *šì-bar* unken, "books of the assembly," and numerous copies have been recovered. Here are the first 20 lines as attested in TM.75.G.1304 containing words beginning with the element nì:

obverse

I 1) [*šì*-] *bar*-unken
2) [nì-d] u
3) [nì-g]ú-du
4) ⌜nì⌝-šu-du
5) nì-šu-du-du
6) nì-da-da

7) nì-kas$_4$
8) nì-[t]a-du
9) [nì-d]u
10) [nì-] ⌈x⌉-du

II 1) nì-è
2) nì-BI-UR.du
3) nì-gúg-du
4) nì-mùš-du
5) nì-gú
6) nì-ba
7) nì-gal
8) nì-é-gul
9) nì-é-gul-gul
10) nì-GIxGI-a-di

At Ebla monolingual dictionaries both in Sumerian and in Eblaite have been found, but the latter are more indicative of the efficiency and autonomy of the Ebla school which with good claim set itself up against the Mesopotamian schools.

But it is the bilingual vocabularies which show Ebla at its cultural best. These list Sumerian words, that is, words belonging to the language of the dominant culture of the third millennium, and then give their translation into old Canaanite, the language spoken in Ebla.

A large tablet with 31 columns preserved, TM.75.G.2000 will pass into history as the bilingual par excellence vocabulary of Ebla. At least 36 duplicates have been identified to date and show how much this text was studied in the schools. The vocabulary is arranged according to the principle of the monolingual dictionaries and offers the same characteristics of organic wholeness and methodicalness that might well be termed modern.

Examples drawn from the vocabularies include the following:

al-du$_{11}$-ga	=	*ì-rí-sa-tum*	desire
dumu-sag	=	*bù-kà-ru$_x$*	firstborn son
ur-sag	=	*qá-ra-dum*	hero
eme-bala	=	*tá-da-bí-lu*	translator
nì-nam	=	*me-na-ma-ma*	everything
al-kešda	=	*kì-sí-lum*	bond
geštu	=	*ḫa-si-sum*	wise
a-aba$_x$	=	*ti-'à-ma-tum*	ocean abyss
kú	=	*a-kà-lum*	to eat
šu šu-ra	=	*ma-ḫa-ṣí-i-da*	to strike with the hand[8]

Among the many surprises encountered in these vocabularies is the insertion, between the Sumerian word and its Eblaite equivalent, of the pronunciation of the foreign (Sumerian) word.

Three examples of this may be given here:

a)	níg-gig	(Sumerian word)
	ne-ki-ki	(pronunciation of the Sumerian word)
	ni-gi-tum	(Eblaite translation)
b)	níg-uru	(Sumerian word)
	ne-gú-ru$_x$-ù	(pronunciation of same)
	ne-gú-ru$_x$-um	(Eblaite translation)
c)	ka-ag	(Sumerian word)
	ga-a-gi	(pronunciation of same)
	ri-gi-tum	(Eblaite translation)[9]

This usage, together with the existence of Sumerian syllabaries mentioned above, underscores the extraordinary importance of the Ebla texts not only for the knowledge of the oldest Semitic tongues, but also for research on Sumerian itself.

2.4. ENCYCLOPEDIAS

The vocabularies point up the strong linguistic interest of the Ebla academy, whether for the conservation of the lexical patrimony, the learning of foreign languages, or for practical purposes such as abetting Ebla's commercial relationship with other countries.

Other types of documents, which might be called "encyclopedias" or more simply "lists of words arranged by subject," organized what was then knowable and made it available. These texts most likely served as handbooks for the school, but their scientific lists give a glimpse into their knowledge of botany, zoology, minerology, etc. There are lists of animals —among which are two of birds—several lists of fishes, of precious and nonprecious stones, lists of plants and trees and objects of wood, lists of metals or objects of metal.

To give some idea of the high level of knowledge regarding divers kinds of birds then found in Ebla and the Near East, I transcribe part of the bird list in TM.75.G.1415, a tablet of 8 columns which enumerates 142 birds which are identifiable as such, thanks to the determinative mušen set alongside each name:[10]

túg-túg^{mušen}
sar-sar-gur$_4$^{mušen}
šár^{mušen}
ná^{mušen}

um^{mušen}
um-ḫur^{mušen}
um-nun^{mušen}
ú-naga-ga^{mušen}
dar^{mušen}
dar-ì^{mušen}
igi-lá^{mušen}
še+lagab^{mušen}
ku-ru^{mušen}
am^{mušen}
da^{mušen}
igi-nita^{mušen}

In addition to these handbooks there are rolls of geographic names, personal names, lists of professions, all exhibiting the same characteristics of methodicalness and arranged according to the principle of acography. It must also be noted that besides transmitting Sumerian lists strictly bound to the Mesopotamian tradition documented at Uruk, Fara, and Abu Salabikh, the Eblaites began to draw up their own lists in Old Canaanite, some of which, such as the geographic list to be treated presently, were transmitted and recopied even in Mesopotamia.

2.5. LITERARY TEXTS

Literary texts are the highest expression of every culture. The "school" of Ebla too produced literary works testifying to the high degree of maturity achieved and to its desire to transmit the religious concepts of the people of the time.

Among the literary compositions figure some 20 myths, several preserved in more than one copy; these shed quite a new light on religious tenets of the third millennium. The divinities who act in these myths are the great Mesopotamian gods Enlil, Enki, Utu, Suen, and Inanna, but there are very strong indications that other major Mesopotamian gods such as Marduk and Tiamat take their origins in a West Semitic ambience.

The other literary works include epic narratives, hymns to gods, incantations, rituals, and collections of proverbs. In the mythological introduction to the hymn of praise to "the lord of heaven and earth" occurs a fragment of the creation of the universe that bears some resemblance to the account in the first chapter of Genesis.[11] Among the literary texts it has been possible to identify two copies of the Gilgamesh Epic. These deal with the oldest version of the poem as well as with a new version that describes the relationships between Uruk and Aratta.

3. SCIENTIFIC CONGRESSES AND CULTURAL EXCHANGES

Some idea has been formed of the workings of the school of Ebla, its function, and cultural weight which enabled it to vie with the schools—all in Mesopotamia—of the third millennium such as Uruk, Fara, Abu Salabikh, and Nippur, once considered as the only forges of thought radiating culture throughout the then known world.

The Ebla tablets furnish evidence that its school maintained fruitful and dynamic cultural contacts with several important Sumerian centers of learning and that it even became a pole of cultural attraction.

Two lexical lists, in addition to the normal colophon consisting of the scribe's signature, carry the annotation:

in
u$_4$
dumu-nita dumu-nita
dub-sar
e$_{11}$
áš-tù
ma-rí^{ki} [12]

"(tablet written) when the young scribes went up from Mari."

Among the various possible interpretations of this annotation, this appears to be the most plausible: scribes from other cities were visiting Ebla and on this occasion some symposium or scientific congress was being held during which they composed some scientific documents.

Should this hypothesis bear up, it would prove the vitality of cultural exchanges in the third millennium and the esteem in which the school of Ebla was held.

An explicit mention of Mesopotamian scribes being guests at the school of Ebla is not lacking; the mathematics professor Išma-Ya, who drafted the only mathematical text identified thus far, comes from the city of Kish.

This text, as beautiful as it is difficult, must be cited in its entirety. It deals with a sequence of numbers that constitute a mathematical problem which, as we are assured by the fifth line of the first column, must still be solved, obviously, by the students. The problem was formulated by the professor who describes himself as "scribe of Kish."

Obverse

I	1)	600 gal	600 large
	2)	3,600 gal	3,600 large
	3)	36,000 gal	36,000 large

	4)	360,000 gal	360,000 large
	5)	360,000 x 6 gal	360,000 x 6 large
		nu-da-šid	not done;
II	1)	ki-gar	problem
	2)	dub-sar	of the scribe
	3)	kis^{ki}	of Kish,
	4)	*iš-má-ìa*	Išma-Ya.[13]

Numerous other elements in the texts demonstrate broad cultural contacts between Ebla and foreign schools.

Quite a few lexical texts, especially the encyclopedic lists, are identical with documents attested mainly at Uruk, Fara, and Abu Salabikh. Thus far at least 50 Ebla texts have exact counterparts in the three Sumerian seats of learning.

An unusually significant text concerning Ebla's cultural exchanges with the other regions of the Near East and some identities between the different cultures is a list of professions.

This list has been found in almost identical form in some cities of southern Mesopotamia, in a city in northern Mesopotamia, Gasur, and in Ebla. The perfect preservation of the Ebla tablet permits the filling out of lacunae caused by breaks in the tablets stemming from other places.

The first two columns of TM.75.G.1488 read:

I	1)	dub-ṣar
	2)	sanga
	3)	sagi
	4)	šabra
	5)	ensí
	6)	nu-bànda
	7)	šagina
	8)	kuš$_x$
II	1)	gal-sukkal
	2)	gal-unken
	3)	eme-bala
	4)	sa$_{12}$-du$_5$
	5)	muḫaldim
	6)	šandana
	7)	gal$_5$:lá
	8)	gal-kinda
	9)	gal-nimgir
	10)	nagar[14]

Thus contacts with other schools were frequent, but it would be a mistake to think that Ebla only received Mesopotamian culture passively. Many are the significant data showing that Ebla was a creative center of considerable importance and that it not only absorbed but also bestowed some of its genius on Mesopotamia. A few examples out of many should suffice to illustrate this statement.

At Abu Salabikh a geographical list was found that proved to be an insoluble crux for its modern editor. The loss of the first lines, in fact, has impeded a sure and clear localization of the 289 cities mentioned in it. The same list has turned up as a school tablet from Ebla and is doubly important; the Ebla tablet, written syllabically, differs from the Abu Salabikh copies which prefer the logographic writings, and thus permits the recognition of the cities with fewer difficulties. Second, it is intact so that one can definitively reconstruct the geographic list, which may more properly be termed the Gazetteer of the Ancient Near East since it embraces the entire area of the Fertile Crescent with particular attention to the cities of Syria-Palestine. These considerations point to Ebla as the site of its original composition whence it was transmitted to Mesopotamia.

Here follows a list of cities that appear in the Ebla list placed alongside their correspondents from Abu Salabikh:[15]

236	E.	*su-ḫu*^{ki}
	AS.	*sa*-AN^{ki}
237	E.	*na-mar*^{ki}
	AS.	*na:mar*^{ki}
238	E.	*na-ma-ra-at*^{ki}
	AS.	*na:ma:ur*$_4^{ki}$
239	E.	*ù-du-at*^{ki}
	AS.	*ù-at*^{ki}
240	E.	*ma-sa-a*$_5^{ki}$
	AS.	*ma:sá-*⌜*x*⌝^{ki}
241	E.	*ma-dar*^{ki}
	S.	*ma dar*^{ki}
242	E.	KI.KI^{ki}
	AS.	*qaq-qá-ra*^{ki}
243	E.	*da*$_5$*-nu-a*$_5^{ki}$
	AS.	*tab-nu*^{ki}
244	E.	*'à*-AN.AN^{ki}
	AS.	*'à-ir-rìm*^{ki}

While Ebla received Sumerian lexical lists, Sumer in turn copied scholastic texts from Ebla.

This further underlines the intensity of cultural exchanges in the third millennium, something unthinkable till now. We have reason to believe that Ebla exported, so to speak, not only its culture but also its scribes. Should numerous scribes of Abu Salabikh with distinctly West Semitic names turn out to hail from Ebla, the wonder would be small.[16]

Notes

1. In this connection, see *RPARA* 48 (1975–1976), pp. 47–57.
2. See above on p. 43.
3. See above on pp. 48f.
4. TM.75.G.2231.
5. TM.75.G.2318.
6. TM.75.G.2260, obv. V 12–19.
7. TM.75.G.1907.
8. *RPARA* 48, p. 54.

The following examples taken from the bilingual vocabularies nicely illustrate some of the characteristics of the Ebla Semitic vocabulary:

baḫar	=	*wa-ṣí-lu-um*	"potter"
pà	=	*na-ba-um*	"to call"
nì-tur-du$_{11}$-ga	=	*pá-tá-ru*$_x$	"to speak softly"
ezen	=	*i-sí-ba-tù*	"feast"
nì-gig	=	*qá-dì-šum*	"taboo"
urudu	=	*kà-pá-lu*	"copper"
ud	=	*da-la-lum*	"day"
šà-ḫul	=	*é-la-lum*	"black heart, evil"
ḫul	=	*ba-rí-um*	"evil"
di-ku$_5$	=	*ba-da-qù da-ne-um*	"to judge"
erén-ki-gar	=	*maš-bí-tù*	"encampment"
sal	=	*ì-ma-tum*	"woman"
nì-géme	=	*a-kà-lu*	"food"
	=	*bù-ur-tum*	"food"
á-zi	=	*i-me-tum*	"right hand"
a	=	*ma-wu*	"water"
áb	=	*ma-ni-lum*	"cow, possession"
al-gin	=	*é-a-gú-um*	"to go"
tu-gur$_4$^{mušen}	=	*ḫu-la-tum*	"phoenix"
šà-gi$_6$	=	*ṭì-é-mu*	"depth"
šà	=	*é-da-ru*$_x$*-um*	"heart"

9. TM.75.G.2008.
10. TM.75.G.1415, obv. III 1–18. A photograph of this tablet has been published by P. Matthiae, *Ebla. Un impero ritrovato* (Torino, 1977), plate 49.
11. See p. 244.
12. *RPARA* 48, p. 57.
13. TM.75.G.1693.
14. *OrAn* 15 (1976), pp. 169–78.
15. For the publication of this gazetteer, see *OrNS* 47 (1978), pp. 50–73.
16. Consult R. D. Biggs, *OrNS* 36 (1967), pp. 55–66 and *IAS*, pp. 34–35.

CHAPTER IX

Religion

1. The pantheon. 1.1. The gods. 1.2. Forms of syncretism. 1.3. Borrowings. 2. Worship. 2.1. Priests and places of worship. 2.2. The offerings. 2.3. The feasts. 2.4. Incantations, hymns, and myths. 3. Popular religion.

Lord of heaven and earth:
the earth was not, you created it,
the light of the day was not, you created it,
the morning light you had not [yet] made exist.

These words echoing the first chapter of Genesis have not been taken from the Bible but rather from a literary text found in three copies in the royal library of Ebla of 2500 B.C.

The subject of religion could scarcely be introduced more fittingly, since these four lines synthesize the Eblaite concept of how the cosmos originated. A superior Being exists, the Lord of heaven and earth who created the earth, the light of day.

What profundity of thought, how much religious sentiment are hidden in the expression "Lord of heaven and earth"! Artificers of a very modern state structure, creators of a successful economic system, as detailed in an earlier chapter, the Eblaites were not less gifted in the realm of religion, where their profound insights command our admiration and reveal how superficial is our understanding of their civilization.

Not without reason has the chapter on religion been saved for the end of the book. Religion not only integrates Eblaite culture, but does so in a new and unexpected manner.

One familiar with the contemporary world of Mesopotamia appreciates the religiosity of the Sumerians and the distinctness of their religious concepts but at the same time does not overlook the political element in the centers of religion and in the economic-administrative activity. In fact, this cultural phase has been identified as *cité-temple sumérienne,* "the Sumerian city-temple."[1] In Sumer, religious power permeated the political field and supplanted politics in the management of the economy. The king was merely the representative of the city god, the sole owner of the land property of the city. To use an anachronistic phrase, in Sumer a "temporal power of the clergy" made itself felt.

In view of this situation in Mesopotamia, one would have expected something similar at Ebla, but once again the Eblaites point up the fragility of hypotheses elaborated in the study. What has emerged from the tablets so far suggests a sharp distinction between the political and the religious spheres. To be even more explicit, the civilization of Ebla was essentially lay or secular. This does not call into question the profound religious sense of its people but only denies that the clergy and the temple enjoyed a key role in political and economic affairs.

Thus Ebla's autonomy with respect to Mesopotamia in the concept of kingship, in the use of its own language in writing, and in its model of economy, is further asserted, and this comes as a surprise with regard to religious conceptions.

1. THE PANTHEON

The lack of local written sources kept the West Semitic divinities of Syria-Palestine in the third millennium beyond the ken of modern scholars. The fragmentary notices gathered mainly from name lists in Mesopotamian texts could not yield the comprehensive view rendered possible by the new textual finds. The literary religious texts are not alone in presenting the divinities; the economic tablets, especially the lists of offerings, and the very extensive onomastica make their contribution as well.

Two essential points stand out clearly: 1) the Eblaites were polytheists; 2) the divinities of the pantheon of Ebla are predominantly Canaanite. The first point creates no surprise, but the second bears importantly on the history of religions in the ancient Near East. Gods considered recent turn out to be most ancient, as in the case of Baal, and others, such as Chemosh whose origin was unknown, find their natural habitat at Ebla, and still others, such as Dabir, witnessed in the Bible but without divine qualities, are in reality divinities.

1.1. THE GODS

The available sources put membership in the Ebla pantheon at about 500 divinities, but they do not spell out its structure or the relationships between the individual gods.

The curious reader may like to know how scholars identify a god and distinguish him or her from other beings. Borrowing from the Sumerians the cuneiform system of writing, the Eblaites also employed the ingenious system of "determinatives"; these are wedge signs which characterize the various entities, such as giš, "wood," placed before a word tells you that it is of wood, while ki, "place," marks a word as a place name. For gods the Sumerians, followed by the Eblaites, employ the determinative or marker DINGIR, "god"; hence when we find the sequence

DINGIR.DA.GAN, we can be confident that the Eblaites consider Dagan a god.

Only a few members of the pantheon and their part in the life of an Eblaite can be singled out here. Among the male gods—the pantheon was populated by male and female deities—the god Dagan enjoyed a preeminent position, perhaps the first position itself.[2] Well known in the second and first millennia as the head of the pantheon, this Canaanite god receives such titles at Ebla as to warrant the conclusion that his subsequent prerogatives were not an innovation.

In Ebla a whole quarter and one of the city gates bear the name of Dagan; in the new calendar the first month of the year is dedicated to him under the generic appellative of "lord." In the onomastica, too, this god commonly appears as "lord," while in the lists of offerings he is further specified by the addition of a city name or of another complement which also serves to stress the centrality of Dagan in the third millennium. If "lord of the city X" reveals the strict bond between Dagan and a city in the sense that he is its protecting deity, other expressions such as "lord of the land" or "lord of Canaan" raise Dagan to the rank of the principal god of the kingdom of Ebla or of the land of Canaan. When, finally, he is called "lord of the gods," then there can be no doubt about Dagan's role as true head of Ebla's pantheon.

Dagan's companion is called belatu, "lady," quite a general term that does not permit identification with a specific goddess. To conclude this description of Dagan, it might be observed that one of his appellatives, ṭi-lu ma-tim, "the dew of the land," sustains that etymology which sees in the name "Dagan" the meaning "cloud, rain."[3]

Among the other male divinities Sipiš (Sumerian UTU), the sun god, deserves special mention, as do Hada, the storm god, who along with the important but still unidentified gods Kura, and Kakkab, the star god, guarantee international treaties and important decisions in general. In the international treaty between Ebla and Ashur "the god sun, the god storm, and the god star" are explicitly called "witnesses" of the accord and must, in the case of nonobservance of the clauses by Ashur's king, set the dire maledictions in motion.[4]

Even on the occasion of Ebrium's dividing possessions among three of his sons, the gods listen in on the decision, evidently in the capacity of witnesses.

The text is TM.75.G.1444:

du_{11}-ga	the decision
en	of the king
giš-ba-tuku	has heard
^{d}*ku-ra*	the god Kura
wa	and

^{d}U T U	the god sun
g i š - b a - t u k u	has heard
wa	and
g i š - b a - t u k u	has heard
^{d}*'à-da*	the god storm
wa	and
g i š - b a - t u k u	have heard
d i n g i r - d i n g i r	(all) the gods.[5]

Here in the place of the god star are found the god Kura and all the gods. The god sun and the god storm, on the other hand, are present in both documents and enact a role not unlike that assigned them in Mesopotamian culture of later periods.

Too important to be passed over in silence are Kamiš, the principal god of Moab; Rasap, the Resheph of later tradition; Aštar, the male god of war and of love; Lim, the great Amorite god famous in the Mari tablets; Kašaru, attested frequently at Ugarit; Baal, the highly popular Canaanite god; Milk, the god king; and two divinized rivers: the Euphrates, called ^{d}*ba-ra-du ma-du,* "the great cold river," which explains the incomprehensible *purattu/furat* of Mesopotamian-Arabic tradition, and the river Baliḫ (^{d}*ba-li-ḫa*).

Thus far divinities mostly known from the Canaanite tradition of the second and first millennia have been mentioned, but at Ebla are also attested gods hitherto unknown. First, there is Dabir, who appears in the Bible as "the plague," who together with Resheph serves as the scourger sent by Israel's God. But at Ebla, Dabir is the patron god of the city:

^{d}*da-bí-ir* d i n g i r *-eb-la*^{ki}

"Dabir, the god of Ebla" in the sense that he is the tutelary divinity of the city and of the dynasty.[6] Then follow other gods such as ^{d}*a-gú,* ^{d}*'à-ma-ri-ik,* ^{d}*da-i-in,* ^{d}*da-lum,* ^{d}*ga-ra-i-nu,* ^{d}*NE-la,* ^{d}*ni.da.kul,* etc., whose nature and sometimes even the reading of their names are unknown. The last-cited divinity ^{d}*ni.da.kul* must have been particularly important as he received many sacrificial offerings, but he resists identification altogether.

In connection with Dagan the fact was touched upon that his name is frequently followed by the name of a city, which means that he was the protective numen of that specific city raised to a definite hypostasis or more generally to a particular manifestation of God. An example from modern times may illustrate this phenomenon: Catholics venerate the Madonna, the Mother of God, but how many Madonnas there are! There is the Madonna of Lourdes, the Madonna of Fatima, the Madonna of Syracuse, etc., but we all know that there is but one Madonna though her manifestations are diverse. This phenomenon is already attested in antiquity; the Mesopotamian Ištar and the Syro-Palestinian Baal are cases in point.

The novelty furnished by Ebla consists in already manifesting in the third millennium the same divine figure brought into relationship with definite cities. Four examples prove instructive:

1) Dagan:

^{d}*Be bù-la-nu*^{ki}	Lord of Bulanu
^{d}*Be du-du-lu*^{ki}	Lord of Tuttul
^{d}*Be kà-na-na*	Lord of Canaan
^{d}*Be ì-rìm*^{ki}	Lord of Irim
^{d}*Be* kalam^{tim}	Lord of the land
^{d}*Be má-NE*^{ki}	Lord of Ma-NE
^{d}*Be Zàr-ad*^{ki}	Lord of Zarad
^{d}*Be* u_9*-gú-a-áš*^{ki}	Lord of Uguaš
^{d}*Be sí-wa-du*^{ki}	Lord of Siwad
^{d}*Be sí-pí-šu*^{ki}	Lord of Sipišu

2) Hada:

^{d}*'à-da a-ba-ti*^{ki}	Hada of Abati
^{d}*'à-da 'à-ta-ni*^{ki}	Hada of Atanni
^{d}*'à-da ḫa-lam*^{ki}	Hada of Ḫalam
^{d}*'à-da lu-ub*^{ki}	Hada of Lub

3) ^{d}*ni.da.kul:*

^{d}*ni.da.kul a-ru*$_{x}$*-ga-tù*	Nidakul of Arugatu
^{d}*ni.da.kul* sa-MI+ŠITA$_{x}$^{ki}	Nidakul of the governorate
^{d}*ni.da.kul é-ma-tù*^{ki}	Nidakul of Ḥama
^{d}*ni.da.kul lu-ba-an*^{ki}	Nidakul of Luban

4) ^{d}Rasap:

^{d}*ra-sa-ap 'à-tá-ni*^{ki}	Rasap of Atanni
^{d}*ra-sa-ap ar-mi*^{ki} *ar-mi*^{ki}	Rasap of the cities
^{d}*ra-sa-ap gú-nu*^{ki}	Rasap of Gunu[7]
^{d}*ra-sa-ap tù-ne-éb*^{ki}	Rasap of Tunip
^{d}*ra-sa-ap ši-é-am*^{ki}	Rasap of Shechem
^{d}*ra-sa-ap* sa-MI+ŠITA$_{x}$^{ki}	Rasap of the governorate

Passing to the feminine divinities—mention has been made of Belatu, the companion of Dagan—we add Aštarte, with the same characteristics as the male Aštar, Išatu, the fire-goddess, and Tiamat, the goddess of the primordial ocean waters.

The two gods Il and Ya, attested chiefly in the onomastica, present an interesting historico-religious problem. Il, in fact, is the Semitic term to indicate a "deity" as well as the name of a particular god of the Semitic pantheon, the *'il* of the Ugaritic-Hebrew tradition, while Ya has till now been considered only a hypocoristicon or abbreviated form of a longer name. In 1976[8] when I advanced the hypothesis that Ya could be an abbreviation of Yau and that it could indicate a particular divinity, there was almost a general uprising among scholars. What is the situation now? Further study reveals that Ya, in addition to being interpreted as a simple hypocoristicon, that is, when it occurs at the end of a personal name, could also stand for a particular divinity and the best proof of this appears in the personal name ^{d}*ìa-ra-mu,* "Ya is exalted," where it begins the name and is accompanied by the determinative d i n g i r, "god." Further evidence that Ya is an abbreviation of Yau emerges from a comparison of the name *šu-mi-a* with *šu-mi-a-u,* "name of Ya(u)." It becomes clear at this point that not all the names can be explained as hypocoristica and that a careful examination is needed.

The second observation is even more unsettling. Until the reign of Ebrium there are very many names composed with Il, but under Ebrium Ya replaces Il as the divine component in personal names. The names on the left are pre-Ebrium, those on the right date to his reign:

en-na-il	*en-na-ìa*
iš-ra-il	*iš-ra-ìa*
iš-má-il	*iš-ma-ìa*
mi-kà-il	*mi-kà-ìa*
ḫa-ra-il	*ḫa-ra-ìa*
ti ra il	*ti ra ìa*
tám-ṭa-il	*tám-ta-ìa*
eb-du-il	*eb-du-ìa*

Why this change in the onomasticon? Is it possibly connected with a religious reform? A certain reply does not lie to hand, but subsequent studies will surely provide some interesting hypotheses.

At the beginning of this chapter the Eblaites were described as essentially polytheistic, but certain considerations such as the appellative "lord" for Dagan and the preponderance of the elements Il and Ya in the onomastica, though not authorizing the term ur-monotheism of the Semitic peoples, do suggest that the Eblaites had a quite advanced concept of the divine and were very near to henotheism, that is, the special worship of some one particular divinity among others existent. To this point we shall return when discussing in detail the hymn to the "Lord of heaven and earth."

1.2. FORMS OF SYNCRETISM

Coming into contact with other peoples, the Eblaites had the chance to compare their gods with those of other cultures. As a matter of fact, Ebla's contacts with Sumer were so direct that a lack of interchange in the field of religion would be surprising indeed. The choice of the term "interchange" is deliberate; as above when culture was discussed, the exchanges with Mesopotamia were not one-way. Mesopotamia gave much to Ebla, but it also learned much from her.

The Ebla rising from the royal archives does not present the characteristics of a Sumerian colony but rather those of a person of imposing appearance. After having studied the qualities of Sumerian deities, the savants of Ebla accepted some of them into their pantheon and others, who appeared to correspond closely to their own gods, they identified with their own.

The highly sophisticated process of religious syncretism, thought to have been inaugurated in Mesopotamia when the Semites came into contact with the Sumerians,[9] can now be traced back to Ebla in northern Syria.

In the bilingual vocabularies, in fact, an entire section is reserved for the Sumerian divinities with counterparts in the Eblaite pantheon. Before giving the complete list, it should be stressed that it is the product of deep study by Eblaite thinkers. Some Sumerian gods are not equated with Eblaite gods, and this indicates that they did not appear in such a manner as to be even remotely compared. The most interesting instance is that of ^{d}en-líl, the supreme god of the Sumerian pantheon, who in the second millennium is equated with Dagan, the supreme god of the West Semitic pantheon. Hence one would have expected the equation ^{d}en-líl=^{d}*dagan,* but such is not the case. This means that the Eblaites did not see Enlil as Dagan, but differently. Instead of the Semitic god for Enlil and two other Sumerian divinities, the Sumerian name is given, spelled out syllabically.

From the five vocabularies the following sequence of Sumerian divinities with their Semitic equivalents has been drawn up:[10]

^{d}gibil$_{4}$	*ì-sa-tù*
^{d}eden-ak	*te-rí-iš-tù*
^{d}mul	*kab-kab*
mul-mul	*Ga-ma-tù*
dingir-kalam^{tim}	*be-lu ma-tim*
^{d}en-zi/u	*zu-i-nu*
^{d}en	*ma-é-um*
^{d}en-en	*tù-uš-tá-i-i-lu-um*
^{d}en-ki	*é-um*
^{d}en-te	*aš:tár:tá*
^{d}inanna	*aš-tár*
^{d}né-eri$_{10}$	*ra-sa-ap*
^{d}eden	*wa-pí-um*
^{d}BARA$_{10}$-ra	*iš-ḫa-ra*
^{d}ak	*sà-du-um*

Some of these equations were taken for granted, such as Nergal=Rasap and Inanna=Aštar, but others are entirely new and highly interesting for the problem of religious syncretism in the third millennium B.C.

Reference was made above to several Sumerian divinities who find no Eblaite counterparts and whose names are transcribed syllabically; these are:

^{d}en-líl	*i-li-lu*
^{d}nin-kar-du	*ni-ga-ra-du*
^{d}ašnan	*a-sà-na-an*

Instead of furnishing the Semitic correspondent, the scholars of Ebla merely wrote out the Sumerian god-names syllabically. These syllabic spellings confirm the reading of these three names documented in Mesopotamia seven centuries later and offer a good example of the continuity of religious traditions in the area of the Fertile Crescent.

1.3. BORROWINGS

To have found points of contact between their gods and those of Sumer bespeaks the maturity of Eblaite thinkers, and to have accepted into their own pantheon foreign gods shows the great openness and religious sensibility of this civilization vis-à-vis other religions.

Thanks to the presence of foreign divinities in the Eblaite pantheon, one can prove the presence already in this period in the Near East of peoples thought to have arrived somewhat later. The most interesting case regards the Hurrians, an Indo-European people attested for the first time toward 2300 B.C. The Eblaites accepted at least four deities of the Hurrian pantheon: ^{d}Adamma, ^{d}Aštabi, ^{d}Ḫapat, and ^{d}Išḫara. The presence, above all, of Aštabi, the great war god, leaves little doubt that the Hurrians were active in this period and had strict ties with Ebla.

Numerous are the bloody and unbloody sacrifices offered to these four Hurrian gods and to two of them, Adamma and Aštabi, months of the new calendar are dedicated, namely, the second and the ninth:

itu nidba$_{x}$-^{d}aš-ta-bi$_{5}$	month: Feast of Aštabi
itu ^{d}*a-dam-ma-um*	month: (Feast) of Adamma[11]

The discourse concerning Sumerian divinities, however, is a bit more complex. Granted, in fact, equations established by the vocabularies, the Sumerian name of the god attested in the lists of offerings does not always indicate worship of the foreign deity. Hence when we find Sumerian ^{d}UTU written, it is most likely that the Eblaite equivalent Sipiš, the sun god, is intended; similarly in other cases as well. Only in the case of ^{d}en-ki and ^{d}nin-ki would I be inclined to see a borrowing from the

Sumerian pantheon precisely because in addition to Enki, his companion Ninki is also venerated at Ebla.

The complete absence both in the cult and in the name lists of the Sumerian high god Enlil would indicate that the Eblaites felt no empathy for this deity who figures centrally in Sumerian myths, which, for the rest, were translated with considerable care.

Studies carried out thus far show that the Eblaites introduced Hurrian and Sumerian gods into their pantheon. Further research will doubtless enlarge the horizon, bringing into view not only gods of other peoples but also other peoples themselves.

2. WORSHIP

How did the Eblaites express their devotion to the gods, where and under what form did they turn to them? To these questions both the economic tablets and the literary texts supply answers: both types are important, the former recording the offerings and the pertinent places of worship and revealing the degree of popularity of the various divinities, and the latter granting a view of this people's lucubrations in the religious field.

2.1. PRIESTS AND PLACES OF WORSHIP

Though the archaeologists have not brought to light any sacred edifices of the period of the royal archives, the texts reveal that Ebla had several temples dedicated to individual gods; the name for these buildings is é-é-dingir-dingir, "the houses of the gods." In some texts, though, it seems that the complex of temples hides under the expression é-mul, "house of the star."

It is not yet possible to furnish a complete list of the temples of the separate deities, even though one has the impression that Ebla must have teemed with sacred places; a number of temples must have been consecrated to Dagan, and there were temples of Kura, Hada, Nidakul, Aštar, etc. In addition to temples, chapels set in the administrative center of the "governorate" and dedicated to different divinities are mentioned by the tablets.

Among the priests and priestesses who performed the rites, pride of place belongs to the *pašīšu,* "the anointed," being either male or female.[12] To cite three examples:

pa₄:šeš ᵈku-ra	pašīšu-priest of Kura
pa₄:šeš ᵈra-sa-ap	pašīšu-priest of Rasap
pa₄-šeš sal ᵈBe SAL	pašīšu-priestess of Belatu

Types of priests are also indicated by the expressions Aširatum and Išartum, more precisely "priestesses."

But the most pleasant surprise is finding attested in this early period holy men not bound to the worship of a particular god but rather representing a new kind of religiosity. These are the "prophets" belonging to the category of the prophesiers of the divine word. These holy men, specified by the country of origin, moved from one city to another announcing the divine message.

Existing already in the prebiblical world, the prophets are called *nabiutum* from the root *nb'/nby,* "to call, announce," and come from Mari.[13]

This section would be incomplete without mentioning a problem to which no satisfactory answer has been forthcoming. In Sumerian civilization the terms e n and e n t u m designate two kinds of priests, but at Ebla e n indicates only the king just as *maliktum* designates the queen. In some texts, however, en and *maliktum* quite possibly refer to persons connected with the cult and not to political authorities.

2.2. THE OFFERINGS

To present offerings to the gods manifests a close relationship between the offerer and the Being to whom a gift is made. But how did the Eblaites represent the divinity?

Mention was made above of the place of worship where the god was venerated; within this place the god or goddess was present in the form of a statue often made of gold and silver. Thus one tablet speaks of five kilograms of silver for preparing a white statue of Dagan:

10 *ma-na* ku:babbar	10 minas of silver
UNKEN-aka	for preparing
1 an-dùl	1 statue
babbar	white
nì-ba	gift
[d]*be kà-na-na-im*	for the Lord of Canaan[14]

Another text speaks, however, of 40 shekels of gold to make a statue of the god Aštabi:

ša-pi gín-dilmun guškin	40 Dilmun shekels of gold
UNKEN-aka	to prepare
1 an-dùl	1 statue
nì-ba	gift
[d]*aš-ta-bi*$_5$	for the God Aštabi.[15]

Ebla's opulence is thus shown in the realm of worship as well. What a welcome discovery it would be were these statues mentioned by the tablets to emerge from the mound of Tell Mardikh!

The offerings presented to the gods are of various kinds. Above all, there are the unbloody (bread, beer, oil) and bloody offerings (smaller livestock), as well as ex-votos properly speaking, consisting for the most part of golden or other metallic objects and cloths. The Sumerian term denoting "offering" is $nidba_x$, literally "unbloody offering," but which at Ebla takes on a wider range of meanings, even coming to signify "feast."

The tablets with information about offerings are so numerous that it is necessary to make a choice. Earlier chapters also cite documents listing gifts to the gods.

Bread is the most common type of offering and in the lists of rations for the personnel in the city, there is frequent mention of rations for the god Kura and for the god Mul. TM.75.G.306 lists as many as 4,450 loaves of both barley and wheat as offerings for the feast of the gods Agu. As drink, beer was offered and occasionally wine.

A series of texts from the reign of Ibbi-Sipiš furnish, on the other hand, a detailed list of sheep offerings by members of the royal family to the official gods of the kingdom. Here are some examples:

2 udu	2 sheep
^{d}*ša-ma-gan*	for the god Šamagan;
2 udu	2 sheep
^{d}*ni-da-kul*	for the god Nidakul
lu-ba-an^{ki}	of Luban
en	from the king
$nidba_x$	as an offering;
3 udu	3 sheep
^{d}*ni-da-kul*	for the god Nidakul
a-ru_x*-ga-tù*^{ki}	of Arugatu
en	from the king
$nidba_x$	as an offering
in ud	for one day.[16]

The tablet continues with the mention of 12 sheep for the god Nidakul of the "governorate," 3 sheep for the god Rasap of Atanni, 2 sheep for the god Rasap of the "governorate," 2 sheep for the god Hada, 1 sheep for the god Amu, etc. After the king comes Ir'ak-Damu, and then the queen:

2 udu	2 sheep
^{d}*ku-ra*	for the god Kura
in 8	for 8 days
ma-lik-tum	from the queen
$nidba_x$	as an offering;
3 udu	3 sheep

^{d}*ni-da-kul*	for the god Nidakul
lu-ba-an^{ki}	of Luban
ma-lik-tum	from the queen
nidba$_x$	as an offering;
2 udu	2 sheep
^{d}*ni-da-kul*	for the god Nidakul
a-ru$_x$*-ga-tù*^{ki}	of Arugatu
ma-lik-tum	from the queen
nidba$_x$	as an offering;
2 udu	2 sheep
^{d}*ni-da-kul*	for the god Nidakul
sa-MI+ŠITA$_x$^{ki}	of the governorate
ma-lik-tum	from the queen
nidba$_x$	as an offering.[17]

The offerings are seen to be very detailed and look to a specific month.

Other tablets, such as TM.75.G.2096,[18] enumerate the sheep allocated to the divinities taken together under the designation é-mul, "house of the star"; the 2,717 sheep mentioned (actually 2,607) are subdivided as follows:

MONTHS:	I	II	III	IV	V	VI	VII	VIII	IX	X
SHEEP:	231	194	371	185	328	67	363	145	310	413

In addition to smaller livestock, oxen were also sacrificed to the deities, though rarely, as TM.76.G.223 informs us:

2 gu$_4$	2 oxen
^{d}*ḫa-a-pá-tù*	for the goddess Ḫapatu;
2 gu$_4$	2 oxen
^{d}*aš-tá-bi*$_5$	for the god Aštabi;
2 gu$_4$	2 oxen
^{d}*ni-da-kul*	for the god Nidakul
a-ru$_x$*-ga-tù*^{ki}	of Arugatu;
2 gu$_4$	2 oxen
^{d}*ra-sa-ap*	for the god Rasap.

The documents amply report what was offered to the gods but are totally silent about the manner and the rite of the sacrifice itself.

As noticed above, precious objects and materials, besides perishable goods, were also presented to the gods. Gifts of precious metals, gold and silver, either in the form of plates or in the shape of objects made of such metals, lead the list. A few examples must suffice:

2 *ma-na* 23 gín-dilmun guškin	2 minas and 23 Dilmunite shekels of gold,
1 díb-maḫ$_x$	1 large plaque

lú-^{giš}gidri-^{giš}gidri	the men of the scepter
in-na-sum	have given
^{d}*'à-da*	for the god Hada
ḫa-lam^{ki}	of Ḫalam
in AMA-ra	in the month of Amara;
en	the king
šu-mu-dúb	has consigned
6⅔ gin-dilmun-guškin	6⅔ Dilmunite shekels of gold
2 *gú-li-lum*	(for) 2 bracelets
nì-ba	property
^{d}*ku-ra*	of the god Kura;
2 *ma-na* guškin	2 minas of gold
šir$_{x}$-za 1 AB	. . . 1 object—AB
é	for the temple
^{d}*'à-da*	of Hada
lú *lu-ub*^{ki}	of the city of Lub;
6⅔ gín-dilmun guškin	6⅔ Dilmunite shekels of gold
^{d}*áš-tá-bi*$_{5}$	for the god Aštabi.[19]

Along with gold bracelets Amorite daggers are mentioned quite often, as are chariots and various figurines of animals as ornaments of the temple.

Cloths were also donated to the temple, on occasion to adorn the statue of the god as TM.75.G.1467 reports:

1 gada-tug kur$_{6}$	1 linen garment, material
an-dùl kù:babbar	for the silver statue
^{d}*be du-du-lu*^{ki}	of the "Lord of Tuttul."

No further specifications are given.

From the tablets one gains the distinct impression that the Eblaites considered the gods an integrating part of their daily life and that the temple teemed with precious gifts and hummed with sacrificial activity.

2.3. THE FEASTS

The Sumerian term for "feast" is nidba$_{x}$, and the observation made in the preceding paragraph that the Eblaites were profoundly religious finds further confirmation in the number of month-names in the new calendar of Ebla which bear the name of a divinity.

1)	Feast of Dagan	First month
2)	Feast of Aštabi	Second month
3)	Feast of Hada	Third month
4)	Feast of Adamma	Ninth month
5)	Feast of Ištar	Eleventh month
6)	Feast of Kamiš	Twelfth month

To these two more (itu *er-me* and itu *ḫulumu*) may be added since they surely refer to religious events which will be discussed presently.

Nor do these names exhaust the list; other feasts crop up in the cursory reading of the archives, such as feasts in honor of the gods Agu, of the god Nidakul, of Rasap, etc.

Certain feasts have a particular name and hence are perhaps more identifiable. Such are the feast Sikil and the feast i-giš. The first is the feast of the purification and the second of the anointing. Though further details are lacking, the meanings of the terms are sufficiently clear so that for the first time we can fix on the profundity of the religious rite, without, however, knowing how it was performed. To these a third feast may be added, called izi-gar in Sumerian and *ḫul/rumu,* literally "consecration" in Eblaite, which, as observed by my colleague M. Dahood, could well refer to the sacrifice of children, a widespread practice among the Punic peoples of the first millennium B.C.

The texts cited below refer to the three feasts just mentioned.

Feast of the purification:

1 udu	1 sheep
^{d}lugal	for the god "Lord"
du-du-lu^{ki}	of Tuttul
in	on (the feast)
sikil	of purification
en	from the king
nidba$_x$	as offering.[20]

Feast of the consecration:

2 udu	2 sheep
^{d}*be*-dingir-dingir	for the god "Lord of the gods"
in	in
Giš-bar-du^{ki}	Gišbardu,
2 udu	2 sheep
^{d}*ku-ra*	for the god Kura
i-bí-sí-piš	from Ibbi-Sipiš
nidba$_x$	as an offering
in u$_4$	on the day
izi-gar	of the (feast) of the consecration.[21]

Feast of the anointing:

1 *é-da-um*-tùg-2 1 gu-súr-túg 2 aktum túg
2 íb-túg $ša_6$-dar
1 íb-lá guškin
1 aktum-túg 1 íb-túg 1 nì-lá-gaba 2 nì-lá-sag
nì-ki-za
lugal
ma-rí^{ki}
in ud
$nidba_x$ ì-giš
eb-la^{ki}
wa
ma-rí^{ki}

"1 Edaum fabric of second quality, 1 Gusur fabric, 2 Aktum fabrics, 2 Ib fabrics, top quality and multicolored,//1 gold crown,//1 Aktum fabric, 1 Ib fabric, 1 belt and 2 foulards,//property//of the king//of Mari//on the day//of the feast of anointing//of Ebla//and// Mari."[22]

Other documents specify that the head is anointed, and when this fact is related to the members of the royal family mentioned in these same documents, one may infer that the rite is bound up with kingship.

The documents also speak of processions of the gods from the capital to other villages of the kingdom. The month name itu *er-me,* "month: the cities," seems to conceal, in fact, a religious practice such as a procession which brought the periphery into contact with the center. Even one of the year names alludes to a procession of Dagan:

DIŠ-mu	the year in which
Be	the Lord
du-du-a	went
ar-mi^{ki}	to the cities.[23]

This obviously refers to an extraordinary event for which the statue of Dagan left the city; in any case, it confirms that the Eblaites were familiar with processions.

At the risk of repetition, the feasts discussed here fit Ebla into its natural Northwest Semitic ambience. Under the religious aspect, too, the Eblaites are Canaanites and the true forebears of the Phoenicians.

2.4. INCANTATIONS, HYMNS, AND MYTHS

What has been said thus far concerns more the manifestations of the Eblaites' deep religious sentiments. But what did they think of their gods? How did they explain the divine action in the universe and in daily life?

Only a thorough study of the literary texts of a religious character will supply answers to these queries. To date different genres have been identified, such as myths, hymns, rituals, and incantations, but their decipherment and interpretation are such a slow process that little can be hazarded about them at present.

Another equally serious obstacle is thrown up by the fact that most of the literary texts are translations of Sumerian works, so that a very careful evaluation is required before concluding whether a particular concept is Eblaite or merely Sumerian.

When, for instance, the protagonists of the myths are gods like Enlil and Enki, the two major divinities of the Sumerian pantheon, it becomes difficult to argue that the content of the myth in question is Eblaite. Other myths dealing with the god Sun appear to be more interesting since in these Tiamatum, "the ocean water," plays a role; this element is surely local and points to original compositions in Ebla.

The incantations (é n - e - n u - r u) present the same ambivalence as the myths: some are clearly Sumerian, other Eblaite. The goddess of the conjuration is, however, always the same, ^{d}n i n - g i r i m$_{x}$, well known from incantations discovered in Fara. Thus far 28 incantations have come to light; one tablet alone numbers 14 incantations, which suggests that the contents are merely "titles or incipits of conjurations." Deserving special mention are those against serpents and scorpions on the one hand, and against the evil spirits, on the other, which invoke the special intervention of gods like Baliḫ, the divinized river, and the god Hada, the storm. The mention of serpents, scorpions, and the god Baliḫ situate these charms in the natural ambience of northwestern Syria, and today the real inhabitants of the ruins of Ebla are the scorpions.

This chapter opened with the citation of a text, preserved in three copies, which reveals some of the Eblaite religious notions. Though written in Sumerian, some elements betray its purely Eblaite character. This hymn to the "Lord of heaven and earth," with a passage referring to the origin of the cosmos as the creation of God, contains a series of appellatives which set off the divinity itself:[24]

> Lord of heaven and earth:
> the earth was not, you created it,
> the light of day was not, you created it,
> the morning light you had not [yet] made exist.
> Lord: effective word
> Lord: prosperity
> Lord: heroism
> Lord: . . .
> Lord: untiring
> Lord: divinity
> Lord: who saves
> Lord: happy life.

The text speaks for itself; under the form of a litany the Eblaite theologians reveal their concept of God, Lord of heaven and earth and hence of the cosmos. God is seen as a superior being but continually present upon the earth and in daily life.

At this point it becomes clear that the Eblaite was profoundly religious and believed in his own gods; indeed, this hymn makes it plausible that this culture, to be sure polytheistic, was on the way to a henotheism virtually declared. Who, in fact, is the Lord of heaven and earth? Certainly not Dagan or Rasap or Sipiš, but GOD written in capitals.

3. POPULAR RELIGION

From pure henotheism we pass to rank polytheism when we look at the religion of the masses. The available data come from the state archives and refer to official worship and reflection of some thinkers but scarcely reflect the popular beliefs that in every culture present some peculiarities.

The only means to pinpoint the differences between official and popular religion is furnished by the lists of personal names. The first observation concerns the divine elements in the personal names: some gods are witnessed here but are absent from the cultic texts. The most glaring cases are those of Malik and Damu, the two most popular gods in Ebla, if we credit the enormous number of personal names composed with these divine elements, and of the pair Il and Ya, equally frequent among the names of Eblaites.

Less frequently attested are some secondary gods, such as Daban, Da'ar, Ba'al, Ḫalu, Erra, Mani, Na'im, ^{d}Ì-GIŠ, Palil, Ti, etc.

The examination of the personal names themselves reveals the true religious sentiments of the Eblaite and how he conceived of his relationship with the divine. Here follow some names whose theophorous components are Malik, Damu, Il, and Ya:

1)	*a-dam-ma-lik*	the man of Malik
	du-bù-ḫu-ma-lik	feast of Malik
	ib-na-ma-lik	Malik has created
	eb-du-ma-lik	servant of Malik
	a-bù-ma-lik	Malik is father
2)	*i-a-da-mu*	Damu exists
	iš-má-da-mu	Damu has heard
	ìr-^{d}da-mu	servant of Damu
	i-ad-da-mu	hand of Damu
	in-da-mu	eye of Damu

3)	*i-ti-il/ìa*	Il/Ya has given
	en-na-il/ìa	Il/Ya has shown favor
	puzur₄-ra-il/ìa	Protection of Il/Ya
	ip-ḫur-il/ìa	Il/Ya has united
	mi-kà-il/ìa	Who is like Il/Ya?

These names grant an insight into the intimate relationship between the common man and his god; he is the servant of god but in recompense the god watches over him, indeed, he is like a father who protects, provides, and listens.

Notes

1. A. Falkenstein, *La Cité temple sumérienne*, in *CHM* 1/4 (1954), pp. 784–814.
2. G. Pettinato, "Dagan e il suo culto in Ebla. Un primo bilancio," (in press).
3. M. H. Pope and W. Röllig, *WdM*, 1, p. 277.
4. For the text of the malediction, see p. 105.
5. TM.75.G.1444, obv. IV 5–17.
6. TM.75.G.1464.
7. M. Dahood and G. Pettinato, "Ugaritic ršp gn and Eblaite rasap gunu (m)^{ki}" in *OrNS* 46 (1977), pp. 230–32.
8. *BA* 39 (1976), p. 48.
9. J. J. van Dijk, "Les contacts ethniques dans la Mésopotamie et les syncrétismes de la religion sumérienne," in *Syncretism*, Åbo, 1969, pp. 171ff.
10. TM.75.G.1825; 2003; 3131; 3171.
11. G. Pettinato, "Elementi ḫurriti ad Ebla nel 3. millennio av.C.," (in press).
12. TM.75.G.525; 1764.
13. TM.75.G.454.
14. TM.75.G.1376, rev. II 7 – III 3.
15. TM.75.G.1402, obv. II 2–6.
16. TM.75.G.11010, obv. I 1–13.
17. *Ibidem*, obv. VI 4–23.
18. See p. 147.
19. TM.75.G.1696, obv. I 1 – III 4.
20. TM.75.G.2075, obv. II 13–19.
21. *Ibidem*, rev. I 19 – II 3.
22. TM.75.G.1261, obv. VIII 8 – IX 9.
23. TM.75.G.410.
24. TM.75.G.1682, and parallels.

CHAPTER X

Conclusion: Problems and Prospects Raised by the Discovery of Ebla

These pages should suffice to show that the march of science is an ongoing process where every goal is only a stage which in turn becomes a point of departure for further researches. The well-worn saying that every discovery raises more problems than it solves also applies to Ebla.

One problem which will engage savants is the position of Eblaite society with regard to other Near Eastern societies, and in general to antiquity. We have already underlined how we looked for a form of Oriental absolutism which characterizes the political organization of ancient Egypt and the different political entities that succeeded one another in Mesopotamia, with the necessary distinctions, however. Hence it was logical to expect an absolute monarch invested from on high in keeping with a religious concept which, with characteristic differences, informs the abovementioned societies.

Ebla, on the other hand, appears as essentially lay, where lay must not be understood as antireligious. The organization of power is in no way absolutist or personalized. The laicality of Ebla—an extremely modern and present fact—is a new reality but perfectly natural, striking but normal. One is not dealing with an experiment but with something very precise, historically and dynamically assimilated, stable, successful in its exceptionality, which makes Ebla stand out in a panorama dominated by the figure of the king-god or the priest-official.

Modernity and balance also appear from the unfortunately scarce data on the model of economic production. The archive discovered is that of state, but there are proofs that along with the economy of state a private industry flourished; given the nature of the sources now available, very little can be learned about the private sector.

The very organization and distribution of labor can reserve some surprises; for example, the large number of texts treating of consignment of barley rations for the women workers in the spinning mills require a special study that would place these texts in diachronic succession, on the one hand, and in parallel with the data of production, on the other.

Too little is known, in fact, about the structure of farm labor and about the exploitation of the produce. Nonetheless, the fact remains unusual that the smallest productive agricultural unit, consisting of 20 persons, bears the name "village." The grouping, in turn, of several hundred of these villages (on the average, 500) was put under the jurisdiction of an official called l u g a l, a term designating the king in Mesopotamia, the holder of supreme power. These l u g a l number 14 and are responsible to the head of the administration, the *adon,* who was elected at the same time as the king to a seven-year term.

The achievement of such a bureaucratic structure goes back to an organization of the economic life predominantly rural in character—as noted by Maurizio Tosi—in contrast with the other sphere of the productive world composed of 4,700 functionaries (ugula), each one the head of a village and all directly dependent upon the head of the administration. Therefore this sector no longer mirrors the territorial division but is placed on a different level.

A much debated question among scholars concerns the "mode of Asiatic production." At the present stage of research it would be unwise, however, to attempt collocating the data furnished by Ebla within such a vast controversy. Still, the peculiarities which have been registered urge caution when assessing Eblaite society, so different not only from the societies contemporary with it but also from those that developed later in the ancient Orient.

The documentation furnished by the Ebla texts, the expression of a well-defined social system, necessarily supposes an older diffusion of writing, a refinement of which is encountered in the tablets exhumed. The most surprising datum is, in fact, the tendency to semitize the Sumerian cuneiform writing.

As is well known, a written Semitic language based on the triconsonantalism of the roots is much more practically and easily expressed by simply registering the consonants. From the Ugaritic texts to current Arabic newspapers the practicality of this custom has steadily dominated. Now in the Ebla texts one cannot but notice the tendency to use the Sumerian sign (obviously with the value of a syllable) to indicate the consonant without concern for the vowel; thus one can find in the body of a word the signs *TA, TU,* and *TI* used indifferently, since the scribe was interested only in indicating the consonant *t* with little regard for the accompanying vowel of the syllabic sign.

The offhand manner and the mastery of Sumerian writing that permit such a practice can only represent the final or mature phase of an ancient and widespread development. Surely more ancient tablets exist which witness this process, and the question must be asked if the date when writing was invented should not be raised. At present, the oldest texts come from stratum IV, the oldest level at Uruk, where the characters are certainly not primitive. With the advance of epigraphic studies, will it not be necessary to push back before the middle of the fourth millennium the time when this essential instrument of communication was invented?

But the language expressed by the writing on the Ebla tablets poses serious problems for the Semitists in particular because of the type of language used. This question, extremely "esoteric" for the nonspecialist, will not be treated here, but many accepted explanations in the field of Semitic philology are going to be confuted by these new finds. The totally unexpected spoken and written use of Northwest Semitic in this form and the very structure of Eblaite are going to undermine, for example, many reconstructions of Proto-Semitic based almost exclusively on Arabic.

Another serious problem derives from the reconstruction of the geography of third-millennium settlements. If before this discovery the exact location of Ebla resembled the game of blindman's buff, the commercial dockets furnish so many data on human settlements that it becomes necessary to take down that painting mentioned at the beginning of this book. Localities inhabited by humans, previously known only by name or completely unknown, await fixing on the geographical map of the ancient Near East that archaeologists and philologists must now draw. The discovery of Ebla marks, then, the beginning of a new adventure across time and space; Ebla opens new paths to the younger archaeologists who have made or are making of archaeology an anthropological science. Thanks to the indications provided by the royal archives of Ebla, a complete panorama of that part of that world that saw the rise of urbanism may come into view; the city seems to have found in the Near and Middle East its most congenial habitat.

If it is true that every scientific discovery entails a mass of problems, it is also true that scientific progress is intimately connected with such dynamics where every goal reached constitutes the basis for further advances and researches—hence new problems—in a development whose outcome cannot be seen.

Speaking of new problems implies therefore speaking of new prospects, a thought that does not upset the genuine scholar but, on the contrary, generates in him greater enthusiasm to uncover what is still wrapped in mystery. This needs to be said because the instability of "assured results" obtained by herculean efforts is the driving force of free thought, which while developing itself shatters every prejudice born of convictions accepted once and for all as absolute truths.

Begging the reader's indulgence for these divagations on the ideal of a scholar's life—but which applies not to him alone—I conclude this survey of Ebla by outlining some research prospects for various disciplines opened up by this remarkable discovery.

The first direct repercussion will involve the resumption of the excavations at sites where researches have been long suspended or proceed at a snail's pace. Such is the case of the city Kish, located a few kilometers north of Babylon, which has yielded monumental traces of an imposing royal palace, thus lending support to the Sumerian legends about kingship before and after the flood.

Until the epoch of the Persian kings, it will be recalled, all the sovereigns of Mesopotamia were embellished by the ancient title of "king of Kish," even long after this city had lost its political importance.

The texts of Ebla speak of a rival kingdom, strong and mighty, a perennial threat to the security of the Eblaite empire. None other than Kish. So feared was this threat that the shrewd Syrian rulers formed an alliance with the kingdom of Ḫamazi, a city of northern Iran that awaits discovery. The soundness of this military and diplomatic strategy recommends it to this day; the privileged relationships France maintained with Russia to contain Germany are an example of this strategy.

Now excavations are being resumed at Kish as the result of the enthusiasm provoked by the Ebla finds, and the recovery of a similar archive illuminating Mesopotamian culture during a period devoid of documentation does not seem to be an unreasonable hope.

The numerous *tells* of Syria, frontier posts or terminals of commercial traffic radiating from Ebla, must surely conceal some archives. These *tells* have at best been subjected to surface exploration. In an ambience still dazzled by the results achieved during the golden era of Near Eastern archaeology, Ebla may have the merit of detonating a burst of light that will illuminate the face of the third-millennium Near East heretofore unknown.

The resumption of interrupted excavations should be followed by the patient exploration of new, important sites still to be identified, as well as by the systematic exploration of corridors of areas and sites unaccountably considered till now of little importance. To each of these sites must be brought those modern techniques that will spare them that "stagnant approach of traditional archaeology oriented toward the object" (Dales 1971:146).

Beyond these medium- and long-range prospectives we can right now begin considering the question of the Sumerian language. This partially deciphered language poses such problems that even Adam Falkenstein deemed it premature to write a general grammar and chose instead to limit himself to analyzing peculiarities of the language in a very restricted sector of the available documentation. But Ebla gives us not only economic and historical texts, but also vocabularies, lexicons, texts in translation, and the representation of the Eblaite-Sumerian pronunciation, as in a modern bilingual dictionary.

New elements unexpectedly rise up under the epigraphist's eyes, clarifying—or complicating—problems unresolved or blocked at the level of working hypotheses.

As remarked earlier, the discoveries springing from these texts shed light not only on the contemporary phase but also on earlier and posterior periods.

Several examples may serve as illustration. A few years ago some tablets written in cuneiform characters of Uruk IV type (ca. 3500 B.C.) came to light in Transylvania (see Fig. X, 1). The Uruk IV tablets have not yet been deciphered and this new find in such a remote region raises

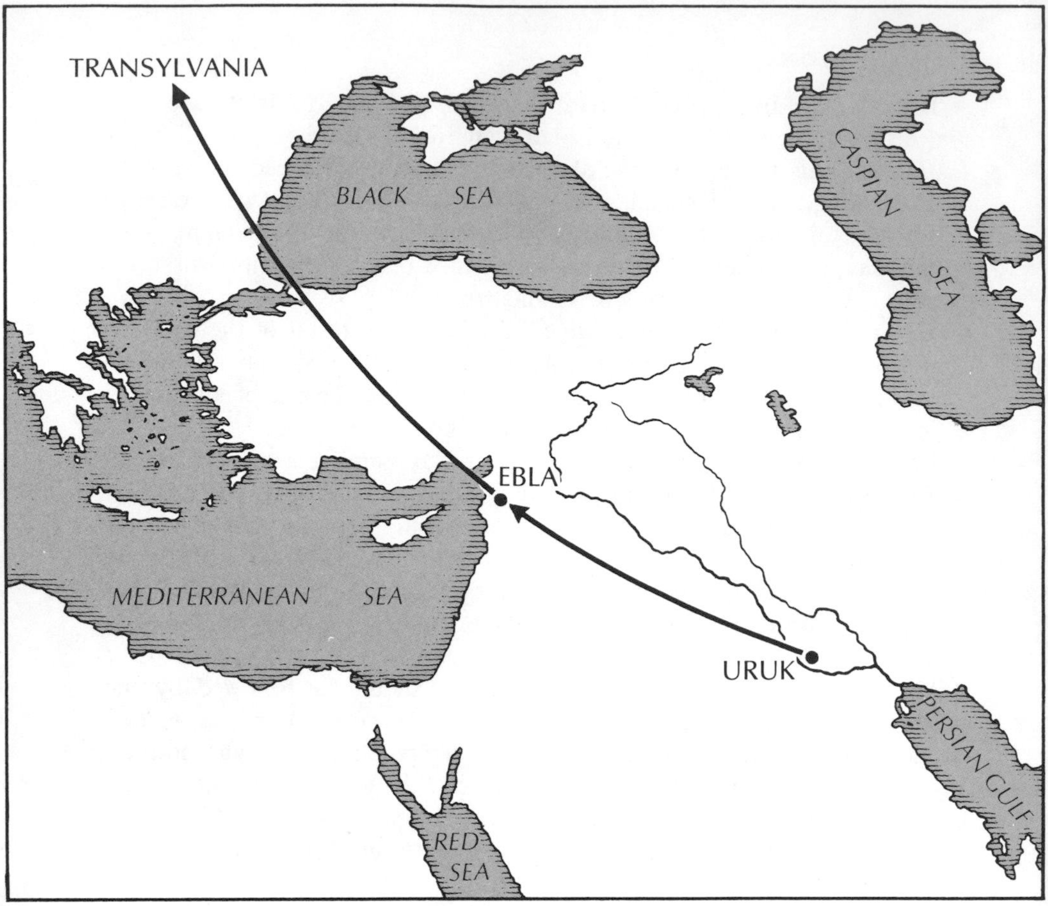

Figure X, 1 Lines of expansion of cuneiform writing in the third millennium

serious questions. For the moment the enigma remains, but exploration of lower levels at Ebla may well yield new elements with which to confront the cuneiform of Uruk IV; at the time of the Ebla archives the extent of commercial traffic, not having risen from scratch, presupposes a much older tradition which renders the discovery in Romania less surprising.

But if Ebla of 2500 B.C. is beginning to throw light on the preceding millennium, many shadowy zones of the second millennium are also coming to assume clearer shapes. The chief beneficiary is the West Semitic world in which fourteenth-century Ugarit stands out, to be followed by Phoenician culture and the world of the Old Testament of the first millennium.

Here might be mentioned the work of the Rome school of Mitchell Dahood which, on the basis of Ugaritic philology and prosody, has succeeded in clarifying numerous biblical passages especially in the poetic books of the Old Testament. The world of the Bible did not rise up in isolation like a solitary mushroom, but is a particular culture, a limb of the tree that is Syria-Palestine of which Ebla, Ugarit, and Phoenicia are related branches.

Such discourse does not wish to suppress the Bible's originality which distinguishes it sharply from the other branches of the tree, but intends to consider it within the whole complex in which it originated, an essential condition for understanding it adequately.

Reading this work the reader has been able, through this common background, to identify the points of contact between the Syro-Palestinian cultures of succeeding centuries and the world of Ebla. His appetite will doubtless be whetted to know what the ultimate consequences of the Ebla discoveries will be. He hopes too that the textual data from this treasure trove will be accompanied by the publication of the analogous riches issuing from the archaeological context, so that the blending of philological and archaeological information will enable him to paint a full portrait of Ebla.

AFTERWORD

Ebla, Ugarit, and the Bible

MITCHELL DAHOOD, S.J.

In February 1978, during a meeting in Washington, D.C., of the American Association for the Advancement of Science, astronomers named Senator William Proxmire, Democrat-Wisconsin, an honorary member of the Flat Earth Society. The award was made a week after Senator Proxmire gave his Golden Fleece award to NASA (National Aeronautics and Space Administration) for its upcoming $14 million, seven-year search for extraterrestrial intelligence. Dr. Frank Drake of Cornell University commented, "When Columbus left Spain, there was no evidence the New World existed, let alone Wisconsin. Even if we discover a dead civilization, the information they leave us could in a week surpass everything in the Library of Congress."[1] Eminent scholars of the ancient Near East have long held that there was no Canaan, let alone Canaanites, in the third millennium B.C., but dogged digging by the Missione Archeologica Italiana in Siria has unearthed a dead Canaanite city dating to circa 2500 B.C. Though dead, the city of Ebla lives on through the language and culture it has transmitted to the Canaanites of the second millennium as reflected by the people of Ugarit, some 55 miles west on the Mediterranean coast, and by the authors of the Hebrew Bible in Palestine. Assessing the Phoenician contribution to the Bible, the late Professor W. F. Albright concluded: "There can no longer be any doubt that the Bible has preserved some of the best in Phoenician literature, especially lyric and gnomic poetry. Without the powerful influence of the Canaanite literary tradition, we should lack much of the perennial appeal exerted by Hebrew poetic style and prosody, poetic imagery and vivid description of natural phenomena. Through the Bible the entire civilized world has fallen heir to Phoenician literary art."[2] Albright died in September 1971, just three years before the first discovery of tablets at Ebla, which reveal that the powerful Phoenician-Canaanite literary tradition already had deep roots in the third millennium B.C. and that its influence on the composition of the Bible may turn out to have been greater than even he could have imagined.

In 1957 John Gray published his volume *The Legacy of Canaan,* with the subtitle *The Ras Shamra* [=*Ugarit*] *Texts and Their Relevance to the Old Testament*. A second, revised edition expanded by more than a hundred pages appeared in 1965. In these volumes Gray gathered an impressive amount of literary material showing how much more intelligible the language and thought of the Old Testament—basically a first-millennium B.C. document—become when studied in the light of the Ugaritic tablets discovered from 1929 on and dating to circa 1375–1190 B.C. The Prophet Isaiah in 19:18 terms the Hebrew language *śᵉpat kᵉna'an,* literally "the lip of Canaan," and the newly discovered language of Ugarit turned out to be closely kindred. As a result, biblical scholars had to readjust their concept of Canaan so as to have it include Ras Shamra on the north Syrian shore, seven miles north of modern Latakia. Now Canaan appears to extend slightly farther north and inland from Ugarit to include Tell Mardikh-Ebla whose recovered tablets reveal a third-millennium dialect of Canaanite and whose people call their principal god *Dagan kananaum,* "Dagan the Canaanite," or *Be-kà-na-na,* "the Lord of Canaan," underscoring the land of his provenance. Back in 1929 at the time when the first Ugaritic tablets were discovered, Charles Virolleaud, the epigrapher responsible for their publication, was initially handicapped in deciphering the new script and classifying the new language, possibly because he had not reconciled himself to the fact that a major coastal settlement in the northern extremity of Syria could be ascribed to Phoenicians or Canaanites. Today some scholars are experiencing the same difficulty with regard to the classification of Eblaite as Canaanite because for them Canaan has in effect become coterminous with the Promised Land or Palestine.

In the Bible the terms "Canaan" and "Canaanite" are used somewhat indiscriminately to cover those areas of Palestine which eventually became the kingdoms of Israel and Judah. The Canaanites were thought of as the major but by no means the only element in the Semitic population dispossessed or absorbed by the Israelites. Archaeological discoveries, however, now indicate that "Canaan" embraced a much larger area, from the borders of Egypt in the south to the north Syrian coast, including the land-bridge, so to speak, between Egypt and Mesopotamia. Geographically, this variegated area had no natural centralizing or unifying feature such as the Nile in Egypt or the Tigris and Euphrates in Mesopotamia. In the second millennium it was not a coherent political unity. It consisted of numerous city-states under feudal kings who constantly sought to assert their independence by political maneuvering, aligning themselves with Egypt to the south or with the Hittite empire to the north. For the third millennium, however, the Tell Mardikh discoveries suggest the existence of a great commercial empire unifying Canaan under the hegemony of Ebla.

For the past fifty years many biblical scholars and Semitists have been studying the Hebrew text of the Old Testament, which bristles with difficulties, especially in the poetic books, in the light of the Ugaritic poetic and prose texts discovered at Ras Shamra and dating to circa 1375–1190 B.C. After considerable resistance because of the chronological disparity between these tablets and the Hebrew Bible, the results of these comparative studies are gradually finding their way into biblical exegesis, Hebrew lexica, and modern translations of the Bible. One reviewer of the 1976 *Supplementary Volume* written to update the 1962 four-volume edition of *The Interpreter's Dictionary of the Bible* correctly noted that "Many of the new and revised Old Testament articles demonstrate the importance of the Ugaritic material for an understanding of the background of the religion of Israel."[3] If the Ugaritic documents of the second millennium have had to struggle so to gain academic respectability in biblical circles, what chance do North Syrian tablets of 2500 B.C. have of claiming the attention of scholars bent on solving textual and exegetical problems in works composed in Samaria or Judea in the first millennium B.C.? One of my Roman colleagues has flatly assured me, "The Ebla tablets are simply much too early to be relevant for Old Testament studies," and a University of Chicago professor has gone on record to the effect that the Ebla tablets will be of supreme importance for our understanding of the Near East in the third millennium, but those who expect new light on the Old Testament will surely be disappointed. How a savant can determine how relevant to the Bible a new discovery may be before the tablets have been published must remain a mystery.

A more generous outlook will probably lead to essentially different results, especially when pertinent material is brought into the discussion from second-millennium Ugarit, which may serve as a bridge between third-millennium Ebla and the Old Testament. In recent years the tenacity of linguistic and religious traditions in Canaan, documented as far west as Carthage and as late as Roman times, has been established on point after point and warrants the careful employment of early material to elucidate later expression and practice.

Of course the time has not come to write a volume of the proportions of Gray's on the legacy of Ebla, but the following comments will attempt to extract from Professor Pettinato's contribution some points bearing on the biblical text and to veer the discussion along the Ebla-Ugarit-Bible axis. This route is taken because it seems that all three bodies of texts reflect Canaanite language and culture in three succeeding millennia. The original plan to divide this Afterword into two parts, Ebla and Ugarit, and Ebla and the Bible, was dropped in favor of the reader who would doubtless prefer to have the Ebla and Ugaritic evidence combined under headings that follow the biblical text by book, chapter, and verse. The Hebrew text is cited in transliteration when such seems needed to facilitate the discussion; in other cases only the translation will be given. The translation tends to be literal and adheres, so far as English idiom permits, to the order of the Hebrew words. In some instances the numbering of the Hebrew verses may differ by one from English Versions. The word or words placed between brackets are those illuminated by Eblaite parallels.

◆

Gen. 1:26 *naʿaśeh* [*ʾādām*] *beṣalmēnû*
Let us make man in our image.

Till not the only attestation of *ʾādām,* "man, Adam," outside the Bible appeared in Old Akkadian texts from the period of Sargon the Great (circa 2350 B.C.) in the form of the personal names *A-da-mu, ʾÁ-da-mu,* and *A-dam-u.*[4]

Now from Ebla comes the personal name *A-da-mu,* one of the 14 governors of the provinces under King Igriš-Ḫalam; see Chapter VI 1.2. In Ugaritic one of the titles of El, the head of the pantheon is *il ab adm,* "El, the father of mankind."

Gen. 2:5 *wekol śîaḥ haśśādeh* [*ṭerem*] *yihyeh bāʾāreṣ*
No shrub of the field was yet in the earth.

The Hebrew adverb of time, *ṭerem,* "not yet, before," does not occur in the other Semitic languages, but it seems to be present in the personal name *ṭarmia,* one of the 14 governors under king Irkab-Damu; see Chapter VI 1.2. On this supposition *ṭarmia* would mean "Ya is my primeval one," and could be compared semantically with the biblical personal name *qadmîʾēl,* "El is my ancient one," which is comprised of the adverb *qedem,* "before," and *ʾēl,* "El."

◆

Gen. 2:7 [*wayyiṣer*] *yahweh ʾelōhîm ʾet hāʾādām*
ʿāpār min-hāʾadāmāh
And Yahweh God molded man,
clay from the ground.

In one of the bilingual vocabularies[5] the Eblaite equivalent of Sumerian *baḫar,* "potter," is *wa-ṣí-lu-um.* Since the scribes often used the sign *-lu-* for *-ru-, wa-sí-lu-um* may fairly be equated with the qal participle of this root in Hebrew, *yōṣēr,* "potter." See below at Judg. 5:20 where the Ebla personal name *sà-sà-lum* is compared with the name of the Canaanite general Sisera. The preservation of initial *waw* in Eblaite, here in *wa-ṣí-lu-um,* is discussed by Pettinato in Chapter IV, 3.1.

Gen. 2:14 *w^{e}hannāhār har^{e}bî'î hû'* [*p^{e}rāt*]
And the fourth river it is the Euphrates.

Gen. 15:18 *minnāhār miṣrayim 'ad hannāhār* [*haggādōl*]
n^{e}har-[*p^{e}rāt*]

Buranun in Sumerian, *purattu* in Akkadian, the name Euphrates has lacked a compelling etymology. Ebla bids fair to fill this lacuna when terming the Euphrates *ba-ra-du,* "the Cold River," and *ba-ra-du ma-ad,* "the Great Cold River," the first answering to biblical *p^{e}rāt,* and the adjective *ma-ad* of the second semantically equaling Hebrew *gādōl,* "great." The doubling of the consonant in the final syllable of Akkadian *purattu* shows that the process of assimilation has been at work, *baradtu* becoming *barattu;* further assimilation takes place when mute *-attu* changes sonant *ba* to mute *pu* with the final result *purattu* in Akkadian and *p^{e}rāt* in Hebrew.[6] The name is altogether fitting since the Euphrates originates from the snows of the Armenian highlands. Flowing down from the snows of Lebanon, the river which forms the oasis of Damascus is today called in Arabic *Barada,* "The Cold River." The far-reaching implications of this Northwest Semitic etymology for the Euphrates cannot be dwelt upon here; suffice it to note that many of the unexplained names of rivers, mountains, and lands in the Near East may turn out to be Semitic and that the Semites may have been indigenous.

Gen. 2:20 records that "Adam gave names to all the beasts and to the birds of heaven and to all the wild animals of the field. But by Adam no helper was found like to himself."[7] This interest in naming and classifying accords with the scientific concerns of Ebla where encyclopedic lists of birds, fishes, plants, trees, metals, precious and nonprecious stones were drawn up at the scribal school, as pointed out by Pettinato in Chapter VIII.

The Eblaite personal name *iš-tá-a-nu,* "I am at ease,"[8] reveals the verbal use of the root *š'n,* "to be at ease," that may clarify Gen. 4:7, "Look, if you have behaved well, you will be at ease, but if you have not, sin will be lurking at your door." Here the problem is created by MT *ś^{e}'ēt* which simply does not parse and consequently gets emended to something else by the textual critics. These same consonants *š't* can be read *šā'attā* from *šā'antā,* the root being *š'n,* "to be at ease," with an assimilation of *-nt* to

-tt. A similar instance of assimilation has been cited above with regard to Gen. 2:14 and another will be noted in connection with the month name *ṣa-'à-tum,* that is discussed at Deut. 28:4.

◄►

Gen. 4:26 At that time men began to call upon the name of Yahweh.

This is a disconcerting assertion in view of Exod. 3:14 and 6:3 which claim that God first revealed his name Yahweh to Moses at a much later period. Yet the author of Genesis employs this divine name throughout the book and ascribes the usage to the beginnings of the human race. Gerhard von Rad states that this reference to an original revelation cannot easily be reconciled with the dominant literary tradition of the Old Testament. Some biblical theologians would see here a theologoumenon, that is, a theological insight; the biblical writer wanted to make the point that Israel's God is the Lord of history whose benevolent designs embrace all mankind to which Israel had a special mission. To establish the exact relationship between the theological intuition and historical truth is rarely a simple task, though the reconciliation of Gen. 4:26 with Exod. 3:14 and 6:3 appears less formidable. Gen. 4:26 might well preserve a northern or Syrian tradition where the name Yahweh was known early on, whereas the Exodus texts may reflect the Egyptian tradition in which this divine name does not figure in the onomasticon. No problem, in fact, is created by Exod. 3:15 when it is scanned and translated as poetry:

> *zeh šš^{e}mî l^{e}'ōlām*
> *w^{e}zeh zikrî l^{e}dōr dōr*
> This has been my name from eternity,
> and this will be my title from generation
> to generation.

Numerous authors have observed that one aspect of the Ebla finds that is bound to provoke endless debate in the future are the personal names ending in *-yà.* Is this ending to be identified with the name of Israel's God which appears in the forms *yāh, yāhû, yô,* and most frequently as *yahweh?* The problem at Ebla stands forth in the comparison of *mi-kà-il,* "Who is like El?" with *mi-kà-yà,* "Who is like Ya?" *iš-má-il,* "El has heard," and *iš-má-yà,* "Ya has heard," *en-na-il,* "Show favor, O El," and *en-na-yà,* "Show favor, O Ya." That *-yà* corresponds to *-il* appears obvious, but some savants urge caution because in Mesopotamia, in particular, the ending *-yà* could mark several different functions, such as being a caritative ending like Mickey for Michael, or it could simply stand as an abbreviation for any deity. But does this usage obtain in Canaan?

A glance at Ugaritic personal names creates the same impression as the comparison of Eblan personal names. Thus *amril,* "El sees," *amrb'l,*

"Baal sees," would point to "Ya sees," as the meaning of Ugaritic *amry*. Or again, *ḏmrb'l,* "Baal is my sentinel," *ḏmrhd,* "Hadd is my sentinel," make it difficult to avoid the conclusion that *ḏmry* signifies "Ya is my sentinel." Lingering doubts will surely be dispersed by the refrain first encountered in the very ancient (thirteenth century B.C.?) poem, Exod. 15:2, *'ozzî wᵉzimrat yāh,* "My strength and sentinel is Ya." Alongside *yrm'l* "the Most High is exalted," and *yrmb'l,* "Baal is exalted," *yrmy,* whose consonants are identical with those of the name Jeremiah, should signify "Ya is exalted." Of course, what would go far toward settling the dispute is an Eblaite personal name with *yà* in the initial position and prefixed by a determinative or semantic marker informing us that the name is divine. Ebla again obliges with the personal name dingir-*yà-ra-mu*, with determinative and all.[9] ᵈ*yà-ra-mu* equates with the biblical name *yôrām,* "Joram," one of the kings of Judah, and means "Ya is exalted." In Ugaritic appear the personal names *iltm,* "El is perfect," *tmy,* "Perfect is Ya," and *ytm,* which elicits biblical *yôtām,* "Jotham," meaning "Ya is perfect." In brief, the evidence for the pre-Israelite existence of the name Ya for a Canaanite deity grows ever more impressive.

Gen. 10:8–11 reports that the first warrior on earth was named Nimrod. For this name no satisfactory explanation has been found, but current opinion tends to favor a Mesopotamian origin of the personal name. The study of the patterns of Eblaite and Ugaritic personal names reveals a frequency of the sequence animal name plus the name of a god. Thus Eblaite *da-sí-ma-ad,* "the he-goat of the Grand,"[10] *en-ṣí-ma-lik,* "the goat of Malik,"[11] and Ugaritic *ibrd,* "the bull of Hadd," *ni-mi-ri-yà,* "the panther of Ya," illustrate this pattern and suggest that Nimrod breaks down into *nmr,* "panther," and *-d,* "Hadd." Which is to say that with this good Canaanite name the founder of Babel, Erech, and Akkad (Gen. 10:10) may well have been a Canaanite.

According to Gen. 11:5, Yahweh went down (*yērēd*) to see the city and the tower that men had built. One of the men at Ebla was named *ri-da-li-im,* "Come down, O Lim!" and in Ugaritic the king is commanded by El, the chief god, *šrd b'l bdbḥk,* "Make Baal come down by your sacrifice" (*UT,* Krt: 77–78). In Exod. 3:8 Yahweh states "I have come down (*'ērēd*) to deliver them out of the hands of the Egyptians." Thus the biblical writers' use of the verb *yārad,* "to descend," to describe God's movement down from heaven has a long history in Canaan.

Gen. 11:30 *watt^{e}hî śāray '^{a}qārāh*
'ên lāh [*wālād*]

Now Sarah was barren,
she had no child.

Since the form *wālād,* instead of the more common *yeled,* preserves initial *wa-,* many critics propose to emend the text to *yālād.* But the preservation of the initial *wa-* at Ebla (see Chapter IV, 4.0) urges caution; the form *wālād* may well be a survival from the period when Hebrew or a dialect of Hebrew preserved, like Eblaite, the initial *wa-.*

Gen. 20:7 *kî* [*nābî'*] *hû' w^{e}yitpallēl ba'ad^{e}kā*
For he is a prophet and he will intercede for you.

This is the first of the more than 300 biblical occurrences of the term *nābî',* "prophet." In recent decades scholars have turned to Mesopotamia for early light on prophecy because the Mari tablets discovered in 1935 and dating from circa 1800–1700 B.C. speak not infrequently of prophets and prophetic activity.[12] In a bilingual vocabulary[13] the Sumerian word p à, "to speak, recite," is translated into Eblaite by *na-ba-um,* the root of Hebrew *nābî',* "prophet."

When recounting the story of Hagar, the author records in Gen. 21:19 that "God opened her eyes and she saw a well of water." The verb employed here, *yipqaḥ,* "he opened," appears in the Ebla personal name *ip-qá-yà,* "Ya has opened."[14] Of course, the name calls to mind *p^{e}qaḥyāh,* the king of Israel mentioned in II Kings 15:22. Cf. Gen. 3:5 where the opening of the eyes is the prelude to divinity: *w^{e}nipq^{e}ḥû 'ênêkem wīhyîtem kē'lōhîm,* "and your eyes will be opened and you will become like gods."

Gen. 23:6 *š^{e}mā'ēnû '^{a}dōnî*
[*n^{e}śî'*] *'^{e}lōhîm 'attāh b^{e}tôkēnû*
Hear us, my lord:
you are the prince of God among us.

C. H. Gordon has recently pointed out that neither Egyptian *nsw,* "king (of upper Egypt)," nor Sumerian *ensí,* "ruler," enjoys a clear etymology.[15] This lack, he noted, may now be supplied by Eblaite *na-se*$_{11}$ which Pettinato translates "prefects." Since *na-se*$_{11}$ has a clear etymology in *nś',* "to lift up," it would seem to be the source of both Egyptian *nsw* and Sumerian e n s í. While Gordon urges caution in drawing premature conclusions, he does note that the archives show that Ebla exerted political and military supremacy over Mari and Ashur, so that it is quite possible that at even earlier dates Syro-Palestinians imposed their rule, as well as their word for "ruler," over Sumer and Egypt.

In the story about Laban, Jacob, and the speckled sheep in Gen. 30:31ff., one encounters the adjective *nāqōd,* "speckled," that occurs only in chapters 30–31 of Genesis. In an Ebla bilingual vocabulary *ma-ku-tum* answers to the Sumerian word for "spotted." Morphologically, *ma-ku-tum* analyzes as the *maqtul* passive participle formation of *nqd,* "to be speckled." Through assimilation of the *nun, manqudum* becomes *maqqūdum,* written *ma-ku-tum* in the cuneiform script but to be normalized *ma-qú-dum.*

Gen. 32:15 [*'izzîm*] *mā'tayim* [*ût^eyāšîm*] *'eśrîm*
two-hundred she-goats and twenty he-goats.

Though *'izzim,* "she-goats," occurs quite frequently in the Bible, *t^eyāšîm,* "he-goats," is attested only four times. Illuminating the cultural background of this episode in the life of Jacob is the fact that these two nouns probably have antecedents in the Eblaite personal names *en-ṣí-ma-lik,* "the goat of Malik" (*en-ṣí* probably stems from *'nz,* the root of Hebrew *'ēz,* "goat"), and *da-sí-ma-ad,* "the he-goat of the Grand," cited above in connection with Gen. 10:8–11.

The verb *pātar,* "to interpret," and the noun *pitrôn,* "interpretation," are found only in the Joseph story narrated in Gen. 40–41. In a bilingual vocabulary[16] the Semitic equivalent of Sumerian *nì-tur-du$_{11}$-ga,* "to speak softly," is *pá-tá-ru$_x$,* "to interpret."

In the butler's description of his dream in Gen. 40:9–10, he uses the word *'eškōl,* "bunch of grapes," now appearing in Eblaite as *aš-kà-lum* and *aš-qa-i-lu.*

Gen. 35:8 *wattāmot* [*d^ebōrāh*] *mêneqet ribqāh*
And Deborah, Rebecca's nurse, died.

Judg. 5:1 *wattāšar* [*d^ebôrāh*]
And Deborah sang.

Borne by Rebecca's nurse and by the charismatic leader and prophetess, the personal name Deborah signifies "Bee." Josh. 19:12 mentions the Levitical city *dāb^e^rat,* "Daberath," the present Deburiyeh to the west of Mount Tabor in central Palestine. Its name also means "Bee" or, better, "Bee-town." The geographical atlas of the ancient Near East from Ebla mentions a town *dub-bar-at*^{ki} [TM.75.G.2231, obv. XI 1], which also signifies "Bee-town," and may well be identical with the place mentioned in Josh. 19:12. Thus far "Bee" as a personal name has not been identified at Ebla but will probably turn up when more tablets have been studied.

Similar in formation and in genre is the name of the town *na-ma-ra-at*^{ki} [TM.75.G.2231, obv. XI 8] that occurs in the same column as *dub-bar-at*^{ki}. Its meaning is "City of Panthers." Num. 32:3 lists *nimrāh,* a place east of the Jordan river, and while some scholars interpret the name in the light of *nāmēr,* "panther, leopard," others show some hesitation. Ebla place names such as *dub-bar-at* and *na-ma-ra-at,* which are based on insect or animal names, should diminish the doubt attaching to the explanation of the biblical place name *nimrāh;* hence it may be rendered "Place of Panther" or, better, "Panther Place."

Gen. 38:14 *wattēšeb b^e^petaḥ* [*'ênayim*]
'^a^šer 'al-derek timnātāh

And she (Tamar) sat down by the gate
of Enaim,
which is on the road to Timnah.

Attested only here and in vs. 21 as an apparent place name, *'ênayim* conjoined with *b^e^petaḥ* has given rise to two major interpretations. In the footsteps of the Targums, the Syriac, and the Latin Vulgate, the phrase *b^e^petaḥ 'ênayim* has been understood as a parting of the road or crossroads and the *NEB* translates "where the road forks in two directions." Others, following the LXX, take *'ênayim* as a place name; Chicago Bible renders the phrase "the gateway of Enaim," and the *Jewish Publication Society Version* (1962) reads: "the entrance to Enaim."

The existence of a place name *'ênayim* may possibly be deduced from the Ebla geographical atlas where the name of one of the cities in Syria-Palestine is written with the Sumerian logograms IGI.IGI^{ki}. Since IGI is the Sumerian word for "eye," the name would doubtless have been read in Eblaite as dual *'ênayim* [TM.75.G.2231, obv. III 23].

In addition to "eye," *'ayin* signifies "spring," so that *'ênayim* would signify "twin springs." The precise location of Eblaite *'ênayim* cannot be made out, but the mere existence of such a place name in Syria-Palestine in the third millennium lends support to those who understand *'ênayim* as a town and not merely as a crossroads.

In Gen. 41:43 Joseph is hailed as *'abrēk,* a hapax legomenon which the *RSV* translates "Bow the knee!" and explains it as an Egyptian word similar in sound to the Hebrew word meaning "to kneel." Another possibility now lies to hand in the Sumerian term a g r i g é e n, "the superintendent of the royal palace," occurring in the letter of Ibubu to the king of Ḫamazi, translated above in Chapter V, 4.1. The Sumerian word a g r i g is also found written syllabically *'à-ga-ra-gu-um* with the variant *'à-ba-ra-gu-um,* which immediately evokes biblical *'abrēk,* now to be rendered "superintendent, steward." See above, Chapter IV, 3.1, on the b/g interchange. So while the Joseph episodes were enacted in Egypt, the stories told about him were composed in ancient Hebrew, a Canaanite dialect sharing many terms in common with its older relative, Eblaite. Another illustration of this can be seen in Gen. 50:26, "They embalmed him and he was placed in a coffin in Egypt," where *'ārôn,* "coffin, sarcophagus," is a Canaanite word attested only in Canaan, i.e., Ugaritic, Hebrew, and Phoenician. Egyptian had several words for "coffin," and one might have expected one of them to be used here.

Exod. 1:1 *wᵉ'ēlleh šᵉmôt* [*bᵉnê yiśrā'ēl*]
habbā'îm miṣraymāh 'et ya'ᵃqōb

These are the names of the sons of Israel
who came to Egypt with Jacob.

Old Testament writers employ the phrase "the sons of Israel" 613 times. Here referring directly to the sons of the patriarch Israel-Jacob, the phrase *bᵉnê yiśrā'ēl* later came to designate the people of the Israelite nation. As Pettinato has noted in Chapter VI, 1.1, the people of Ebla who enjoy the full rights and privileges of citizens are called d u m u - n i t a d u m u - n i t a *eb-la*^{ki}, "the sons of Ebla." This usage is also witnessed at Ugarit in the Akkadian phrase *mārû ú-ga-ri-it,* "the sons (citizens) of Ugarit,"[17] but it must not be thought to be an exclusively Canaanite usage since it is attested elsewhere.[18]

Exod. 3:1 *ûmōšeh hāyāh rō'eh 'et ṣô'n* [*yitrô*] *ḥōtᵉnô*
Now Moses was tending the flock of his
father-in-law Jethro.

The personal name *yitrô,* borne in the Bible only by Moses' father-in-law, has heretofore not been documented in nonbiblical sources. It may now possibly be identified in the Eblaite personal name *wa-ti-lu* = *wa-ti-ru.*[19] Lacking the divine component, *wa-ti-ru* is probably a shortened form of **wa-ti-ru-i-lu,* "El is generous," or **wa-ti-ru-'à-da,* "Hadd is generous." In any case, the Ugaritic personal names *ytr* and *ytrhd* become more intelligible, the former being materially identical with Eblaite *wa-ti-ru* (initial *wa-* becomes *ya-* in Ugaritic) and biblical *yitrô,* "Jethro"; the latter name *ytrhd* would signify "Hadd is generous."

◆

Exod. 22:5 *w^e^ne'ekal* [*gādîš*] *'ô haqqāmāh*
so that the stacked grain
or the standing grain is consumed.

Job 5:26 *ka'^a^lôt* [*gādîš*] *b^e^'ittô*
like the stacking of grain in its season.

Found but four times in the Bible, *gādîš,* "stack of grain," is now attested in one of the bilingual vocabularies where Sumerian n ì - g i g, "something of grain," is rendered into Eblaite by *ga-dì-šúm.*[20]

◆

Exod. 30:12 *w^e^nāt^e^nû 'îš* [*kōper*] *napšô*
layahweh bipqōd 'ōtām
Each shall pay to Yahweh a ransom
for himself on being enrolled.

In recent years a number of studies have been dedicated to the root *kpr,* which underlies *kōper,* "ransom, payment," *kipper,* "to atone, purge, expiate," and *kippûr,* best known from *yôm kippûr,* "the Day of Atonement."

Etymological derivations from putative cognates in Arabic with the meaning "to cover" or in Akkadian with the sense "to rub, wipe," have long been admitted into Hebrew lexica and enjoy widest support, though the view that the *kipper* is denominative and derives from *kōper,* "ransom," is not without its adherents. The latter will surely find new ammunition in the bilingual vocabulary where Sumerian URUDU, "copper," is reproduced by Eblaite *kà-pá-lu* = *kà-pá-ru.*[21] In Akkadian lists Sumerian URUDU is translated *erû,* "copper." Here, then, is another lexical argument for distinguishing Eblaite from Akkadian. Hence biblical *kōper* could originally have meant "copper," and since the settling of differences between Israelites themselves or between Israelites and God involved the transfer of something of value (a person, an animal or commutation of such in the form of commodity or currency), this etymology would accord with the subsequent development of this institution. It also sheds light on *kappôret,* a slab of gold placed on top of the ark of the testimony. This slab may have been of copper but coated with gold.

Lev. 24:11 *wayyiqqōb ben-hā'iššāh*
hayyiśrᵉ'lît 'et [*haššēm*]
and the son of the Israelite woman
blasphemed the Name.

In the light of vs. 16, *šēm-yahweh,* "the name of Yahweh," some critics would also read that here. Others, however, feel that "the Name" here has been substituted in the text for an original *yahweh* which was already beginning to be thought ineffable. How old is the use of *šēm,* "the Name," as a surrogate for *yahweh?* On the basis of such texts as Ecclus. 23:10 and Wisd. Sol. 14:21, many see it as a later development, but now two personal names from Ebla give one pause as to its lateness. Comparison with the names *ṭù-bí-da-mu* "my good is Damu," and *ṭù-bí-šum,* "my good is Šum," reveals that *šum* is the divine element in the names *ṭù-bí-šum,* "my good is the Name,"[22] and *iš-má-šum,* "the Name has heard."[23] This may be taken as another indication of the movement in Ebla toward the henotheism discussed briefly in Chapter IX at the end of 2.4. Hence one may with less hesitation than that found in current Hebrew lexica interpret the personal name *šᵉmîda'* in Num. 26:32 as "the Name knows." Similarly, the Aramaic form *šūm,* "name," found 11 times in the books of Ezra and Daniel, which has sometimes been ascribed to Akkadian influence, may well be an alternate Canaanite form already documented at Ebla.

Deut. 28:4 [*šᵉgar*] *'ᵃlāpêkā*
wᵉ'aštᵉrôt ṣō'nekā
the offspring of your large cattle,
and the breeding of your sheep.

In these objects of divine blessing, three of the words have a background in Canaanite religion. The first, *šᵉgar,* "offspring," appears in tandem with *'ṯtrt* in a Ugaritic list of gods,[24] and designates the god responsible for the increase of cattle. In the new calendar at Ebla, described above in Chapter VI, 3.2.2, the name of the eleventh month (July–August) is i t u ᵈA M A-*ra* where the logogram AMA hypothetically stands for goddess Ištar, the guardian of small livestock. In the old calendar, however, the name of the eleventh month is i t u *ṣa-'à-tum,* "the month of sheep." The biblical writer has demythologized Ištar and transmuted her into a common noun signifying "breeding, calving," and united her in a construct chain to the common noun *ṣō'n,* "sheep."

That the Canaanite gods have traits quite distinguishable from those of

Mesopotamian deities is demonstrated by the details of sacred iconography in the glyptic art discovered at Ebla. The great goddess who tames the beasts and protects the flocks is a dominant figure of this artistic patrimony, typically Northwest Semitic, which will have a long and complex history in Syria in later periods. The name of the protecting goddess is not forthcoming from the glyptic art itself but must be identified with the aid of texts. Here, then, would be an illustration of wedding art to philology to the advantage of both.

◀▶

Deut. 32:31 *kî lō' k^{e}ṣûrēnû ṣûrām*
w^e'ōy^{e}bênû [*p^{e}lîlîm*]
For their rock is not like our Rock,
or our foes like our Mediator.

It was noted in Chapter IX, 3, in connection with popular religion, that among the minor deities figures Palil, who is attested only in personal names, such as *i-da-palil,* "the Mediator knows" (TM.75.G.336, rev. I 12). The second half of our verse has been rendered very variously, but a poetically viable version results when the comparative *k^e,* "like," in the first colon is seen extending its force into the second colon, and *p^{e}lîlîm* understood as a plural of majesty designating God. It thus balances *ṣûrēnû,* "our Rock." The verb *pālal,* "to intercede," is also predicated of God in poetic I Sam. 2:25 which is commonly printed and translated as prose.

'im yeḥ^{e}ṭā' 'îš l^e'îš
ûpil^{e}lô '^{e}lōhîm
w^e'im layahweh yeḥ^{e}ṭā' 'îš
mî yitpallel-lô
If a man sin against a man,
God will mediate for him;
but if a man sin against Yahweh,
who will mediate for him?

◀▶

Judg. 5:19 [*b^{e}ta'nak*] *'al mê m^{e}giddô*
At Taanach near Megiddo's waters.

Judg. 5:20 *nilḥ^{a}mû 'im-*[*sîs^{e}rā'*]
They fought against Sisera.

Just as the root of Deborah's name is now witnessed in the place name *dub-bar-at*^{ki}, "Bee-town," in the atlas from Ebla, so the name of the

Canaanite royal city Taanach in central Palestine also appears in the atlas written *mar-tá-na-ak*^{ki}, "the Exchange (or Market) of Taanach."[25]

To find an explanation of the name of the Canaanite general Sisera, scholars have looked as far west as Illyria (Yugoslavia), though why a man of Canaan should bear an Illyrian name seems not to have disturbed researchers. In the most recent study on the cultural and historical background of the Canticle of Deborah (Judg. 5), G. Garbini[26] insists that the name Sisera is non-Semitic and probably Cretan in origin. But this theory runs into the roadblock thrown up by the Ebla personal name *sà-sà-lum,* an official in charge of 600 workers.[27] Since cuneiform *-lum* at Ebla is often to be read *-rum,* the equation of the name (not the person!) *sà-sà-lum* with Hebrew *sîsᵉrā',* "Sisera," does not appear far-fetched. See above at Gen. 2:7, *wa-ṣí-lu-um=wu-ṣí-ru-um.*

◆

Judg. 16:4 *wayye'ᵉhab 'iššāh bᵉnaḥal śōrēq ûšᵉmāh* [*dᵉlîlāh*]
He fell in love with a woman from the valley
of Sorek whose name was Delilah.

The Israelite hero in the skirmishes with the Philistines bore the etymologically transparent name *šimšôn,* "Samson," signifying "sun's man" or, better, "Sunny." His girlfriend Delilah has not fared so well etymologically, and savants still argue whether Delilah owes her name to Arabic *dallatum,* "flirtation"—not out of character—or is the outcome of a pun on Heb. *laylāh,* "night," hence "the one of night." Ebla furnishes a new possibility that puts Delilah into the same semantic category as Samson and gives her equal etymological rights. As the equivalent of Sumerian UD, "day," an Eblaite bilingual vocabulary gives the totally new Canaanite word *da-la-lum,* "day."[28] If one may call Samson "Sunny," then "Daisy," from "day's eye" may fairly reflect the meaning of Delilah.

◆

I Sam. 2:3 *kî 'ēl dē'ôt yahweh*
wᵉlē' (MT *lō'*) *nitkᵉnû 'ᵃlîlôt*
For a God of all knowledge is Yahweh,
and by the Almighty are actions weighed.

When pairing *'ēl,* "God," with our proposed reading *lē',* "the Almighty," the poet plays on names and epithets that contain the same consonants but in different order. The same two roots *l'* and *'l* appear to concur in the Ebla personal name *lí-é-ì-lu,* "El is the Almighty."[29]

◆

I Sam. 2:10 *yahweh yēḥattû m^e^rîbāw*
[*'ālû*] (MT *'ālāw*) *baššāmayīm y^e^rō'ēm* (MT *yar'ēm*)
Yahweh—his challengers have been shattered,
the Most High crushed them from heaven.

More and more, scholars and versions recognize in consonantal *'lw* the divine epithet "Most High," which with first-colon Yahweh forms the composite divine name *yahweh-'ālû,* "Yahweh Most High." The clue to the recognition of this epithet here and in numerous other biblical verses was provided by the composite Canaanite name *b'l 'ly,* "Baal Most High," appearing in Ugaritic poetry (*UT,* 126:III:5–6). That the word has an even longer history may be inferred from the Ebla man's name *a-lu-a-ḫu,* "the Most High is a brother,"[30] the semantic equivalent of the Phoenician king's name Aḥiram, "my brother is the Exalted."

◆

I Sam. 25:3 Now the man's name was Nabal,
and the name of his wife Abigail;
the woman had good sense and a fine figure,
but the man was uncouth and [evil] in his
actions (*ra' ma'^a^lālîm*),
for he was just like his [heart] (*kalibbô*).

The versions, ancient as well as modern, usually alter *kālibbô,* "like his heart," to *kalibbî* and render "he was a Calebite," i.e., of the clan of Caleb. But the consonantal text *klbw* becomes more difficult to impugn because the bilingual vocabulary gives as the definition of Sumerian šà-ḫul, "evil heart," the Eblaite word *é-la-lum,*[31] which probably answers to Heb. *'ollal,* "to deal wantonly," *'^a^lîlâh,* "wantonness, deed," and *ma'^a^lāl,* "evil practice." It would thus appear that in context with *ra' ma'^a^lālîm,* "evil in his actions," the reading *kālibbô,* "just like his heart," has the superior claim.

◆

When Ammon planned to ravish his sister Tamar, he asked the king, "Pray let my sister come and make a couple of cakes in my sight, that I may eat from her hand" (II Sam. 13:6). The word traditionally rendered "cakes" is *l^e^bībôt,* literally "heart-shaped cakes." This usage may help explain the Eblaite term *luppu* which Pettinato, Chapter VIII, 3.2, translates "wineskin." *Luppu* is apparently to be read *lubbu* (cuneiform writing does not distinguish between mute *p* and sonant *b*) and related to *lēb, lēbāb,* "heart." The skin may originally have been heart-shaped; hence its name *lubbu.*

◆

I Kings 10:17 *šelōšet [mānîm] zāhāb*
three minas of gold

Considered by some to be of Babylonian origin, *mīnāh,* a unit of weight varying according to place and period, recurs repeatedly in the economic texts examined in Chapter VII. Since these attestations are considerably older than those heretofore at our disposal, the term *mīnāh* may well be Canaanite in origin.

Isa. 1:10 *šimeʿû debar-yahweh*
qeṣînê [sedōm]
ha'azînû tôrat 'elōhênû
'am [ʿamōrāh]
Hear the word of Yahweh,
you rulers of Sodom!
Give ear to the teaching of our God,
you people of Gomorrah!

Hos. 11:8 *'êk 'ettenekā [ke'admāh]*
'aśîmekā [kiṣebō'yīm]
How can I make you like Admah,
treat you like Zeboim?

Parallel word pairs are a basic building block of Hebrew and Canaanite poetry; these word pairs can be divine names and titles, common nouns, or, as in the present instances, names of cities. When pairing Sodom and Gomorrah, Isaiah cited the first two of the five cities of the Plain mentioned in Gen. 14:2. This word pair will be used in parallelism by subsequent prophets and poets and will be cited by Christ himself. But Hosea remains unique when reaching down to cities three and four of the infamous pentapolis and making a poetic pair of them to achieve the desired parallelism. Two of these cities may have counterparts in *sí-du-mu*ki (TM.76.G.524) or *sa-dam*ki (TM.75.G.2231, obv. X 4) and *sa-bí-im*ki (TM.75.G.2231, obv. I 7).

Isa. 9:4 *kî kol-[se'ôn sō'ēn] beraʿaš*
Indeed every boot of tramping warrior in battle tumult.

Among the prepositions attested at Ebla (see Chapter IV, 3.4) *ší-in,* "to, toward," is completely new and awaits an etymology. Being contrasted with *áš-tù,* "from," in some contexts such as "from (*áš-tù*) the month X to (*ší-in*) the month Y," it leaves no doubt as to its meaning. Perhaps the root *s'n,* "to tramp, march," witnessed as a noun in Ugaritic *s'in,* "boot," and as a participle and noun in the biblical citation, provides a clue. Some prepositions are known to derive from verbs of motion, like biblical *derek,* "toward," from *dārak,* "to march."

◆

Isa. 27:1 *'al liwyātān nāḥāš* [*bārīªḥ*]
wᵉ'al liwyātān nāḥāš 'ªqallātôn
Leviathan the evil serpent,
Leviathan the crooked serpent.

The source of the imagery in this verse came to light in 1934 with the publication of a mythological tablet from Ras Shamra which begins, *ktmḫṣ ltn bṯn brḥ/tkly bṯn 'qltn/šlyṭ d šb't rašm,* "When you smote Lotan the evil serpent/made an end of the crooked serpent/Shalyat of the seven heads" (*UT,* 67:I:1–3). On the basis of the Hebrew adjective *bārîªḥ,* "fleeing," scholars have regularly rendered both *nāḥāš bārîªḥ* and Ugar. *bṯn brḥ* as "fleeing serpent," though C. H. Gordon has opted for "evil serpent" in the light of Arabic *barḥu,* "evil."[32] This latter choice appears preferable now that the root hitherto witnessed only in Arabic is found in Northwest Semitic as well. In a bilingual vocabulary the Sumerian word *ḫul,* "evil," is defined by *ba-rí-um,* "evil";[33] not having a sign to represent the pharyngal consonant *ḥ,* the cuneiform scribes found a surrogate in the vowel *-i-;* hence one recognizes in *ba-rí-um* the adjective *ba-riḥ-um.* This example nicely illustrates how new discoveries at Ugarit and Ebla can conspire with Arabic to elucidate a phrase in biblical poetry. Scholars today, it will be recalled, are understandably hesitant to admit an Arabic etymology into a Biblical Hebrew lexicon unless it is employed in Canaanite dialects as well; this hesitation arises in part from the excesses of past decades when Arabic roots were widely invoked without sufficient discrimination to determine biblical etymologies.

◆

Isa. 48:19 *wayᵉhî kaḥôl zar'ekā*
wᵉṣe'ᵉṣā'ê mē'êkā [*kimᵉ'ōtāyw*]
Your offspring would have been like the sand,
and the issue of your body like its hundred thousand grains.

The obscure word *mᵉ'ōtāyw*—so obscure that the Isaiah Scroll from Qumran simply omitted it—may tentatively be identified with the Eblaite word *ma-i-at,* "100,000." The resultant version recalls the prayer in Gen. 24:60, "Our sister, be the mother of thousands of ten thousands, and may your descendants possess the gate of those who hate them." My colleague Pettinato (Chapter VII, 3.4) thinks that *ma-i-at* is the plural of *mi-at,* "100," but I suspect that the root of one hundred thousand is *m'y* and not *m'y.* What is more, *ma-i-at,* "100,000," follows *ri-ba*$_x$, "10,000"

(Heb. *ribbô*), in several texts, and this same pairing may be recognized in Ps. 4:8:

nātattā śimḥāh b^e^libbî
mā'ōt (MT *mē'ēt*) *d^e^gānām*
w^e^tirôšām rabbû
Put joy in my heart;
a hundred thousand fold be their wheat,
and their wine ten thousand fold.

Isa. 60:18 You shall call your walls Salvation, and your gates Praise.

The practice of naming city gates has a long history, and its earliest documentation is perhaps supplied by Ebla, whose four gates are named after four principal deities: Rasap, Sipiš, Dagan, and Baal; see Chapter VI, 2.2.1.

Exegetes have long recognized the polemic tone of Isa. 60:19–20, but only with the textual discoveries at Ras Shamra has it become possible to spell out the details. Verse 19 reads:

The sun shall no more be your light by day,
  nor for brightness shall the moon give you light;
but Yahweh shall be for you the everlasting light,
  and your God your glory.

The publication of the Ugaritic tablets revealed the pervasiveness of the cult of the sun-goddess Shapsh in Canaanite religion during the second millennium, and now the Ebla documents advertise this cult as no less popular in third-millennium Canaan. This appears from the frequency of Sipiš in personal names, as well as the name of a city, and especially from the fact that one of the four gates of Ebla was called "the gate of Sipiš." In verse 20 Isaiah continues, "Your sun shall no more go down, nor your moon withdraw itself." With Yahweh their God, the Israelites had no further need of divinities like the transient sun and moon. The Ugaritic nuptial blessing couched in the chiastic or "x" pattern *ar yrḫ wyrḫ yark,* "Let shine the Moon, yes, may the Moon shine for you," (*UT,* 77:38–39) is one that the prophet does not want to hear from the lips of an Israelite. And when Isaiah states *kî yahweh yihyeh-llāk l^e^'ôr 'ôlām/w^e^šāl^e^mû y^e^mê 'eblēk,* "For Yahweh shall be your everlasting light/and your days of mourning shall set," he uses the verb *šāl^e^mû,* "shall set," unexampled with this meaning, doubtless to evoke the Canaanite myth of *Šaḥar,* "Dawn," and *Šalim,* "Sunset," preserved on tablet 52 from Ras Shamra.

To make their point the prophets often resorted to punning, and one of the more successful word-plays occurs in Isa. 65:11–12:

O you who forsake Yahweh,
who forget my holy mountain,
who spread a table for Fortune (*gad*)
and fill the wine vat for Destiny [(*m*ᵉ*nî*),]
I will destine [(*mānîtî*)] you for the sword.

Before recent research on the god *m*ᵉ*nî* in the Bible (see below on Pss. 61:8, 65:4, 74:22) the closest extrabiblical parallel was located in Surah 53:20 of the Koran which mentions the deity Manat worshipped in Arabia before Islam. The Eblaite personal name *en-na-*ᵈ*ma-ni,* "Have mercy, O Mani,"[34] suggests that Mani was an ancient Canaanite god still worshipped by nonobservant Israelites at the time of Third Isaiah in the sixth century B.C. This attestation in turn sheds light on the till now unexplained Ugaritic personal names *pn-mn,* "the presence of Destiny," *p-mn,* "the decree of Destiny," *abmn,* "my father is Destiny," and *mny,* "My destiny is Ya." Putting approximate dates on the sources, one can now trace Mani or Destiny from 2500 B.C. (Ebla) to 1300 B.C. (Ugarit) to 550 B.C. (Third Isaiah) to A.D. 625 (Koran). The tenacity of this tradition perduring over three millennia may be compared with the reference in Surah 89 of the Koran to three cities or communities which suffered judgment at the hands of God. Just as Sodom and Gomorrah have become proverbial for sinful cities, so Šamuta, ʻAd, and Irma were held up by the Koran as examples of divine justice. All three are listed in Ebla tablets[35] and are probably to be located in Syria; in Islamic tradition they are linked to Dạmascus. Between Ebla and the Koran there is no other reference to this triad of cities.

Jer. 4:30 *kî tilb*ᵉ*šî šānî*
kî [*taʻdî*] *ʻ*ᵃ*dî zāhāb*
that you dress in scarlet,
that you deck yourself with ornaments of
gold.

The road that leads from Ebla to the Bible also leads from the Bible to Ebla. The parallel verbs *tilb*ᵉ*šî,* "you dress," and *taʻdî* "you deck yourself," may help explain a phrase recurring in the economic texts, *é-da-um-*

túg, which Pettinato usually renders "Edaum garment" or "Edaum fabric"; in other words, he translates Sumerian túg, the word for garment which has its Semitic counterpart in the root *lbš,* "garment," and leaves *é-da-um* untranslated. But the biblical pair *lbš//'dh* attested in Jer. 4:30, Job 40:10, etc., makes it difficult to dissociate *é-da-um* from Heb. *'ādāh,* "to deck oneself, put on festive garb." Hence the recurrent Eblaite phrase *é-da-um*-túg may justifiably be rendered throughout "festive clothes" or "festive fabrics." This, again, would be an illustration of how the biblical text can elucidate Eblaite phraseology; the following text also shows how the Bible is repaying its debt to the new discoveries.

◆

Jer. 10:6–7 *mā'ēn* (MT *mē'ēn*) *kāmôkā yahweh* . . .
ûbᵉkol-malkûtām [*mā'ēn*] (MT *mē'ên*) *kāmôkā*
There is absolutely no one like you, Yahweh . . .
and among all their royalty, there is
absolutely no one like you.

For the history of the interpretation and classification of Eblaite, these two verses of Jeremiah may in future have a claim on our interest. When studying a commercial treaty between Ebrium, the king of Ebla, and the king of Ashur, Professor Pettinato was at a loss to explain the phrase *ma-in* tuš occurring in the midst of a series of curses with which the treaty ends. He saw that tuš was Sumerian and meant "abode," but for *ma-in,* which he recognized as non-Sumerian, no light was forthcoming from the Semitic languages. When asked my opinion, I replied that a plausible solution might be found in *mā'ên,* a double negative, in Jer. 10:6–7, about which I had just published a short note entitled "The Emphatic Double Negative *m'yn* in Jer. 10:6–7" in the *Catholic Biblical Quarterly* 37 (1975), 458–59. As a result, the Ebla phrase *ma-in* tuš is rendered in the *Biblical Archaeologist* 39 (1976), 48, "May you have no stable abode!" As a further consequence of this equation *mā'ên*=Eblaite *ma-in,* numerous other biblical texts, such as Isa. 41:24, 63:3; Mal. 2:13; Lam. 3:45, have been shown to employ this emphatic double negative.[36] Unfamiliar with this usage, the Masoretes added vowels to the consonantal text of the Hebrew Bible which have impeded the understanding of this idiom.

◆

In the Old Testament the god of the Moabites is mentioned eight times; seven times his name is written *kᵉmôš,* "Chemosh," but in Jer. 48:7 it is written *kᵉmîš* "Chemish." As one would expect, textual critics have rushed to set matters right, changing consonantal *kmyš* to *kmwš*. But now the Ebla tablets caution the critics to stay their emending hand; the tablets spell his name ^{d}*kà-mi-iš* and ^{d}kà-me-iš. These spellings reveal the antiquity of this cult (see Chapter IX, 1) and at the same time provide a sound etymology of the famous city Carchemish as "the market of Chemish."[37] The notion that the national god of Moab in Transjordania was a latecomer was corrected by the appearance of his name *kmṯ* in a god list from Ugaritic, and now his documentation reaches back into the third millennium. Of not infrequent occurrence in the Ebla tablets is the personal name *i-ti-*^{d}*kà-mi-iš,* "with me is Chamish."[38]

Ezek. 16:40 [*ûbitt*^{e}*qûk*] *b*^{e}*ḥar*^{e}*bôtām*
They will hack you to pieces with their
swords.

Occurring only here in the Bible, the verb *bitt*^{e}*qû* "they will hack to pieces," finds early attestation in the infinitive absolute *ba-ta-qù da-ne-um,* literally "to cut a judgment," which reproduces Sumerian di-ku$_{5}$, with the same meaning in a bilingual vocabulary.[39] Cognate with *bātaq,* "to cut," is the root *bdq,* "to split," attested in *UT,* 51:VII:19, *wypth bdqt ʻrpt,* "He opened cracks in the clouds," and in Ezek. 27:9 where Tyre is compared to a ship:

ziqnê g^{e}*bal waḥ*^{a}*kāmêhā*
hāyû bāk
maḥ^{a}*zîqê* [*bidqêk*]
The elders of Byblos and her skilled men were in you
the repairers of your cracks.

Ezek. 27:17 Judah and the land of Israel
traded with you;
with wheat from [Minnit] (*ḥiṭṭê minnît*), wax,
honey, oil, and balsam they supplied you.

Being a single occurrence word in the Bible, *minnît* is not easily defined. One savant has traveled as far as India and claims to have found the answer in Tamil, a language of southern India and Sri Lanka. Canaanite tablets nearer home may prove more enlightening. The Ugaritic city name *mnt* and Eblaite *my-nu-ti-um* in an economic tablet[40] prompt the suggestion that *mnyt* in Ezek. 27:17 may be the name of a town known for a distinctive kind of wheat. In Chapter VII, 1.1, Pettinato observes that 17 kinds of wheat were cultivated in the towns and villages surrounding Ebla. Just as in Song of Songs 2:13 (see below) the town name *s^e^mādar* seems to describe a certain type of vine, so it seems quite natural to describe a wheat by the town of its origin. Compare Isa. 16:9, *gepen śibmāh,* "the vine of Sibmah," where Sibmah is a city in Moab famous for its vineyards.

One may proceed further and attempt to identify this word in a poetic couplet from Ras Shamra. *UT,* 2 Aqht: I:32–33 reads:

spu ksmh bt bʿl
mnth bt il

In this couplet *ksmh* is usually rendered "his grain" or "his emmer" and its counterpart *mnth,* "his portion." But biblical *ḥiṭṭê minnît,* "wheat from Minnit,"[41] suggests that *ksmh//mnth* represent the breakup of the hypothetical construct chain **ksm mnt,* "grain from Minnit," so that the couplet would now be translated:

Who consumes his grain in Baal's house,
his Minnit grain in the house of El.

◆

Hos. 4:19 *w^e^yēbōšû [mizzib^e^ḥôtām]*
And they shall be ashamed of their banquets.

This is the only time that the plural of *zebaḥ,* "sacrifice, banquet," is feminine *zib^e^ḥôt;* elsewhere it is always masculine *z^e^bāḥîm.* The Hosean feminine plural form now becomes explicable, thanks to bilingual vocabularies from Ebla which give as the equivalent of Sumerian EZEN, "feast," the Canaanite word *ì-zi-ba-tu.*[42] This syllabic writing seems to reproduce the consonants *zbḥt,* "sacrifices, banquets," which coincide with those in the hapax legomenon form in Hos. 4:19, *zbḥt.*

A millennium later, a quadrilingual vocabulary from Ugarit lists singular *da-ab-ḫu,* "sacrifice, feast," as the Ugaritic equivalent of Sumerian EZEN.[43]

◆

Hos. 7:14 They did not cry to me from their hearts,
but wailed upon their beds;
of Dagan and [Tirosh] they became guests,
having turned their back on me.

Differing from ancient and current versions especially in the third and fourth cola or parts of the verse, this translation sees in *dāgān w^e^tîrôš,* commonly taken as "grain and wine," the proper names of the Canaanite deities Dagan and Tirosh, from which the common nouns "grain and wine" originated.[44] In Near Eastern records the god Dagan is widely documented, and in the Ebla tablets he appears as the head of the pantheon. The wine divinity Tirosh, however, has been so sparsely attested that its gender cannot be determined, though some few have suggested that it was feminine because of its pairing with masculine Dagan.

In the sequence of Sumerian divinities with their Semitic equivalents established on the basis of five vocabularies (see Chapter IX, 1.2), Sumerian ^{d}e d e n - a k is matched by Canaanite *te-rí-iš-tù*. The feminine form *te-rí-iš-tù* can scarcely be dissociated from Heb. *tîrôš*, "Tirosh," and Ugar. trṯ, and shows the gender to be female. In the same sequence the Sumerian goddess of fire ^{d}i z i is paired with feminine *ì-sa-tù*, "fire." In Hebrew, too, *'ēš*, "fire," is feminine though the form is masculine.

In this connection it may be noted that the root of *yitgôrārû*, "they became guests," probably appears in the personal name *gir-da-mu*, "the guest of Damu," one of the sons of King Ebrium; see Chapter V, 2.

An impressive number of names of biblical prophets were borne many centuries earlier by citizens of Ebla and Ugarit. Thus far the name *'āmôs*, "Amos," has been witnessed in Phoenician *'mskr* and Ugaritic *bn 'ms*, "the son of Amos." To judge from the available documentation, Amos is an exclusively Canaanite name. The name of the minor prophet Zechariah, *z^{e}karyāh*, "Yah has remembered," can now be identified in Ugaritic *ḏkry*, thanks to the identification of the divine element *yà* at Ebla; like the biblical name, Ugaritic *ḏkry* means "Ya has remembered." The name Elijah can be identified in Ugaritic *ily*, "my god is Ya" (*UT*, 321:II:22).

Amos 7:1 *w^{e}hinnēh-[leqeš] 'aḥar [gizzê] hammelek*
And, lo, it was the latter growth
after the king's mowings.

This parenthetic detail about the time of year when the locusts were eating the grass of the earth acquires a special interest when compared with the sequence of two month names in the old calendar treated in Chapter VI, 3.2.1. The tenth month of the year (June) is named i t u *ig-za*, "the month of the grain harvest," where *ig-za* has been explained by Heb. *gāzāh*, "to cut," and *gāzaz*, "to shear, mow." This would correspond to *gizzê* in the biblical phrase *gizzê hammelek*, "the king's mowings." The eleventh month (July) is called i t u *ig-za*-m ì n, "the month of the second grain harvest," and this would seem to equal biblical *leqeš*, "the latter growth."

Amos 9:13 *w^eniggaš [ḥôrēš] baqqōṣēr*
And the plowman shall overtake the reaper.

In this prophecy of the restoration Amos uses the rhetorical figure of merismus or the expression of totality by the listing of two members or parts of the series. In the agricultural cycle the plowman represents the beginning of the process and the reaper its end. In the old calendar the second month of the year (October) is termed itu *i-rí-sá* which is rendered "the month of sowing" in Chapter VI, 3.2.1 on the basis of Akkadian *erištu*, "season of seeding." Since seed was drilled into a furrow by means of a seeder plow, the underlying root appears to be *ḥrṯ*, "to plow," preserved thus in Ugaritic and as *ḥāraš* in Hebrew. Hence itu *i-rí-sá* may also, and more probably should be, rendered "month of plowing," since this is the meaning commonly attested in West Semitic.

Jonah 1:3 But [Jonah] arose to flee to Tarshish from
Yahweh's presence. So he went down to Joppa.

Till Ebla the personal name Jonah, *yônāh* in Hebrew, had not been found outside the Bible. One of the functionaries at the royal palace—hence a citizen of Ebla and not a foreign merchant stopping there—bears the strange-looking name *wa-na* which at first blush does not even appear Semitic. And yet according to phonetic rules it is identical with the biblical name, though not with the prophet! Ebla preserves initial *wa-* which in Hebrew shifts to *ya-*, and the long *-ā-* sound which becomes *-ô-* in Hebrew; hence *wā-na* equals Hebrew *yô-nāh*. The name of the seaport town of Palestine, Joppa or Jaffa, has, however, been well attested in extrabiblical sources of the second millennium. The first evidence for the existence of this town in the third millennium comes from Ebla in the form *i-yà-pu*^ki, "Coastal Jaffa."[45]

Hab. 2:5 *w^eap kî hayyayin bôgēd*
[gūbār] (MT *geber*) *yāhîr w^elō' yinweh*
'^ašer hirḥîb kiš^e'ôl napšô
w^ehû' kammāwet w^elō' yiśbā'
Even though the wine is treacherous,
the jar overflowing, nothing remains;
because he opens his jaws like Sheol,
and he like Death is never sated.

Though one of the obscurest lines in a very obscure book, the first two cola acquire a certain coherence and consistency of metaphor when MT *geber,* "man," is repointed *gūbār* and equated with Eblaite *gubar,*[46] the name of the standard-size jar used for the storage or shipment of wine, oil, or grain; see Chapter VII, 3.1.

Hab. 3:5 *l^epānāyw yēlek* [*dāber*]
w^eyōṣī' (MT *w^eyēṣē'*) [*rešep*] *l^eraglāyw*
Before him marches Pestilence,
and Plague provides light for his feet.

Two of the principal deities at Ebla were Dabîr, the patron god of the city who is called ^d*da-bi-ir* dingir-*eb-la*^ki, "Dabir, the god of Ebla" (see Chapter IX, 1.1), and Rasap or Resheph to whom one of the four city gates was dedicated. Dabîr, the name of a god, came to signify "pest," in Ugaritic and biblical texts. His name is preserved in the name of the city Debîr in southern Palestine. That the rulers and citizens of Ebla would want the god of pestilence as their tutelar deity arises from the conviction that he who causes the plague can also keep it distant from the city placed under his aegis. In the Bible both these divinities are reduced to the common nouns "pestilence" and "plague" or to attendants to Yahweh on his journeys. The repointing of MT *yēṣē',* "he goes forth," to causative *yôṣī',* with the meaning "he provides light," is suggested and supported by Arabic, Ugaritic, and biblical usage in Isa. 63:1; Ps. 37:6; 73:7, etc.

Ps. 27:4 *laḥ^azôt* [*b^enō'am*]-*yahweh*
to gaze upon the loveliness of Yahweh.

In the Ugaritic poems the noun *n'm,* "loveliness," is predicated of the goddess of love and war, Anath, whose beauty was proverbial: *dk n'm 'nt n'mh,* "whose loveliness is as the loveliness of Anath" (*UT,* Krt: 145). The pagan associations of *nō'am* and other derivatives from this root have long been appreciated in view of the complaint expressed by Isa. 17:10, "For you have forgotten the God of your salvation/and have not remembered the Rock of your refuge; for this you have planted gardens of the lovely gods (*niṭ'ê na'^amānîm*)/and set out slips of an alien deity." Among the secondary deities of the Ebla pantheon is the god Na'im, "the Lovely One," as noticed in Chapter IX, 3. Much dispute surrounds the biblical phrase which I have rendered "gardens of the lovely gods," but there can be little doubt from the parallelism with "alien deity" that the Prophet is alluding to some forbidden Canaanite cult.

Ps. 36:7 *ṣidqātekā keharerê ['ēl]*
Your generosity is like the towering mountains.

Literally "the mountains of God," *harerê 'ēl* illustrates the use of the name of God in function of expressing the superlative. This not uncommon poetic usage is now known to have had Canaanite antecedents in the Ugaritic texts where the name of the head of the pantheon *il,* "El," also served as the marker of the superlative as exemplified by such phrases as *ṯlḥn il,* "a magnificent table," and *hdm il,* "a magnificent footstool." The ancestry of this usage can now be traced even further back into the third millennium where túg *ì-lí,* literally "a garment of El," really signifies "a costly garment."[47] Another small but instructive illustration of the continuity of lingustic usage in Canaanite poetry. One also encounters in Akkadian *kasap ilim,* "the finest silver," or "silver reserved for the gods," but only in Mari and in an El Amarna letter from Cyprus.[48]

Ps. 46:2 (1) *'elōhîm lānû maḥaseh wā'ōz*
'ezrāh beṣārôt nimṣā' [me'ōd] (or *[mā'ōd]*)
God for us is refuge and stronghold,
the liberator from sieges have we found the Grand.

Before the recent Ebla discoveries it was suggested[49] on the strength of the chiastic or "x" construction of this line that the final word *me'ōd,* "much," should correspond to the first word *'elōhîm,* "God"; *lānû,* "for us," should pair with *nimṣā',* "have we found," and the military metaphors in the center of the verse pair off. This analysis contrasts sharply with current renditions of the verse, such as that of the *RSV,* "God is our refuge and strength, a very present help in trouble," where *me'ōd* is rendered by "very." The existence of the divine epithet *me'ōd,* "the Grand," has lacked extrabiblical documentation but is now sustained by the Ebla names *da-sí-ma-ad,* "The he-goat of the Grand," in which *ma-ad* marks the divine element. This occurrence in turn illuminates the Old Akkadian names from Mesopotamia *en-na-ma-ad,* "Have pity, O Grand One," and *i-dur-ma-ad,* "Everlasting is the Grand." The recognition of this divine name improves the understanding and poetic analysis of Ps. 78:59, "God heard them and was enraged/and so the Grand rejected Israel," and Ps. 109:30, "I will thank Yahweh the Grand with my mouth/and amid the elders will I praise him" where, as in Ps. 46:2, the word order is chiastic or in the "x" pattern.

Ps. 46:10 (9) *mašbît milḥāmôt ʻad q^eṣēh hāʼāreṣ*
who makes wars cease to the end of
the earth.

In this achievement the psalmist recognizes one of God's great works: the cessation of warfare. A new insight into the alliterative phrase *mašbît milḥāmôt,* "who makes wars cease," is afforded by the bilingual vocabulary from Ebla which lists *maš-bí-tù* as the Canaanite equivalent of Sumerian *erén,* "soldier." A hiphil causative participle from *šābat,* "to cease, desist," *maš-bí-tù* would mean that the soldier's role was to suppress riots or insurrections.

Ps. 50:13 *haʼôkal b^eśar ʼabbîrîm*
w^edam ʻattûdîm ʼešteh
Do I eat the flesh of bulls,
or drink the blood of goats?

The full force of the irony appears when one considers Canaanite beliefs in this regard. The parents at Ebla who named their child *a-kà-al-ma-lik,* "Eat, O Malik!" or "food of Malik," apparently believed that the god Malik ("King") had need of food. As the Creator of all creatures, the God of Israel makes light of such pagan beliefs.

Ps. 51:7 (6) *hēn b^eʻāwôn ḥôlātî*
ûb^eḥēṭʼ [*yeḥ^ematnî*] *ʼimmî*
Indeed, I was brought forth in inquity,
and in sin did my mother conceive me.

The uncommon verb *yāḥam,* "to conceive," is registered only here and in Gen. 30–31 which recount the story of Jacob's flock and its breeding time. In our verse the juxtaposition *yeḥ^ematnî ʼimmî,* "my mother conceived me," is particularly noteworthy in view of the equation of Eblaite *ì-ma-tum* and Sumerian s a l, "woman." In the syllabic writing *ì-ma-tum* one recognizes Semitic *ḥmt;* the reduplicated form in Ugaritic, *ḥmḥmt,* signifies "impregnation" and in Egyptian *ḥm.t* is the word for "woman, wife." In this and in other examples cited above can be seen the history of the Canaanite language traced in forms and meanings of the third, second, and first millennia B.C.

Ps. 61:3 *miq^{e}ṣēh hā'āreṣ*
'ēlêkā 'eqrā'
ba'^{a}ṭop libbî
b^{e}ṣûr-yārûm
[mīmānî] t^{e}nīḥēnî (MT *mimmennî tanḥēnî*)
From the brink of the nether world
I call to you,
as my heart grows faint.
Upon the lofty mountain,
O Destiny, give me rest.

Ps. 61:8 *yēšēb 'ôlām lipnê '^{e}lōhîm*
ḥesed we'^{e}met [mānī] (MT *man*) *yinṣ^{e}rūhû*
May he sit enthroned forever before God,
may the kindness and fidelity of Destiny
safeguard him.

Ps. 65:4 *gāb^{e}rû [mānî]* (MT *mennî*) *p^{e}šā'ênû*
'attāh t^{e}kapp^{e}rēm
Though our crimes, O Destiny, are enormous,
you will remit them!

Ps. 74:22 *qûmāh '^{e}lōhîm*
rîbāh rîbekā
z^{e}kōr ḥerpāt^{e}kā [mānî] (MT *minnî*)
nābāl kol-hayyôm
Arise, O God,
defend your cause;
remember how you are insulted, O Destiny,
by the fool all day long!

In connection with Isa. 65:11 it was pointed out that the god *m^{e}nî,* "Destiny," condemned by the prophet, was worshipped at Ebla. But the psalmists seem not to have had qualms about using this name of a now defunct Canaanite deity to designate their own divinity. Thus Ps. 16:5 professes, *yahweh mānītā* (MT *m^{e}nat*) *ḥelqî w^{e}kôsî,* "O Yahweh, you have destined my lot and my cup." In the four verses cited above the consonants *mn* and *mny* have created syntactic difficulties still unresolved. When the Ebla information about the god Mani is transferred to these four verses, the grammatical problems begin to yield and the poetic parallelism comes into clearer view. In Ps. 61:3, *mīmānî,* "O Destiny," preceded by the vocative particle *mī-,* balances vocative *'^{e}lōhîm,* "O God," in verse 2 with which it forms an inclusion or envelope figure. In Ps. 61:8, *'^{e}lōhîm,* "God," is again balanced by *mānī,* "Destiny," and in Ps. 65:4 *mānî* in the vocative case forms an inclusion, as in Ps. 61:2–3, with vocative *'ᵉlōhîm,* "O God," in vs. 2. The emerging composite divine title distributed over the parallel cola in Ps. 74:22 recalls the pairing in Ps. 61:8.

◀▶

Ps. 68:10 (9) *[gešem nᵉdābôt] tānîp 'ᵉlōhîm*
Your generous rain pour down, O God.

Teeming with words and phrases of single occurrence in the Bible, Psalm 68 represents one of the greatest challenges to the translator and interpreter of the Psalter. One of these single-occurrence phrases is *gešem nᵉdābôt,* literally "rain of nobility," here rendered "generous rain," and which other versions translate "abundant rain." Both the components of this phrase have antecedents in Ebla. The name of the third month in the old calendar (see Chapter VI, 3.2.1) is *ga-šúm,* which can readily be identified with Hebrew *gešem,* "rain." Since the rains in Syria-Palestine normally begin in November, the name *ga-šúm* is apt indeed since the third month of the autumnal calendar is November. This word for rain—*ga-šúm* or *gešem*—is also attested in Ugaritic *gšm,* with no vowels written, and in no other languages. This means that it is a typically Canaanite word and further points up the close relationship between Eblaite, Ugaritic, and Hebrew.

The name of the fourth month, December, is given only as Sumerian i t u ì - n u m, literally "noble oil," but the variant i - n u n $^{\text{na-at}}$ shows that the name was read as Semitic.[50] In Ugaritic poetry *šmn,* "oil," is a term for rain; thus *UT,* 'nt: IV: 86–87, *tḥspn mh wtrḥṣ/ṭl šmm wšmn arṣ,* "She drew water for herself and washed/with the dew of heaven and the oil of earth." Since the fertility of the earth depends upon the rain, the poet calls the rain the oil or fatness of the earth.

The Sumerian epithet n u n, "noble," applied to oil or rain becomes more comprehensible when compared with biblical *gešem nᵉdābôt,* literally "rain of nobility." As noted above at Deut. 28:4, this would be another instance of a biblical phrase elucidating Eblaite month names.

◀▶

Ps. 69:22 (21) *wayyittᵉnû [bᵉbārûtî] rō'š*
wᵉliṣmā'î yašqûnî ḥōmeṣ
They put poison in my food,
and for my thirst they gave me vinegar to drink.

The noun *bārût,* "food," is of single occurrence, though Lam. 4:10, *lᵉbārôt,* "for eating," seems to have been read *lᵉbārût,* "for food," by some ancient versions.[51] In one of the bilingual vocabularies a student scribe gave *a-kà-lu,* "food," as the equivalent of Sumerian KÚ, "mouth, food," but another scribe, perhaps to show off his knowledge of literary language, put down *bù-ur-tum* as the definition of Sumerian KÚ. We presume that the latter received a higher mark from Ipṭur-Išar the teacher (see Chapter VIII, 1.1) than the scribe who put down the ordinary prose word *a-kà-lu,* Heb. *'ōkel,* "food."

◆

Ps. 103:12 [*hirḥîq*] *mimmennû 'et pᵉšā'ênû*
He has made distant from us our crimes.

Job 13:21 *kappᵉkā mē'ālay* [*harḥēq*]
Keep your hand distant from me.

Sentiments such as these containing the causative forms of *rāḥaq,* "to be distant," help identify the verbal root and meaning of the Eblaite personal name *zàr-i-iq-da-mu.* The inadequacy of the cuneiform syllabic system of writing a Semitic language with sounds proper to itself means that the philologist must resort to other Semitic languages to attempt the identification of the underlying root, in this case, of *zàr-i-iq-da-mu.* The initial syllable doubtless represents the Semitic sound *šar-,* the simple vowel *-i-* stands for *-ḥi-,* and the entire name may now be transcribed *šar-ḥiq-da-mu,* "make distant, O Damu," where the shaphel causative imperative *šarḥiq* is the semantic equivalent of Job 13:21, *ḥarhēq.* Just what the god Damu is asked to keep distant is not explicitly stated by the name, but biblical usage suggests a number of possible direct objects, such as sin, punishment, calamity. Ugaritic attests the shaphel conjugation in *UT,* 'nt: IV: 84, *šrḥq aṯt lpnnh,* "He removed the women from his presence."

Ps. 106:20 [*wayyāmîrû*] *'et kᵉbôdām*
bᵉtabnît šôr 'ōkēl 'ēšeb
They exchanged their Glorious One
for the figure of a bull eating grass.

The commercial term *yāmîrû,* "they exchanged," from the root *mwr* may help explain the element *mar-* in Ebla place names such as *mar-tá-na-ak*ᵏⁱ; "the exchange (or shopping center) of Taanach," and *mar-a-bí-ak*ᵏⁱ "the exchange of Apheq (?)."[52]

◆

Ps. 107:3–4 And from the lands he gathered them,
from the east and from the west,
from the north and from [the south.]

In the final phrase *miṣṣapôn ûmiyyām,* "from the north and from the south," *yām,* literally "the sea," is often emended to *yāmīn,* "the south," since this sequence of cardinal points requires "the south" in the final position. In other biblical texts "the sea" usually refers to the Mediterranean and often connotes "the west." In the bilingual vocabulary[53] Sumerian á-zi, "the right side," is translated *i-me-tum* where one recognizes at once *yimittum* from *yimintum,* with the assimilation of *-n* by *-t.* In Hebrew orthography this would appear as *ymt* and since verse 4 begins with a *t-* in *tā'û,* "they strayed," one may appeal to the practice of shared consonants and read *miṣṣapôn ûmiyyāmīt* (*tā'û*), "from the north and from the south (they strayed)." In other terms, *miṣṣāpôn ûmiyyāmīt* would equal Ps. 89:13, *ṣāpôn wᵉyāmîn,* "north and south."

Ps. 112:4 Out of the darkness will dawn
the Light [*'ôr*] for the upright,
the Merciful [*ḥannûn*] and Compassionate and Just One.

Two of these titles of God, *'ôr,* "the Light" and *ḥannûn,* "the Merciful," may probably be identified in the personal names *en-àr-yà,* "Ya is mercy (*en*), light (*àr*),"[54] where *en* stands for *ḥēn,* "mercy," the root underlying *ḥannûn,* "the Merciful," and *àr* equals Heb. *'ôr,* "light."

Job 5:18 He makes a bruise, but he dresses it;
he smites, but his hands also heal.

The biblically unique juxtaposition of *yimḥaṣ,* "he smites," and *yādāw,* "his hands," has had its closest parallel in *UT,* 1 Aqht: 220–221, *yd mḫṣt aqht ǵzr/tmḫṣ alpm ib,* "The hand that smote Aqhat the hero/will smite thousands of foes." An even older attestation is now supplied by the equation of Sumerian šu-šu-ra, "to smite with the hand," with Eblaite *ma-ḫa-ṣi i-da,* "to smite with the hand(s)."[55]

Job 9:7–9 Who commands the sun that it rise not,
and seals up the stars [*kôkābîm*].
Alone he stretched out the heavens,
trod on the back of Sea;
Maker of the Bear, Orion,
and the Pleiades [*kîmāh*] and the Chambers of the South.

Occurring here, in Job 38:31, and in Amos 5:8, *kîmāh* has been rendered "the Pleiades" by many ancient and modern versions, though there is no agreement about the etymology. The 1907 *Hebrew Lexicon* of Brown-Driver-Briggs subsumes it under the root *kwm,* "to accumulate," and cites Arabic *kûmun,* "a herd of camels," whereas the 1974 *Hebräisches und aramäisches Lexikon zum Alten Testament* by Walter Baumgartner adds Akkadian *kimtu,* "family," to the list of cognates and also renders *kîmāh* by "the Seven Stars, Pleiades." New evidence from Ebla sustains this line of reasoning. In Chapter IX, 1.2 Pettinato presents the sequence of Sumerian divinities with their Canaanite equivalents as reconstructed from five vocabularies. The god ^{d}m u l equals *kak-kab,* in Hebrew *kôkāb* (see Job 9:7), and is followed by m u l - m u l, "Pleiades," which equals *kà-ma-tù.* This latter easily connects with *kîmāh,* "Pleiades," a conspicuous group or cluster of stars in the constellation Taurus. The Akkadian equivalent of Sumerian m u l - m u l is *Zappu,* "Pleiades"; here Ebla distinguishes itself from Mesopotamia, using its own Canaanite term *kà-ma-tù* for the Pleiades, a term reappearing centuries later in the Canaanite of the Bible as *kîmāh.*[56]

Job 9:30 If I wash with water from snow [*b^{e}mw šāleg*],
and cleanse my hands with lye.

There is a conflict between the original consonantal text *mw* and the Masoretes who want to read *mê,* that is, changing *mw* to *my.* Again the consonantal text proves sound as the Eblaite word for "water" is *ma-wu* whose consonants are identical with biblical *mw.*[57]

Job 15:29 He will not be rich,
nor will his wealth endure,
nor will his [*mnlm*] descend to the netherworld.

The consonants *mnlm,* vocalized *minlām* by the Masoretes, are a hapax legomenon or a word of single occurrence. Thanks to the parallelism with *ḥêlô,* "his wealth," the sense of *mnlm* can be divined, though the ancient versions seem not to have done so. The Greek renders it "He shall not cast a shadow on the earth" and the Latin Vulgate reads "Nor shall he send roots into the earth." New evidence from Ebla sustains the derivation from a root *nyl,* "to acquire," attested in Arabic and, more importantly for present purposes, in Phoenician, which is a Canaanite dialect whose testimony has more immediate relevance than Arabic. In one of the bilingual vocabularies Sumerian á b, "cow," is rendered by *ma-ni-lum,* which apparently means "property" or "wealth," and corresponds to biblical *mnlm,* now perhaps to be vocalized plural *m^{e}nīlīm* and translated "his property."[58] But how does one make the semantic leap from "cow" to "property"? Analogies from several different languages spring to mind: Heb. *miqneh,* "cattle," came also to signify "property"; Heb. *n^{e}kāsîm,* "riches," relates to Aramaic *niksâ,* "riches, herds of cattle"; Latin *pecus,* "sheep, cattle," and *pecunia,* "money," are related; English "stock" means either "livestock" or holdings on Wall Street, and in rural Ireland relative wealth is assessed in such terms as "a woman of three cows," "a woman of five cows."

How did this hapax legomenon get into Job, a book dating to perhaps the eighth or seventh century B.C.? A chronological chasm of some eighteen centuries separates Ebla from Job. The evidence for the tenacity of linguistic terms and traditions daily becomes more impressive and below on Job 29:18 and Prov. 26:23 further instances of cultural continuity will be discussed.

◆

Job 22:25 Let Shaddai be your gold,
pale silver for you.

Here one of Job's so-called friends, Eliphaz, speaks possibly with a recollection of his own name which means "my God is fine gold." The identification of *ya* as a divine name in Ebla permits the explanation of the Ugaritic personal name *aktmy* as "I consider Ya my precious gold," in which *aktm* parses as a denominative verb from *ktm,* "precious gold," which now appears as *kutim* at Ebla.

◆

Job 24:13 *hēmmāh hāyû b^{e}mōr^{e}dê*—[*'ôr*]
lō' hikkîrû d^{e}rākāyw
w^{e}lō' yāš^{e}bû bin^{e}tîbōtāyw
These are the rebels against the Light,
they acknowledge not his ways,
nor settle in his paths.

Though most modern versions translate *'ôr* as the common noun "light," Ibn Ezra and others understood *'ôr* to refer to God as the light of the world. This latter view appears correct because in biblical usage *mārad,* "to rebel," means to rebel against a person. In Canaanite religion, *ar,* "Light," was the daughter of the god Baal according to *UT,* 51:I:17, but a male divinity at Ebla, as may be deduced from the personal name *ìr-kab-ar,* "Light rides (his chariot)," in TM.75.G.1353, obv. VII 2. Recent studies have shown that virtually all of God's epithets and titles in the Old Testament have antecedents in the nomenclature of the Canaanite pantheon.

II Kings 23:11 relates that King Josiah destroyed the horses that the kings of Judah had set up in honor of the Sun and that *mark^{e}bôt haššemes śārap bā'ēš,* "he burnt the chariots of the Sun," a clear reference to idolatrous worship of the Sun. Since *šemeš,* "sun," and *'ôr,* "light," occasionally appear as poetic synonyms, the name *irkab-ar,* "Light rides," may fairly be compared to "the chariots of the Sun." The personal name *ar-ra-sí-piš,* "Shine. O Sun!" is also witnessed at Ebla.

◆

Job 24:14 *ûballaylāh yāhîk gannāb* (MT [*y*ᵉ*hî kaggannāb*])
and at night the thief prowls.

The difficult phrase *y*ᵉ*hî kaggannāb,* "he becomes like a thief," apparently is the result of the misunderstanding of the rare verb *hâk,* "to walk," which is related to *hālak,* "to walk." In the bilingual vocabulary TM.75.G.2001 rev. VIII 3, Sumerian a l-DU, "to walk," is paired with Eblaite *é-a-gú-um,* which looks like cuneiform writing for *hâku*. In an unpublished Akkadian word list, *ḫu-u-qu* equals *a-la-ku,* "to walk."[59]

Job 24:15 *lō' [t*ᵉ*šûrēnî] 'āyin*
No eye will behold me.

As several Hebrew dictionaries observe,[60] the verb *šûr,* "to behold," occurs with especial frequency in the Book of Job; ten of the sixteen biblical occurrences are in this composition, and often the verb is predicated of God. So in Job 35:13, *šadday lō' y*ᵉ*sûrennāh,* "Shaddai does not behold." This usage will surely bear on the interpretation of the Ebla personal name *šu-ra-da-mu* in which *šu-ra* may be parsed as the emphatic imperative of *šûr,* "to behold," so that the name may be translated "Behold, O Damu!" Till now the verb *šûr,* "to behold," has not been clearly witnessed outside of biblical Hebrew. Should the present proposal prove sound, another link between the language of Ebla and that of the Bible will have been forged.

◆

Job 26:13 *ḥōl*ᵃ*lāh yādô nāḥāš [bārî*ᵃ*ḥ]*
His hand transfixed the evil serpent.

Customarily rendered "the fleeing serpent," *nāḥāš bārî*ᵃ*ḥ* is now preferably rendered "the evil serpent" in the light of the Ebla equation ḫ u l, "evil," equals Canaanite *ba-rí-um.*[61]

Job 29:18 *wā'ōmar 'im-qinnî 'egwā'*
*[w*ᵉ*kaḥôl] 'arbeh yamîm*
And I thought, "Though I perish like its nest,
I shall multiply my days like the phoenix."

The bone of contention in this verse is the word *ḥôl,* here rendered "phoenix," but "sand" by many ancient and modern versions and commentators. To be sure, there is a very frequent noun *ḥôl,* "sand," but does it meet the needs of the present context? Some rabbis in antiquity saw in *ḥôl* a reference to the phoenix, the symbol of death and resurrection, a motif which enjoyed great popularity and wide geographic distribution.[62] Where there is a nest (*qinnî*), there must be a bird! Support for the phoenix interpretation was supplied by the Ugaritic epithet of the god Baal, *ḥl rḥb mknpt,* "phoenix broad of wingspread,"[63] and now Ebla makes a threefold contribution. In the bilingual vocabulary Sumerian tu-gur$_4$^{mušen} equals Eblaite *ḫu-la-tum,* which is the feminine form of Hebrew *ḥôl.* Though the precise meaning of Sumerian tu-gur$_4$ remains to be determined—"wood pigeon" being commonly given as its definition[64]—the presence of the determinative mušen leaves no doubt that a bird is meant. Just as connection with *mknpt,* "wingspread," served to specify the meaning of *ḥl* in Ugaritic, so the determinative mušen indicates the species to which *ḫu-la-tum* belongs.

In the old calendar (see Chapter VI, 3.2.1) the name of the first month, September, is feminine *ḫa-li-tù* or masculine *ḫa-li;* in the new calendar (see Chapter VI, 3.2.2) the name of September is *be-li,* "my lord," a title referring to Baal (or Dagan). Since Baal is the dying and rising god, one understands this interchange of *ḫa-li-tu* and *be-li:* the phoenix is the symbol of death and resurrection. At Ugarit, too, one of the months is called *yrḫ ḥlt,* "the month of the phoenix," a further illustration of the tenacity of tradition in Canaan.

The third piece of evidence comes from the personal name *aḫ-ḫa-lum,*[65] which may tentatively be rendered "the Phoenix is my brother," an interpretation which suggests that the bird had already been divinized, since in personal names one of the components is usually a god.

Job 31:6 Should he weigh me on honest scales,
God would know my full weight.

Job insists that he is not a fraud; if weighed he will be found full weight. The verb *yišqᵉlēnî,* "Should he weigh me," predicated of God may well have an antecedent in the Ebla personal name *iš-gú-lu* in TM.76.G.523, obv. IX 19. The name is an apocopated or abbreviated name with the name of the god omitted; its meaning would be "(the god) weighs."

Job 39:4 *[yaḥlᵉmû] bᵉnêhem*
yirbû babbār
yāṣᵉʾû wᵉlōʾ-šābû lāmô
Their young are healthy,
they grow more quickly than wheat,
they go forth and do not return to them.

The verb *yaḥlᵉmû,* "they are healthy," occurs but four times; in Isa. 38:16 it is predicated of God, *taḥlîmēnî,* "You restore me to health." It now appears in the name of Igriš-Ḫalam, the first king of the Ebla dynasty; the name may be interpreted "Drive out (the malady), O Ḫalam!" The verbal element *igriš* can be seen in context with gods in *UT,* 126: V:20–21, *my bilm ydy mrṣ/gršm zbln,* "Who among the gods will expel the sickness/driving out the malady?" Ḫalam would be the god of health and seems still to have been revered at Ugarit where the name *bn ḫlm,* "son of Ḫalam," was borne by one of the citizens.

◆

Job 40:30 *yikrû 'ālāyw ḥabbārîm*
yeḥeṣûhû bên kᵉnaʿᵃnîm
Will wholesalers haggle over him,
divide him among the merchants?

This verse begins with a form of the verb *kārāh,* "to trade, bargain," and ends with the term *kᵉnaʿᵃnîm,* literally "Canaanites," the biblical word for "trader, merchant," in Prov. 31:24, Zech. 14:21, as well as here. The antiquity of both words is documented by their occurrence at Ebla in the name of the city *kàr-kà-mi-iš* [TM.75.G.1806, obv. II 1], "Carchemish," on the Euphrates near the Syrian-Turkish border, and in the epithet *kà-na-na-um,* "the Canaanite," which characterizes Dagan, the chief god of Syria. He is called *da-ga-nu kà-na-na-um,* "Dagan the Canaanite," a title which stresses his provenance and land of rule. The name Carchemish means "the trading center of the god Chamish," and as Pettinato has suggested (*OrAn* 15 [1976] p. 15), the city may well have been founded by the Eblaites.

◆

Prov. 2:9 *'āz tābîn ṣedeq ûmišpāṭ*
[*ûmêšārê-m*] (MT *ûmêšārîm*) *kol-maʿgal-ṭôb*
Then you will understand righteousness and justice,
and the directness of every path to virtue.

One of the most exciting discoveries that emerged from the Ugaritic tablets half a century ago was, paradoxically, the tiny enclitic particle *-ma* or *-mi* that was inserted for reasons of euphony or prosody in a construct chain or was attached to other parts of speech. For example, "son of El" could be written *bn il* or with the enclitic particle inserted between the two nouns: *bn-m il.* This revelation enabled biblical philologists to explain numerous *m's* in the text which had been grammatically troublesome. Ebla also employed this particle with different parts of speech, such as *a-dì-ma,* "until," for *a-dì; an-ti-ma,* "you," for *an-ti; aš-tù-ma,* "from," for *aštù; lu-ma,* "I beg you," for *lu.* This widespread usage in Eblaite and Ugaritic authorizes the Hebraist to recognize this particle in numerous passages where neither the sense nor the grammatical analysis prove satisfactory. Prov. 2:9 would seem to be a case in point. As it stands, it is not a poetical couplet in Hebrew, as some commentators have noted. But instead of altering *mêšārîm* to a verb, it seems preferable to maintain the consonantal text intact and to parse the second colon as a four-component construct chain with the enclitic *-m* inserted between the first two components.

◆

Prov. 8:30 *wā'ehyeh 'eṣlô* [*'āmôn*]
I was beside him, the Master Architect.

The rare biblical word *'āmôn,* "Master Architect," has a long history in Mesopotamia, where it signifies "an expert," and now turns up as the title of the dean of the scribal school at Ebla: AB.BA *tám-ta-il* u m - m i - a, "the Elder, Tamta-Il the dean"; see Chapter VIII, 1.1. The biblical wisdom writer predicates this Sumerian word of Yahweh the Creator of the universe.

◆

Prov. 11:22 A gold ring in a pig's snout,
a beautiful woman teaching discretion.

Commonly rendered "discretion" or "good taste," Hebrew *ṭa'am* answers to Sumerian š à - g i $_6$, "depth of heart," in the master bilingual vocabulary TM.75.G.2000, rev. II 22′; it is written *ṭì-é-mu* in Eblaite which, employing syllabic cuneiform, had no exact consonantal symbol for the letter *'ayin* and as a surrogate used the vowel *-é-*.

◆

Prov. 18:8 *dibrê nirgān k^emitlah^amîm*
w^ehēm yār^edû [*ḥadrê-bāṭen*]
A gossip's whispers are like savory morsels,
and they go down into the innermost belly.

The phrase *ḥadrê-bāṭen,* literally "the rooms of the belly," evokes the equation in TM.75.G.2000, rev. III 9, where Sumerian š à, "heart, interior," is translated by Eblaite *é-da-ru*$_x$*-um,* which equals Heb. *ḥeder,* "room, chamber." This archaic usage of *ḥeder* as "interior" bespeaks the antiquity of the proverb which the biblical redactor may have culled from Canaanite collections of proverbs. Of course, the prepositional phrase *mēḥ^adārîm* in Deut. 32:25 and elsewhere simply means "within."

Prov. 22:1 *nibḥār [šēm] mē'ōšēr rāb*
mikkesep ûmizzāhāb ḥēn ṭôb
The Name is to be preferred to great riches,
to silver and gold the favor of the Good One.

The noun *šēm* is usually interpreted in the light of Eccles. 7:1, *ṭôb šēm miššemen ṭôb,* "Better a (good) name than good oil," and the final phrase *ḥen ṭôb* has been handled in several different ways. *NEB* simply paraphrases by "esteem." Above at Lev. 24:11 some evidence was cited for the use of Eblaite *šúm,* "name," as a surrogate for a divinity and hence to be rendered with capital "Name." If this is the usage in our verse, then it becomes possible to translate the construct chain, *ḥēn ṭôb,* "the favor of the Good One," since *ṭôb* is one of Yahweh's epithets in Prov. 13:21–22; 24:25; Hos. 8:3, etc.[66] In other words, the biblical poet has balanced in *šēm,* "the Name," and *ṭôb,* "the Good One," the two components appearing in the Eblaite personal name Ṭubi-Šum, "my good is the Name." One might object that the proposed version results in a religious sentiment much too altruistic and sublime for the pragmatic Book of Proverbs, but such an objection loses much of its force when compared with religious aspirations enunciated by Canaanites in the third millennium and reflected in the names they bore. It might also be noted that the following verse, Prov. 22:2, states, "Rich and poor have this in common: Yahweh made them both," so that the new version of Prov. 22:1 accords with the context.

This usage of *šúm,* "the Name," in Ebla and of *šēm* in Hebrew bears importantly on the translation and interpretation of Ps. 54:8–9 (6–7):

bin^{e}dābā 'ezb^{e}ḥāh-llāk
'ôdeh [ššim^{e}kā] yahweh kî-ṭôb
kî mikkol-ṣārāh hiṣṣîlānî
ûb^{e}'ōy^{e}bay rā'^{a}tāh 'ênî
For your generosity I will sacrifice to you,
I will thank your Name, Yahweh, truly good,
Because from all my adversaries He (Name) rescued me,
and mine eye feasted on my foes.

The problem lies in the third-person singular verb *hiṣṣîlānî* in verse 9: who is the subject of this verb? It can hardly be Yahweh who is addressed in verse 8 in the second person; were he the subject one would expect second-person *hiṣṣaltā,* "you rescued." And yet *RSV* without a textual note indicating that it was departing from the consonantal text renders it, "I will give thanks to thy name, O Lord, for it is good. For thou hast delivered me from every trouble." The third-person verb *hiṣṣîlānî* parses without difficulty when its subject is construed as third-person "your

Name." The Name is conceived as an attribute of Yahweh endowed with a personal identity and acts as the subject of "rescued me." Among recent versions appreciating the role of the Name may be cited the *Book of Psalms: Sepher Tehillim* of the Jewish Publication Society of America (Philadelphia, 1972), "I will acknowledge that Your name, Lord, is good, for it has rescued me from my foes, and let me gaze triumphant upon my enemies."

This is more than an example of personification for poetic effect. This theological development also affects the dispute whether Wisdom in Proverbs 8–9 is a hypostasis with an independent existence and activity.

Prov. 22:8 *zōrē^{a}' 'awlāh yiqṣôr 'āwen*
w^{e}šēbeṭ 'ebrātô [*y^{e}kīlēhū*] (MT *yikleh*)
He who sows injustice will harvest disaster,
and will measure for himself the rod of his fury.

A very difficult verse, especially in its second half, it became more intelligible when compared with line 5 of the tenth-century B.C. Gezer Calendar from central Palestine which reads *yrḥ qṣr wkl,* "the month of harvesting and measuring." Before the harvest was stored, it was apparently measured. Unintelligible MT *yikleh* standing parallel to *yiqṣôr* evidently camouflages the root *kyl/kwl* that occurs in the Gezer Calendar phrase *qṣr wkl.* Repointed from *yikleh* to *y^{e}kīlēhū,* the verb would mean that the evil man measures for himself the rod of divine punishment. In the old calendar the name of the twelfth month or August is itu *qì-lí,* which Pettinato once interpreted in the light of common Semitic *qly,* "to scorch," so as to render it "month of summer heat," but since in cuneiform writing GI-lí can also be read *kí-lí,* one prefers the "month of measuring," attested at Gezer, as the name of August.

Prov. 26:23 [*k^{e}sapsîgî-m*] (MT *kesep sîgîm*) *m^{e}ṣuppeh 'al-ḥereś*
ś^{e}pātayim dōl^{e}qîm w^{e}leb-rā'
Like glaze spread on earthenware
are ardent lips with an evil heart.

Ugaritic *spsg,* "glaze," supplied the solution to the long-standing difficulty created by MT's false reading *kesep sîgîm,* "silver of dross." When the goddess Anath promises Aqhat immortality in exchange for his bow, Aqhat disdains the offer in the conviction that *spsg ysk lriš/ḥrṣ lẓr qdqdy,* "Glaze will be poured on my head/plaster on top of my skull." He does not believe in immortality. Several scholars have connected this literary description with the ten skulls covered with plaster that were discovered by Kathleen Kenyon in the neolithic (late seventh millennium) level at Jericho. In the twenty years since this connection was made, several scholars have endorsed it in print, but recently three savants[67] have rejected this proposal as fantastic since it would mean that at least part of the Ugaritic Legend of Aqhat in which the description is found goes back to neolithic times. Ebla may now have something to contribute to this dispute; time and again these new textual discoveries bear witness to the conservatism and continuity of customs and traditions throughout millennia in Canaan, so one should pause and not reject out of hand a proposal to relate plastered skulls from Jericho in southern Canaan to a later literary description from northern Canaan. After all, this unique mortuary cult of reburying these plastered skulls under the floors of houses is strangely paralleled, according to Herodotus, by an account of a partly similar practice in Ethiopia.

Prov. 27:24 *kî lō' l^{e}'ôlām* [*ḥōsen*]
w^{e}'im-[*nēzer*] *l^{e}dôr dôr*
Wealth does not endure forever,
nor the crown for generation to generation.

While employing the figure of merismus to deny the perpetuity of all power as represented by two of its manifestations—financial and political—the writer pictures the situation of a Phoenician city-state where wealthy merchants and the king shared authority. The king's power was severely circumscribed by the commercial magnates. In Ebla a similar situation seems to have obtained; here the king was elected for a period of seven years, and he shared power with the group that the tablets constantly refer to as "the Elders," without further specifying their character. They doubtless corresponded to the leaders of the merchant class that limited royal sway in Canaanite-Phoenician city-states of the second and first millennia. In Israel, on the other hand, dominion was exercised chiefly by the king, though the priestly class also wielded some authority; little is reported about the influence of the merchants.

Song of Songs 1:14 [*'eškōl hakkōper*] *dôdî lî*
b^{e}karmê 'ên gedî
A cluster of henna flowers is my beloved to me
from the vineyards of En-gedi.

Though occurring in the Bible only here and in 4:13, *kōper*, "henna flowers," or "cypress," is a term found widely in the Mediterranean world: Ugaritic *kpr*, Hebrew *kōper*, Arabic *kāfūr*, Greek *kipros*, and

Latin *cyprus*. It designates a shrub or small tree growing to a height of eight to ten feet with fragrant whitish flowers growing in clusters like grapes. Unfortunately, the clarity of its meaning has not been matched by the certainty of its derivation, and Hebrew lexica generally refrain from positing an etymology.

This restraint may no longer be necessary in view of the Eblaite word for "copper," which would seem to answer the lexicographer's prayer. In one of the bilingual vocabularies the Sumerian word URUDU, "copper," is reproduced by Eblaite *kà-pá-ru*. The dried leaves of the henna are used for making a reddish-orange cosmetic dye with which women in the Levant stain their hair, hands, feet, and nails. Since copper is a reddish-orange metal, a relationship between *kà-pá-ru,* "copper," and kōper, "henna flower," becomes highly probable.

The word forming the other half of the phrase *'eškōl hakkōper* "a cluster of henna flowers," is also attested in the bilingual vocabularies as *aš-kà-lum,* "cluster," so that both biblical words are now seen to have a venerable lineage in Canaan.

◀▶

Song of Songs 2:13 *w*^{e}*hagg*^{e}*pānîm* [*s*^{e}*mādar*] *nāt*^{e}*nû rê*^{a}*ḥ*
and the Semadar vines give scent.

2:15 *m*^{e}*ḥabb*^{e}*lîm k*^{e}*rāmîm*
ûk^{e}*rāmênû* [*s*^{e}*mādar*]
who ravage the vineyards,
yes, our Semadar vineyards.

7:13 *naškîmāh l*^{e}*kōr*^{e}*mîm* (MT *lakk*^{e}*rāmîm*)
nir'eh 'im pār^{e}*ḥah haggepen*
pittaḥ [*hass*^{e}*mādar*]
hēnēṣû hārīmmônîm
Let us awake before the vinedressers
to see if the vine has sprouted,
if the Semadar has budded,
if the pomegranates have flowered.

Found in just these three passages, the term *s*^{e}*mādar* still awaits an explanation; the most recent discussion by M. H. Pope[68] has not palpably advanced our understanding of this elusive noun. Being a quadriliteral, *s*^{e}*mādar* should not be difficult to identify should it crop up in a new text. This now seems to be the case in TM.75.G.2231, a large, well-preserved tablet which Pettinato has recently published under the title "L'Atlante geografico del Vicino Oriente Antico attestato ad Ebla e ad Abū Ṣalābīkh.[69] In column II 8 of the obverse occurs the place name *zú-mu-dar*^{ki}. Its four consonants coincide with those of *s*^{e}*mādar* since cuneiform zú- may also be read su$_{11}$, but all that can be said about its location is that it was probably in northern Syria; none of the immediately preceding or following towns or cities are readily identifiable, though the mention of Arvad off the north Syrian coast in the next column gives some idea of the region where one must look for Sumudar. It may have been famous for its vines whose slips were carried to different parts of Syria-Palestine so that the Semadar vines acquired fame far and wide. Ezek. 27:18 mentions the wine of Helbon as imported into Tyre, so to speak of Semadar vines appears biblically appropriate.

In the Song of Songs 7:13 the construct chain *gepen hassᵉmādar* "the Semadar vine" (cf. 2:13), has been broken up and its components distributed over the parallel cola to produce the rhetorical figure commonly called the breakup of the composite phrase. See the discussion at Ezek. 27:17 where a similar phenomenon in Ugaritic is cited.

Song of Songs 5:14 *yādāyw [gᵉlîlê] zāhāb*
mᵉmullā'îm battaršîš
His hands are golden bracelets,
studded with gems.

Occurring only in Esther 1:6, *gᵉlîlê kesep,* "silver rings," and here, *gᵉlîlê* probably signifies rings also in our verse. The more unusual definition "rods, cylinders," obliges one to understand *yādāyw* as "arms," and Pope[70] renders the phrase "His arms rods of gold." Well attested in the Ebla tablets is the noun *gú-li-lum,* "bracelet."[71]

Eccles. 4:13 *ṭôb yeled [miskēn] wᵉḥākām*
mimmelek zāqēn ûkᵉsîl
Better a lad poor and wise
than a king old and foolish.

Recurring in 9:15, *miskēn,* "poor, miserable," has through Arabic channels entered the romance languages as *meschino* in Italian, *mesquin* in French, but a satisfactory etymology for this adjective has been lacking. Perhaps an etymology is now at hand in Eblaite *mu-sa-ga-i-núm* which may parse as the shapel causative participle, *mu-ša-qá-i-núm,* of the root *qyn,* "to lament," and signify "the one who emits laments."[72]

Eccles. 5:7 (8) *[gābōᵃh] mē'al gābōᵃh šōmēr*
[ûgᵉbōhîm] ʿᵃlêhem
One high official watches over another high official,
and the All High over them.

Here the plural form *g^e^bōhîm* parses as the plural of majesty and refers to God as the All High who keeps an eye on all. In Ps. 138:6 the singular form *gābōah* is predicated of Yahweh: "Though Yahweh is the Exalted, he regards the lowly one/and though the All High, he heeds even from afar." The root *gbh* seems to underlie the personal name written *gú-ba-ù* in TM.75.G.1357, rev. VIII 28 and to be normalized Gubahu; it would be a hypocoristicon or abbreviated form of the full name (such as *gú-ba-ù-i-lu*) whose divine element has been omitted. Compare Job 22:12, *halō'-'elōah gōbah šāmāyīm,* "Is not God the All High of heaven?" where the vocalization *gōbah* corresponds with Eblaite *gú-ba-ù* in the first and second syllables.

Eccles. 7:1 *ṭôb šēm* [*miššemen ṭôb*]
Better a (good) name than good oil.

The antiquity of this punning proverb may be guaged by the appearance of *šemen ṭôb,* "good oil," in Ebla as *sa-ma-nu ṭa-bù,* "good oil," and of the terms *ṭôb šēm,* "Better a (good) name," jointly in the Ebla personal name *ṭù-bí-šúm,* "my good is the Name."

Eccles. 9:1 The just and the wise and their deeds
are from the hand of God (*beyad 'elōhîm*).

Usually rendered "in the hand of God," *beyad 'elōhîm* may also and perhaps preferably be understood as "from the hand of God." In Ugaritic poetry the preposition *min,* "from," was lacking so that the idea of separation was commonly expressed by *b,* "from." To a certain extent the same obtains in Hebrew, so that one must often translate *be* as "from." The Ugaritic personal name *bdil* is correctly interpreted by C. H. Gordon[73] as "From-the-hand(s)-of-god," and now Ebla witnesses the name *ba-ti-lum,*[74] which at first blush looks like "the daughter of El" but, since it is borne by a man, should be read *ba-dì-lum,* "from the hand of El," and compared with the Ugaritic personal name *bdil* and biblical *beyad 'elōhîm,* "from the hand of God."

Eccles. 11:7 *ûmātôq hā'ôr* [*weṭôb*] *la'ênayim*
lir'ôt 'et-[*hāššameš*]
Light is sweet, and it is good for the eyes
to see the sun.

For the background of this typical sentiment (cf. Eccles. 6:5) of Ecclesiastes, the Ebla personal name *ṭù-bí-sí-piš,* "my good is the Sun," is not devoid of interest.

◆

Eccles. 12:11 *dibrê ḥ*ª*kāmîn [kaddor*ᵉ*bōnôt]*
The words of the wise are like goads.

Occurring elsewhere only in I Sam. 13:21, *dor*ᵉ*bōnôt,* "goads," served to clarify the meaning of Ugar. *drb,* "goad," without the ending *-ôn,* and now may help elucidate the place name *dar-áb*ᵏⁱ in TM.75.G.1353, rev. III 6. The town's situation on the spur of a mountain may have given rise to its name.

◆

Eccles. 12:12 [*w*ᵉ*lahag*] *harbēh y*ᵉ*gīʿat bāśār*
and much reflection is weariness of the flesh.

The hapax legomenon *lahag* has taxed the ingenuity of translators and philologists; the word has no clear cognates in the other Semitic languages. Its sense can, however, be conjectured from the context and St. Jerome's *meditatio* cannot be too wide of the mark. Its etymological isolation may now be at an end with the appearance of the personal name *íl-'à-ag-da-mu/yilhag-Damu,* "(the god) Damu reflects," or "Damu is pensive." The latter interpretation accords with what is known about this god from other sources.[75]

GENERAL CONSEQUENCES

Professor Pettinato has closed his contribution with 'Problems and Prospects," and after this review of individual points of contact between the texts found in Canaan and biblical passages, the reader may want to know what the overall impact is going to be on biblical studies.

The first general effect may turn out to be psychological. Since the discoveries at Ras Shamra beginning in 1929, many biblical scholars have shown a certain reluctance to exploit this new textual material because they felt that it was too early (circa 1375–1190) and too far away to be relevant for solving problems in texts composed in Hebrew and in Palestine in the first millennium B.C. In his review of L. Sabottka, *Zephaniah,* a work which attempts to apply Ugaritic data to the text of the prophet which bristles with difficulties, F. C. Fensham[76] writes, "One must, however, be very cautious in comparing Ugaritic material from the fourteenth to the twelfth centuries B.C. with the Hebrew of Zephaniah (ca. 612 B.C.), with the interval of about six hundred years in which the meaning of a word or a literary device could have changed enormously. In cases where one has no choice but to compare Ugaritic and Hebrew so far apart, it would be wise to put a question mark after one's solution." But Ugaritic and Hebrew no longer seem to be so far apart, thanks to the Ebla tablets of 2500 B.C. which illumine the Hebrew text on point after point and which in turn are elucidated by the biblical record. Scholars are, in fact, beginning to remark facetiously that the Ugaritic texts may be much too recent to be relevant for biblical research! Not the least of Ebla's contributions will be the gradual demolition of the psychological wall that has kept the Ras Shamra discoveries out of biblical discussions in some centers of study and from committees convened to translate the Hebrew Bible into modern tongues. That a word or phrase or poetic device could have changed its meaning over the centuries few will deny, but one must also learn to appreciate the continuity of linguistic and religious traditions in Canaan; preliminary studies of the bilingual vocabularies from Ebla reveal that words are preserved with the same meanings centuries later in the Book of Job, for example. This lexical and linguistic conservatism is matched by social and religious phenomena witnessed both at Ebla and in the Bible despite the chronological chasm. Once this conservatism is properly evaluated, biblical scholars will begin to show less diffidence vis-à-vis the Ras Shamra materials. Hence Ugaritic specialists welcome the Ebla discoveries for rendering their own discipline more credible and relevant in the eyes of hesitant biblical scholars. When a colleague recently assured me that the new finds have made Ugaritic passé, I replied that, *au contraire,* they have rendered Ugaritic research respectable again.

The second general effect may concern the attitude of biblicists toward the literary capacity of Old Testament writers. A century ago writing was considered a relatively late cultural arrival in Israel, so that there was a marked tendency to date most of the biblical books to a late period; preferably to the sixth-century Exile and to the immediately following period. The discovery in 1929 of the Ras Shamra tablets with their long poems composed with exquisite skill and refinement led to a reevaluation of the age and level of writing skills in Canaan. As a result, critics are raising the dates of many of the poetic compositions in the Old Testament. The history and practice of writing in Canaan are now seen to be even older, going back to the beginning of the third millennium; this means that the sacred poets had fallen heir to a venerable literary tradition, and the modern critic would be well advised not to underestimate their technical capacity. Several years ago after a lecture at Cambridge, England, on the formal devices of Hebrew poetry, I was asked if I was not giving too much credit to the biblical writers as craftsmen, and one listener commented that the lecture was "too clever by half" for precisely this reason. Today one would hesitate to raise such an objection in view of the literary skills and interests already in evidence in the third millennium.

Today the density of the Hebrew language can be appreciated to a greater degree than was possible before these recent discoveries. Take, for example, the phrase in Deut. 28:4, *'ašt^erôt ṣō'nekā,* "the breeding of your sheep." With the publication of the two calendars from Ebla it appears that the name of the eleventh month in the old calendar was *ṣa-a-tu,* "sheep," but in the new calendar Ištar. With exquisite irony the biblical author joined these two month names into a construct chain to express the reproduction of sheep. What a comedown for the great goddess Ištar to be reduced to a common noun! Hence the literary critic is now authorized to look for meanings and allusions much deeper and far-reaching than heretofore has been possible or warranted.

The third overall consequence looks to biblical philology and lexicography. Till now it has been possible to write grammars of Hebrew and to compile Hebrew lexica. In the decades ahead such projects will hardly be feasible because for such grammars and lexica to be credible they must include grammatical and lexical data made available by the recent discoveries in the area of Northwest Semitic. In other terms, it will become necessary to write grammars of Canaanite or Northwest Semitic that will include examples from Eblaite, Ugaritic, Phoenician, and Hebrew, and to compile lexica incorporating words from all these sources. The Hebrew words and phrases will thus acquire historical and linguistic dimensions that will render them more comprehensible. In recent years I have come to understand why students of biblical Hebrew experience such difficulty in reading and translating the text. They have been schooled in grammars which have virtually ignored developments, especially with regards to prepositions and particles, in Northwest Semitic philology over the past forty years. According to early reports, the bilingual vocabularies from Ebla contain almost 3,000 syllabically spelled Canaanite words; the Ugaritic glossary contains some 2,600 roots. For a Hebrew lexicon to be truly useful and informative, it should include this relevant nonbiblical material to provide more contexts from which one may deduce with greater precision the nuances of a word.

Twenty years ago A. Jirku published a short article with the significant title "Eine Renaissance des Hebräischen"[77] in which he tried to show how new grammatical usages in Ugaritic poetry were permitting Hebraists adequately to explain for the first time numerous biblical constructions that had eluded exact analysis. The net result was an improved translation of the Hebrew text in hundreds of verses, especially in the poetic books, and more scientific description of the Hebrew language. Jirku could justifiably speak of a rebirth of Hebrew philology in 1958, thanks to the Ugaritic discoveries.

The Ebla finds can hardly be expected to affect grammatical and prosodic research in Hebrew to the same extent because about 75 percent of the tablets are economic and formulaic in character and contain a limited amount of morphology and syntax. The bilingual vocabularies, on the other hand, bid fair to place Hebrew lexicographers in their debt, and one can on the basis of what has already been learned from these recent finds envision a renascence of biblical lexicography to parallel the progress in grammatical and prosodic research made possible by the poetic texts from Ugarit. Not a few of the more than 1,700 hapax legomena or words of single occurrence in Hebrew are happily being deprived of their solitary status by the appearance of their counterparts in Eblaite vocabularies.

Much of Old Testament poetry, which is very dense and elliptical, has eluded precise analysis and exact translation because of the lack of extrabiblical material in the past with which to compare and study these literary phenomena; the two great discoveries from northern Syria, Ugarit and Ebla, are beginning to fill that lacuna so that in the not too distant future it should be possible to put into the hands of readers more rigorous and coherent translations of the Old Testament.

Notes

1. My information comes from the *International Herald Tribune* (Paris) for February 22, 1978.
2. In *The Bible and the Ancient Near East,* ed. by G. Ernest Wright (Garden City, N.Y., 1961), p. 351.
3. Michael D. Coogan, *CBQ* 39 (1977), p. 556.
4. Consult Ignace J. Gelb, *Glossary of Old Akkadian* (Chicago, 1957), p. 19.
5. TM.75.G.3433, obv. II 5'.
6. A similar instance of assimilation can be seen in the single-occurrence noun in Hab. 3:17, *r^{e}pātîm*. Apparently signifying "stalls," as the balance with *mikleh,* "sheepfold," suggests, *r^{e}pātîm* has lacked an etymology. The analogy of Eblaite *baradu* becoming *p^{e}rat* in Hebrew would point to *rābad,* "to spread out," as the root of *r^{e}pātîm*. In Arabic *rabada* signifies "to confine, tie," and this too would satisfy as the root. By subsequent dissimilation *r^{e}bādîm* because *r^{e}pātîm,* "stalls."
7. Reading qal passive *mūṣā'* for the qal active *māṣā'* of MT, and parsing of *l^{e}* of *l^{e}ādām* as *lamedh* of agency with the passive verb. This way Adam remains the agent both at the beginning and at the end of the verse.
8. TM.75.G.1863, rev. VII 13.
9. In TM.75.G.522, rev. II 2, published by G. Pettinato, *AfO* 25 (1974–77), p. 32.
10. TM.75.G.336, obv. VI 11, published by G. Pettinato, *RSO* 50 (1976), p. 5.
11. TM.74.G.120, rev. III 6, published by G. Pettinato, *OrNS* 44 (1975), p. 370, where he interprets *en-ṣi* as "my protection," following a suggestion of G. Gar-

bini who sees in *en-ṣi* a metathesis or inversion of consonants of the root *ḥsn,* "to be strong."

12. In his study, "Origins of Prophecy," in *BASOR* 221 (1976), pp. 125–28, V. W. Rabe concludes that "the question of whether prophecy came to Israel from Phoenicia-Canaan or from Mesopotamia (Mari) is not indicated by the data." The appearance of *na-ba-um,* "to speak," and *na-bí-u-tum,* "prophecy," at Ebla would point to Canaan as the more promising region in which to search for the origins of Hebrew prophecy.
13. TM.75.G.2000, rev. VII 36.
14. TM.75.G.1353, obv. VI 6.
15. In *The Bulletin of the American Society of Papyrologists* (Studies presented to Naphtali Lewis) 15 (1978), pp. 65–66.
16. TM.75.G.2284.
17. J. Nougayrol, *Palais royal d'Ugarit, III* (Paris, 1955), text 16.270:12, p. 42.
18. See *CAD,* vol. 10 (M) (Chicago, 1977), p. 315.
19. TM.75.G.1353, rev. XI 4.
20. TM.75.G.2284.
21. TM.75.G.1648, obv. III 6.
22. The name of one of the 14 governors: see Chapter VI, 1.2.
23. TM.75.G.1352, obv. VIII 24.
24. See C. Virolleaud in *Ugaritica V* (Paris, 1969), text 9: rev. 9 (p. 584); see also L. R. Fisher, ed., *Ras Shamra Parallels* I (Rome, 1972), p. 305. On the parallel pair *'^{a}lapêka,* "your large cattle," and *ṣō'nekā,* "your small cattle," that also occurs in Ugaritic, *ibidem,* pp. 113–14.
25. TM.75.G.2231, obv. V 1.
26. "Il cantico di Debora," in *La Parola del Passato* (Naples), Fasc. 178 (1978), pp. 5–31.
27. TM.75.G.2284, obv. IV 4.
28. TM.75.G.3162+3163, obv. V 5.
29. TM.75.G.336, obv. VII 8. Pettinato, *RSO* 50 (1976), p. 5, reads *ni-é-ì-lu,* but the initial sign may also be read *lí.*
30. TM.75.G.336, rev. I 7.
31. TM.75.G.11312, III 2'.
32. *UT,* p. 376, under *brḥ* II.
33. TM.75.G.11312, III 5'.
34. TM.75.G.336, rev. I 4.
35. See G. Pettinato, *Rivista biblica italiana* 25 (1978), p. 236.
36. For further discussions of this double negative, consult M. Dahood, *OrNS* 45 (1976), p. 347; *Biblica* 59 (1978), pp. 187–88.
37. G. Pettinato, *OrAn* 15 (1976), pp. 11–15.
38. E.g., TM.75.G.336, rev. III 4.
39. TM.75.G.10023, rev. II 21. See also *Ugaritica V,* pp. 244–45, on Ugaritic *ba-ta-qu,* "to cut, break," where the scribe has annexed to Sumerian GUL the value of k u$_5$ (TAR), "to cut."
40. TM.75.G.1520, obv. VIII 19.
41. In the light of Eblaite *mu-nu-ti-um,* MT *minnît* may have to be repointed *mūnît* or *m^{e}nît.*
42. TM.75.G.3162+3163, obv. III 5. The initial vowel or consonant plus vowel *ì-* is probably a prothetic *aleph.*
43. Consult J. Nougayrol in *Ugaritica V,* pp. 244–45. The Akkadian word for "feast" in this quadrilingual dictionary is *i-zi-nu,* obviously a Sumerian loanword. Once again Eblaite distinguishes itself lexically from Akkadian and reveals its affinity with Ugaritic.

44. On this interesting development, cf. W. F. Albright, *Archaeology and the Religion of Israel* (Baltimore, 1946), p. 220, n. 115; M. Dahood, *Ephemerides Theologicae Lovanienses* 44 (1968), pp. 53–54.
45. TM.75.G.1591, obv. III 10.
46. Probably the same word as Late Hebrew *g^e^rāb,* "large clay jar," the metathetic (inverted consonants) form of *gú-bar.*
47. G. Pettinato, *OrAn* 15 (1976), p. 12, n. 7.
48. Cf. P. Artzi and A. Malamat, *OrNS* 40 (1971), p. 84, n. 23.
49. In M. Dahood, *Psalms III* (AB 17a; Garden City, N.Y., 1970), p. XXVI.
50. Consult G. Pettinato, *OrAn* 16 (1977), p. 273.
51. As recently as 1968 Robert Gordis, *Jewish Quarterly Review* 58 (1967–68), pp. 30–31, defended the long-standing suggestion that *l^e^bārôt,* "for eating," concealed the Mesopotamian deity *labartu* which does not exist since the Akkadian word must be read *la-maš-tu,* not *la-bar-tu.* In the future scholars will exercise greater caution when appealing to Mesopotamian phenomena to clarify biblical obscurities, now that an abundance of relevant material is available from Canaan itself. After all, it was in Canaan that the language of the Old Testament and its imagery originated and developed.
52. TM.75.G.2231, obv. V 1 and 16, published by G. Pettinato, *OrNS* 47 (1978), p. 56. In the summer of 1978 a 41-line tablet written in Akkadian by a man from Ugarit was found at Tell Apheq in central Palestine. It dates to the twelfth century B.C. and gives an idea of the far-reaching communications in Syria-Palestine that correspond to the picture drawn by the Ebla tablets more than a millennium earlier.
53. TM.75.G.1426, rev. II 8.
54. TM.75.G.1359, obv. V 1. Compare also the name Ar-ennum, the second king of the dynasty, which appears to be related semantically to the name *en-àr-yà.*
55. See *BA* 39 (1976), p. 50.
56. In the gazetteer tablet TM.75.G.2231, obv. IV 14, the town name *ki-ma*^ki^ may well signify "Pleiades."
57. A. F. Rainey, *Tel Aviv* 3 (1976), pp. 137–40, has published a trilingual cuneiform inscription from Tell Apheq which gives *ma-wu* as the Semitic equivalent of Sumerian a-meš, "water." In Job 6:15–16, *mw,* "water," and *šāleg,* "snow," doubtless concur as they do in Job 9:30.
58. If one points the noun as plural *m^e^nīlīm,* "his property," the principle of the double-duty suffix authorizes the attachment of the suffix of *ḥêlô,* "his wealth," to its counterpart *m^e^nīlīm.* This usage is aptly illustrated by Prov. 27:23 where *ṣō'nekā,* "your flock," lends its suffix to its balancing partner *'^a^dārîm,* "herds," which may accordingly be rendered "your herds."
59. *CAD,* vol. 6 (H), p. 87a.
60. E.g., Brown-Driver-Briggs, *A Hebrew and English Lexicon,* p. 1003b.
61. See the discussion above relating to Isa. 27:1.
62. In his 485-page book, amply illustrated, *The Myth of the Phoenix according to Classical and Early Christian Traditions* (Leiden: Brill, 1972), R. van den Broek collects much of the relevant material.
63. For fuller discussion consult M. Dahood, *CBQ* 36 (1974), pp. 85–88.
64. Some of the representations of the phoenix gathered in van den Broek's work look much like a pigeon, so that "wood pigeon" proves satisfactory as a definition.
65. TM.75.G.336, obv. V 3, published in *RSO* 50 (1976), p. 4. The oscillation between the masculine form *ḫali* and feminine *ḫalitu* credits the report of Lactantius, the Christian apologist of the fourth century, that the phoenix was either sexless or hermaphroditic. In three of the Ebla tablets the first month is

called *ḫa-li-tu,* but in fifteen texts it appears as masculine *ḫa-li;* for precise references see G. Pettinato, *OrAn* 16 (1977), p. 272.

66. Cf. Lorenzo Viganò, *Nomi e titoli di YHWH alla luce del semitico del Nord-ovest* (Rome: Biblical Institute Press, 1976), pp. 182–93.
67. A. F. Rainey, *UF* 3 (1971), p. 154; M. Dijkstra and J. C. de Moor, *UF* 7 (1975), p. 190.
68. *Song of Songs: A new Translation with Introduction and Commentary* (AB 7c; Garden City, N.Y., 1977), pp. 398–99.
69. In *OrNS* 47 (1978), pp. 50–73.
70. *Song of Songs,* pp. 502, 542, discusses in detail the various proposals.
71. E.g., TM.75.G.1353, obv. V 15; see also Chapter IX, 2.2 where a *gulilum,* "bracelet," is listed as the property of the god Kura.
72. For a different analysis, cf. I. J. Gelb, *Thoughts About Ibla: A preliminary Evaluation,* March 1977 (Undena Publications, Malibu, 1977), p. 23.
73. *UT,* p. 370.
74. TM.76.G.523, obv. VII 22
75. Consult Thorkild Jacobsen, *Toward the Image of Tammuz and Other Essays on Mesopotamian History and Culture* (Harvard, 1970), p. 73–103.
76. *JBL* 92 (1973), p. 598.
77. *Forschungen und Fortschritte* 32 (1958), pp. 211–12.

Bibliography

All works mentioned in this bibliography are by Giovanni Pettinato.

A) *General Survey:*

a. *Ebla. Un impero inciso nell'argilla.* Milano: Mondadori, 1979, p. 320. Illustrazioni 21+12.
[The archaeological discovery of Ebla. The royal archives. The writing and language of Ebla. The dynasty of Ebla and its historical documents. Society. Economy. Culture. Religion]

b. "The Royal Archives of Tell Mardikh-Ebla," in *BA* 39 (1976), pp. 44–52.
[Archives. Political history. Religion. Language]

c. "Ibla" (Ebla).A. Philologisch, in RlA V (1976), pp. 9–13.
[Name and location of the city. Ebla in Mesopotamian and non-Mesopotamian literature. Archives and dating. Typology and language of the texts of Ebla. List of the kings of Ebla. Political history]

d. "Ebla. Immagine di una nuova civiltà del III millennio av. Cr." in *Atti della Società Leonardo da Vinci,* Firenze, 1979 (in press).

B) *Archives:*

a. *Catalogo dei testi cuneiformi di Tell Mardikh-Ebla* (= Materiali Epigrafici di Ebla,l; Istituto Universitario Orientale di Napoli, Seminario di Studi Asiatici, Series Maior, I). Napoli, 1979. Pp. XLII+290.
[Epigraphic discoveries of 1974–76. Typology of the texts. Their dating. Methodical catalogue of 6,643 inventory numbers]

b. "Testi cuneiformi del 3.millennio in paleo-cananeo rinvenuti nella campagna di scavi 1974 a Tell Mardikh-Ebla," in *OrNS* 44 (1975), pp. 361–74.
[Contents of the tablets. Eblaite language. Grammar]

c. "Gli Archivi Reali di Tell Mardikh-Ebla: Riflessioni e prospettive," in *RBI* 25 (1977), pp. 225–43. 2 Tables.
[Contents of the texts found in 1974–76. New chronology proposed. Grammar of Ebla. Elaboration of TM.75.G.2342]

C) *Inscriptions:*

a. "Inscription de Ibbiṭ-Lim, roi de Ebla," in: *AAAS,* 1970, pp. 19–22.

b. "Il torso di Ibbiṭ-Lim, re di Ebla. II. L'iscrizione," in *MAIS,* 1967–68, Roma 1972, pp. 1–38, tavv. I–V (advance offprint).
[Elaboration of the inscription on the statue with philological and historical commentary. Epigraphic documentation of Ebla. Identification and location of Ebla]

D) *Politics:*

a. "Una lettera diplomatica degli Archivi Reali di Tell Mardikh-Ebla," in *AAAS* (in press).
[Elaboration of TM.75.G.2342]

b. "Relations entre les royaumes d'Ebla et de Mari au troisième millénaire, d'après les Archives Royales de Tell Mardikh-Ebla," in: *Akkadica,* 2 (1977), pp. 20–28.
[Cultural, economic and political relations. Translation of TM.75.G.2367: military bulletin of the campaign of Enna-Dagan against Iblul-Il, king of Mari and of Ashur]

E) *Geography:*

a. "L'Atlante geografico del Vicino Oriente Antico attestato ad Ebla e ad Abu Ṣalabikh (I)," in *OrNS,* 47 (1978), pp. 50–73. Tavv. VII–XII.
[Texts: TM.75.G.2231=*IAS,* 1974, p. 71 ff. (289 geographical names of the Fertile Crescent with syllabic and logographic writing); TM.75.G.2136: a list of countries under the sway of the cities with which Ebla traded in TM.75.G.1591]

b. "TSŠ 242. Fondazione della città UNKEN^{ki}," in: *OrAn,* 16 (1977), pp. 173–76.

c. "Carchemiš—Kar-Kamiš. Le prime attestazioni del III millenio," in: *OrAn,* 15 (1976), pp. 11–15.
[Attestations of Carchemish in the Ebla texts and reflections on the geographical name]

d. "Le città fenicie e Byblos in particolare nella documentazione epigrafica di Ebla," in *Atti del I Congresso Internazionale di Studi Fenici e Punici,* Roma, 5–10 Nov. 1979 (in press).

F) *Administration:*

a. "Aspetti amministrativi e topografici di Ebla nel III millennio av. Cr. A. Documentazione epigrafica," in: *RSO,* 50 (1976), pp. 1–15.
[Text: TM.75.G.336. Administrative organization of the city of Ebla]

G) *Calendars:*

a. "Il calendario semitico del 3. millennio ricostruito sulla base dei testi di Ebla," in: *OrAn,* 16 (1977), pp. 257–85. Tavv. XI–XII.
[Texts: TM.75.G.1629, 1630, 2096. Calendar of the months and its meaning. Geographical horizon of the old calendar]

b. "Il calendario di Ebla al tempo del re Ibbi-Sipiš sulla base di TM.75.G.427," in: *AfO,* XXV (1974–77), pp. 1–36.
[Elaboration of TM.75.G.427 and reconstruction of the new calendar]

H) *Economy:*

a. "Il commercio internazionale di Ebla. Economia statale e privata," in *OIA,* 5, 1979 (in press). Tavv. I–II.
[Models of exchange and the geographical extent of Ebla's commerce. Elaboration of TM.75.G.1377 and of TM.76.G.523]

I) *Culture and Language:*

a. "I testi cuneiformi della biblioteca reale di Tell Mardikh-Ebla," in: *RendPARA,* 48, 1975–76, pp. 47–57.
[Literature, language, school, and lexicography]

b. "Ebla und Sumer: kulturelle und wirtschaftspolitische Beziehungen" (Relazione alla XXV Rencontre Assyriologique Internationale, 3–7 July 1978) (in press).
[Cultural relations between Ebla, Fara, and Abu Salabikh, as well as the political and economic relations with Kiš]

J) *Religion and cult:*

a. *Culto ufficiale ad Ebla durante il regno di Ibbi-Sipiš.* Con Appendice di P. Mander (= Orientis Antiqui Collectio—XVI), Roma, 1979, pp. 131. Tavv. I–XII.
[Typology of the offering texts. Those offering. Gods worshipped in the cult. Regular offerings and particular festivities. Terminology relating to the offerings. Edition of TM.75.G.1764, 2238, and 11010+]

b. =*OrAn,* 18 (1979), pp. 85–215. Tavv. I–XII.

c. "Dagan e il suo culto ad Ebla. Un primo bilancio" (in press).
[The problem of Dagan at Ebla: Dagan and Enlil; Dagan=ᵈbe. Dagan in the name lists and in the cult]

d. "Politeismo ed enoteismo nella religione di Ebla," in: *Atti del Simposio su Dio nella Bibbia e nelle culture ad essa connesse* (in press).
[Polytheism at Ebla. The problem of Il and Ya. Elements of henotheism. Translation of the Hymn to the Lord of heaven and earth]

e. "Elementi hurriti ad Ebla" (Relazione alla XXIV (Rencontre Assyriologique Internationale 4–8 July 1977 (in press).
[Religion and cult: presence of Aštabi, Adamma, Ḫepat ed Išḫara. Names: Arennum and Ebrium]

f. "Pre-Ugaritic Documentation of Ba'al" in: *Festschrift C. H. Gordon* (in press).
[Presence of Ba'al in Abu Salabikh, Ebla, Ur III, and Mari. Personality of Baal]

K) *Lexicography:*

a. "ED Lu E ad Ebla. La ricostruzione della prime 63 righe sulla base di TM.75.G.1488," in: *OrAn,* 15, (1976), pp. 169–78. Tav. III.
[Lexical list with names of professions]

b. "Liste presargoniche di uccelli nella documentazione di Fara ed Ebla," in: *OrAn,* 17 (1978), pp. 165–78. Tavv. XIV–XVI.
[Edition of TM.75.G.1415 and 1636 in relationship to the text collated for the occasion in Berlin]

c. "Ugaritic ršp gn and Eblaite rasap gunu(m)^{ki}," in: *OrNS,* 46 (1977), pp. 230–32.

d. "Die Lesung von AN.IM.DUGUD. MUŠEN nach einem Ebla-Text," in: *JCS* (in press).
[The reading an-zu established on the basis of TM.75.G.3439, a duplicate of *IAS,* pp. 62ff.]

e. "dingir kalam^{tim} at Ebla," in: *JCS* (in press).
[The bilingual vocabulary TM.75.G.3171 furnishes the equation dingir kalam^{tim} = be-lu ma-tim]

L) *Literary texts:*

a. "Le collezioni én-é-nu-ru di Ebla," *OrAn,* 18 (1979) pp. 329–51.
[Preliminary edition of texts containing incantations: TM.75.G.1501, 1519, 1619, 1627, 1722, 1816, 2038, 2195, 2217, 2459]

Indexes

1. NAMES OF PERSONS

a-a-bù-ìr-ku$_8$ 141
a-ba-šu 140
Abatu 88, 110
abmn 290
a-bù-^{d}*gu*$_5$*-ra* 138, 139, 142
Abu-Gura 215
Abu-Kura 219, 221
a-bù-ma-lik 260
Abu-Malik 169
a-bù-sí 142
Acquaro, E. xvi
Adadu 224
'ā d ā m 274
a-dam-ma-lik 260
Adamu 123, 128, 130, 274
Adulu 215
Adulum 168
Agga 218
Aḫa-Ar 122
aḫ-ḫa-lum 139, 306
a-kà-al-ma-lik 139, 298
a k t m y 304
*a-la-sa-*GÚ 141
Albright, W. F. 21, 271, 320, (n. 44)
AL.DA.BÀD.KI 138
Alexander 36
a-lu-a-ḫu 140, 286
Alu-Aḫu 143
a-lum 139
Alum 212
Amar-Suena 16
Ammitaku 17
'ā m ô s 294
Amudu 215
amrb'l 276
amril 276
amry 277
Anaba 213
Ana-Lugal 216
a-na-ma-lik 62
Ana-Malik 171
Anut 110
a:píl-ma-lik 138
Apri-Aḫu 207
Arcari, E. xvi
Ar-Ennum 69, 70, 71, 73, 121, 122, 123, 125, 127, 128, 129, 130, 192, 320 (n. 54)
ar-ra-sí-piš 140, 305
ar-šè 140, 141
ar-šè-a-ḫu 139, 141
Arši-Aḫa 128, 130
Arši-Aḫu 209
Artzi, P. 320 (n. 48)
Arwa 110
Ashur-Ya 209
Asi-Malik 209
A-Sipiš 116
Astour, M. C. 21, 28
Aśba-Il 187
áš-ba-ìa 140
Awa-Išar 219, 221
Azi 232
Azubada 212

Badulum 121
Bahnassi, A. xvi
ba-qá-da-mu 44, 64
Bari 218, 221
Barth, T. F. 227
Barzamau 167
ba-ṣa-a 139
Batilum 209, 314
Bauer, J. 51, 65
Baza 135
bdil 314
be-du-núm 138
Biga, G. xvi
Biggs, R. D. 51, 242
b n ḫ l m 307
Bottero, J. 21
Böhl, F. M. Th. 66
Bounni, A. xvi
Brock, R. van den 320 (nn. 62, 64)
Buda-Ya 219, 221
Buda-Malik 224

Budu 110
Bugan 211
Bulau 166
Burakam 220
Burrows, E. 51
Butz, K. xvi, 227

Cagni, L. xvi
Cheops 107
Chephren 107
Childe 196
Civil, M. xvi
Coogan, M. D. 318 (n. 3)

Daba'u 83
Dada-Ar 224
Dahood, M. xvi, 66, 257, 261, 268
Dana-Lugal 88, 110
Danalum 94
Dani 223
da-ni-lum 140
Dar-Malik 88, 110
Darmia 128, 163, 190
da-sí-ma-ad 136, 139, 218, 277, 279, 297
d^e^bôrāh 279–80
Deimel, A. 51, 196
della Valle Pietro 8
d^e^lîāh 285
Deller, K. xvi
Dijkstra, M. 321 (n. 67)
Dossin, G. 51
Drower, H. S. 32
Dubuḫu-Hada 4, 69, 75, 77–79, 90, 94, 167, 222
Dubuḫu-Malik 161
du-bù-ḫu-ma-lik 260
DU.GÚ 140
Durenezu 218, 221
Dušigu 187
ḏkry 294
ḏmrb'l 277
ḏmrhd 277
ḏmry 277

Eannatum 37
eb-du-ìa 140, 142, 249
Ebdu-Ya 203
eb-du-il 249
Ebdulu 223
eb-du-ma-lik 260
eb-du-^d^*ra-sa-ap* 141
eb-la-a-num 17
Ebrium 4, 61, 69–71, 74–77, 80, 81, 83, 84, 86–88, 92, 96, 98, 109, 120, 122, 123, 125, 127–30, 136, 147, 172, 180, 187, 246, 249
é-da-ša 138, 140
Edaša 215
Edzard, D. O. 28, 29
é-gi-a-lum 141
Ekhli-Teshup 17, 19
Emišum 203
Emurugu 218, 220
Enarya 123, 128, 302, 320 (n. 54)
en-àr-da-mu 44
Enmerkar 95
en-na-be 138
Enna-Be 216
Enna-Dagan 46, 99, 101, 102, 129
en-na-ìa 136, 138, 139, 142, 249, 261
Enna-Ya 191, 215, 216, 217, 219, 221, 224, 276
en-na-il 249, 261, 276
Enna-Il 128, 161, 192, 232
en-na-ma-lik 139
en-na-ma-ni 140, 290
en-na-ni-il 138, 142
Ennani-Il 203
en-na-^d^*ra-sa-ap* 140, 141
Ennu-Ya 117
Enzi-Malik 208, 209, 277, 279
Enzuwerum 213
Ewara 212, 213
Ezi 218, 222

Falkenstein, A. 21, 51, 66, 196, 261, 267
Farber, G. 28, 29
Fensham, F. C. 315
Ferrara, A. J. 29
Fisher, L. R. 319 (n. 24)
Fozzati, L. xvi
Fransos, M. xvi
Fronzaroli, P. 66

Gada 212
Gadana 219, 221
Gadd 21
Gadum 86, 110, 215, 218
Gaduwedu 116
Garbini, G. xvi, 65, 66, 285, 318 (n. 11)
Garra 164
Gelb, I. J. xvi, 21, 51, 59, 66, 318 (n. 4), 321 (n. 72)
GIBIL.ZA-*il* 163
Gigi 123, 128, 191
Gilgamesh 37, 74, 75, 95, 238
Gir-Damu 84, 110, 294
Giri 83, 84, 110, 122
Goetze, A. 21
Gordis, R. 320 (n. 51)
Gordon, C. H. 278–79, 288, 314
Grandi, E. 227
Gray, J. 272
Guba 219, 221
Gubalum 219

Gubau 222
Gudea 16, 18, 21, 39, 314
Gugian 223
Gugianu 217
Gugiwan 153
Gula 216
Gulilu(nu) 219, 221
Gulla 187
Gura-Damu 110
Guraya 18
gú-ra-sí 142
Guza-Malik 207
Guzuzi 116

Harmatta, J. 29, 51
Heltzer, M. 28, 29
Heretani, M. xvi
Herodotus 8
Hirsch, H. 29

Ḫaba 211
ḫa-ba-rí 139
ḫa-bil 141
Ḫaluṭ 110
ḫa-ra-ìa 142, 249
Ḫara-Ya 161
ḫa-ra-il 249
Ḫazari 117
ḫa-zu-ru$_x$ 140
Ḫubara 161

i-a-da-mu 260
i-ad-da-mu 260
í-a-du-ud 105
^{d}ìa-ra-mu 152, 194, 249
i-bí-da-mu 44
i-bí-ni-li-im 63
Ibbi-Sipiš 4, 43, 45, 69–71, 74–78, 80, 81, 90, 93, 102, 110, 121–23, 128–30, 133, 146, 147, 150, 152, 173, 187, 192, 207, 210, 227, 254, 257
i-bí-iṭ-li-im 24, 25
Ibbiṭ-Lim 21, 23, 25, 27, 32, 46
ibln 17
Iblul-Il 46, 73, 83, 99, 101, 102
ib-lul-il 146
ib-na-ma-lik 260
i b r d 277
i-bù-bu$_6$ 65
Ibubu 97, 119
Ibumut 123, 128, 192
Ida-NE 213
i-da-NI 142
i-da-nu 140
i-da-núm 138
ì-da-palil 140, 284
Ida-Palil 144
Idunanuni 224
Idununa 117
Iga-Lim 70, 109
Igi 171
Igriš-Damu 110
Igriš-Ḫalam 69–71, 122, 123, 125, 129, 147, 307
ig-ri-iš-ḫe-epa$_x$ 24
Igriš-Ḫepa 27
iḫ-su-up-da-mu 61
Iḫsup-Damu 224
Iḫušzinu 128, 133, 163
i-i-da-du 140
ik-su-up-da-mu 61
Iksup-Damu 86, 110
Iku-šar 129
i l - ʾà - a g - d a - m u 315
i l a b a d m 274
Ile-Išar 218
Ili-Dagan 16
Iltagar 171
i l t m 277
Ilumagarnu 117
Ilum-Aḫi 110
ì-lum- b a l a 136, 138
Ilum-Bala 207, 224
i l y 294
Ilzi-Damu 124, 128, 191
in-da-mu 260
In-Damu 110
Ingar 84, 110, 121
Inilum 210
ip-ḫur-^{d}*gu*$_5$*-ra* 141
ip-ḫur-ìa 139, 261
Ipḫur-Ya 211, 217
ip-ḫur-il 261
Ippiḫir 224
Ipqa-Ya 208, 278
Ipqa-Išlu 211
Ipte-Damu 87, 110, 218
Iptula 161
ip-ṭù-ra 139
Ipṭura 78, 79, 122, 154
ip-ṭur-ìa 141
Ipṭur-Ya 224
Ipṭur-Išar 135, 232
ip-ṭur-iš-lu 136
Iqnaʼum 215
Iqna-Damu 124, 128, 191
Irda-Malik 128, 133
ír-^{d}*da-mu* 260
Ir-Damu 84, 85, 110
Ir-Dumuzi 225
Irʼeak-Damu 90
Irʼe-Damu 87, 110
ìr-ì-ba 140, 141
Iriba 219, 224
Irib-Aḫu 213
Irib-Damu 70, 71
Irigunu 124, 128, 133, 191

Irisa 216
Irkabar 124, 129, 133, 191, 304
Irkab-Damu 69, 70, 71, 97, 98, 122, 123, 125, 129, 130
Irkab-Dulum 122, 124, 172
Ir-Malik 222
ìr-MI+ŠITA$_x$-*ni* 140
ìr-^{d}*na-im* 140
Irra-Dimu 217
Irti 84, 110
Iṣṣi(n)-Dagan 18
Ishbi-Erra 17
Iš'a-Malik 224
i-šar 138
iš$_x$-ar-Damu 44
Iš'ar-Damu 110
Iš-Damu 83
Išga 219
Išgi-Barzu 209
Išgidar 128, 133
i š - g ú - l u 306
iš-la-ìa 136
Išla-Ya 222
Išlutu 116
Išma-Daban 203, 210
iš-má-da-mu 260
iš-má-ìa 249
Išma-Ya 214, 239, 240, 276
iš-má-il 249, 276
Išma-Šum 211, 283
Išqulu 211
iš-ra-ìa 249
iš-ra-il 249
iš$_x$-ru$_x$-ut-Damu 44
i š - t á - a - n u 275
Išta'al 163
Ištup-šar 101
Iti-Aštar 203
Iti-Dašin 172
Iti-Hada 159
i-ti-ìa 261
Iti-Ya 224
i-ti-il 261
i-ti-kà-mi-iš 141, 292
Iti-Kamiš 128, 191
Iti-Malik 210
Iti-Nidakul 216, 222

Jacobsen, Th. xvi, 109, 111, 321 (n. 75)
Jestin, R. 51
Jirku, A. 317

KA-banu 214
Kammenhuber, A. 28, 32
kà-ra-ba-il 64
kà-za-na 138
Kešdut 208
Khayata, W. xvi
Khuziru 16
Kienast, B. 29
ki-ni-lum 141
Kinum 117
Kirsut 88, 110
Kitir 209, 218, 223
Klengel, H. 21, 28
Komoroczy, G. 29, 51
Kramer, S. N. 109
Kupper, J. 21

Lactantius 320 (n. 65)
Ladad 123, 128, 190
Landsberger, B. 21, 65
Langdon, S. 51
Legrain 21
Leontief, W. W. 227
Lewy, J. 21
l í - é - ì - l u 285
Liverani, M. 21
lu-a-ìa 139
Luduna 117
Lugal-Aba 212
Lugalbanda 95
Luningirsu 16

Ma'e'u 224
ma-gal-lu 139
Malamat, A. 320 (n. 48)
Mander, P. xvi
Matthiae, P. 22–25, 28, 29, 48, 49, 51, 109, 110, 242
Mau'ut 110
Mesalim 73
me-sà-li-ma 73
mi-kà-ìa 138, 139, 212, 249, 261, 276
mi-kà-il 63, 249, 261, 276
Milabite 19
Milano, L. 110
Minali 208, 213
MI-NE 207
m n y 290
Moor, J. C. de 321 (n. 67)
Moran, W. L. xvi
Moscati, S. 66

Naga'um 110
Napa 19
Napḫa-Il 84, 85, 110
Naram-Sin 14–16, 18, 35, 80
Nazi 219, 221
NE-A'a 212
Niba 116
ni-ba-ìa 138
Niba-Ya 219, 221
Niebuhr, C. 8
NI-*é-ì-lu* 140, 319 (n. 29)
n i - m i - r i - y à 277
Nimrod 277

Ninušḫu 171
ni-qì 139
NI-*ṣa-ra-nu* 140
Nougayrol, J. 319 (n. 17), 319 (n. 43)
Nur-Ili 16

Palil 284
Parrot, A. 51
Pennacchietti, F. xvi
pᵉqaḥyāh 278
Pettinato, G. 29, 51, 66, 109, 111, 261
Picchioni, S. xvi
pmn 290
Poebel, A. 21
Pomponio, F. xvi
Pope, M. H. 261, 312, 313
Puglia, A. xvi
Puḫi 217
Pušu 218, 221
pù-tá-be 142
pù-tá-ìa 138, 141
Puwu 217
puzur$_4$*-ra-a-gú* 140
puzur$_4$*-ra-be* 138
puzur$_4$*-ra-ìa* 42, 43, 61, 138, 140, 261
Puzur-Ya 222
puzur$_4$*-ra-il* 261
puzur$_4$*-ra-ma-lik* 138, 140
puzur$_4$-URU 136, 138

qadmî'ēl 274
qur-da-núm 138
qú-ti-núm 139

Rabe, V. W. 319 (n. 12)
Rad, G. von 276
Rainey, A. F. 320 (n. 57), 321 (n. 67)
Rebecca 77
Rid(a) Hadad 15, 18
ri-da-li-im 277
Ridut 88, 110
Rigaḫalu 116
Roccati, A. xvi
Röllig, W. 261
ru$_x$*-ba-nu* 138
Rupušlim 128, 133

Sabottka, L. 315
Sag-Damu 87, 110, 218
Sargon 15, 16, 18, 21, 109
Sasalum 128, 133, 208, 274, 285
Shennam 27
Shuri-Hadad 16, 18
Shusin 16
Sibatum 116
sí-ma-^{d}*gu*$_5$*-ra* 140
sí-mi-na-ìa 139
sí-piš-ar 142
Sipiš 289
Sipiš-Ya 224
sîsᵉrā' 284–85
Sollberger, E. xvi, 29
Sulum 219, 221

Ṣi-Damu 86, 110
Ṣib-Damu 87, 110, 211

Šama 213
Šamši-Adad 101
ša-NAM-*gi-nu* 109
ša-ri-gi-nu 109
šᵉmîda' 283
Ši'aum 224
Šima-Kura 94
Šubur 128, 133
šu-ì-lum 139
Šuilum 223
šu-mi-a 249
šu-mi-a-ù 249
Šura-Damu 83, 102, 110, 146, 305

Takeš-Malik 88, 110
tám-tá-ìa 249
tám-tá-il 249
Tamta-Il 232
Tamur-Damu 110
Tarib-Damu 110
Tawananna 77
Tešma-Damu 88
Thutmosis III 18
Tia 211
Tia-Barzu 87, 88, 110
Tia-Damu 110
ti-dì-nu 136, 139
Tidinu 87, 120, 128, 191
Tikeš-Malik 94
ti-la-ìa 138, 139, 141
Tiludu 110
tmy 277
ti-ra-ìa 249
ti-ra-il 64, 249
Tira-Il 98, 232
[illegible]ṭ 294
[illegible]m 87, 96, 110
[illegible]amu 110
Tišt[illegible]amu 88, 110
Tosi, M. xvi, 265
Tubil-Malik 88, 110
Tudia 73, 105
Tueir, K. xvi
Tuṣi-Išar 88, 110

Ṭabi 110
ṭarmia 274
ṭūbī-Ab 44
ṭù-bí-da-lu 63
ṭūbī-Dalu 44
ṭù-bí-da-mu 283
ṭūbī-Damu 44

ṭù-bí-sí-piš 140, 315
Ṭubi-Sipiš 187, 218, 224
ṭù-bí-šum 283, 309, 314
Ṭubi-Šum 128, 156
ṭūbī-Ti 44

Ubillum 219, 221
Uḫub 107
Umlulu 117
Unger, E. 21
Ungnad, A. 21
Uriḫamu 219, 221
UR.PI 140
Uti 110
Utnapishtim 37

van Dijk, J. J. 261
Viganò, L. 321 (n. 66)
Virolleaud, C. 272, 319 (n. 24)
Visicato, G. xvi
von Soden, W. 65, 66

Wada'e 218, 221
wa-da-la-NI-*mu* 139
Waetzoldt, H. xvi
wa-na 138, 295
wa-ṣl-lu-um 274
Watilu 224, 282
wa-ti-ru-'à-da 282
Wedulum 138
Weidner, E. 21
Wirth, E. 226
Wright, G. E. 318 (n. 2)

^{d}yà-ra-mu 122, 277
yitrô 281
yônāh 295
yôrām 277
yôtām 277
yrmb'l 277
yrm'l 277
yrmy 277
ytm 277
ytr, ytrhd 282

Zama'aru 218, 220
Zamilu 224
Zariq-Damu 172, 301
z^{e}karyāh 294
Zirušu 219, 221
Zizi 97, 98
Zorell, F. 109
Zubalum 161
ZU.MA.NE 116
Zuzugamu 219, 221

2. NAMES OF PLACES AND RIVERS

A'a 85
A'ada 160
'*à*-AN.AN^{ki} 241
Abati 248
Abrum 202
Absu 84
Aburu 102
Abu Salabikh 10–12, 37, 39, 40, 46, 54, 72, 148, 230, 237, 239–41
Adab 17, 37, 73, 226, 230
Adaš 135
Adazu 207
Addali 101
A.EN.GA.DU^{ki} 109
Afghanistan 169
Aḫa-Damu 220
'*à-ir-rìm*^{ki} 241
Akkad 14, 15, 17, 21, 35, 37, 73, 80, 95, 106, 109
Akko 226
Ala 208, 209
Alalakh 17, 18, 226
Aleppo 3, 18, 21, 22, 28, 35, 41, 196, 201
Alexandria 48
Alsum 106
Alu 203
Amanus 14, 21
Ambar-Ambar 192
Anatolia 6, 95, 96, 103
Angai 99
Ara 224
Arabia 57
Aramu 217
Aratta 238
Arga 103, 209, 217
Arisum 101
Arman 14, 15
ar-mi^{ki} 78, 258
ar-mi^{ki}-*ar-mi*^{ki} 248
Arra 224
Arramu 84
Arugatu 211, 213, 248, 254, 255
Arulu 135
Ashur 6, 17, 36, 45, 73, 101, 103–16, 114, 121, 184, 226, 246
Assyria 17
Ašaltu 99
Ašdod 226
Atanni 248

Azidu 209
Azu 223

Babylon 17, 266
Babylonia 8, 37
Badul 99
Baghdad 37
Bahrein 182
Bailan 21
Balikh 21, 96
Bananatu 224
b a - r a - d u 275, 318 (n. 6)
Barama 102
Bargau 85
Batin 83
Batinu 209
Beirut 226
Belan 99, 102
Bidadar 106
Birecik 21
Boghazköy 36
Bulanu 248
Burman 101, 161, 203
Buzuga 116
Byblos 73, 209, 226

Canaan 56, 246, 248, 253, 271–73, 307
Cappadocia 17, 18
Carchemish, see Karkemiš
Chagar Bazar 2
Commagene 21
Cyprus 6, 96, 201, 226

Da'awa 164
d ā b^{e} r a t 280
Dagbaal 135
Dagu 157, 160
Damascus 3, 166, 226
Dammium 101
du$_5$*-nu-u*$_5^{ki}$ 241
Dapinu 211
Darab 192, 315
Dara'um 208, 213
Daripanu 85
Dazaba 103
Diyala 37, 148
Dilmun 182
d u b - b a r - a t 280, 284
Dunanan 84
Dunu 106
Duwum 106

Ebal 120
Ebla 3, 4, 6–12, 14–25, 27–29, 32–37, 39, 40, 42–48, 50, 54–55, 57–59, 61, 62, 65, 68–77, 79–81, 83, 86–88, 91–99, 101, 103–8, 114, 115, 117–23, 134, 136, 144, 145, 147, 156, 157, 160–62, 164–67, 174, 176, 179–82, 184–86, 188, 195, 196, 200–3, 225, 230–37, 239–42, 244–47, 250–53, 256, 258, 259, 264–69, 271–73
Ebsu 83, 86
Eden 209
Edu 45, 98, 99, 103, 120, 217
Egypt 2, 73, 95, 96, 103, 107, 200, 201, 230, 264
El Amarna 64
Elašune 103
Emar 17, 45, 87, 96, 101, 102, 161, 162, 226
ê n a y i m 280
Erbilum 226
Eresh 37
Ethiopia 57
Euphrates 2, 14, 21, 32, 96, 162, 226, 247, 275
Ezan 121

Fara 10–12, 37, 39, 46, 54, 55, 230, 237, 239, 240, 259
France 267

Galalabi 101
Ganane 102
Garamu 103
gàr-mu^{ki} 43
Garmu 161, 216
Garru 220
Gasa 161
Gasur 37, 102, 148, 226, 240
Gemdet Nasr 37, 55
Germany 267
Gezira 226
Gibiu 85
Gidu 160
Girsu 37
Giš 84
Gišbardu 257
Gizanu 85, 106
Gudadanum 103, 162, 194, 195, 206, 207, 217
Gunu 225, 248
gu-ra-kul^{ki} 61
Gurakul 223
Gurarab 86
Gurarakul 194
gu-ra-ra-kul 61
Gurdabitu 213
Guwalu 159, 160, 164

Ḫabur 3
Ḫalam 188, 248, 256
Ḫalazu 85
Ḫamazi 6, 73, 96, 98, 107, 108, 119, 226, 267
Ḫarran 73, 120, 226
Ḫašuwan 101

Ḫub 221
Ḫubušan 106
Ḫušu 106
Ḫutimu 206, 212, 214

Hama 3, 22, 35, 45, 215, 226, 248
Homs 35, 226

Iamatium 16
Iarmuti 15
Ibutum 205, 210
Igi 103, 210, 217
Ikdulu 134
Ilgi 99
Ilibi 216
Ilmada 84
Ilwi 99
Inebuni 161
Iran 3, 6, 95, 107, 226, 230
Iraq 8
Iribitu 216, 222, 224
Irim 99, 248
Iritum 213, 214
Irraku 170
Isin 17
Issos 21
i-ya-pu 295
Izu 160

Jaffa 226

Kablul 103, 170, 201
Kab-sipa 84
Kadesh 35
Kakmium 84, 207, 216, 217
kà-na-na 272
Kaniš 17, 106, 226
Kanišu 106
Karaman 85
Karkamis 21
Karkemiš 103, 209, 226, 292, 307
Karnak 18
KI.KI^{ki} 241
Kilis 21
ki-ma 320 (n. 56)
Kish 17, 18, 43, 73, 74, 75, 107, 119, 226, 230, 239, 240, 266, 267
Kulban 135
kur^{ki} 163

Labanan 99
Lachiš 226
Lada 85
Ladabi 202
Ladainu 103
Lagab 103
Lagash 16, 17, 37, 148
Lagu 85
Lalanium 101
Lebanon 15, 74, 95, 226

Litiba 223
Luban 96
Luatum 106
Luatim 164
Lub 248, 256
Luban 248, 254, 255
Lumnanu 161

ma-dar^{ki} 241
Madu 85
Madulu 85
Ma-NE 248
Manuwat 212, 216, 222
mar-a-bí-ak 301
Marbe 85
Mardin 21
Mari 2, 6, 15, 16, 17, 18, 29, 35, 36, 37, 43, 46, 55, 57, 73–74, 83, 98, 99, 101, 102, 106, 119, 120, 129, 146, 148, 166, 187, 201, 208, 210, 214, 216, 217, 220, 221, 226, 239, 247, 253, 258
mar-tá-na-ak 285, 301
Martu 120, 210
ma-sa-a$_5^{ki}$ 241
ma:sá:⌈*x*⌉^{ki} 241
Mašdanium 192
Megiddo 226
Meskene 162
Mesopotamia 2, 3, 6, 8, 15, 18, 22, 36, 37, 44, 46, 47, 57, 73, 74, 75, 95, 96, 103, 106, 107, 119, 122, 146, 148, 152, 179, 181–84, 201, 226, 230, 235, 238, 239, 240, 241, 244, 245, 250, 264–66
Mitum 85
Mugrini 84
mu-nu-ti-um 292, 319 (n. 41)
Muraru 84
Muriq 85
Muru 217
Mušilu 210

Nagar 43, 73, 121, 219
Naḫal 99, 102
Nai 222
na-mar^{ki} 241
na-ma-ra-at^{ki} 241, 280
na:ma:ur$_4^{ki}$ 241
Nasariya 37
Neer 202
Nema 101
Nenedu 135
Nerad 101
Nibarat 85
Nidur 192
Nile 2, 3
nimrāh 280
Nin 85

Niniveh 36
Nippur 16, 17, 37, 230, 239
NI-ribi 106
NI-šigu 216
Nizimu 164
Nugamu 134
Nuzi 37

Palestine 6, 57, 76, 96, 106, 226, 241, 245, 269, 271–72
Paris 6
p^e^rat 275, 318 (n. 6)
Persepolis 8
Phoenicia 269
Pugi 85

qaq-qá-ra^{ki} 241

Raaš 103
Radda 103
Raeak 99, 161
Ras Shamra 272–73
Ridu 164
Romania 268
Rome 114, 268
Russia 267

sa-AN^{ki} 241
sa-bi-im^{ki} 287
sa-dum^{ki} 287
Sadur 84
Sag 217
sa-ḫa^{ki} 241
sa-MI+ŠITA$_x$^{ki} 83, 84, 135, 144, 151, 152, 220, 248, 255
Sanarilum 86
Saraqeb 35
s^{e}mādar 293, 312–13
Sheba 76
Shechem 248
Shuruppak 37
si-da-mu^{ki} 287
Sidon 226
Sinai 226
Sipišu 248
Siriba 106
Sistan 201
Siwad 248
Sukurrim 101
Sumer 16, 17, 37, 54, 75, 226, 241, 244
Syria 2, 5, 6, 15, 16, 18, 21, 22, 27, 32, 35, 36, 42, 57, 65, 74, 76, 91, 92, 95, 96, 106, 107, 166, 226, 241, 245, 250, 259, 267, 269

Šabadu 83
Šada 101, 102
Šagu 159, 160
Šaniktu 106
Šaran 101
Šarane 222
Šeladu 84
Šeradu 83
Šizu 216, 223
Šizugu 213
Šubugu 216
ŠUM.URU^{ki} 224
Šutigu 210, 214

Taanach 285
tab-nu^{ki} 241
Taurus 21
Tell Abu Salabikh 37
Tell Afis 22
Tell Brak 2
Tell el-Biya 21
Tell Mardikh 3, 8, 20, 21, 22, 23, 27, 28, 32, 34, 35, 41, 157, 253
Tibalat 99, 102
Tigini 202
Tigris 2
Tin 215, 217, 223
Tinamazu 106
TIN.KASKAL^{ki} 212
Tinnu 103
Tišum 212
Transylvania 267
Tripoli 21
Tub 161, 204, 205, 210
Tunanapa 21
Tunip 248
Turkey 15, 18, 21, 36, 106, 226
Turkiman 201
Tuttul 15, 16, 43, 248, 256, 257

ù-at^{ki} 241
ù-du-at^{ki} 241
Udulum 83
Ugarit 17, 18, 35, 36, 268, 269, 271–73
Uguaš 248
Ul 191
Ulisum 14
Umersadu 84
Unagu 218
Unub 209
Unu-NI 214
Ur 16, 17, 18, 32, 36, 37, 230
Urlu 84
Urlum 159, 164
Ursa'um 161, 205, 220
Urshum 27
Ursu 16, 28
Ursum 20
Uruk 36, 37, 46, 54, 74, 75, 95, 107, 230, 237–40, 265, 267, 268
Uzilatu 103

Yapinu 209

Zaar 103
Zabalum 43
Zabatu 159, 164
Zaburrim 106
Zagros 2, 201
Zaḫiran 101
Zalulu 84
Zamidanu 218
Zamium 84
Zarad 248
Zidalu 186
zú-mu-dar 312
Zumur 107
Zuramu 164
Zušagabu 215

3. NAMES OF GODS

A'ama 171
Aba 14
^{d}'*à-da* 150, 151, 152
^{d}'*à-da* + NP 248
$^{(d)}$Adamma 251, 257
^{d}*a-dam-ma-um* 118, 150–52
^{d}*a-gú* 247
Agu 254, 257
^{d}ak 250
^{d}'AMA-*ra* 150–52, 188
^{d}'*à-ma-rí-ik* 247
Amon 18
a-sà-na-an 251
^{d}ašnan 251
^{d}*aš-tá-*pi_5 150–52
$^{(d)}$Aštabi 251, 253, 255, 256, 257
aš-tár 250
Aštar 247, 248, 251, 252
aš-tár:tá 250
Aštarte 248

Baal 44, 58, 245, 247, 248
ba-al 143
Baliḫ 259
^{d}*ba-li-ḫa* 247
^{d}*ba-ra-du ma-du* 247
^{d}$BARA_{10}$-*ra* 250
^{d}*be*-dingir-dingir 257
^{d}*be* + NP 248, 256
belatu 246, 252
be-lu ma-tim 250

Chemosh 245

Dabir 245, 247, 296
Dagan 14, 15, 44, 58, 143, 152, 246–48, 250, 253, 257, 259, 272, 307
^{d}*da-i-in* 247
^{d}*da-lum* 247
Damu 260
dingir-kalam^{tim} 250

^{d}eden 250
^{d}eden-ak 250
^{d}en 250
^{d}en-en 250
Enlil 47, 238, 259
^{d}en-líl 250, 251
Enki 47, 238, 259
^{d}en-ki 250–52
^{d}en-te 250
^{d}en-zi 250
^{d}en-zu 250
^{d}$eš_4$-*tár* 24, 25
Eštar 25
é-um 250

ga-ma-tù 250
^{d}*ga-ra-i-nu* 247
^{d}$gibil_4$ 250

Hada 105, 169, 188, 246–48, 252, 256, 257, 259

^{d}Ḫapat 251
Ḫapatu 255
Ḫepat 61
Ḫuwawa 74

il 4, 248, 249
i-li-lu 251
Inanna 47, 238, 251
^{d}inanna 250
ì-sa-tù 250
Išatu 248, 294
iš-ḫa-ra 250
^{d}Išḫara 251
Ištar 152, 248, 257, 283, 318

Kakkab 246, 303
kak-kab 250
^{d}*kà-mi-iš* 150–52, 292
Kamiš 247, 257, 291–92
Kašaru 247
Kura 169, 246, 247, 252, 254, 256, 257

Lim 247
^{d}lugal-*du-du-lu*^{ki} 257

ma-é-um 250
Malik 260
Marduk 47, 238
Milk 247
mul 172, 252, 254
^{d}mul 105, 209, 211, 250
mul-mul 250

Na'im 296
Nanna 17
^{d}nè-eri$_{11}$ 250
^{d}NE-*la* 247
Nergal 14, 251
Nidakul 215, 252, 254, 255, 257
^{d}*NI.DA.KUL* 247
^{d}*NI.DA.KUL* + NP 248
ni-ga-ra-du 251
^{d}nin-girim$_{x}$ 259
^{d}nin-kar-du 251
^{d}nin-ki 251, 252

^{d}*ra-sa-ap* 143
^{d}*ra-sa-ap* + NP 248
ra-sa-ap 250

Rasap 225, 247, 251, 252, 255, 257, 259
Resheph 44, 58, 247

sà-du-um 250
Sin 15
Sipiš 44, 246, 251, 259
Suen 47, 238

Šamagan 254

te-rí-iš-tù 250, 294
Tiamat 47, 238, 248
Tiamatum 259
tù-uš-tá-i-i-lu-um 250
ṭi-lu ma-tim 246

Utu 47, 105, 143, 238, 246, 247, 251

Ya 4, 248, 249
Yahweh 276–77, 283
Yau 4, 249

wa-pí-um 250

Zababa 73
zu-i-nu 250

4. EBLA TEXTS CITED

TM.68.G.61 23
TM.74.G.120 56, 230, 318 (n. 11)
TM.75.G.217 226
TM.75.G.220 89, 154
TM.75.G.221 89
TM.75.G.245 154
TM.75.G.247 110
TM.75.G.273 115, 153
TM.75.G.306 254
TM.75.G.308 153
TM.75.G.309 120
TM.75.G.336 88, 89, 136, 143, 153, 154, 184, 318 (n. 10), 319 (n. 29), 319 (n. 30), 319 (n. 34), 319 (n. 38)
TM.75.G.344 72
TM.75.G.400 153
TM.75.G.408 153
TM.75.G.410 261
TM.75.G.411 72, 78–80, 90, 110, 154
TM.75.G.427 71, 90, 109, 146, 150, 153
TM.75.G.441 153
TM.75.G.454 153, 261
TM.75.G.519 153
TM.75.G.520 153
TM.75.G.522 318 (n. 9)
TM.75.G.525 261
TM.75.G.527 79, 154
TM.75.G.1237 109
TM.75.G.1261 261
TM.75.G.1263 153
TM.75.G.1264 110, 153
TM.75.G.1265 110
TM.75.G.1267 227
TM.75.G.1276 110
TM.75.G.1285 153
TM.75.G.1286 153
TM.75.G.1289 153, 200
TM.75.G.1293 153
TM.75.G.1296 125, 130, 227
TM.75.G.1299 154
TM.75.G.1304 235
TM.75.G.1317 153
TM.75.G.1319 153
TM.75.G.1335 109
TM.75.G.1344 153
TM.75.G.1345 110
TM.75.G.1352 319 (n. 23)
TM.75.G.1353 304, 315, 319 (n. 14), 319 (n. 19), 321 (n. 71)
TM.75.G.1357 125, 154, 190, 314
TM.75.G.1358 109

TM.75.G.1359 123, 125, 154, 188, 320 (n. 54)
TM.75.G.1362 110
TM.75.G.1366 153, 154
TM.75.G.1371 109, 154
TM.75.G.1373 154
TM.75.G.1374 154
TM.75.G.1375 153
TM.75.G.1376 72, 110, 146, 154, 261
TM.75.G.1377 227
TM.75.G.1383 110
TM.75.G.1389 110
TM.75.G.1390 200, 227
TM.75.G.1392 134, 156
TM.75.G.1393 110
TM.75.G.1398 231
TM.75.G.1402 120, 153, 154, 261
TM.75.G.1406 185, 200
TM.75.G.1413 110
TM.75.G.1414 110, 153
TM.75.G.1415 237, 242
TM.75.G.1417 109
TM.75.G.1426 320 (n. 53)
TM.75.G.1435 109
TM.75.G.1436 110
TM.75.G.1442 110
TM.75.G.1443 109, 110
TM.75.G.1444 84, 109, 110, 136, 246, 261
TM.75.G.1446 110
TM.75.G.1464 261
TM.75.G.1467 256
TM.75.G.1470 83, 110
TM.75.G.1474 156
TM.75.G.1479 166, 227
TM.75.G.1488 240
TM.75.G.1513 153
TM.75.G.1520 319 (n. 40)
TM.75.G.1522 110
TM.75.G.1525 109
TM.75.G.1536 109
TM.75.G.1558 227
TM.75.G.1559 153
TM.75.G.1570 227
TM.75.G.1582 162
TM.75.G.1591 109, 320 (n. 45)
TM.75.G.1599 168, 169
TM.75.G.1608 153
TM.75.G.1625 110
TM.75.G.1629 147, 226
TM.75.G.1630 147, 148, 226
TM.75.G.1643 110
TM.75.G.1648 110, 319 (n. 21)
TM.75.G.1655 125
TM.75.G.1656 168, 227
TM.75.G.1659 153
TM.75.G.1678 227
TM.75.G.1680 153
TM.75.G.1681 71, 72, 109, 110
TM.75.G.1682 261
TM.75.G.1688 109, 110
TM.75.G.1691 109
TM.75.G.1693 242
TM.75.G.1696 187, 261
TM.75.G.1735 153
TM.75.G.1743 110
TM.75.G.1749 110
TM.75.G.1764 110, 261
TM.75.G.1766 66
TM.75.G.1767 160
TM.75.G.1781 109
TM.75.G.1806 200, 307
TM.75.G.1812 109
TM.75.G.1817 153, 154
TM.75.G.1825 261
TM.75.G.1841 166, 227
TM.75.G.1846 162
TM.75.G.1847 160
TM.75.G.1852 227
TM.75.G.1860 173, 176–78, 227
TM.75.G.1863 318 (n. 8)
TM.75.G.1881 74, 109
TM.75.G.1907 242
TM.75.G.1918 173, 174, 200
TM.75.G.1953 102
TM.75.G.2000 47, 154, 236, 308, 319 (n. 13)
TM.75.G.2001 305
TM.75.G.2003 261
TM.75.G.2008 242
TM.75.G.2033 164
TM.75.G.2065 227
TM.75.G.2068 227
TM.75.G.2070 202
TM.75.G.2075 261
TM.75.G.2086 154
TM.75.G.2094 87
TM.75.G.2096 147, 226, 255
TM.75.G.2112 227
TM.75.G.2121 153
TM.75.G.2133 153
TM.75.G.2136 111
TM.75.G.2200 233
TM.75.G.2231 242, 280, 287, 312, 319 (n. 25), 320 (n. 52), 320 (n. 56)
TM.75.G.2236 109
TM.75.G.2260 234, 242
TM.75.G.2284 319 (nn. 16, 20), 319 (n. 27)
TM.75.G.2290 70
TM.75.G.2318 242
TM.75.G.2321 111
TM.75.G.2342 9, 111
TM.75.G.2367 111
TM.75.G.2420 111, 154
TM.75.G.2428 200
TM.75.G.2429 173, 177, 200
TM.75.G.2505 172, 173, 177, 200

TM.75.G.2561 111
TM.75.G.2658 109
TM.75.G.3131 261
TM.75.G.3162 and 3163 319 (nn. 28, 42)
TM.75.G.3171 261
TM.75.G.3242 109
TM.75.G.3433 318 (n. 5)
TM.75.G.6030 84, 110
TM.75.G.10023 319 (n. 39)
TM.75.G.11010 261
TM.75.G.11126 153
TM.75.G.11312 319 (nn. 31, 33)
TM.76.G.89 111
TM.76.G.151 227
TM.76.G.187 227
TM.76.G.188 157
TM.76.G.189 227
TM.76.G.199 153
TM.76.G.223 255
TM.76.G.281 160
TM.76.G.523 186, 195, 306, 321 (n. 74)
TM.76.G.524 287
TM.76.G.528 227

5. BIBLICAL TEXTS CITED

Gen. 1:26 274
Gen. 2:5 274
Gen. 2:7 274
Gen. 2:14 275, 276
Gen. 2:20 275
Gen. 3:5 278
Gen. 4:7 275
Gen. 4:26 276
Gen. 10:8–11 277
Gen. 11:5 277
Gen. 11:30 278
Gen. 14:2 287
Gen. 15:18 275
Gen. 20:7 278
Gen. 21:19 278
Gen. 23:6 278
Gen. 30:31 ff. 279
Gen. 32:15 279
Gen. 35:8 279
Gen. 38:14, 21 280
Gen. 40:9 10 279
Gen. 41:43 281
Gen. 50:26 281
Exod. 1:1 281
Exod. 3:1 281
Exod. 3:8 277
Exod. 3:14–15 276
Exod. 6:3 276
Exod. 15:2 277
Exod. 22:5 282
Exod. 30:12 282
Lev. 24:11, 16 283, 309
Num. 26:32 283
Num. 32:3 280
Deut. 28:4 276, 283, 317
Deut. 32:31 284
Josh. 19:12 280
Judg. 5:1 279
Judg. 5:19 284
Judg. 5:20 274, 284
Judg. 16:4 285
I Sam. 2:3 285
I Sam. 2:10 286
I Sam. 2:25 284
I Sam. 10:18 109
I Sam. 25:3 286
II Kings 15:22 278
II Kings 23:11 304
Isa. 1:10 287
Isa. 17:10 296
Isa. 19:18 272
Isa. 27:1 288
Isa. 48:19 288
Isa. 60:18 289
Isa. 60:19–20 289
Isa. 65:11–12 290, 299
Jer. 4:30 290–91
Jer. 10:6–7 291
Jer. 48:7 291–92
Ezek. 16:40 292
Ezek. 27:9 292
Ezek. 27:17 292
Hos. 4:19 293
Hos. 7:14 293
Hos. 8:3 309
Hos. 11:8 287
Amos 7:1 294
Amos 9:13 295
Jonah 1:3 295
Hab. 2:5 295
Hab. 3:5 296
Hab. 3:17 318 (n. 6)
Ps. 4:8 289
Ps. 27:4 296
Ps. 36:7 297
Ps. 46:2 (1) 297
Ps. 46:10 (9) 298
Ps. 50:13 298
Ps. 51:7 (6) 298
Ps. 54:8–9 (6–7) 309–10

Ps. 61:3 299
Ps. 61:8 290, 299
Ps. 65:4 290, 299
Ps. 68:10 (9) 300
Ps. 68:33 109
Ps. 69:22 (21) 300
Ps. 74:22 290, 299
Ps. 78:59 297
Ps. 103:12 301
Ps. 106:20 301
Ps. 107:3–4 301
Ps. 109:30 297
Ps. 112:4 302
Ps. 138:6 314
Job 5:18 302
Job 5:26 282
Job 6:15–16 320 (n. 57)
Job 9:7–9 302–3
Job 9:30 303, 320 (n. 57)
Job 13:21 301
Job 15:29 303
Job 22:12 314
Job 22:25 304
Job 24:13 304
Job 24:14 305
Job 24:15 305
Job 26:13 305
Job 29:18 304, 305–6
Job 31:6 306
Job 39:4 306–7
Job 40:30 307
Prov. 2:9 307
Prov. 8:30 308
Prov. 11:22 308
Prov. 13:21–22 309
Prov. 18:8 308
Prov. 22:1–2 309
Prov. 22:8 310
Prov. 24:25 309
Prov. 26:23 304, 310
Prov. 27:23 320 (n. 58)
Prov. 27:24 311
Song of Songs 1:14 311–12
Song of Songs 2:13, 15 292, 312–13
Song of Songs 4:13 311
Song of Songs 5:14 313
Song of Songs 7:13 312–13
Eccles. 4:13 313
Eccles. 5:7 (8) 313–14
Eccles. 7:1 309, 314
Eccles. 9:1 314
Eccles. 11:7 314–15
Eccles. 12:11 315
Eccles. 12:12 315
Lam. 4:10 300

6. INDEX OF SUBJECTS

absolutism 264
academy 230 ff.
acrography 46–47
Acropolis 22–23, 32, 145
administration 122 ff.
adverbs 63
agriculture 45, 157 ff.
Akkadians 3
alliances 96–98
allocations of sheep 91
alloys 172 ff., 176
allusions 316–17
alphabetical principle 47
ambassadors 122
Ammonite 57
Amorite 27, 56
animal name plus name of a god 277
animals 46
anointing 258
anointing, feast of 257
anthropology 266
Arabic 266
Arabic etymology 288
archive science 48–49
archives 38–39
area of commerce 6
artifacts 40
artisans 114–15
Asiatic production 265
assimilation 275–76, 279, 318 (n. 6)
atonement 282
"axes" 4, 173

b, "from" 314
Babylonian 8
baking of tablets 40
barley 45, 157, 254
barter 45, 185 ff., 188
beasts of burden 165
beer 44, 91–92, 254
Bible 271–73
Biblical Hebrew 316–18
bicameral system 75
Biga 41
bilingual vocabularies 41, 46–47, 236–37, 242, 250, 317–18
bilingualism 56–57
birds 46
bitumen 187
borders, geographic 226

borrowings 251
bovids 164
bracelets 92, 169, 187, 256, 313, 321 (n. 71)
bread 44, 91
bread, offering 254
breakup of construct chain or of composite phrase 293, 313
breeding of cattle 162–64
bronze 168
bronze alloys 173
bull calves 164
burden, beasts of 165

cakes 286
calendars 45, 147, 306, 317
calendar, new 4
Canaan 56, 248, 271–73, 320 (n. 51)
Canaanite languages or dialects 272–73, 281, 288
Canaanites 271–73
"canal of Ebla" 16–17
carats 166
cardinal points 302
carnelian 168, 202
"cart" 181
case-endings 62
catalogue 41–42
cattle 160
cattle breeding 162–64
cattle-raising 45
causative conjugation 64
cereals 160
chasm, chronological 316
chiasmus or chiastic construction 289, 297
child sacrifice 257
children 121
citizens 118
city gates 143
city gates, naming 289
city states, Canaanite-Phoenician 311
civil servants 122–23
classification, linguistic 58–59
classification of Eblaite 65
clergy 244
clothes 7
cloths 256
colophon 231, 232
commerce 6, 184 ff.
commercial empire 225 f.
commercial goods 202 ff.
commercial traffic 268
commissars 122
commodity prices 200
congresses, scientific 239–40
conjunctions 63
consecration, feast of 257
conservatism 311, 316
consonantal writing 265
consonantism 62
continuity 297, 316
copper 168, 173, 227, (n. 27), 282, 312
cosmos 244
cows 164
creation 238
crops 197
cult, Canaanite 296
cult of the sun-goddess 289
cultivation 197 f.
culture 230
culture, higher 233 ff.
culture, urban 22
cuneiform signs 8, 54, 234
currency 195 ff.
curriculum 231 f.
cypress 311

daggers 169, 187, 256
"daggers of gold" 92
daily fare 89–90
daily rations 89–91
damask 166
date palms 162
dating 73–74, 145–47
daughters of Ebrium 87–88
dean 232
decimal system 183
decipherment xv, xvi, 34–35, 56
deities, West Semitic 245
density of Hebrew 317
determinatives 245
dialect, Hebrew 278
dictionaries 7, 235–36
diplomatic correspondence 96
discovery, scientific 266
dissimilation 318 (n. 6)
distribution 196
division of city 136 ff.
double-duty suffix 320 (n. 58)
double negative 291
dry measures 181–82
duration of dynasty 72
dynamics of prices 196
dynasty 69 ff.
Dynasty, Akkad 15, 95

earrings 187
Ebla *passim*
Ebla, location 3, 20–21, 28
Ebla-Ugarit-Bible axis 273
economic resources 156 ff.
economic tablets 45
economy of state 180
edicts 45
Edomite 57
Egypt 107
Egyptian word 281

Elders 74–75, 79–80, 92–95
election of king 71–72
electrum 176
emmer 293
empire 6
empire, commercial 225 f.
encyclopedias 46, 237–38, 275
epenthesis 61
epic narratives 47, 238
epithets 27
epithets and titles of God 304–5
ethnic composition 27–28, 32
exchange 45, 185
exchange, cultural 239–40
expansion, political 106 ff.
exports 7
ex-votos 254

fabrics 165 ff., 202 ff.
Fara xiv
farmers 118
fasces 4
feasts 256–58, 319 (n. 43)
female gods 248
Fertile Crescent 2, 107
fig 162
fire-goddess 248
fishes 46
flax 162, 165
flour 90
foreign priests 119
foreigners 4, 118–19
"forest of Ebla" 17
foundry bronze 179
functionaries 114 ff.
fusion of metals 176

garments 92
gates of city 44, 289
gazetteer 106–7
gemination 61
Genesis 238
geographic borders 226
geographical list 241
glyptic art 284
goats 164
"goddess of Ebla" 17
gods 245 ff.
God's movement down from
  heaven 277
gold 166 ff., 201
gold bars 187
Good One, the 309
governors 122–30
grammar 59
grapes 162
"green eyes" 173, 178
gubar 181, 183

Hanseatic League 4
hapax legomenon 281, 293, 303–4, 315
head, anointing of 258
heaps of corpses 101–2
Hebrew lexica, grammars 316–18
Hebrew poetry 318
henna 311–12
henotheism 249, 260, 283
herds 164
hermaphrodite 320 (n. 65)
hierarchy of state 78–79
historical texts 45, 48, 68
Hittites 32
hoes 173, 178
Hurrian 27
husbandry 196
hybrid conjugation 64
hymns 47, 258–59
hypocoristicon 249
hypostasis 247

imagery 288
imperative, emphatic 305
imports 6–7
import-export 202 ff.
incantations 47, 238, 258–59
industry 165
infixed *-t-* 64
inflation 195
inflection 62
inscription 24–25
intensive conjugation 64
interchange of gods 249
international commerce 45
inventory numbers 40
Iran 3

jars 181
jewels 92
judges 122 f.
juridical texts 45–46

king 4, 69–70, 74–75, 92–93
king-god 264
king pays taxes 190

lack of case-endings 62
laicality 264
lamb 90
lances 173
language, Eblaite 7–8, 55 ff.
lapis lazuli 168–69, 170, 186, 202
lead 168, 227 (n. 27)
"Legend of Sargon" 15
letters of state 45–46
lexical texts 38, 46, 231 ff.
lexicography 318
library 48–49, 231
library, palace 34

linen 162
linen weaving 42
linguistic tradition, tenacity of 273, 297, 298, 300, 304, 306, 315–16
liquid measures 181–82
lists, encyclopedic 275
litany 260
literary texts 231, 238
livestock 148–49
location of Ebla 28
locusts 294
logograms 55, 57
lord 122
loveliness 296
lower city 145
luppu 181

-m, enclitic 307–8
mace head 178
maces 173
malediction 105, 261, (n. 4)
mallets 173, 178
malt 162
Mari tablets 55
marker 233
"martu" daggers 173, 174
Masoretes 291
mass media 34–35
mathematics 73
measures 7
measures of area 200
mercenaries 119–20
merchants 114 ff., 311
merismus 295, 311
messengers 44, 114 f.
metal industry 166 ff.
metallurgy 173 ff., 201
metals 7, 256
metathesis 318 (n. 11), 320 (n. 46)
military campaign 46
mina 166 ff., 181–82, 183–84
Missione Archeologica Italiana in Siria 271
Moabite language 57
Moabites 291
models of exchange 18 f.
models of production 179 ff.
molds 178–79
monetization 7
money 196
months, names of 283, 294–95, 300, 306, 310, 317
Most High, the 286
multicolored cloth 201
multicropping 227 (n. 46)
mutton 90
myths 238, 258–59, 290

nails 173, 178
name of God expressing superlative 297
Name, the 283, 309–10
negative, emphatic double 291
nepotism 4
new calendar 150–53
"noble shekel" 182
Northwest Semitic 59, 266, 316–18
noun 61–62
numbering systems 182–83

offerings 253–54
offspring of King Ebrium 81–87
oil 44, 160–62, 300
oil skin 181
Old Akkadian 55–56
old calendar 147 ff.
Old Canaanite xv
olive groves 160
olive-growing 45
olive trees 160–61
ordinances 45
organization of labor 264
oxen 164

palace, royal 15
palaces 144–45, 227 (n. 16)
pantheon 244
parallelism 65
parīsu 181
peasants 118
personal names 56
personification 310
pharyngal 288
philologist's task 41
philology and lexicography, biblical 318
Phoenician 7, 57, 317
Phoenician contribution to the Bible 271–72
Phoenician literature 271
Phoenicians 6
phoenix 305–6, 320 (nn. 62, 64, 65)
phonetics 60–61
pigs 44, 164
pins 173, 178
place names based on insect or animal names 280
places of worship 252 f.
plaques 173
Pleiades 302–3, 320 (n. 56)
plow tip 178
plowing 295
plowshares 173
plural of majesty 314
pocket vocabularies 234
polemic tone of Isa. 60:19–20 289
polytheism 245 ff., 249, 260
pomegranate 162

popular religion 260–61
population 118, 134 ff.
prebends 45
precious stones 168
preformatives 62
prepositions 63
prepositions derived from verbs
of motion 287–88
price-list 195
prices 187 ff., 195 ff.
priestesses 252–53
priests 252 f.
primitive democracy 75
prisoners of war 120
private economy 180
processions 258
professor of mathematics 72
pronouns 62–63
prophet, prophecy 278, 319 (n. 12)
prophetess 279
prophets 119, 253
prophets' names 294
Proto-Semitic 266
proverbs 47, 238
Punic 57
punning 290
"purchase and sale" 45, 188
purification, feast of 257

quadrilingual vocabulary 293
queen 4, 75–76
queen mother 75–76
queen of Sheba 76

rain 300
rams 187
Ras Shamra discoveries 316–17
ratio of gold/silver 200
rations 44
razors 173, 176, 178
reactions 28–29
Rebecca 77
religion 244 ff.
religion, popular 260–61
religious tradition, tenacity of 273, 290, 291–92, 306, 311, 316
Renaissance 4
rhyme 65
rituals 238
Rome School 268
royal inscriptions 46

sacred iconography 284
sacrifice of children 257
scholastic exercises 233
scholastic tradition 44
school 230 ff.
school documents 232
school tablet 43
schoolboy exercise 231
scientific lists 46
scribal school 231
Sea Peoples 6
seed 197
Semitic languages 58, 265
senate 4
settlements 134 ff., 266
seven-year reign 72
sexagesimal system 183
shared consonants 302
sheep 44, 162–63, 202, 254
sheep-rearing 45
shekels 170 ff., 181–82
shelves 49–50
sibilants 60
signs, cuneiform 8, 54, 234
sila 183
silver 7, 185 ff., 201
skepticism xv, xvi, 28, 32, 35
skulls glazed or plastered 310–11
slave 5
smelting 178
social classes 114 ff.
spinning mill 165 ff.
spokesmen 122
star 247
starches 90, 91
state economy 180
state, structure of 3, 44, 78
state treasury 180, 190
statue 23–24, 169, 173, 178
stones, precious 168
storage 197, 200
storing of tablets 50
style 65
stylus 39, 54
Summerian language 267
Sumerians 3
submultiples 183
suffixes 63
sun 247
superintendent 131
superlative 297
surfaces 182
syllabograms 55
syllabaries 46, 234 f.
syncretism 249–51
syntax 65

-t-, infixed 64
table 191
tablets 9–10
tablets, discovery of 35–36
tablets, lexical 11
tablets, manufacture of 39
teacher 232
technique, poetic 318
technology 172–75, 201

tells 267
temple offerings 91
temples 252 f.
tenses 64
textbooks 234
textile industry 165
textiles 4, 92, 197, 201
theologoumenon 276
tin 168, 173, 176, 179
"tooth" 178
topography of Ebla 145
tradition, Egyptian 276
traditions, tenacity of 273, 290, 291–92, 297, 298, 300, 304, 306, 311, 315–16
translation of Bible 315–18
treaties 45, 96, 103 ff.
"tributes" 189 ff.
tunics 92
tutelar divinity 247
typology 42

Ugaritic 57, 271–73
Ugaritic studies 317–18
Ugaritic texts 56
units of measures 181 ff.
utensils 173, 176

value of goods 196
vases 173
verbs 63–64
village 133–36, 264
vine 293
viticulture 45, 91, 160
vocabularies, bilingual 41, 235 ff., 267, 317
vulture stela 38

wagon-barn 227 (n. 16)
wagon tongues 173, 178
wards 143
wars 99 ff.
weights 7, 181–82
weights, bronze 176–78
West Semitic 56
wheat 45, 254, 293
wheat, kinds of 157
wine 44, 91, 160, 254
wineskin 181, 286
Wisdom in Proverbs 8–9 310
"woman" 298
women 4
wool 162, 165
word-play 290
workers 115 ff.
worship 252 f.
writing 54
writing, consonantal 265
writing, origin of 265
writing skills in Canaan, in Israel 316–17

Yahweh 276–77, 283

Zakirratum vase 176
Zagros 2
Zephaniah 315–16

7. HEBREW WORDS IN AFTERWORD

(Hebrew order)

'abrēk 281
'ōkel 301
'āmôn 308
'ôr 304
'ārōn 281
'eškōl 279, 311–12
bdq 292
b^{e}yad '^{e}lōhîm 314
b^{e}nê yiśrā'ēl 281
bārût 300–1
bārî^{a}ḥ 288, 305
bitt^{e}qû 292
gābō^{a}h, g^{e}bōhîm 313–14
gōbah 314
gūbār (MT *geber*) 295–96
gādîš 282
gizzê 294
g^{e}lîlê 313
g^{e}rab 320 (n. 46)
gešem n^{e}dābōt 300
dāber 296
dāgān w^{e}tîrôš 293–94
dor^{e}bōnôt 315
wayyiṣer 274
wālād 278
zib^{e}ḥôt 293
ḥadrê-bāṭen 308
ḥôl 305–6
ḥôrēš 295
ṭôb 309
ṭôb šēm 314
ṭa'am 308
ṭerem 274
yāh, yāhû, yô, yahweh 276–77, 283
y^{e}hî kaggannāb 305
yôm kippûr 282

yaḥlᵉmû 307
yeḥᵉmatnî 'immî 298
yᵉkīlēhū (MT *yikleh*) 310
yām 302
yāmīt 302
yōṣēr 274
yārad 277
yišqᵉlēnî 306
kôkāb 303
kîmāh 302–3
kᵉsapsîgî-m (MT *kesep sîgîm*) 310–11
kippûr 282
kappôret 283
kpr 282
kipper 282
kōper (ransom) 282
kōper (henna flowers) 311–12
lᵉbārôt 300, 320 (n. 51)
lahag 315
leqeš 294
mᵉ'ōd, mā'ōd 297
mā'ên (MT *mē'ên*) 291
mw (MT *mēw*) 303, 320 (n. 57)
mīnāh 287
mᵉnî, mānī, mānî 290, 299
minnît 292, 319 (n. 41)
minlām 303
miskēn 313
mā'ōt (MT *mē'ēṭ*) 289
mᵉ'ōtāyw 288
nābî' 278
nāḥāš bārîᵃḥ 288, 305
nāmēr 280
nō'am 296
nāqōd, nqd 279
nś' 278
'ādāh 291
'ēz, 'izzîm 279
'ālû 286
'aštᵉrôt ṣō'nekā 283, 317
pᵉlîlîm 284
pālal 284
pātar, pitrôn 279
rābad 318 (n. 6)
rāḥaq 301
rᵉpātîm 318 (n. 6)
rešep 296
śᵉ'et 275
š't, šā'attā 275
šᵉgar 283
šûr 305
šāleg 320 (n. 57)
šālᵉmû 289–90
šēm, (*šūm*) 283, 309–10
šemen ṭôb 314
tîrôš 293–94
tᵉyāšîm 279

8. EBLAITE WORDS IN AFTERWORD

'à-ba-ra-gu-um 281
a-dì-ma 308
'à-ga-ra-gu-um 281
a-kà-lu 300–1
an-ti-ma 308
aš-kà-lum, aš-qa-i-lu 279, 312
aš-tù-ma 308
ba-rì-um 288, 305
ba-ta-qù 292
be-li 306
bù-ur-tum 301
da-la-lum 285
dumu-nita *eb-la*ki 281
é-a-gú-um 305
é-da-ru$_x$-um 308
é-da-um-túg 290–91
é-la-lum 286
en-ṣi 318 (n. 11)
ga-dì-šúm 282
gašum 300
gú-bar 296, 320 (n. 46)
gú-li-lum 313, 321 (n. 71)
ḫa-li-tu, ḫa-li 306, 320 (n. 65)
ḫu-la-tum 306
ì-ma-tum 298
i-me-tum 302
d*AMA-ra* 283
ig-za 294
*ig-za-*mìn 294
i-rí-sá 295
qì-lí 310
ṣa-'à-tum 283
ì-zi-ba-tu 293
kà-ma-tù 303
kà-na-na-um 307
kà-pá-lu, kà-pá-ru 282, 311–12
kutim 304
lu-ma 308
luppu 286
ma-ad 297
ma-ḫa-ṣi i-da 302
ma-i-at 288
ma-in tuš 291
ma-ku-tum 279
ma-ni-lum 303
maš-bí-tù 298
ma-wu 303
mu-ša-gá-i-núm 313

na-ba-um 278, 319 (n. 12)
na-bí-u-tum 319 (n. 12)
na-se$_{11}$ 278
pá-tá-ru$_x$ 279
ṣa-a-tu 317
ṣa-'à-tum 276
sa-ma-nu ṭa-bù 314
ší-in 287
šum 283
ṭì-é-mu 308
t ú g *ì-lí* 297
-yà 276

9. UGARITIC WORDS IN AFTERWORD

brḥ 288
da-ab-ḫu 293
drb 315
yrḫ-ḥlt 306
mnth 293
spsg 310–11

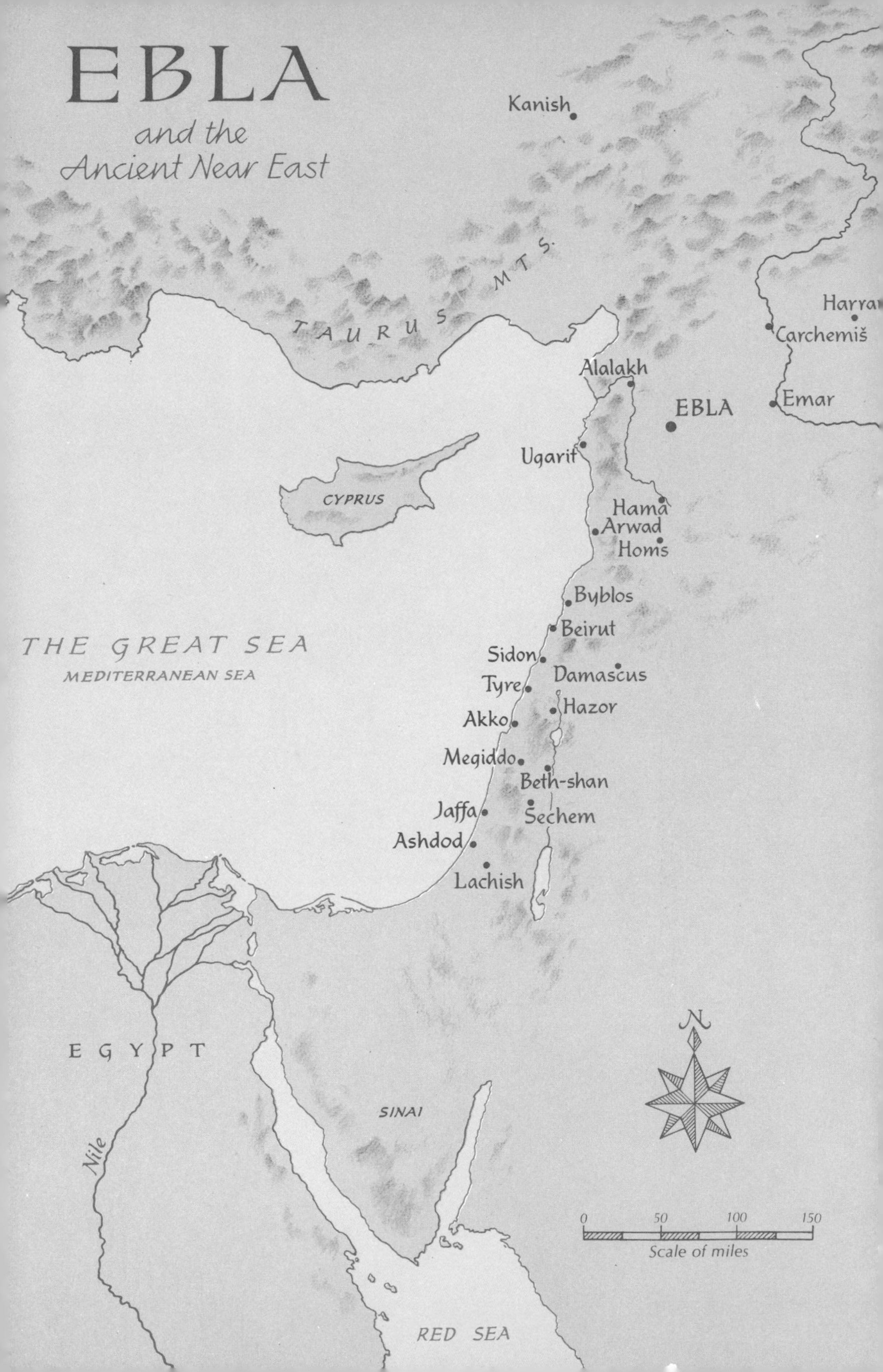
EBLA
and the
Ancient Near East
Kanish
TAURUS MTS.
Harra
Carchemiš
Alalakh
EBLA
Emar
Ugarit
CYPRUS
Hama
Arwad
Homs
Byblos
Beirut
THE GREAT SEA
MEDITERRANEAN SEA
Sidon
Damascus
Tyre
Hazor
Akko
Megiddo
Beth-shan
Jaffa
Šechem
Ashdod
Lachish
N
EGYPT
SINAI
Nile
0
50
100
150
Scale of miles
RED SEA